P9-CDM-391

ADHD WITH COMORBID DISORDERS

ADHD with Comorbid Disorders

Clinical Assessment and Management

Steven R. Pliszka, MD
Caryn L. Carlson, PhD
James M. Swanson, PhD

THE GUILFORD PRESS
New York   London

A Division of Guilford Publications, Inc.
72 Spring Street, New York, NY 10012
http://www.guilford.com

Printed in the United States of America

This book is printed on acid-free paper.

Last digit is print number: 9 8 7 6 5 4 3 2

Library of Congress Cataloging-in-Publication Data

Pliszka, Steven R.
ADHD with comorbid disorders: clinical assessment and management / Steven R. Pliszka, Caryn L. Carlson, James M. Swanson.
p. cm.
Includes bibliographical references and index
ISBN 1-57230-478-2
1. Attention-deficit hyperactivity disorder. 2. Comorbidity. I. Carlson, Caryn L. II. Swanson, James M. III. Title. IV. Title: Attention deficit hyperactivity disorder with comorbid disorders.
[DNLM: 1. Attention Deficit Disorder with Hyperactivity—diagnosis. 2. Attention Deficit Disorder with Hyperactivity—therapy. 3. Comorbidity. WS 350.8.A8 P728a 1999]
RJ506.H9P55 1999
618.92'8589—dc21
DNLM
for Library of Congress 99-29748
CIP

To my wife, Alice, and to my parents,
whose enormous patience and encouragement
made this book possible. This book is also a tribute
to James W. Maas, MD, Hugo A. Auler Professor
of Psychiatry and Pharmacology,
who did so much to guide my career.
—S. R. P.

To my mother, and in loving memory of my father.
—C. L. C.

To the memory of Dennis P. Cantwell, MD.
Although on the faculty at UCLA,
Denny spent considerable time
at the University of California, Irvine,
and he had major influences on the clinic, school,
and research programs at the UCI-CDC.
He and I were coinvestigators on grants, coauthors
on papers, close friends, and ideal collaborators
in combining the disciplines
of psychology and psychiatry.
The clinical and research programs at the UCI-CDC
are part of his rich legacy.
—J. M. S.

About the Authors

Steven R. Pliszka, MD, is Associate Professor and Chief of the Division of Child and Adolescent Psychiatry at the University of Texas Health Science Center at San Antonio. Dr. Pliszka was the recipient of a National Institute of Mental Health Physician Scientist Award and conducts research in the areas of psychopharmacology and the comorbidity of psychiatric disorder with ADHD. He has recently been active in examining inhibitory control in ADHD children using neuroimaging techniques and has studied the role of mental disorders in juvenile delinquency. He lives in San Antonio with his wife, Alice, and his son, Andrew.

Caryn L. Carlson, PhD, received her doctorate in psychology from the University of Georgia and completed her postdoctoral training at Indiana University. Her research has been funded by the National Institute of Mental Health, and she has published numerous articles and book chapters on the assessment and treatment of children with ADHD. Her primary current research interests concern children with the Predominantly Inattentive subtype of ADHD, and the motivational, social, and attentional correlates of ADHD. Dr. Carlson is currently an Associate Professor at the University of Texas at Austin, and she lives with her greyhound, Luna.

James M. Swanson, PhD, Professor of Pediatrics and Cognitive Sciences at the University of California Irvine, received his doctorate from Ohio State University. In 1983, Dr. Swanson founded the UCI Child Development Center (UCI-CDC), which has specialty programs for ADHD children. The UCI-CDC school programs include a school-based day-treatment program and a paraprofessional program for delivering school-based interventions for ADHD students in regular classrooms in public schools. The UCI-CDC research program includes investigations of multimodality treatment of ADHD children, investigations of the neurobiology of ADHD, and pharmacological investigations of new medications for ADHD. Over the past 20 years, his work with ADHD children has been supported by the Ontario Mental Health Foundation, the MacArthur Foundation, the Irvine Community Foundation, the Educational Foundation of America, the Sackler Foundation, the U.S. Department of Education, the National Institute of Mental Health, and the National Institute on Child Health and Development.

Contents

I

Introduction

1

Overview of Issues in Comorbidity

Children and adolescents with attention-deficit/hyperactivity disorder (ADHD) are quite often most gratifying to treat. If there are no associated problems such as learning disabilities, aggression, or mood problems, and if the family is intact and cooperative, treatment is straightforward. Very often the child will respond within days to stimulant medication, and the positive response is maintained for months or years. Yet many clinicians have had to deal with cases of ADHD that seem to frustrate every effort to intervene effectively.

> Justin was one such challenge. A 13-year-old seventh grader, he was first diagnosed with ADHD when he was 5 years of age. He doctor prescribed methylphenidate (Ritalin), but that lead to increased agitation. He was then managed without medication until the age of 7, when his severe hyperactivity and aggression lead to a suspension from school. He was treated with dextroamphetamine (Dexedrine) with modest results. Psychological testing at age 8 showed marked reading delay; Justin had particular difficulty sounding out words. His handwriting was very poor. He began attending special education classes 2 hours a day. In the fifth grade, he exploded and threw a chair at a teacher, which lead to a 5-day psychiatric hospitalization. An electroencephalogram (EEG) showed "right temporal slowing" but no actual seizure activity. He was started on carbamazepine (Tegretol) in the hope this would reduce the aggressive out-

> bursts. After 6 months of treatment, however, it was still unclear if the anticonvulsant was helpful and it was eventually discontinued. Justin barely passed the sixth grade; repeat of psychological testing showed he was reading at the third-grade level. During the seventh grade his aggressive outbursts increased and he began making suicidal statements such as "How'd you feel if I wasn't around any more." He was caught with a small amount of marijuana in his school locker and was expelled. In the midst of an argument with his mother that night he made a cut on his wrist and was hospitalized again. The managed care company approved a 3-day stay.

Justin's case typifies the complex challenges facing clinicians. Does Justin simply have a "severe" case of ADHD? Is there an underlying mood disorder? Is a mood disorder in fact the primary problem? How do his learning problems influence his behavior? Finally, how do the neurological factors (i.e., abnormal EEG) relate to his ADHD, if at all? The final sentence of the case description illustrates another dilemma for the modern clinician: these complex questions must be answered in a very short time frame, whether in the hospital or in the office. We hope this volume will help the busy practitioner develop three major skills to help manage children like Justin: (1) a practical working knowledge of the research examining ADHD children with different comorbid psychiatric conditions, (2) a state-of-the-art knowledge of the complex psychopharmacological interventions these children require, and (3) familiarity with the appropriate psychosocial treatments for the wide variety of disruptive and mood symptoms that these children show. First, we must examine some important theoretical issues.

WHAT IS COMORBIDITY?

In its simplest terms, comorbidity is the condition whenever two different disease processes are present in an individual patient. Often, the two disease processes do not interact and can each be treated without regard to the other. For example, if a child with ADHD catches a cold, there is comorbidity of a viral illness. The pediatrician will not treat the cold any differently because his patient also has ADHD. When dealing with the more complex comorbidity of a psychiatric disorder with ADHD, there are two principle concerns: First, how are the clinical presentation, course of illness, and treatment options different in the comorbid child relative to the child with either disorder alone? Secondly, what is the degree of comorbidity between ADHD and a given psychiatric disorder? If it is much greater than chance alone would predict, what is the explanation for this overlap? This problem has been pondered at length in several recent reviews (Angold & Costello, 1993; Biederman, Newcorn, & Sprich, 1991; Caron & Rutter, 1991; Lilienfeld, Waldman, & Israel, 1994; Pliszka, 1998), and we direct readers wanting an in-depth theoretical treatment of this question to them. From these reviews, we identify four important issues about comorbidity relevant to this volume, as discussed in the following subsections.

Problems with the Diagnostic Criteria

The fourth edition of the *Diagnostic and Statistical Manual of Mental Disorders* (DSM-IV; American Psychiatric Association, 1994) operationalizes criteria for mental disorders. The criteria themselves may produce comorbidity because of symptom overlap or vagueness in defining a symptom. There are many examples of symptom overlap in DSM that will concern us in later chapters. Restlessness is symptomatic both of ADHD and generalized anxiety disorder; similarly poor concentration is present in depressive disorders as well ADHD. Increased motor activity and distractibility are listed in the criteria for both ADHD and mania. As Angold and Costello (1993, p. 1786) point out, this leads to the situation in which having one disorder "constitutes a partial fulfillment of the criteria for the second disorder." Suppose a clinician evaluates a highly exuberant child with high self-confidence who only sleeps 5 hours a night. The child does not have ADHD, so there is no distractibility or increased motor activity. If there are no other symptoms such as delusions of grandeur, pressured speech, or hypersexuality, the clinician would not diagnose mania. Now assume the child does have ADHD and is both distractible and restless. These ADHD symptoms now push the child over the diagnostic line into mania. If every case of ADHD with comorbid mania arose because of such overlap, the comorbidity would be an artifact of the criteria. This would obviously require a change in DSM rather than a change in the child's treatment plan. (We will discuss the controversy over ADHD and mania in detail in Chapter 8.) While DSM provides symptom lists, it rarely defines the symptoms precisely and reasonable clinicians may differ sharply on whether a symptom is present or absent. Even if they agree that it is present, they may differ on which diagnostic category to assign the symptoms. For instance, if a child is irritable, is it due to a major depressive episode, a manic episode, or oppositional defiant disorder (ODD)? DSM does not say, and there is a wide variation among clinicians on this issue. Such difference will lead to marked differences about the degree to which different disorders are comorbid with each other (Biederman, 1998; Klein, Pine, & Klein, 1998).

Difference among Informants

This is a particular problem in work with children, as we always have at least two informants, usually the parent and child. Suppose the parent states that the child has severe symptoms of ADHD but is not depressed, while the child says she is sad but denies being inattentive or restless. Different approaches to combining this information will lead to different rates of comorbidity. If the clinician accepts only one of the informants as valid (whether that informant is the parent or child), there is no comorbidity. On the other hand, if the clinicians "adds" the two interviews, comorbidity (ADHD with depression) is present. We will ponder the issue of child–parent congruence as it relates to symptoms in Chapter 3.

Which Disorder, If Either, Is Primary?

If a child has both ADHD and conduct disorder (CD), has one disorder served as a risk factor for the other? Because children with ADHD are impulsive and use poor judgment, perhaps they are more likely to respond to suggestions of peers to engage in antisocial behavior. Do children with ADHD develop depression because of the demoralization of dealing with negative feedback from parents, teachers, and peers? In this view, comorbidity results from one disorder being an etiological agent for the other.

Is the Comorbid Condition a Clinical Subtype Distinct from ADHD Alone?

Based on the work of Cantwell (1995), Jensen, Martin, and Cantwell (1997) proposed seven criteria that can be used to determine if ADHD plus the comorbid condition (ADHD/CM) should be viewed as truly distinct from ADHD alone.

1. *Distinctive clinical picture.* Children with ADHD/CM should differ in substantial ways from children with ADHD on measures other than the diagnostic criteria themselves. For instance, ADHD children with social phobia should be seen as withdrawing from social interactions on the playground by observers blind to the child's diagnostic status. If ADHD children with and without a comorbid diagnosis differ

only on the clinician's interview, without any "real-world" differences on behavior rating scales, peer interactions, educational achievement, etc., then the validity of the distinction is questionable.

2. *Distinctive demographic factors.* The ADHD/CM group may differ from the ADHD children alone in terms of sex, ethnicity, or social class.

3. *Differences in psychosocial factors.* The ADHD/CM group may have a differential exposure to major societal stressors such a poverty, crime, urban decay, or exposure to violence.

4. *Differences in biological factors.* Are there differences between the ADHD/CM and ADHD groups in terms of genetic markers, brain anatomy neuroimaging, or physiology? This approach is still in its infancy but holds great promise for the future.

5. *Distinctive family genetic factors.* Does the ADHD/CM condition "breed true"? That is, if a child has ADHD/CM, is there an increased prevalence of both ADHD and CM in his/her relatives? Furthermore, do the ADHD and CM almost always occur in the same relative or does the child have some relatives with CM and others with ADHD? In the former situation, the case for ADHD/CM being distinct genetic subtype is strengthened. In the latter case, the child most likely inherited two independent disorders from separate relatives and ADHD/CM is not distinct.

6. *Distinctive family environmental factors.* Has the ADHD/CM child been exposed to certain family experiences not shared by the child with ADHD alone? Have ADHD children with anxiety disorders experienced more divorce or separation than those with ADHD alone? Are children with ADHD and CD more likely to have been exposed to domestic violence?

7. *Distinctive clinical course and outcome.* Are ADHD children with and without comorbid disorders different at follow-up? Do ADHD/CD children have more criminal convictions? Do ADHD children with depression have a higher rate of adult affective disorder than nondepressed ADHD children? Are there differences in the life course of the ADHD itself for comorbid and noncomorbid children? Does the presence of the comorbid disorder make continuation of ADHD into adulthood more or less likely?

8. *Unique response to specific treatments.* Do ADHD children with and without comorbid disorders differ in their response to either psychopharmacological or psychosocial interventions?

Throughout Chapters 6–13, we review the evidence (where it is available) on whether the comorbid disorder meets the test to be regarded as a distinct entity.

PITFALLS IN THE STUDY OF COMORBIDITY

There are two areas of misunderstanding in the study of ADHD with comorbid psychiatric disorder.

First, some clinicians use the term comorbidity to refer to fact that the child has experienced a particular stressor, rather than meeting DSM-IV criteria for two different disorders. Suppose a child meets DSM-IV criteria for only ADHD, but during the interview the parent reports that the child witnessed his father being killed in a car accident 3 years ago. The child is interviewed and states that he was sad at the time but has "gotten over it," and he denies any flashbacks, intrusive memories, or symptoms of posttraumatic stress disorder (PTSD). The clinician, working from a psychodynamic perspective, is convinced that such a traumatic event must have left some mark and recommends play therapy for the comorbid disorder of PTSD. In other cases, children are diagnosed as depressed or anxious because they are presumed to be having unconscious emotional conflicts because of divorce or some other psychosocial stressor. This is not the definition of comorbidity we use in this volume: while we discuss the debates about how best to elicit from a parent DSM symptoms in a child, we always assume that if a child with ADHD has a comorbid disorder, he/she meets full, overt, symptom-based DSM-IV criteria for that disorder.

A second concern is the role of referral bias in determining rates of comorbidity of different psychiatric disorders with ADHD. As a general rule of thumb, the lowest rates of comorbidity are found in large community/epidemiological samples. The majority of ADHD children in these samples have no comorbid diagnosis at all. No cases of bipolar disorder emerged in a large epidemiological study (August, Realmuto, MacDonald, Nugent, & Crosby, 1996), and no cases were found in a community sample of over 600 children with ADHD recruited for the National Institute of Mental Health (NIMH) multimodality treatment of ADHD study. In contrast, studies of ADHD children in tertiary care centers or institutional settings yield very high rates of mood and conduct disorders. Thompson, Riggs, Mikulich, and Crowley (1996) found that nearly one-third of institutionalized ADHD boys meet criteria for mania. We mention this because clinicians, particularly those in primary care settings, read about high rates of comorbidity in some studies and worry that they are "missing" diagnoses. By the same token, clinicians in community mental health centers or long-term residential units may feel as though they never see a case of ADHD that is not comorbid with some psychiatric disorder. It is incumbent upon investigators in this area to describe their referral patterns thoroughly and not to overgeneralize their findings to dissimilar populations. Readers should consider the referral bases of their practices when comparing their experience to the results of studies.

COMORBIDITY AND DOMAINS OF FUNCTIONING

Historically, the study of abnormal behavior has been linked to the field of medicine. As such, medical or psychiatric approaches have focused on establishing diagnoses that then dictate specific pharmacological treatments. The goal of treatment is to reduce or eliminate diagnostic symptoms, and treatment efficacy is based on symptom remission. In the medical model, the history is taken to elicit symptoms, for example, of poor concentration. The physician must determine (by looking at the patient's full range of symptoms) if the poor concentration is due to ADHD (for which stimulants are indicated) as opposed to major depressive disorder (in which case antidepressants would be prescribed). The "either–or" approach is that of "differential diagnoses." The physician must also consider the possibility of "dual diagnoses," that is, when it is more appropriate to diagnose the patient with both conditions rather than choosing between them. (This process will be discussed in detail in Chapter 2.) In any case, making a categorical diagnosis is critical to selection of the appropriate pharmacological agent.

In contrast to the medical approach to treatment, the behavioral approach focuses on domains of impairment rather than psychiatric diagnoses. The goals of behavioral assessment and behavioral treatment are directed by the impact of psychiatric symptoms on functioning in multiple areas, including well-defined domains of school, home, and playground settings; this approach is closely related to the evaluation of impairment in a psychiatric assessment. For example, instead of verifying the presence, onset, and number of inattentive and hyperactive–impulsive symptoms, the purpose of evaluating symptoms of ADHD in a behavioral assessment would be to define the impact of inattention and hyperactivity–impulsivity on functioning in the classroom, in the home, and on the playground. Also, the effectiveness of behavioral treatment is evaluated in terms of improvement of functioning across domains rather than in terms of changes in the specific symptoms and/or criteria of diagnosis of ADHD.

Accordingly, the same behavioral interventions target problem behaviors that may occur across comorbid conditions. Furthermore, decoding the etiology of a specific problem behavior is not necessarily required for intervention. For example, whether school refusal stems from the oppositional behavior associated with a disruptive behavior disorder or from apprehension associated with separation anxiety disorder, sanctions and reinforcements are appropriate and effective treatment components. This is not to say that etiological considerations may not at times be relevant aspects of treatment planning; in the previous situation, the child with separation anxiety may also benefit from adjunctive treatment components including education (i.e., about the situational components that contribute to school anxiety and the natural course of separation anxiety) and interventions that directly target decreased anxiety. The behavioral model addresses this issue in its consideration of antecedent events as relevant aspects of treatment planning; in the foregoing example, different antecedents would have been identified for the oppositional child than for the anxious one.

Traditionally, behavior problems have been classified as involving behavioral excesses or behavioral deficits (although some problems, such as poor academic skills, do not clearly map onto this distinction). As a disruptive behavior disorder, ADHD (as well as ODD and CD) is defined by behavioral excesses, such as high rates of talking out in class and teasing peers. In contrast, some of the comorbid disorders (e.g., depression and anxiety) are defined by behavioral deficits, such as social withdrawal and avoidance of feared situations. The goals of combined pharmacological and behavioral treatments may be additive, with both interventions addressing similar symptoms or target behaviors. Alternatively, the goals may be complementary, such that the combined treatments address different target symptoms. Complementary goals, however, are often involved to address behavioral deficits. Thus, treatment with stimulants alone may decrease negative interactions but not increase positive interactions at home, at school, or on the playground. Specific targets of behavioral interventions (cooperation, participation, communication, and validation) and specific behavioral techniques (shaping and prompting with positive reinforcement) may address the complementary goal of taking advantage of time-limited reductions in behavioral excesses to address behavioral deficits.

The basic premise of our approach is that psychiatric diagnoses and domains of functioning are related. For each diagnostic category, the specific psychiatric symptoms defining the disorder and relevant medications will be delineated. In addition, the associated problem domains will be identified, with specific target behaviors and examples of behavioral interventions (across categories of reinforcement, punishment, stimulus control, and extinction) outlined. Let us return to the symptom of Irritability in an ADHD child. From a categorical perspective, the physician must determine whether the irritability is part of a comorbid ODD or whether there is a comorbid mood disorder (either depression or mania). This distinction will influence the choice of psychotropic medication—stimulants versus antidepressants versus mood stabilizers.

For the behavior therapist, however, it is critical to explore the context of the irritability and the behaviors it produces (temper outbursts, crying, verbal aggression). What triggers these behaviors? What are the consequences of them? What factors are reinforcing them? Then a behavior plan can be devised to help parents and teachers cope with the behavior. This aspect of the treatment proceeds independent of the DSM diagnosis but parallel with it.

ORGANIZATION OF THIS BOOK

The primary emphasis of this book is on issues faced by clinicians in practice; implications of this practical focus include less detailed coverage of research issues, recognition of constraints related to managed care, and the necessity for brief assessments and interventions in many cases. In Part II, we provide a discussion of psychiatric and behavioral assessment, and provide assessment instruments that can be utilized both in establishing diagnoses and in identifying areas of behavioral impairment. Part III provides an overview of pharmacological and behavioral treatment approaches. In Part IV, we discuss the various comorbid diagnoses and specific treatments for them, including disruptive behavior disorders (including substance abuse), neurological disorders, affective disorders, anxiety disorders, mental retardation and pervasive developmental disorders, medical disorders, learning disorders, and obsessive–compulsive and tic disorders. In Part V, we identify potential areas of impairment and their specific treatments, including problems in home, classroom, and playground. Finally, the Epilogue discusses future directions in comorbidity research and treatment. We assume throughout that the reader has basic familiarity with ADHD in terms of its diagnostic criteria and basic treatment principles.

II

Assessment

2

Psychiatric Assessment

This chapter focuses on the best ways to elicit signs and symptoms and classify them into diagnostic categories. The subsequent chapter, on behavioral assessment (Chapter 3), discusses techniques for assessing maladaptive behaviors across different diagnostic categories. When assessing the child with multiple problems, the clinician faces a variety of issues:

1. Should the clinical interview have an open-ended or highly structured format? What kinds of data are to be more heavily weighed: data about signs and symptoms or information about the child's life history and psychological dynamics? What kinds of formal structured interviews are available to aid the clinician in this process?
2. Which of the possible informants (parent, teacher, or child) are most helpful in eliciting symptoms? Does the reliability of informants vary depending on the type of symptom one is inquiring about (i.e., inattentiveness vs. depression)?
3. Since, as noted in the Chapter 1, DSM-IV can assign the same symptom to two (or more) diagnostic categories (e.g., distractibility is a symptom of both ADHD and bipolar disorder; poor concentration is a symptom of both depression and ADHD), how can the interview process proceed so that the clinician can determine whether the symptom "counts" toward one particular diagnosis or to both (or all) of them? Here the clinician must struggle with two processes: *differential diagnosis*—that is, assigning a symptom complex to one of many diagnoses—versus *dual (or multiple) diagnoses*—wherein it is decided that the symptoms complex represents two (or more) separate diagnoses.

INTERVIEW STYLE: OPEN-ENDED VERSUS STRUCTURED FORMATS

In a traditional open-ended mental health interview, the informant (whether parent or child) is allowed to set the pace and describe his/her problems. The clinician speaks as little as possible, except to ask for clarification. The open-ended interview places more emphasis on the informant's affect than on the facts of the history per se. The clinician pays attention to facial expression and emotional responses as the informant speaks. In an open-ended format, informants often mix descriptions of symptoms ("My child won't sit still") with information about life events ("My husband won't spend any time with him"). The open-ended interview is a helpful way to uncover psychological processes in the parent, family, or child. If the informant is a good historian, the open-ended interview may yield adequate data about the child's specific behavior problems. Advantages of the open-ended interview include its relaxed style, as well as its ability to make patients (or, more importantly, their parents) feel at ease and listened to. It sets the tone for future psychotherapy, if this is the clinician's goal. Also, families may spontaneously report events that they attach no importance to but which the clinician might wish to explore further.

Open-ended interviews have their disadvantages, however, particularly for the type of child we are focusing on in this book. Informants vary dramatically in the amount and type of data they offer. Some individuals will spend a great deal of time describing life events that may not in fact turn out to be relevant to the child's problems. Others will fail to mention important symptoms (e.g., suicidal ideation) unless specifically asked. Finally, in an open-ended interview symptoms may be described in no particular order, making it difficult for the clinician to keep track of the number and age of onset of symptoms. As we shall see, such data are critical in the determining the presence of comorbid disorders. All of these factors suggest that a more structured approach is needed in the complicated ADHD child. To these clinical issues are added practical ones: clinicians increasingly have a limited amount of time to spend with patients. It is rare that the physician can spend 2–3 hours with a family; even bringing a family back for multiple history-taking visits before treatment is started is often not possible. This forces the clinician to use a more efficient structured approach.

Such efficiency is paramount in the modern health care environment. In many cases, the physician's role in the treatment of the ADHD child is limited to medication management. The physician may be part of a multidisciplinary team where other mental health professionals provide the psychosocial treatment. When a patient is referred to a physician for medication management only, the focus of the interview is different from when the physician is the only clinician treating the child. Physicians become concerned that they do not have the time to evaluate the "whole child" and that the briefer, more structured clinical interview might cause them to "miss" important psychosocial information that would influence their decision to use medication. Suppose a physician evaluates a 7-year-old and learns that the child has been hyperactive and inattentive for the past 2 years, during which period the parents have been getting divorced. Could psychological stress from the divorce be "causing" the ADHD symptoms? Would family therapy be a better treatment than stimulants? The physician might well argue that this cannot be determined by a "medication evaluation" and time is needed to completely assess the psychodynamics of the family.

Such concerns arise from the notion that psychosocial variables, as opposed to symptoms, predict whether or not a child will respond to a psychotropic medication. The issue of whether psychosocial variables influence stimulant response has been thoroughly examined in a study from the United Kingdom whose results should be better disseminated among American clinicians. E. Taylor et al. (1987) evaluated 38 boys with serious disruptive behavior. As part of the baseline assessment, a wide variety of family life measures were obtained: parental coping and consistency, expressed warmth and criticisms, quality of parents' marriage, socioeconomic status, family size, separations from parents, and history of foster care or neglect. All the children underwent a double-blind placebo-controlled crossover trial of methylphenidate. Analyses were performed to determine if the family variables predicted which children would respond to stimulant. One might expect that children from "stressful" family backgrounds might not respond to stimulant since their behavior problems were "caused" by the poor environment rather than anything "biological." In fact, the family variables had no role in predicting stimulant response. If a child had high levels of inattentiveness and hyperactivity, he had an equally good chance of responding to stimulants whether he came from a home that was high or low in adverse family events. We are not arguing that a positive stimulant response absolutely confirms a diagnosis of ADHD, but clearly one should not assume that symptoms of ADHD arise for whatever stressful situation the child is in and therefore are not amenable to pharmacological intervention. Similarly, data in adults with affective disorder have not shown that psychosocial stressors predict which patients are more likely to respond to antidepressants. Thus a major principle in this book is that a symptom pattern (inattentiveness, hyperactivity, depression, anxiety, aggression) will predict which drugs are most likely to be useful in a given child. Structured interviews lend themselves to such a clinical assessment, so we will give a brief overview of those interviews that may be of practical use in the clinician's office.

Structured clinical interviews were originally developed to allow researchers to make reliable diagnoses to include children in a study protocol, as well as to provide a standardized means of making diagnoses in large-scale epidemiological studies. These interviews fall into two categories. In the highly structured format, lists of symptoms are presented to the informant who simply states whether or not the symptom is present or absent. No clinician need be present. The Diagnostic Interview Schedule for Children (DISC; Schwab-Stone et al., 1996; Shaffer et al., 1996), and the Diagnostic Interview for Children and Adolescents (DICA; Welner, Reich, Herjanic, Jung, & Amado, 1987) all fall into this category. In contrast, the Schedule for Affective Disorders and Schizophrenia for School Age Children—Present and Lifetime Version (K-SADS-PL or "Kiddie-SADS"; Kaufman et al., 1997) is a semi-structured interview designed for use by clinicians. The informant is asked by the clinician about a symptom, and the clinician uses his or her own judgment to rate the severity of the symptom on a scale. Each type of interview has advantages and disadvantages.

The DISC has a long history of development, with extensive data on reliability and validity available (Fisher, Blouin, & Shaffer, 1993; Jensen et al., 1995; Piacentini et al., 1993; Schwab-Stone et al., 1993, 1996; Shaffer et al., 1993, 1996). Most of these studies were done on the DISC-2.3 version, which followed DSM-III-R criteria. Recently the DISC-4 has been published, updating all the criteria to DSM-IV. A computerized version is available that makes administration much easier. (Indeed, manual administration of the DISC, which is several hundred pages long, would be impossible in the clinical setting.) The interview covers all 31 DSM diagnoses that are known to occur in children. Questions are grouped into 27 diagnostic groupings (ADHD, depression, bipolar disorders, etc). The computer allows the examiner to administer particular diagnostic modules. The examiner can read the questions off the computer screen to the informant (when the informant is a poor reader) or the informant may sit at the computer and enter the responses him/herself. The informant, whether parent or child, must answer "yes" or "no" to most of the questions. The examiner does not have the leeway to change the questions. If the informant answers "yes," the computer asks if the symptoms has been present in the last year, the last 6 months, or the last 4 weeks. At the end of a diagnostic module, the computer asks questions about the degree of impairment that the symptoms have caused. The computer automatically scores the interview and displays the diagnoses generated. The DISC has a parent and youth version; the latter version *cannot* be administered to children under 12.

It takes an average parent about an hour to complete all the modules, but it can take much longer if a parent is a slow reader or responder, or endorses many symptoms in the child, as this requires the computer to ask many more questions. The DICA-4 is quite similar in format to the DISC, though the research on it in terms of reliability and validity has not been as extensive (Welner et al., 1987). The DICA-4 is also available in a computerized version.

The K-SADS-PL can also generate up to 32 DSM-IV childhood diagnoses and can only be administered by clinicians. After a 10- to 15-minute introductory interview, there are 82 screen questions divided into 20 diagnostic areas. If a child meets the threshold criteria for a disorder during the screen interview, the interviewer then goes on to ask the full range of questions about the disorder. If the screen interview is negative for that diagnosis, then the full interview for that category is skipped. The complete questions are contained in diagnostic supplements, of which there are five: (1) affective disorders; (2) psychotic disorders; (3) anxiety disorders; (4) behavioral disorders; and (5) substance abuse, eating, and tic disorders. The items in the supplements are rated by the clinician on a 0–3 rating scale, with 0 indicating no information, 1 meaning the symptom is not present, 2 indicating subthreshhold level of the symptoms, and 3 meaning that the symptom is definitely present. First the parent is interviewed alone, and then the child is interviewed. The final ratings are a synthesis of the parent report and the child report. Generally, greater weight is given to parental report of disruptive behaviors, while the child is relied upon for reports of his/her own subjective feelings (depression, anxiety). Each clinician, however, is free to use his/her own clinical judgment is integrating parent and child data. Test–Retest reliability data on the K-SADS-PL appear quite good, ranging from .9 for depression to .63 for ADHD (Kaufman et al., 1997). Each site where the K-SADS-PL is used must ascertain that different clinicians are administering the interview in a consistent manner.

The DISC has the advantage of highly standardized administration and extensive reliability data. Lay interviewers can be trained to administer it, or the parent can enter the data directly into the computer. It forms an excellent database, but a clinician must review the interview and integrate the information with other data (teacher report, rating scales, etc.). A computerized DISC diagnosis by itself is not sufficient to make the full clinical diagnosis. As already noted, the DISC cannot be administered to children under 12, and even adolescents must have patience to sit through it. The K-SADS-PL corresponds more to what clinicians do in their offices, but clinicians will come up with different diagnoses if their interview styles differ. Both interviews make clinicians explore the full range of DSM-III diagnoses and develop a sense of the time frame of how the different disorders emerged in a given patients (i.e., did the ADHD symptoms begin before the depression, or vice versa?). This systematic approach is critical to achievement of an accurate diagnosis of the multisymptom child, as we shall see in later chapters.

WHO IS THE BEST INFORMANT?

Disagreements often emerge from separate parent and child interviews. What should the clinician do if the child states she is sad but the parent denied that the child was depressed? If the child denies any hyperactivity, should the clinician give this any weight? According to a longstanding clinical practice, adults (parents and teachers) are presumed to be better reporters of children's disruptive behaviors, whereas children themselves are generally considered more reliable informants when it comes to internalizing symptoms such as depression or anxiety (Edelbrock, Costello, Dulcan, Conover, & Kalas, 1986; Loeber, Green, Lahey, & Stouthamer-Loeber, 1989; Reich & Earls, 1987; Welner et al., 1987). Bird, Gould, and Staghezza (1992) examined this issue empirically. They performed DISC interviews on several hundred parent–child pairs. DISC diagnoses were generated, and then a clinician made a separate diagnosis of the child, which served as the external validating criterion ("the gold standard"). Statistical methods were used to determine if, for a given diagnosis, the parent or child data were most critical to make the diagnosis. For instance, if a child was given a diagnosis of ADHD by the clinician, did the parent or the child endorse the inattention and hyperactivity items on the DISC? Or did they both endorse symptoms of ADHD? For ADHD and oppositional defiant disorder (ODD), *only* the parent DISC predicted the diagnoses, whereas for anxiety and depressive diagnoses, *both* the parent and child DISC contributed to the diagnosis.

The data of Bird et al. (1992) clearly showed that the parents and children only agree about 20% of the time. Using the method of Loeber et al. (1989), Bird and colleagues examined the percentage of time children endorsed a symptom if their parent had said the child had it. Note that if the parent said the child fidgeted, about 45% of the children agreed that they fidgeted; if, however, the parent said the child failed to finish things, only 18% of the children agreed that they had this problem. A similar pattern was found for internalizing symptoms. If the parent stated the child worried a great deal, 58% of the children agreed. If the parent stated the child was depressed, only 20% of the children agreed. If a child says he has a symptom, what percentage of parents agree? The pattern is not any more consistent. Bird et al. (1992) next looked at the prevalence of diagnoses in their sample if they based the diagnoses on the parent interview only, the child interview only, or a combination of the parent and child interview. In the latter method, if the either the parent or the child DISC interview yields a diagnosis, that diagnosis is regarded as present. Basically, the "either–or" method yields somewhat higher prevalence estimates of the disorders. Children will deny they have ADHD or ODD when adults clearly state it is present, but they will report more internalizing symptoms than adults have observed.

In this volume, we accept the "received wisdom" that adults are better reporters of externalizing symptoms and children of internalizing disorders. The reader should be aware, however, that many questions remain unanswered about the discrepancy between parent and child reporting of symptoms, particularly with regard to the internalizing disorders. These issues are discussed further in later chapters.

MULTIPLE VERSUS DIFFERENTIAL DIAGNOSIS

The clinician must have an algorithm in his/her head about how to classify the many symptoms encountered in the psychiatric interview, as well as how to sort them into diagnostic categories. A case example is helpful in illustrating this process:

> Nine-year-old James was brought to the clinic by his mother because of poor school performance. Currently a third grader, he had been described by his teachers throughout elementary school as careless, sloppy, and unable to finish his work. He fidgets and makes noises, but does not get out of his seat or run around the classroom. On the playground he is shy and does not play with the other children. The teacher reported that he has said, "I'm ugly and stupid" when asked why he does not get along with the other children.
>
> The mother also has trouble getting James to complete tasks at home. He seems unable to concentrate on his homework. He throws temper tantrums when pushed to do things. He cries, stamps his feet, and hurls things around. He does not become physically aggressive. He often says, "I hate you" or "I hate my life" when very angry. He does not want to go to bed at night and calls out for water and says he can't sleep. Once asleep, he stays asleep through the night. He has always been a picky eater. He is very nervous in new situations. He has never tried to deliberately hurt himself. His mother states that James is in a "bad mood" much of the time but does not say he is sad.

> During the examination, James is cooperative and friendly. He doesn't seem restless during the interview, but it is difficult to get him to concentrate on the questions asked. He says he hates school because "it is boring and the kids are mean." He states he is sad because there is no one to play with in his neighborhood and his dad does not always visit him. He is scared of the dark and worries that something bad will happen to his mom. He once wished he was dead when his mom grounded him, but he denies any suicidal ideation currently.

This case presents with a mixture of anxiety, depressive, and inattentive/hyperactive symptoms. The clinician must determine whether this a case of ADHD, depression, or a truly comorbid case of ADHD and depression. Figure 2.1 illustrates how a clinician can step through the data to arrive at the appropriate conclusion. After a structured interview, one of several patterns may be evident.

James may meet full criteria for ADHD, with onset of the symptoms before age 7. The interview detects symptoms of depression, but the child does not meet the full criteria for major depressive disorder (MDD) or dysthymia. The depressive symptoms may stem from a variety of issues. They may be centered on the child's unhappiness over the consequences of his ADHD behavior. Children will not play with him because he acts silly or is irritating. He might miss activities because of frequent misbehavior. This pattern was termed "demoralization" by Dennis P. Cantwell many years ago. It does not constitute a true depressive disorder, though it certainly may be the focus of psychosocial intervention. The psychotropic management would focus on the ADHD, most likely beginning with stimulant treatment. Antidepressant medication would not be the first-line treatment in such a child. The primary diagnosis made would be ADHD, though a diagnosis of adjustment disorder with depressed mood might be entertained if the demoralization symptoms were significantly impairing. The child would not be regarded as truly comorbid.

In the middle box of Figure 2.1, a somewhat more complex outcome of the interview is illustrated. The child clearly meets full criteria for MDD, and the child reports pervasively depressed mood. ADHD symptoms are present, but the child does not meet the full criteria for ADHD. He has a number of inattentive symptoms, as well as three impulsive–hyperactive symptoms. Age of onset is a critical issue. If these symptoms were not present before age 7, by definition he does not have ADHD. Equally important is whether these ADHD symptoms had their onset only after the depressive symptoms emerged. If so, it is likely they may be secondary to the MDD. The depression would be the focus of

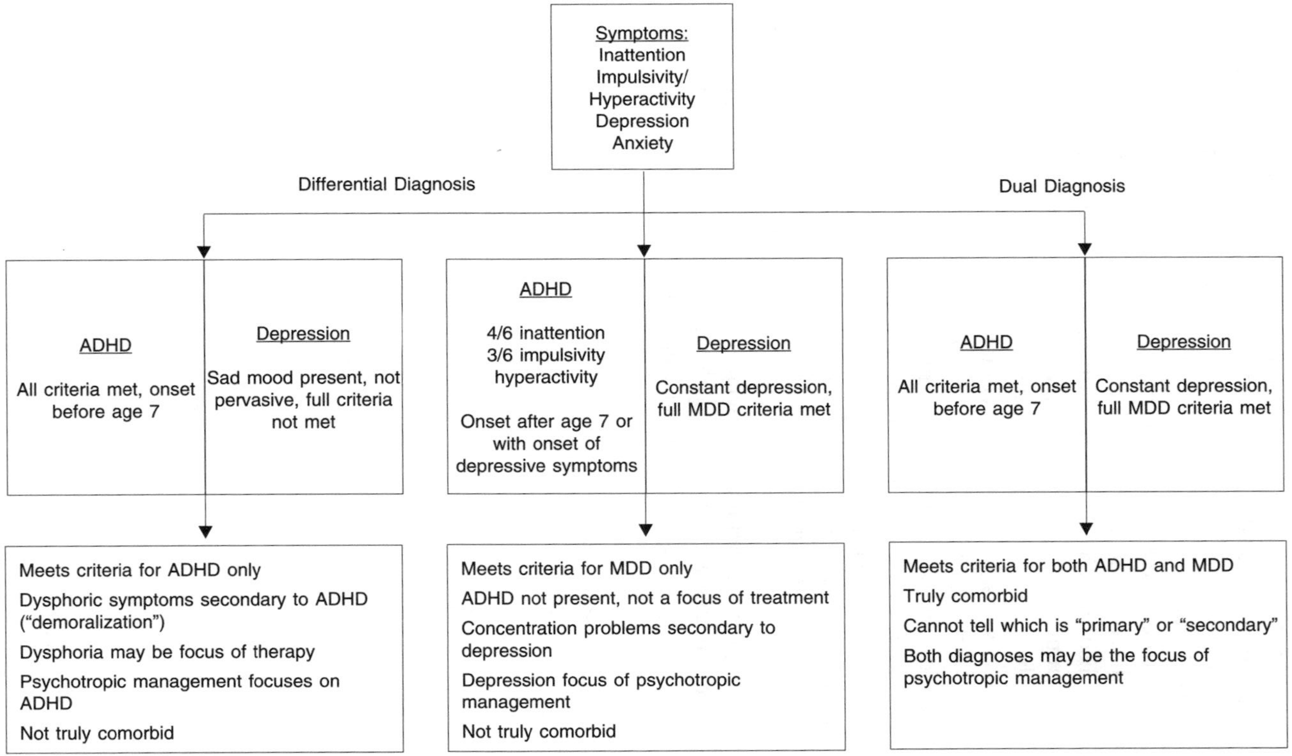

Symptoms:
Inattention
Impulsivity/
Hyperactivity
Depression
Anxiety

Differential Diagnosis

Dual Diagnosis

ADHD
All criteria met, onset before age 7

Depression
Sad mood present, not pervasive, full criteria not met

Meets criteria for ADHD only
Dysphoric symptoms secondary to ADHD ("demoralization")
Dysphoria may be focus of therapy
Psychotropic management focuses on ADHD
Not truly comorbid

ADHD
4/6 inattention
3/6 impulsivity
hyperactivity
Onset after age 7 or with onset of depressive symptoms

Depression
Constant depression, full MDD criteria met

Meets criteria for MDD only
ADHD not present, not a focus of treatment
Concentration problems secondary to depression
Depression focus of psychotropic management
Not truly comorbid

ADHD
All criteria met, onset before age 7

Depression
Constant depression, full MDD criteria met

Meets criteria for both ADHD and MDD
Truly comorbid
Cannot tell which is "primary" or "secondary"
Both diagnoses may be the focus of psychotropic management

FIGURE 2.1. Hypothetical algorithm for differential and dual diagnosis of a child with both ADHD and depressive symptoms.

the psychotropic management, as well as any psychological intervention. It would be expected that the inattentive and impulsive symptoms would resolve once the child's depression lifted. Again, this would not be a truly comorbid case.

The box to the far right of Figure 2.1 illustrates the most complex situation of all. After the interview, the child is found to fully meet criteria for both disorders. The child is inattentive, impulsive, and hyperactive; these symptoms are pervasive and have been present since early childhood. The child is also pervasively depressed and has multiple neurovegetative signs. This is a truly comorbid case. There is no way to tell for sure which diagnosis is "primary" and which is "secondary." Indeed, the child may be suffering from two independent disorders, each requiring its own treatment. Thus both diagnoses may be the focus of psychotropic or psychological treatment. It is this type of case that is the focus of this book. The clinical interview as we have described it is only one (albeit the most important) part of the child's assessment. There are also a variety of standardized instruments to assess child behavior problems that will greatly expand the clinician's grasp of a complex case. The next chapter will review those rating scales that are most likely to be useful in the workup of a complex ADHD child or adolescent.

3

Behavioral Assessment

In Chapter 2, we described procedures for clinical interviews and explained why the structured interview is recommended: this procedure organizes information by sets of symptoms that define disorders, and it is an efficient way to acquire information within the limited time available in modern mental health care settings. In this chapter, we describe some procedures that are based on rating scales, which can be used for three purposes: (1) to screen children for disorders in preparation for the clinical interview, (2) to establish a baseline of symptoms against which the success of treatment can be measured, and (3) to identify specific areas of impairment that are the focus of psychosocial interventions.

A number of rating scales have been developed that aid in the assessment of both behavioral (acting out) and emotional (internalizing) symptoms. Rating scales that are useful in work with children are shown in Table 3.1. We focus on the SNAP-IV Rating Scale, a revision of the Swanson, Nolan, and Pelham (SNAP) Questionnaire (Swanson, Sandman, Deutsch, & Baren, 1983). Over the past 20 years, the SNAP has been revised along with the DSM criteria (American Psychiatric Association, 1980, 1987, 1994). The SNAP has been refined, developed, and used for the evaluation of effects of medication (Swanson et al., 1983), for assessment of school behavior (Atkins, Pelham, & Licht, 1985, 1988; Swanson, 1992), for epidemiological screening (Gaub & Carlson, 1997a), for assessment of gender differences (Gaub & Carlson, 1997b), and for monitoring outcome in treatment studies. The SNAP-IV is based on the symptoms listed in the DSM-IV manual, so its content is the same as that of the DISC-4 structured interview described in Chapter 2. It dif-

TABLE 3.1. Common Rating Scales Used to Assess Childhood Psychiatric Symptoms

Scale name	Information
SNAP/SKAMP	See text
Conners Parent Rating Scale—Revised (CPRS-R)	Most recent revision of Conners Rating Scales (CRS). Has both long (80-item) and short (27-item) versions. Parent rates item as not at all, just a little, pretty much, or very much. Contains ADHD index that includes all 18 DSM-IV symptoms. Long form has 10 subscales: oppositional, cognitive problems, hyperactive–impulsive, anxious–shy, perfectionism, social problems, psychosomatic, DSM-IV subscales, ADHD index, and Conners Global Index (Conners, 1998).
Conners Teacher Rating Scale—Revised (CPRS-R)	Also has long (59-item) and short (28-item) versions. Long form contains all of the above subscales except psychosomatic. Includes ADHD index (Conners, 1998).
Conners–Wells Adolescent Self-Report Scales	Self-report form for adolescents. Long (87-item) and short (27-item) versions available. Normed on adolescents. Long form includes the following subscales: family problems, conduct problems, anger control problems, emotional problems, inattention, hyperactivity, ADHD index (Conners, 1998).
ADHD Rating Scales–IV	18-item scale using ADHD DSM-IV criteria (DuPaul, Power, Anastopoulos, & Reid, 1998).
Children's Depression Inventory (CDI)	27-item scale. On each item, child selects option that best fits him or her: "I am sad all the time"; "I am sad some of the time"; "I am never sad." Not diagnostic, but useful in screening and documenting response to treatment (Kovacs, 1998).
Revised Manifest Anxiety Scale (RCMAS)	37 items written at third-grade level. Child answers "yes" or "no" to each item. Well-established norms, not diagnostic, but useful in screening and documenting response to treatment (Reynolds & Richmond, 1997).
Screen for Child Anxiety Related Emotional Disorders (SCARED)	38-item scale with parent and child forms. Subject responds to each item with 0—not true, 1—sometimes true, or 2—often true. Yields five factors: somatic/panic, general anxiety, separation anxiety, social phobia, and school phobia. Discriminates depressed/anxious children from disruptive behavior disorders; no norms as yet (Birmaher et al., 1997).
Multidimensional Anxiety Scale for Children (MASC)	39-item scale with four factors: physical symptoms, social anxiety, separation anxiety, and harm avoidance. Fourth-grade reading level (March et al., 1997).

fers in how the information about symptoms is acquired. The SNAP-IV questionnaire is not meant to replace the clinical interview. Instead, it is designed to provide advance information to enhance the interview process. Instead of a face-to-face interview with the parent or teacher, as in the DISC-4 interview in which questions are asked about each symptom, the symptoms of the SNAP-IV are listed (by disorder) on a paper form to be sent to these sources for completion before the interview is conducted. The range of responses to each item also differs for the SNAP and DISC. Instead of specifying the presence or absence of each symptom (i.e., by a yes/no answer as in the DISC-4 interview), on the SNAP-IV the respondent (the parent or teacher) is asked to rate how much each symptom is characteristic of the child's typical behavior.

Page 1 of the SNAP-IV is shown in Figure 3.1. Each item is stated as it appears in the DSM manual. Each "source" (the parent or teacher) is asked to rate the same set of items on a 4-point scale—not at all, just a little, quite a bit, or very much. The term "often" usually appears in the DSM format for ADHD items, and this distinguishes the psychiatric symptom from normal childhood behavior.

The items from the DSM-IV (American Psychiatric Association, 1994) criteria for ADHD are included for the two subsets of symptoms: inattention (items #1–#9) and hyperactivity/impulsivity (items #11–#19), with a summary item for each domain (#10 and #20). Also, items are included from the DSM-IV criteria for oppositional defiant disorder (ODD; items #21–#28), since it often is present in children with ADHD, as well as an item from DSM-III-R (#29) that was not included in the DSM-IV and a summary item for the ODD domain (#30).

In addition to the DSM-IV items for ADHD and ODD, the SNAP-IV contains items from the Conners Index Questionnaire and the Iowa Conners Questionnaire (Loney & Milich, 1979, 1982) that are not in the DSM-IV symptom list. The 10-item IOWA questionnaire has separate items that measure inattention/overactivity (I/O—items #4, #8, #11, #31, #32) and aggression/defiance (A/D—items #21, #23, #29, #34, #35). The 10 Conners Index (items #4, #8, #11, #21, #32, #33, #36, #37, #38, #39) was developed by selecting the items that loaded highest on the multiple factors of the full Conners Questionnaire. These items were included to allow the SNAP-IV to provide scores on the historically important and clinically relevant scales.

The 4-point response is scored 0–3 (not at all = 0, just a little = 1, quite a bit = 2, and very much = 3). Subscale scores on the SNAP-IV are calculated by summing the scores on the items in the specific subset (e.g., inattention) and dividing by the number of items in the subset (e.g., 9). The score for any subset is expressed as the average rating per item, as shown for ratings on the ADHD–inattentive (ADHD-I) subset in Figure 3.2.

Name ______________________ Gender ________ Age ________ Grade ________

Ethnicity: African-American ___ Asian ___ Caucasian ___ Hispanic ___ Other ______________

For teacher: Completed by __________________ Type of class __________ Class size _______

For parent: Completed by ___________ No. of parents living in home ______ Family size _______

Period of time covered by rating: Past week __ Past month __ Past year __ Lifetime __ Other _______

For each item, check the column that best describes this child:	Not at all	Just a little	Quite a bit	Very much
1. Often fails to give close attention to details or makes careless mistakes in schoolwork or tasks	_____	_____	_____	_____
2. Often has difficulty sustaining attention in tasks or play activities	_____	_____	_____	_____
3. Often does not seem to listen when spoken to directly	_____	_____	_____	_____
4. Often does not follow through on instructions and fails to finish schoolwork, chores, or duties	_____	_____	_____	_____
5. Often has difficulty organizing tasks and activities	_____	_____	_____	_____
6. Often avoids, dislikes, or reluctantly engages in tasks requiring sustained mental effort	_____	_____	_____	_____
7. Often loses things necessary for activities (e.g., toys, school assignments, pencils, or books)	_____	_____	_____	_____
8. Often is distracted by extraneous stimuli	_____	_____	_____	_____
9. Often is forgetful in daily activities	_____	_____	_____	_____
10. Often has difficulty maintaining alertness, orienting to requests, or executing directions	_____	_____	_____	_____
11. Often fidgets with hands or feet or squirms in seat	_____	_____	_____	_____
12. Often leaves seat in classroom or in other situations in which remaining seated is expected	_____	_____	_____	_____
13. Often runs about or climbs excessively in situations in which it is inappropriate	_____	_____	_____	_____
14. Often has difficulty playing or engaging in leisure activities quietly	_____	_____	_____	_____
15. Often is "on the go" or often acts as if "driven by a motor"	_____	_____	_____	_____
16. Often talks excessively	_____	_____	_____	_____
17. Often blurts out answers before questions have been completed	_____	_____	_____	_____
18. Often has difficulty awaiting turn	_____	_____	_____	_____
19. Often interrupts or intrudes on others (e.g., butts into conversations/games)	_____	_____	_____	_____
20. Often has difficulty sitting still, being quiet, or inhibiting impulses in the classroom or at home	_____	_____	_____	_____

(continued)

FIGURE 3.1. The SNAP-IV Syndrome Rating Scale for Teachers and Parents.

21. Often loses temper				
22. Often argues with adults				
23. Often actively defies or refuses adult requests or rules				
24. Often deliberately does things that annoy other people				
25. Often blames others for his or her mistakes or misbehavior				
26. Often is touchy or easily annoyed by others				
27. Often is angry and resentful				
28. Often is spiteful or vindictive				
29. Often is quarrelsome				
30. Often is negative, defiant, disobedient, or hostile toward authority figures				
31. Often makes noises (e.g., humming or odd sounds)				
32. Often is excitable, impulsive				
33. Often cries easily				
34. Often is uncooperative				
35. Often acts "smart"				
36. Often is restless or overactive				
37. Often disturbs other children				
38. Often changes mood quickly and drastically				
39. Often is easily frustrated if demands are not met immediately				
40. Often teases other children and interferes with their activities				

FIGURE 3.1. *cont.*

		Not at all	Just a little	Quite a bit	Very much	Item score
1.	Makes careless mistakes			×		2
2.	Can't pay attention				×	3
3.	Doesn't listen				×	3
4.	Fails to finish work			×		2
5.	Disorganized		×			1
6.	Can't concentrate				×	3
7.	Loses things		×			1
8.	Distractible				×	3
9.	Forgetful	×				0

Total ADHD-I score = 18; ADHD-I score = 18/9 = 2.0.

FIGURE 3.2. Example of scoring the ADHD-I section of the SNAP.

A scoring template for the ADHD and ODD of items on the SNAP-IV is presented in Figure 3.3. The first two subsets are from assessment of subtypes of ADHD (inattention and hyperactive–impulsive). The third is for assessment of ODD. The next two subsets are for the Iowa Conners dimensions (I/O and A/D). The last subset is for the Conners Index. The Iowa Conners and Conners Index measure ADHD and ODD behavior and thus should correlate with the teacher or parent ratings of inattention or hyperactivity/impulsivity. They may

ADHD inattention		ADHD impulsivity/ hyperactivity		Oppositional defiant disorder		Inattention/ overactivity (I/O)		Aggression/ defiance (A/D)		Conners Index	
#1	_____	#11	_____	#21	_____	#4	_____	#21	_____	#4	_____
#2	_____	#12	_____	#22	_____	#8	_____	#23	_____	#8	_____
#3	_____	#13	_____	#23	_____	#11	_____	#29	_____	#11	_____
#4	_____	#14	_____	#24	_____	#31	_____	#34	_____	#21	_____
#5	_____	#15	_____	#25	_____	#32	_____	#35	_____	#32	_____
#6	_____	#16	_____	#26	_____					#33	_____
#7	_____	#17	_____	#27	_____					#36	_____
#8	_____	#18	_____	#28	_____					#37	_____
#9	_____	#19	_____							#38	_____
										#39	_____

Each subset above is totaled and averaged to produce the scores specified below:

	Inattention	Impulsivity/ hyperactivity	ODD	I/O	A/D	Conners Index
Total	_____	_____	_____	_____	_____	_____
Average:	_____	_____	_____	_____	_____	_____

ADHD—Combined = (Total inattention + Total impulsivity/hyperactivity)/19 = _____

SNAP 95 percentile cutoff scores for ADHD and ODD

	Teacher	Parent
ADHD—inattention	2.56	1.78
ADHD—hyperactivity/impulsivity	1.78	1.44
ADHD—combined	2.00	1.67
ODD	1.38	1.88

FIGURE 3.3. Scoring template for disruptive behavior disorders section of the SNAP.

also be used to track improvements in symptoms following medication treatment.

The SNAP-IV items for ADHD and ODD have been used in surveys of entire schools to produce norms (Gaub & Carlson, 1997a). This allows us to specify a cutoff that separates an abnormal degree of "inattentive and hyperactive/impulsive" behavior from normal behavior in these domains. Two methods have been used to accomplish this: item averaging or item counts.

The *subset average,* calculated by the procedures outlined above, has an unusual distribution in the school population. When the average scores for the individuals of an entire school are graphed, the scores are not normally distributed (i.e., they do not form a "bell-shaped" curve). Instead, since most individuals have very low (or 0) scores, the distribution is "J-shaped." There is an important consequence: the usual descriptive statistics (i.e., the mean and standard deviation) are inappropriate. That is, the usual statistical cutoff based on the mean and standard deviation (e.g., mean + 1.65 *SD,* which in a normal distribution identifies 5% of the cases) produce aberrant results. In the J-shaped distribution, this cutoff identifies over 14% of the cases! It should not be used. Due to this "statistical artifact," our cutoffs are based on percentiles that identified the most extreme 5% of the school population. We present the 95th percentile cutoffs for both "sources" (parents and teachers) for the SNAP-IV in Figure 3.3.

The *item count* procedure is based on a different assumption about the ratings that parents and teachers provide. Instead of a continuous measure of "abnormality," this method assumes that only extreme items contribute. Thus, those items with lower ratings (not at all, just a little, quite a bit) are counted as "absent" and those items with the highest scores (very much) are counted as "present." This item count procedure is aligned better with the criteria for DSM-IV than is the average symptom score procedure. Once the decision is made about what rating category to use for defining "abnormal," the qualifying items are counted and the total is compared to the criterion stated in DSM-IV (i.e., 6 or more symptoms in either or both domains). Using this method, Gaub and Carlson (1997a) obtained the SNAP-IV in 2,744 elementary school children: 221 (8%) meet criteria for one of the subtypes of ADHD based on the fact that teachers rating at least 8 of the inattention or hyperactivity–impulsivity symptoms as "very much"; interestingly, the inattentive subtype was found to be the most common (4.5%), followed by the combined subtype (1.9%), with the hyperactive–impulsive subtype the least common (1.7%). The ratio of males to females was about 2.8:1 for all of the subtypes except the hyperactive–impulsive subtype, where the male predominance was higher (4.1:1). Such diagnoses by rating scale would of course need to be con-

TABLE 3.2. Items on Page 2 of the SNAP-IV and Their Corresponding DSM-IV Diagnoses

#41–#45	Conduct disorder
#46	Intermittent explosive disorder
#47	Tourette's disorder
#48	Stereotypic movement disorder
#49–#50	Obsessive–compulsive disorder
#51–#56	Generalized anxiety disorder
#57	Narcolepsy
#58	Histrionic personality disorder
#59	Narcissistic personality disorder
#60	Borderline personality disorder
#61–#65	Manic episode
#66–#73	Major depressive episode
#74–#76	Dysthymic disorder
#77–#78	Posttraumatic stress disorder
#79–#80	Adjustment disorder

firmed by clinical interview, but the close correspondence between the rates of diagnosis established by the SNAP-IV and that found in epidemiological studies using the DISC 2.3 is encouraging (Shaffer et al., 1996). The SNAP is very user friendly for screening for ADHD as well as other comorbid disorders, as we shall see.

On Page 2 of the SNAP (see Figure 3.4), we have listed symptoms of other disorders that might co-occur with ADHD. Not all symptoms of childhood psychiatric disorders are listed here, but in Table 3.2 we show which items on the SNAP items correspond to 10 non-ADHD disorders. The items that were included on the SNAP-IV were those that overlap or may masquerade as ADHD or ODD. For example, "inattentive" behavior is a symptom of anxiety (item #53) and of depression (item #73) as well as of ADHD (items #1– #9). Thus the SNAP screens for these comorbid disorders, but the clinician must sort them out as described in Chapter 2.

A simple computer program (based on the Access database system and available from one of the present authors, J. M. Swanson) is used to generate a simple report for the SNAP-IV. In addition to the use of the SNAP-IV for information on symptoms of disorders, we have developed other questionnaires for use in the assessment functional impairment at home and school . The first of these was the SKAMP for assessment of classroom manifestations of ADHD in the school setting. The teacher

Check the column that best describes this child.	Not at all	Just a little	Quite a bit	Very much
41. Often is aggressive to other children (e.g., picks fights or bullies)	____	____	____	____
42. Often is destructive with property of others (e.g., vandalism)	____	____	____	____
43. Often is deceitful (e.g., steals, lies, forges, copies the work of others, or "cons" others)	____	____	____	____
44. Often and seriously violates rules (e.g., is truant, runs away, or completely ignores class rules)	____	____	____	____
45. Has persistent pattern of violating the basic rights of others or major societal norms	____	____	____	____
46. Has episodes of failure to resist aggressive impulses (to assault others or to destroy property)	____	____	____	____
47. Has motor or verbal tics (sudden, rapid, recurrent, nonrhythmic motor or verbal activity)	____	____	____	____
48. Has repetitive motor behavior (e.g., hand waving, body rocking, or picking at skin)	____	____	____	____
49. Has obsessions (persistent and intrusive inappropriate ideas, thoughts, or impulses)	____	____	____	____
50. Has compulsions (repetitive behaviors or mental acts to reduce anxiety or distress)	____	____	____	____
51. Often is restless or seems keyed up or on edge	____	____	____	____
52. Often is easily fatigued	____	____	____	____
53. Often has difficulty concentrating (mind goes blank)	____	____	____	____
54. Often is irritable	____	____	____	____
55. Often has muscle tension	____	____	____	____
56. Often has excessive anxiety and worry (e.g., apprehensive expectation)	____	____	____	____
57. Often has daytime sleepiness (unintended sleeping in inappropriate situations)	____	____	____	____
58. Often has excessive emotionality and attention-seeking behavior	____	____	____	____
59. Often has need for undue admiration, grandiose behavior, or lack of empathy	____	____	____	____
60. Often has instability in relationships with others, reactive mood, and impulsivity	____	____	____	____
61 Sometimes for at least a week has inflated self-esteem or grandiosity	____	____	____	____
62. Sometimes for at least a week is more talkative than usual or seems pressured to keep talking	____	____	____	____
63. Sometimes for at least a week has flight of ideas or says that thoughts are racing	____	____	____	____
64. Sometimes for at least a week has elevated, expansive or euphoric mood	____	____	____	____

(continued)

FIGURE 3.4. Page 2 of the SNAP-IV. Screening for Non-ADHD Disorders.

65. Sometimes for at least a week is excessively involved in pleasurable but risky activities ____ ____ ____ ____
66. Sometimes for at least 2 weeks has depressed mood (sad, hopeless, discouraged) ____ ____ ____ ____
67. Sometimes for at least 2 weeks has irritable or cranky mood (not just when frustrated) ____ ____ ____ ____
68. Sometimes for at least 2 weeks has markedly diminished interest or pleasure in most activities ____ ____ ____ ____
69. Sometimes for at least 2 weeks has psychomotor agitation (even more active than usual) ____ ____ ____ ____
70. Sometimes for at least 2 weeks has psychomotor retardation (slowed down in most activities) ____ ____ ____ ____
71. Sometimes for at least 2 weeks is fatigued or has loss of energy ____ ____ ____ ____
72. Sometimes for at least 2 weeks has feelings of worthlessness or excessive, inappropriate guilt ____ ____ ____ ____
73. Sometimes for at least 2 weeks has diminished ability to think or concentrate ____ ____ ____ ____
74. Chronic low self-esteem most of the time for at least a year ____ ____ ____ ____
75. Chronic poor concentration or difficulty making decisions most of the time for at least a year ____ ____ ____ ____
76. Chronic feelings of hopelessness most of the time for at least a year ____ ____ ____ ____
77. Currently is hypervigilant (overly watchful or alert) or has exaggerated startle response ____ ____ ____ ____
78. Currently is irritable, has anger outbursts, or has difficulty concentrating ____ ____ ____ ____
79. Currently has an emotional (e.g., nervous, worried, hopeless, tearful) response to stress ____ ____ ____ ____
80. Currently has a behavioral (e.g., fighting, vandalism, truancy) response to stress ____ ____ ____ ____

FIGURE 3.4. *cont.*

and parent versions of the SKAMP rating scale are presented in Figure 3.5 and 3.6, respectively.

The SKAMP items are not DSM symptom items. Instead, the items were selected based on an analysis of the classroom behaviors that are essential for appropriate and productive performance in a specific settings in the school—a typical classroom period. The basis for this is described in Swanson (1992). We reviewed the literature on school-based interventions to develop a standard token system for the University of California at Irvine—Child Development Center (UCI–CDC) school-based day-treatment program (see Chapter 15). Five behaviors were con-

Check the column that best describes this child:

	None	Slight	Mild	Moderate	Severe	Very severe	Maximal
1. Getting started on assignments for classroom periods	____	____	____	____	____	____	____
2. Sticking with tasks or activities	____	____	____	____	____	____	____
3. Completing assigned work:							
Math	____	____	____	____	____	____	____
Language arts	____	____	____	____	____	____	____
4. Performing work accurately:							
Math	____	____	____	____	____	____	____
Language arts	____	____	____	____	____	____	____
5. Being careful and neat while writing or drawing	____	____	____	____	____	____	____
6. Interacting with others:							
Children (e.g., other students)	____	____	____	____	____	____	____
Adults (e.g., teacher or aide)	____	____	____	____	____	____	____
7. Remaining quiet according to classroom rules	____	____	____	____	____	____	____
8. Staying seated according to classroom rules	____	____	____	____	____	____	____
9. Complying with the usual requests and directions of teachers	____	____	____	____	____	____	____
10. Following the rules established for the school	____	____	____	____	____	____	____

FIGURE 3.5. Teacher SKAMP.

Check the column that best describes this child:

	None	Slight	Mild	Moderate	Severe	Very severe	Maximal
1. Getting up and ready for the day's activities							
2. Sticking to games or activities after school or during the day							
3. Completing assigned work:							
Homework							
Chores							
4. Performing work accurately:							
Homework							
Chores							
5. Being careful and neat (e.g., while cleaning up room)							
6. Interacting with others:							
Children (e.g., friends, siblings)							
Adults (e.g., parents or others)							
7. Remaining quiet when situation requires it							
8. Staying seated and still when the situation requires it							
9. Complying with the usual requests and directions of parents							
10. Following the rules established for the home							

FIGURE 3.6. Parent SKAMP.

sidered essential for appropriate and productive schoolwork: getting started when the teacher gives directions, staying on task for the entire classroom period (usually about 30–45 minutes), interaction with staff and students that is nondisruptive, completing work that is assigned for the period, and stopping and shifting to a new activity or task when requested by the teacher. We expanded this list by adding typical classroom rules about staying seated and remaining quiet, and for following the activity of the group when required to make the SKAMP a 10-item scale.

The SKAMP has been evaluated by a factor analysis (McBurnett, Swanson, Pfiffner, & Tamm, 1997), which verifies the two factors proposed by Swanson (1992): attention and deportment. The SKAMP has been used in several studies of effects of medication (Swanson, Wigal, Greenhill, Browne, Waslick, Lerner, Williams, Flynn, Agler, Crowley, Fineberg, Regino, Baren, & Cantwell, 1998; Wigal, Gupta, Guinta, & Swanson, 1998), in which its reliability and validity have been established. The SKAMP was used in the MTA study for evaluating effects of medication in a large double-blind titration trial (Greenhill et al., 1996). For this study, slightly different versions were used that had been developed for use by teachers and parents. The teacher version of the SKAMP was constructed by specifying general behaviors that occur across the day in the school setting (instead of specific behaviors for each classroom period). The parent version of the SKAMP was constructed by specifying parallel behaviors that occur across the day in the home setting: getting up and getting ready for the day's activities, sticking to games or other activities outside of school, completing work at home, performing accurately at home, being neat and tidy at home, interacting with friends and siblings, interacting with parents and other adults outside of school, remaining quiet in home situations, remaining seated in home situations, complying with parental requests, and obeying the rules of the home.

What information does the SKAMP provide? Since the two versions of the SKAMP (teacher and parent) are based on a typical list of target behaviors for a token system, they provide baselines for classroom behaviors and for home behaviors that may be the focus of intervention. This may help the clinician decide when and where behavioral intervention may be needed. The theoretical position for behavioral assessment and treatment is quite different than the theoretical position for psychiatric assessment and treatment. For the psychiatric assessment of disorders, information is gathered in sets of symptoms to allow for syndrome definition based on onset and number of symptoms present, as well as the impairment that they produce. This emphasis on diagnosis has a specific purpose. It is our position (see Chapter 2) that the diagnosis of a disorder is considered to be important (and perhaps even essential) for choice of the class of medication. Thus, this emphasis on the diagnosis of the primary disorder (defined by it being the focus of treatment) is extremely important. This directs treatment both in the medical and psychosocial realms, but in different ways. This is the topic of Part III (Chapters 4 and 5) of this book.

For behavioral assessment, we focus on the time and place of specific behaviors, not the sets of symptoms that define a syndrome. We call this an evaluation by domain of behavior. Instead of starting with a set of symptoms that seem to go together (to define a syndrome), we start with the events of a typical day. Instead of domains of symptoms (defined by the DSM-IV categorical diagnoses), we address domains of behavior that are required for successful interactions and performance at school and at home. For parents, we start with the events surrounding getting up and getting to school in the morning, Since the child is in school for about 6 hours, we go directly to the events surrounding playing and studying after school. This is a critical problem area for children with ADHD. The next area in this sequence is behavior associated with eating dinner or supper. The next is homework, followed by bedtime, and then overnight sleep. We ask parents about each of these behavioral domains to assure ourselves that parents are not overlooking serious disruptive behavior that impairs functioning at home.

We should state our biases at this point, to avoid any misinterpretations of our somewhat radical point of view. We hold a theoretical view that the etiology of the target behavior matters very little for behavioral treatment. For example, the symptoms of inattention are listed for several disorders (ADHD, anxiety, and depression), and the manifestation of inattention (from all three diagnoses) in the school setting may be the same (failure to complete schoolwork). In the behavioral approach, the same intervention might be used for this common target for all three diagnoses (e.g., shaping of attentive behaviors via the SKAMP) and reinforcement of completion.

The assessment provided by the SKAMP would be of more use to a nonphysician who implements psychosocial treatment than to a physician whose primary role is to prescribe a pharmacological treatment as it is needed in the long term—or even when it is likely to help in the short term. The slant provided here in Chapter 3 is markedly different than the slant provided in Chapter 2. We consider the "behavioral domain" (assessed by the SKAMP) to be distinct from the "symptom domain" (assessed by the SNAP-IV and other instruments). Table 3.1 also includes instruments for assessing internalizing symptoms. Self-report scales of depressive and anxiety scales are not diagnostic but are combined with clinical interview to aid in diagnosis. They are very useful for screening and can be used to assess progress in treatment.

III

Overview of Treatment Approaches

4

Psychopharmacological Interventions

Treatment of children with ADHD invariably involves the use of psychotropic medication, and when other comorbid conditions are present the selection of the appropriate agent or agents becomes much more complex. Virtually every psychotropic available for clinical use has been tried in ADHD, yet well-controlled trials for drugs other than stimulants and tricyclic antidepressants (TCAs) are rarely available to guide the clinician. In this chapter, we focus on two main goals: First, we wish to give the clinician an overview of the stimulant treatment of ADHD. In spite of all the psychotropics available for clinical use, the stimulants remain the drugs of first choice in the treatment of ADHD. Second, since so many different psychotropic agents have been used in ADHD children with comorbid disorders, it is critical for the clinician to understand the use of these medications. In this chapter we consider to what degree a drug has been used in children, review side effect issues, and present an overview of dosages for each agent. Later, in Part IV, studies examining the role of the drug in the treatment of ADHD and/or its comorbid condition are reviewed in each of the appropriate chapters. For instance, while basic information of the clinical use of fluoxetine is found in this chapter, in Chapter 8 the reader can review the use of fluoxetine in the treatment of ADHD and comorbid affective disorder.

STIMULANTS

As has been widely reported in the literature, the stimulant medications (methylphenidate, amphetamine, and pemoline) are highly effective in the treatment of ADHD. Hundreds of double-blind placebo-controlled trials involving thousands of subjects have established this beyond any doubt (Barkley, 1990; Swanson et al., 1993). The placebo response of children with ADHD is extremely small (about 25% in most studies; as low as 0% in some), while around 75% of children respond to active drugs. Thus the stimulants have the most pronounced effect size of any psychotropic. Swanson et al. (1993) found the average effect size of stimulants on behavior and attention from three meta-analyses to be .84. In comparison the effect size for placebo ranged between .07 and .32. (Any effect size over .75 is quite large, indicating a highly effective treatment.)

Treatment of ADHD with stimulants has been rising over the past decade. Outpatients visits for ADHD increased from 1.6 to 4.2 million, and at 90% of these visits, stimulant medications were prescribed (Swanson, Lerner, & Williams, 1995). Approximately 2.8% of the school-age population was taking stimulants in 1995 (Goldman, Genel, Bezman, & Slanetz, 1998). This is well within the expected rates, given the prevalence of ADHD. Goldman et al. (1998) found that snorting of methylphenidate tablets occurs far less frequently than does cocaine or marijuana use and that reports of lifetime nonmedical use of stimulants has remained very low and stable for many years. Thus there is little evidence that stimulants are being abused, and almost all of the increase in stimulant use is likely to be due to greater recognition of clinical cases. Data from long-term studies are beginning to emerge. C. Gillberg et al. (1997) performed a 15-month double-blind placebo-controlled trial of amphetamine; the stimulant groups showed significantly fewer attention and behavior problems than the placebo group through the 15 months of the study. Interestingly, decreased appetite was the only side effect to remain significantly elevated in the stimulant group relative to the placebo group.

Certain questions remain unclear to many clinicians regarding stimulant treatment: (1) What percentage of children with ADHD "respond" to stimulants? (2) What is the best way to define "response" in a clinical setting? (3) Are all the stimulants alike, or do some children respond to one stimulant agent better than another?

Studies reviewed by Barkley (1990) showed that about 75% of children with ADHD (defined in different ways over the years) would show a response to either methylphenidate or dextroamphetamine. "Response" usually means that the symptoms of inattention, hyperactivity, and impulsivity decline (according to the teacher or parent rating scale), while side effects are minimal. The definition of the term "nonresponse" has always been somewhat vague, and most studies have not distinguished between behavioral nonresponse, (i.e., symptoms of ADHD did not decline significantly on administration of the drug) and excessive side effects. In the latter situation, the child's behavior improves but problems with tics, insomnia, appetite decrease, or other side effects cause the physician to discontinue the medication. Over the years, it was gradually assumed that the stimulants methylphenidate and dextroamphetamine were interchangeable, and the use of dextroamphetamine declined (Elia, Borcherding, Rapoport, & Keysor, 1991). Many clinicians assumed that if an ADHD child did not respond to methylphenidate, he would not respond to dextroamphetamine. Children were often treated with a tricyclic agent or clonidine if they failed their initial trial of a stimulant.

Elia and colleagues (1991) challenged this assumption by conducting a double-blind crossover study of placebo, dextroamphetamine, and methylphenidate in 48 boys with ADHD. They also wished to explore a wide range of doses of the stimulant to determine if children who did not respond at in the traditional dose range for stimulant (0.3–1.0 mg/kg for methylphenidate) might respond behaviorally to doses above this. All 48 boys received 9 weeks of treatment: 3 weeks each of placebo, methylphenidate, and dextroamphetamine. A physician blind to the child's drug status titrated the dose upward each week. Up to 19 (~40%) of the subjects could not tolerate an increase to the doses beyond 1.0 mg/kg per day. The children attended a day hospital program through the 9 weeks of the study. Behavioral ratings were obtained from parents, teachers, and clinicians throughout the study. Responder status was defined by a consensus rating (made before the blind was broken). A nonresponder might be so defined either because the drug failed to improve behavior or because side effects were too severe even if the behavior had improved.

Overall 79% of the subjects responded to methylphenidate and 88% responded to dextroamphetamine. Only two subjects failed to respond well to both drugs; even these subjects had a behavioral response to the drugs, but for them the side effects to both stimulants were quite severe. Eight (16%) failed to respond to methylphenidate but did respond to dextroamphetamine; in contrast there were four patients (8.3%) who did not respond to dextroamphetamine but did respond to methylphenidate; 71% of the sample responded equally well to both drugs. Greenhill et al. (1996) performed a meta-analysis using the above data and three other studies that directly compared methylphenidate and dextroamphetamine in the treatment of ADHD. These studies involved a total of 141 subjects: 50 (35%) responded best to dextroamphetamine, 37 (26%) improved more on methylphenidate, while the remaining 38% did equally well on both stimulants.

A wide body of literature exists on the effects of methylphenidate and dextroamphetamine in the treatment of ADHD. Data are just beginning to emerge on Adderall, a combination of 75% dextro- and 25% levoamphetamine. In an open trial of Adderall performed by Shire-Richwood (1997), 4,321 patients with ADHD of all ages were enrolled if they had an unsatisfactory response to a previous trial of medication: 9% were under 6 years of age, 43% were under 12 years of age, 24% were adolescents, and 15% were adults. For the children under 12 years of age, the mean dose of Adderall was 15 mg/day, with a range of 2.5–80 mg/day. For the adolescents, the mean dose was 20.8 mg. The adults took an average of about 30 mg/day. No unusual or dangerous side effects were noted, suggesting that Adderall is as safe as the more commonly used stimulants.

Swanson et al. (1998) performed a study of the acute effects of Adderall on school-age children. Thirty-three boys with ADHD who were responding to methylphenidate were enrolled in a 6-week double-blind placebo-controlled crossover study. During each of the 6 weeks the child received a different medication: placebo; his usual dose of methylphenidate; or a dose of Adderall, 5, 10, 15, or 20 mg. Order was randomized for each child. On the Saturday of each study week, the child received the A.M. dose of medication and attended an all-day school session. Teacher ratings and measures of classroom productivity were obtained every 1.5 hours through the school day. Both Adderall and methylphenidate were superior to placebo in reducing classroom ADHD symptoms and improving classroom productivity. The higher doses of Adderall (15 and 20 mg) had later peak effects during the day (2.6 and 3.0 hours, respectively) than the child's usual dose of methylphenidate (1.9 hours). Methylphenidate duration of action averaged 3.98 hours, whereas the average duration of action for the 5- to 20-mg doses of Adderall were 3.52, 4.83, 5.44, and 6.4 hours, respectively. Further studies of Adderall are currently underway, but it appears to be a useful addition to the list of stimulants routinely used in ADHD. Ultimately, it may not matter which stimulant is selected first, as long both stimulants (methylphenidate and amphetamine) are tried if the first medication utilized is not satisfactory.

Dosing and Assessing Response to Stimulants

What is the best way to dose stimulant medication? If the child meets criteria for ADHD, stimulant medication is usually initiated at a dose based on the child's weight. With methylphenidate, 0.3 mg/kg per *dose* has been viewed as an appropriate starting point. (Some clinicians confuse mg/kg per *dose* amounts with mg/kg per *day*. For instance, a 30-kg child would start on 10 mg twice a day, not a total daily dose of 10 mg.) Generally a week at a given dose is necessary to obtain the data needed to judge efficacy of the dose. For monitoring stimulant response, the physician may simply ask the parent to relay to him/her the teacher's opinion. To be more precise, the teacher can fill another rating scale that is compared to the baseline rating. If there has been a "clinically significant" improvement (usually defined by a statistically significant shift in scores on the rating scale) and no serious side effects, the physician holds the dose steady. Most of the time, the physician will elect to leave "well enough alone" and not try a higher dose. In contrast, if the behavior is still problematic, the dose may be increased and standard practice has been to step through doses ranging from 0.3 to 1.0 mg/kg per day of methylphenidate. For most school-age children, this means absolute doses of 5–20 mg. Interestingly, in older children and adolescents, doses are in fact rarely based on mg/kg per dose. One would not place a 60-kg adolescent on 60 mg twice a day, yet this would work out to 1.0 mg/kg per dose. Indeed, it is quite rare to exceed a single dose of 20 mg, even in an adult patient. Several issues emerge from the above overview of the "typical" clinical practice. Are teacher and parent reports the best way to assess stimulant response? Are there more objective methods to assess the effect of drugs on the child's cognition? Can we reduce the role of parent and teacher bias in the assessment of drug response? Does body weight really matter in the dosing of stimulants?

Dosing of stimulants has been influenced by the work of Sprague and Sleator (1977). Each child in their study received placebo or 0.3 or 1.0 mg/kg per dose of methylphenidate; during each condition teacher ratings of behavior and a laboratory learning task were obtained. For the whole group, mean teacher ratings improved most on the higher methylphenidate dose, while mean performance on the learning task showed the greatest improvement on the lower dose. On the higher methylphenidate dose, the children's performance on the laboratory task was not different from that on placebo. This study was widely cited as showing that "low" doses of stimulant "optimized" learning. At "high" doses the child was better behaved but might not be learning as much as at a lower dose. This conclusion was premature for two reasons: (1) the results referred to mean data of the *group* of ADHD children—*individual* subjects might have quite different dose–response curves; (2) the laboratory "learning" task might not have a relationship to learning in the real classroom. There followed an intensive focus on the "fine-grain" effects of psychostimulants. Several groups of investigators (C. L. Carlson,

Pelham, Milich, & Dixon, 1992; Pelham, 1993; Pelham, Bender, Caddell, Booth, & Moorer, 1985; Rapport, DuPaul, Stoner, & Jones, 1986; Rapport, Stoner, DuPaul, Birmingham, & Tucker, 1985; Swanson, Kinsbourne, Roberts, & Zucker, 1978) developed methods of objectively assessing stimulant response in ADHD children. In these designs, a child with ADHD receives a double-blind placebo-controlled trial of stimulant in a crossover design such that each child serves as his/her own control. For instance, a child receives medication for 5 weeks. During one of the weeks the capsules contain placebo; during the other 4 weeks the capsules contain different doses of methylphenidate (5, 10, 15, or 20 mg). Each of these weeks, teachers and parents, who are blind to medication status, fill out behavior rating scales. Other measures of behavior and attention may also be obtained, such as a laboratory measure of attention (like the Conners Continuous Performance Test, CPT) or an actual measure of classroom performance. In the latter, the amount of classroom work completed can be assessed at a particular time each week of the trial. At the end of the 5-week period, the clinician can examine the dose–response curve for all of the different measures. Figure 4.1 shows hypothetical data for three children, with the mean scores for the three children in the fourth panel; "0 mg" represents placebo, while an increasing value on the *y*-axis represents increasing behavioral or attentional improvement.

When the mean scores for all the patients are considered, one generally finds a linear relationship between dose and improvement. For the whole group, the higher the *mean* dose, the more *mean* improvement one sees on the measure, whatever it is (Rapport et al., 1985). For some measures, particularly some laboratory measures of cognition, there is a "quadratic" effect; that is, the dose–response curve flattens out at the higher doses, such that a further increase in dose does not lead to greater improvement (Rapport & Denny, 1997; Rapport et al., 1985, 1986). Several studies have now show that for *group* data, higher doses of stimulant do not lead to declines in learning or behavior. Measures of both these variables improve with increasing stimulant dose (Solanto, 1991; E. Richardson, Kupietz, Winsberg, Maitinsky, & Mendell, 1988). A number of studies have shown that for some measures of cognition the highest doses of stimulant may lead to deterioration even when behavior improves. Swanson et al. (1978) compared the performance of children with ADHD on a laboratory learning task (Paired Associates Learning Task) on a low and high dose of methylphenidate (mean doses, 10 and 19 mg, respectively). There was a 50% improvement over baseline on the low dose, whereas the higher dose produced an almost 40% impairment. A later study (Swanson et al., 1983) also associated higher doses of stimulants with declines in performance on the Paired Associates Learning Task.

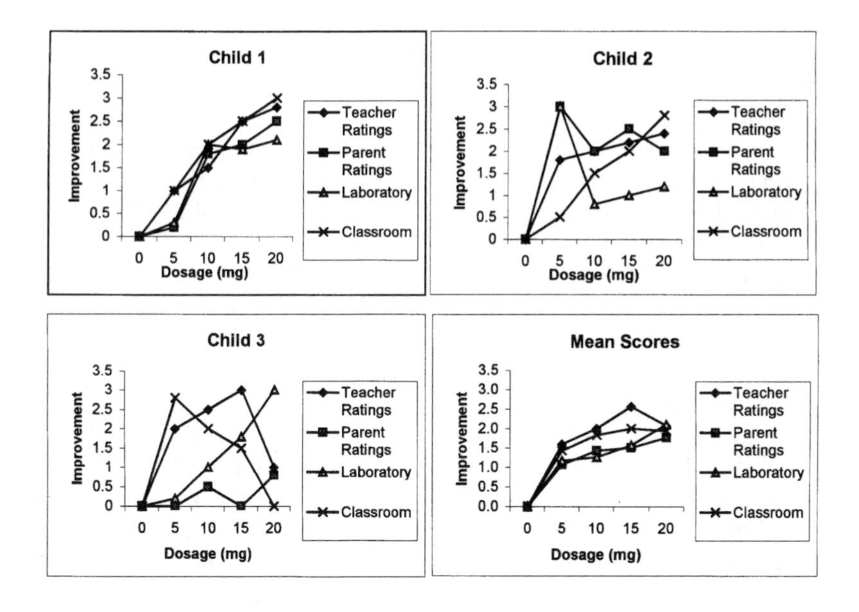

FIGURE 4.1. Hypothetical data illustrating dose response curves of different measures to methylphenidate.

The difficulties of translating these studies into clinical practice are illustrated in Figure 4.1. When we examine the individual curves in the figure, we note several different patterns that are obscured by averaging of the scores. The pattern of child 1 corresponds to the average data; on each of the variables he improves with increasing dose. All clinicians would agree the 20-mg dose is best for him. Child 2 shows a more complex pattern. Parent ratings and the laboratory measure show the greatest improvement at the 5-mg dose, with declines in performance at higher levels. The teacher ratings, on the other hand, show continued improvement in behavior at the higher dosages, and classroom productivity also shows marked gain at the higher levels. It more difficult to say whether the 5- or 20-mg dose is best. The data for child 3 are even more difficult to discern. Classroom productivity is highest at the 5-mg dose, with deterioration at the 20-mg dose. In contrast, the score on the laboratory test was best in the 20-mg condition. Parent ratings showed no significant change at all, whereas teacher behavioral ratings were best at the intermediate (15-mg) dose. Is this child a stimulant responder or not? If he is classified as a responder, what is his best dose?

The case of child 3 in particular points out the difficulty of using multiple measures to assess stimulant response. Each measure has its own dose–response curve, and the measures do not correlate with one another (Pelham & Milich, 1991). Computerized laboratory tests of attention assess about 15 minutes to 1 hour of behavior and thus may not correspond at all to the child's behavior in the "real world." Thus one cannot use tests such as the CPT or the Test of Variables of Attention (TOVA) as the primary measure of psychostimulant response. In the multimodality treatment of ADHD (MTA; Greenhill et al., 1996) study sponsored by the National Institute of Mental Health (NIMH), each subject receives placebo, 5, 10, and 20 mg of methylphenidate over a 4-week period. Teacher and parent ratings are used to determine whether one of the methylphenidate conditions is superior to placebo—and if so, which dose is best. The laboratory measures of attention are not used since there is no consensus as to how to interpret their scores.

In these designs, each child, regardless of weight, receives all the doses. Despite the long-time use of mg/kg formulas in the administration of stimulants, it was found many years ago that this may not be the most optimal way of dosing these agents (Swanson et al., 1978). Rapport and Denney (1997) performed a double-blind placebo-controlled crossover study in which each child received 5, 10, 15, and 20 mg of methylphenidate. The dose for optimal response on a variety of measures of ADHD behavior (classroom on-task behavior, teacher ratings, and classroom productivity) did not correlate with the child's body weight. The aforementioned authors point out that both methylphenidate and ritalinic acid (its metabolite) are highly polar and do not accumulate in fat tissue. The kidneys rapidly clear both metabolites; therefore the fact that body weight does not predict optimal dose is consistent with the pharmacokinetic data on the psychostimulants. Adhering to a strict mg/kg formula could lead to underdosing smaller children and overdosing larger ones. It should be borne in mind, however, that these studies were all performed with school-age children and it is not known whether the results extrapolate to preschoolers or older adolescents. A wide range of doses should be tried regardless of the child's weight.

Algorithm for Stimulant Administration

The MTA study of the NIMH involved 576 school-age children with ADHD who were randomized to treatment as usual, specialized medication management, medication management combined with psychosocial intervention, or psychosocial intervention only. The groups receiving specialized medication management showed a superior outcome to the group receiving treatment as usual (often stimulants administered by the primary-care physician). What made the MTA medication management unique? Mostly, it was careful titration of stimulants using the full dose range, coupled with systematic observations of the child behavior using a standardized rating scale (Greenhill et al., 1996). Children weighing less than 25 kg received 5, 10, or 15 mg of methylphenidate three times a day, while children weighing more than 25 kg received the 20-mg methylphenidate dose. Each child underwent a double-blind crossover trial for 4 weeks with placebo and each of the above doses. Teacher and parent ratings of behavior were obtained on placebo and each dose of methylphenidate, as was an 11-item Side Effect Scale (see Chapter 3). Thus the best dose for each child could be determined. If there was no difference between any of the methylphenidate doses and placebo, and if the child's behavior remained severely impaired, a trial of dextroamphetamine was initiated using the same design. If stimulants failed, the MTA protocol then utilized imipramine.

An office physician in less likely to utilize placebo controls in the initial assessment of stimulant effectiveness. It is possible to use an algorithm as shown in Table 4.1 to find the most effective dose. As noted earlier, it is the physician's and family's choice as to which stimulant is the first line, as long as the alternative stimulant is tried if the first trial is not effective in treating the ADHD symptoms.

TRICYCLIC ANTIDEPRESSANTS

Imipramine was studied as a treatment for ADHD in the early 1970s. A number of double-blind placebo-controlled studies showed it to be superior to placebo but not as effective as stimulants in treatment of ADHD (Pliszka, 1987). Desipramine was found to be superior to placebo in the treatment of ADHD, even if the child was a stimulant nonresponder (Biederman, Baldessarini, Wright, Knee, & Harmatz, 1989). Desipramine began to have widespread use in the treatment of ADHD, but in the early 1990s four cases of sudden death in children treated with desipramine were reported (Riddle, Geller, & Ryan, 1993). The children were aged 8–12; three of the four collapsed while exercising, and one child had a past history of cardiac problems. All were treated with therapeutic doses of desipramine; in some cases the doses were quite low. In 1994 a fifth case of sudden death was reported. That child was found to have an anomaly of his right coronary artery at autopsy (Popper & Ziminitzky, 1995). Recently, a sixth such case has come to light—that of a 9-year-old boy who was treated with 3.3 mg/kg per day of desipramine for depression. After 6 weeks of treatment he had a cardiac arrest and died. Autopsy did not reveal any cardiac abnormality (Varley & McClellan, 1997). Prior to the last two cases, it was calculated that the risk of sudden death for children taking desipramine was 8 per million,

TABLE 4.1. An Algorithm for Stimulant Treatment of ADHD

	Amphetamine		Methylphenidate	
	Weight <25 kg	Weight >25 kg	Weight <25 kg	Weight >25 kg
Week 1	2.5 mg in A.M.	5 mg in A.M.	5 mg	5 mg
Week 2	5 mg in A.M.	10 mg in A.M.	10 mg	10 mg
Week 3	Select option:* (1) 10 mg in A.M. (2) mg in A.M. and noon	Select option:* (1) 15 mg in A.M. (2) 10 mg A.M. and 5 mg noon (3) 7.5 mg A.M. and noon	15 mg	15 mg
Week 4	No week 4	Select option:* 20 mg in A.M. 10 mg in A.M. and noon	No week 4	20 mg
Dosing pointers	*Amphetamine has a longer duration of action; in first weeks, should be dosed A.M. only. In second 2 weeks, doses at noon can be sculpted if individual patient clearly has a short duration of action. If no response to amphetamine, initiate trial of methylphenidate.		Methylphenidate is dosed three times daily (A.M., noon, and 4 P.M.) except when parents clearly indicate P.M. behavior is not problematic for them. Physician may also use lower 4 P.M. dose (one half noon dose). If no response to methylphenidate, initiate trial of amphetamine.	
Rating scales obtained at end of each week (see Chapter 3)	Teacher classroom rating Parent rating (after school) Parent rating (weekend) Side Effect Scale			
Long term	After initial doses, clinician may titrate to maximum doses as side effects permit. Do not exceed 60–80 mg of methylphenidate or 40–50 mg of amphetamine except in special cases. Monitor for cognitive toxicity at higher doses.			

compared to the 4 per million risk of unexplained sudden death in the general population of children (Biederman, Thisted, Greenhill, & Ryan, 1995). The risk must be assumed to be higher in view of the new cases. No satisfactory explanation of this phenomenon has been advanced, particularly in terms of why desipramine should be associated with cardiac problems but not other TCAs used at therapeutic levels. Twenty-four-hour ambulatory (Holter) electrocardiographic monitoring of children on desipramine did not yield any unusual findings; furthermore there was no correlation between a child's baseline ECG and the Holter results (Biederman, Baldessarini, Goldblatt, et al., 1993). It may be that only ECG during stress testing would reveal which of those children on desipramine might be vulnerable to cardiac effects, but such testing is obviously not practical in clinical practice. Most parents do not want to have their child take desipramine when they are informed of the sudden death cases, so many clinicians have turned to imipramine or nortriptyline (Wilens, Biederman, Geist, Steingard, & Spencer, 1993; Spencer, Biederman, Steingard, & Wilens, 1993) for the treatment of children. TCAs should always be viewed as drugs of second choice in the treatment of ADHD, to be used only after a child has failed to respond well to two different stimulants.

For imipramine, children should be started at a dose of 1 mg/kg per day, always in divided doses. Dosing twice a day (early A.M. and evening) is most common in children more than 9 years of age, but dosing three times a day should be considered in children under that age due to their higher rate of metabolism. If children appear to be having classic tricyclic withdrawal symptoms (irritability, somatic complaints) each day, this is more cogent evidence that the dose needs to be further divided. In spite of the fact that baseline ECGs are unlikely to uncover any occult cardiac abnormalities, most major authorities in this area continue to recommend monitoring for such abnormalities in children treated with TCAs. The TCA dosage should be titrated each week until the ADHD symptoms respond or until a dose of 3 mg/kg per day is reached. At this point a steady-state serum level and an ECG should be obtained. Doses of 5 mg/kg per day should never be exceeded in any case, as toxicity is much more likely at these levels. Most children will responded at doses between 2 and 4 mg/kg per day. If ADHD symptoms have remitted even though the serum level of TCA is subtherapeutic, there is no need to push the dosage higher. Blood levels of TCA do not correlate with response of the ADHD symptoms (Biederman, Baldessarini, Wright, Knee, Harmatz, & Goldblatt, 1989). For nortriptyline, the starting dose is 0.5 mg/kg per day; the dose may be titrated to 2.5 mg/kg per day (Wilens et al., 1993).

The dosage of TCA should be reduced if the following findings on ECG are noted: P–R interval > 200 msec, QRS interval increased 30% over baseline, and $Q–T_c$ interval $\not>$ 450 msec. Pulse should not exceed 130 beats/minute. Interindividual variability in the metabolism and elimination of TCAs is extremely high (10- to 30-fold), and serious toxicity can occur at only three times the upper limit of the therapeutic range. The serum level should never exceed 200 mg/ml for all the TCAs, as cardiotoxicity in particular is much more likely at these levels (Preskorn & Fast, 1995). Once a child is at a steady-state serum level, do not need to be repeated until there is a dose increase. It should be emphasized that these laboratory methods do not ensure that the patient will not have a catastrophic event if normal. The cumbersome nature of this monitoring has lead clinicians to prefer the newer nontricyclic antidepressant agents.

NONTRICYCLIC ANTIDEPRESSANTS

These newer agents include several classes of drugs. The most well known and widely used are the selective serotonin reuptake inhibitors (SSRIs). Relative to other neurotransmitters, these drugs potently block the reuptake of serotonin (5-hydroxytryptamine, or 5-HT) in the neuronal cleft, initiating a series of "downstream" neurochemical effects on the brain, which in turn lead to widespread effects on mood, energy level, sleep, and cognition. Serotonin receptors are found in the gastrointestinal tract, leading to common side effects such as nausea, cramping, and diarrhea. The SSRIs are fluoxetine (Prozac), sertraline (Zoloft), fluvoxamine (Luvox), and paroxetine (Paxil). Nefazodone (Serzone) blocks the reuptake of serotonin as well, but it also blocks the action of serotonin at one of the serotonin receptor subtypes (5-HT_{2a}). Nefazodone is the most sedating of the SSRIs; most of the others tend to be behaviorally activating.

Bupropion (Wellbutrin) does not significantly block the reuptake of any neurotransmitter; rather it is metabolized to hydroxybupropion, which potently blocks the reuptake of both norepinephrine and dopamine, but not serotonin. Venlafaxine (Effexor), in turn, blocks the reuptake of both norepinephrine and serotonin. Despite differences in mechanisms of action, on average all of these antidepressants are equally as efficacious as TCAs in treating adult major depressive disorder, though with many fewer side effects.

Table 4.2 summarizes the studies to date of these novel antidepressants in children and adolescents. Several patterns are noticeable: (1) SSRIs appear to be effective in obsessive–compulsive disorder (OCD) and major depression of childhood; (2) doses of SSRIs in pediatric patients are quite similar to adult doses, even in young children; (3) many of the SSRIs are associated with behavioral activation that in some cases can lead to self-injurious behavior or a manic episode. This may be of concern when treating children with comorbid ADHD who may already have a high activation level before treatment. Details on the use of these drugs in specific conditions comorbid with ADHD will be reviewed in subsequent chapters (in Part IV).

LITHIUM

Studies of the effect of lithium on symptoms of aggression and affective disorders in children and adolescents are reviewed in Chapters 6 and 8, respectively. The prelithium laboratory workup is similar to that in adults: electrolytes, thyroid function, hematology studies, and ECG. Ad-

TABLE 4.2. Use of SSRIs in Children and Adolescents

Drug	Authors	Year	*N*	Dose (mg)	Age	Indication	Side effects
Fluvoxamine	Apter et al.	1994	6 14	100–300 100–300	13–18 13–18	Depression OCD	Significant improvement in YBOCS and CGAS scores, 15% had behavioral activation
	Riddle et al.	1996	120	50–200, mean = 173	8–17	OCD	Fluvoxamine superior to placebo in reducing OCD symptoms; no behavioral activation; minimal SE
	Walkup	1998	98		8–17	OCD	Open 1-year follow-up; medication remained effective
Fluoxetine	Boulos et al.	1992	15	5–40	16–24	Depression	64% of sample responded to drug; 27% had behavioral activation
	Simeon, Dinicola, et al.	1990	16	60	13–18	Depression	Fluoxetine not different from placebo
	Jain et al.	1992	31	20–80	9–18	Depression	74% had "some" improvement in depression; 23% had behavioral activation
	Riddle et al.	1992	14	20	8–15	OCD	23% showed behavioral activation
	Geller, Biederman, et al.	1995	38	10–80, mean = 50	6–18	OCD	74% improved OCD symptoms; 21% had behavioral activation
	Barrickman et al.	1991	22	20–60	7–15	ADHD	No behavioral activation; moderate response of ADHD symptoms
	Gammon & Brown	1993	32	<20	9–17	ADHD	No behavioral activation; combined with methylphenidate, improvement of depression, ADHD, and oppositional symptoms
	Birmaher et al.	1994	21	10–60	11–17	Anxiety	81% improved; no behavioral activation

(continued)

TABLE 4.2. *(continued)*

Fluxotine *(continued)*	Emslie et al.	1997	48	20	8–18	Depression	56% of fluoxetine group responded versus 33% of placebo group; three subjects developed mania
	King et al.	1991	42	20–60	10–17	OCD	6 (14%) with self-injurious behavior
	Riddle et al.	1990	24	?	?	OCD	46% behavioral activation
Paroxetine	SmithKline Beecham	1998	275	20–40	12–19	Depression	8-week trial; response rates: placebo, 46%; imipramine, 50%; paroxetine, 66%; paroxetine superior to imipramine
Sertraline	Tierny et al.	1995	33	25–200, mean = 100, 1.6 mg/kg per day	8–18	Depression	65% had fewer depressive symptoms; 21% behavioral activation
	March et al.	1998	187	Up to 200 mg/day	6–17	OCD	Sertraline superior to placebo
Nefazodone	Wilens et al.	1997	7	200–600, mean = 357	7–18	Depression	4 out of 7 responded; 2 manic episodes arose during treatment
Bupropion	Conners et al.	1996	72	Up to 250	<13 years	ADHD	17% nausea in bupropion; 14% nausea in placebo; 8 abnormal EEGs; no behavioral activation
	Barrickman et al.	1995	15	0.7–3.3 mg/kg per day	<13 years	ADHD	Significant reduction in ADHD symptoms; no behavioral activation
Venlafaxine	Olvera et al.	1996	16	25–75, mean = 60	9–13	ADHD	Significant declines in parent hyperactivity ratings; 3 (18.8%) with increased hyperactivity
	Mandoki	1995	32	Not reported	7–17	Depression	"Well tolerated"; specific side effects not reported; venlafaxine not different from placebo
	Derivan et al.	1995	15	1–2 mg/kg per day	6–15	ADHD/CD	"Well tolerated"; 38% with nausea; 46% of children and 58% of teens improved by clinical judgment

olescents weighing at least 100 pounds (45 kg) can be started on 300 mg three times a day, as adult patients would be. Children smaller than this can be started on 300 mg twice a day. Blood levels should be checked weekly until therapeutic levels (0.5–1.2 mEq/liter) are obtained. Many children and adolescents need to be maintained at the higher end of the therapeutic range to achieve adequate response. Lithium toxicity (over 3 mEq/liter) can be life threatening, but even levels over 1.6 mEq/liter can result in neurological disorders. Adolescents engaged in strenuous activities who perspire heavily need closer monitoring of levels, as lithium is extensively excreted in sweat, leading to a decline in lithium levels (Jefferson, Greist, & Ackerman, 1987). Lithium levels and thyroid functions should be checked every 6 months.

Side effects to lithium have been found to be well tolerated in children and similar to those in adults (Campbell et al., 1995). Nausea (24%), vomiting (48%), tremor (16%) and polyuria were the side effects most frequently noted. Lithium has been used in children 4–6 years (Hagino et al., 1995). Twenty preschoolers with weights ranging from 15 to 28.2 kg (mean-21.8 kg) were treated with a mean dose of lithium of 875 mg. Serum lithium levels ranged from 0.65 to 1.37 mEq/liter. Side effects were more common in this age group: half the sample showed CNS (central nervous system) effects such as tremor, drowsiness, and ataxia, while 25% had gastrointestinal upset; two children had polyuria. Children with side effects had higher mean lithium levels than those without adverse events (0.96 vs. 0.81 mEq/liter). Thus, while lithium can be used in this age group, extreme caution is needed and levels may need to be kept at the lower end of the therapeutic range. The aforementioned authors also recommended monitoring of lithium levels every other day during the first 2 weeks of treatment for children aged 4–6 years. In general, however, clinicians should avoid the use of lithium in this age group because of the high level of side effects. DeLong and Aldershot (1987) report that they have successfully maintained older children and adolescents on lithium without long-term developmental problems for up to 10 years. To our knowledge, no more recent case reports of untoward effects of lithium on growth or development have appeared in the literature.

VALPROATE

Valproate (valproic acid) has been widely used as an anticonvulsant in children since the early 1970s (Menkes & Sankar, 1995). Its use in psychiatric disorders of children has accelerated with the advent of studies showing valproate to be effective in treatment of acute mania in adults (Bowden et al., 1994; Freeman, Clothier, Pazzaglia, Lesem, & Swann, 1992; Pope, McElroy, Keck, & Hudson, 1991). It is available as valproic acid (Depakene) or as divalproex sodium (Depakote). The latter is a compound of valproic acid and sodium valproate that reduces gastrointestinal upset and is supplied both as tablets and as a "sprinkle" that can be mixed with food for young children. The limited studies of its use in childhood psychiatric disorders are reviewed in Chapters 6 and 8.

Valproate is generally started at a dose of 15 mg/kg per day in young children, divided three or four times a day. Table 4.3 shows the initial dose as a function of the patient's weight. Valproate's half-life is 6–15 hours, and 4 days are generally required to reach steady-state serum levels. Blood levels should range between 50 and 150 µg/ml, though there is not a clear correlation between higher serum levels and better clinical response. Few epileptic or manic patients respond with serum levels below 50 µg/ml, but some adult manic patients have required levels above 200 µg/ml (McElroy, Keck, Pope, & Hudson, 1992). In no study of children with psychiatric disorders has valproate been administered at such high levels, however. Side effects from valproate consist primarily of nausea and other forms of gastrointestinal upset, though taking the medication with food reduces such problems. Weight gain has been reported in 11% of patients (Bourgeois et al., 1987), and this effect may be more pronounced in females (Pope et al., 1991). Increases in liver enzymes can be seen in up to 44% of patients, but these are most often transient and are resolved with dose reductions (Gram & Bentsen, 1985; Dreifuss, Langer, Moline, & Maxwell, 1989). Hepatic failure has occurred in children under 2 years of age who were taking multiple anticonvulsants (1 in 500 cases). No child over 10 years of age treated with valproate alone has developed liver failure (Dreifuss et al., 1989).

Recently, reports have emerged that valproate may be associated with polycystic ovaries and menstrual difficulties. Isojarvi et al. (1993) performed vaginal ultrasonography and serum testosterone tests in adult female epileptics with (n = 41) and without (n = 57) menstrual distur-

TABLE 4.3. The Use of Valproate in Children and Adolescents

Weight		Total daily dose	
lb	kg	(mg)	How to divide
22–55	10–25	250	Once a day
56–88	26–40	500	Twice a day
89–132	41–60	750	Three times a day
133–165	61–75	1,000	Three times a day
166–200	>75	1,250	Three times a day

bances and in 51 normal women. Of the 31 women receiving valproate, 68% had either polycystic ovaries or elevated serum testosterone levels. In contrast, 22% of the women on carbamazepine and 18% of the controls had polycystic ovaries; none of the women in these groups had increased serum testosterone levels. Of concern here is that 80% of the women who began valproate treatment before age 20 had polycystic ovaries or hyperandrogenism. While further studies are needed to confirm these findings, they suggest the need for caution in prescribing valproate to young females.

CARBAMAZEPINE

Carbamazepine has also enjoyed long use as an effective treatment for childhood seizures (Menkes & Sankar, 1995), though its efficacy in childhood psychiatric disorder has not been adequately established, as we shall see. Carbamazepine is initiated at doses of 10–25 mg/kg per day in children aged 6–12, working out to 100–200 mg twice a day in most cases. Doses are increased until a therapeutic level of 4–12 µg/ml is reached. Usually this results in a dosage of 600–800 mg/day. Autoinduction of liver enzymes is common in the first month, with higher doses being required to maintain the same serum level. It may take 5–10 days to reach steady state, but carbamazepine pharmacokinetics are linear. A 2 mg/kg increase generally results in a 1 µg/ml increase in serum level (Dodsen, 1987). The liver metabolizes carbamazepine to its epoxide; this compound has both anticonvulsant and toxic effects. The epoxide cannot be assayed, and children vary in the degree to which they convert carbamazepine to the metabolite. The breakdown of the epoxide is blocked by valproate; valproate can also decrease the protein binding of carbamazepine. Both these factors can induce toxicity even at therapeutic blood levels of carbamazepine itself. Careful monitoring of drug levels and side effects is required when these drugs are used together.

Diplopia and other neurological effects (drowsiness, motor incoordination, and dizziness) are the most common side effects. Rashes occur in 5% of children taking carbamazepine (Pellock, 1987). Pellock (1987) found nearly 13% of children had a leukopenia of 4,000 white cells mm^3, but 75% of these low white blood cell counts resolved spontaneously. Agranulocytosis and aplastic anemia occur rarely, in about 1 of 50,000 cases. These cases have occurred more frequently in older adult individuals than in children, and it is not clear that routine blood count monitoring will pick up these cases early enough to allow for successful intervention (Menkes & Sankar, 1995). Nonetheless, blood counts should be monitored every 3–6 months, and carbamazepine should be discontinued if the blood count falls below 1,000 white cells mm^3.

ALPHA AGONISTS

The neurotransmitters norepinephrine and epinephrine bind to alpha and beta receptors as shown in Figure 4.2. $Alpha_2$ receptors are found presynaptically; their stimulation leads to decreased release of norepinephrine. $Alpha_2$ agonists (such as clonidine and guanfacine) may down-regulate the noradrenergic system by this mechanism. At higher doses, however, they have effects at postsynaptic $alpha_2$ receptors that may mimic those of norepinephrine. Guanfacine, like clonidine, is an $alpha_2$ agonist but is more specific in terms of receptor binding. Clonidine binds equally to all three subtypes (a, b, and c) of the $alpha_2$ receptor, whereas guanfacine is more specific to the $alpha_{2a}$ site. $Beta_1$ and $beta_2$ receptors are only found postsynaptically; drugs such as propranolol block the action of norepinephrine and epinephrine at these sites. This may result in reduced arousal, which could lead to attenuation of agitation, whether it results from anxiety or impulsiveness.

Clonidine

Swanson et al. (1995) have estimated that in 1994 some 89,000 prescriptions were written for clonidine alone for the treatment of ADHD, while 61,000 children were placed on a combination of methylphenidate and clonidine. Considerable controversy now surrounds the use of antihypertensive agents in the treatment of ADHD and associated symp-

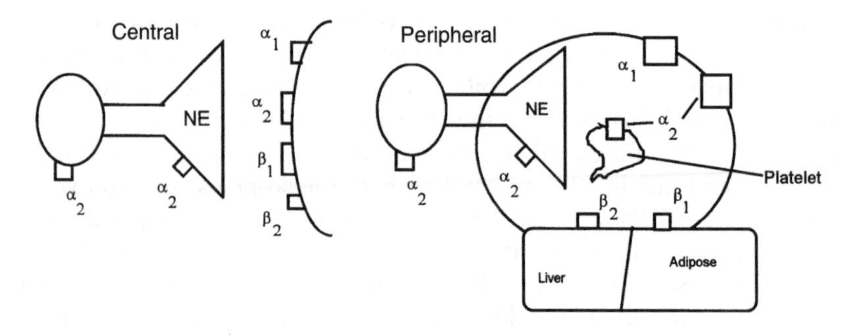

FIGURE 4.2. Alpha and beta receptors in the CNS and in the peripheral nervous system. For clarity, some of the known subtypes are not shown (i.e., alpha 2a, alpha 2b, etc.).

toms such as emotional lability and aggression. This controversy has been raised by four cases of sudden death in children taking methylphenidate and clonidine in combination (Cantwell, Swanson, & Connor, 1997; Fenichel, 1995; Popper, 1995). Each of these cases had unique aspects. One 9-year-old with a history of seizures had been prescribed extremely high doses of methylphenidate, clonidine, fluoxetine, and promethazine. An 8-year-old girl died a week after undergoing general anesthesia, and neither clonidine nor methylphenidate was found in the blood on postmortem examination. It was not clear whether she was taking both drugs at the time of her death. A 7-year-old boy had been taking the methylphenidate–clonidine combination for about a year, but doses are unknown. At postmortem examination, he was found to have fibrotic scarring of the heart. In the most recent case a 10-year-old boy was taking 10 mg of methylphenidate twice a day and was wearing a clonidine patch (0.2 mg every 5 days). His ADHD symptoms were well controlled, but he developed episodes of syncope. Workup procedures for these including computed tomographic scan (CT), ECG, and EEG were within normal limits. While swimming vigorously he complained of faintness, passed out, had a seizure, and died. The autopsy revealed a congenital cardiac malformation that may have caused transient ischemia or arrhythmia.

There have been a further 19 reports of nonfatal cardiac side effects in children taking clonidine, either alone or with stimulant (Swanson et al., 1995). In 11 of these 19 nonfatal cases, clonidine was administered alone; a combination of methylphenidate and clonidine was administered in the remaining cases. In the nonfatal cases, two patterns of cardiovascular side effects were noted: in 10 of the 19 cases, the children suffered sedation and hypotension, whereas in 5 cases activation and hypertension were present. In two-thirds of the cases, the adverse event followed a dose change, either prescribed or due to noncompliance. Most of the time, the dose of clonidine was missed, another medication was adjusted, or a switch to a clonidine patch was attempted. Nonetheless, many clinicians at major psychiatric centers have reported on treating thousands of patients with the clonidine–methylphenidate combination without similar serious cardiovascular side effects.

Clonidine and methylphenidate have differing effects on the cardiovascular system. Methylphenidate is an indirect agonist of both dopamine and norepinephrine. It enhances the release and blocks the uptake of both these neurotransmitters; in the periphery there is a net increase in norepinephrine. Clinical doses will cause an increase in heart rate of about 10 beats/minute as well as increases in systolic blood pressure (mean increase, 8.1 mmHg). These effects peak about 1 hour after administration of methylphenidate. The effect of clonidine also peaks 1 hour after administration; and its half-life is more than 10 hours (D. S. Davies et al., 1977). It is interesting that despite its long half-life, clonidine has often been dosed three and four times a day. This suggests that it is the peak action that is most critical in any therapeutic effect, rather the achievement of a steady state in the body. While blockade of presynaptic alpha$_2$ autoreceptors results in a net decrease in norepinephrine release, in high doses its postsynaptic action can result in hypertension. Indeed, the hypertensive effect predominates early in accidental overdoses, with the hypotensive effect emerging after 2–4 hours (Heidemann & Sarnaik, 1990). A hypertensive rebound after abrupt discontinuation may occur (Weber, 1980). Based on the above data, it is possible that the hypotension–sedation pattern would be particularly likely to emerge when clonidine is administered while methylphenidate is wearing off (e.g., at bedtime). In contrast, the hypertension–activation pattern would emerge whenever the clonidine is wearing off while the methylphenidate effects are increasing.

Hunt, Minderaa, and Cohen (1985) first performed a double-blind crossover study of clonidine in the treatment of ADHD. The study period was 12 weeks; all subjects received clonidine doses for 8 continuous weeks. Some subjects received placebo for 2 weeks before the clonidine treatment and again for 2 weeks after the clonidine phase, whereas others received clonidine for 8 weeks followed by 4 weeks of placebo. Relative to placebo, the investigators found significant decreases on both the parent (34%) and teacher (44%) Conners Hyperactivity Index ratings. The study had a number of flaws, including an atypical crossover design, small sample size, and biases in referral that prevent it from being regarded as conclusive.

One study has compared clonidine to methylphenidate (Hunt, 1987). Ten children with ADHD underwent a placebo-controlled crossover trial of placebo and two doses of methylphenidate. After this study, all the subjects were then entered into an open trial of 8 weeks of oral clonidine. After the open trial of oral clonidine, eight of the subjects then underwent a trial of transdermal clonidine. The length of the time the subjects were on the patch was not specified. Clonidine (both oral and transdermal) and methylphenidate both produced an equivalent reduction in parent and teacher Conners ratings relative to placebo, but without a double-blind design the study cannot support claims that clonidine is as efficacious as methylphenidate in the treatment of ADHD.

Gunning (1992) evaluated the effectiveness of clonidine and methylphenidate in two groups of ADHD children: 32 with ADHD and tic disorders, and 72 with ADHD alone. A double-blind placebo-controlled parallel groups design was used. Curiously, clonidine was not effective relative to placebo in ADHD children with comorbid tic. For the children with ADHD without tics, methylphenidate and clonidine were equally effective (50% response rate in each active drug group), while only 13% responded to placebo. Leckman et al. (1991) found that clonidine significantly reduced both clinician and parent ratings of ADHD symptoms relative to placebo in comorbid ADHD/Tourette's syndrome children.

There are no controlled trials of combining methylphenidate and clonidine in ADHD. Hunt, Capper, Fingeret, and Ebert (1988) performed an open trial of the two drugs individually and in combination in 25 children with ADHD. The age range of the subjects was 7–13 years, and many had comorbid conduct disorder. Each subject received methylphenidate alone (0.3–0.5 mg/kd per day), clonidine alone (3–5 µg/kg per day), and the two drugs in combination. Each condition was administered for a month. Data on blood pressure or pulse were not reported. Only the parent Conners rating scale was used to assess outcome. While all three conditions—methylphenidate, clonidine, and the combination—reduced parent ratings of ADHD symptoms, it is not clear that the combination was superior to either medication alone. The aforementioned authors did report that the methylphenidate dose needed to obtain "optimal improvements" was 40% lower in the combined treatment group, although the open design makes this difficult to interpret.

Further studies of clonidine alone and clonidine in combination with stimulants are needed. Does clonidine truly have direct effects on inattention and impulsivity, or does it exert its effect via sedation? Is it useful for ADHD symptoms per se, or is it really best used to treat aggression or explosiveness?

Guanfacine

The theoretical basis for role of guanfacine in the treatment of ADHD has been reviewed by Arnsten, Steere, and Hunt (1996). Clonidine is equally effective at stimulating all three subtypes (a, b, c) of the $alpha_2$ receptor. $Alpha_{2b}$ receptors are found exclusively in the thalamus, and clonidine's action in this area accounts for its sedative effect. $Alpha_{2c}$ receptors are found in the brainstem and underlie the hypotensive effect of clonidine. $Alpha_{2a}$ receptors are found predominately in the prefrontal cortex and are important in cognitive function. Guanfacine has greater affinity for the $alpha_{2a}$ receptors and improves attention and impulse control in monkeys with much less sedation than clonidine (see Arnsten et al., 1996, Fig. 1). Thus the preclinical data suggest that guanfacine might have a more direct effect on attention with less sedative effect in the treatment of ADHD. Conversely, if guanfacine were ineffective, this would suggest that clonidine achieve its reduction in disruptive behavior through sedation alone. Hunt et al. (1995) first explored the use of guanfacine in ADHD. The 13 subjects underwent an open trial of guanfacine at a mean dose of 3.2 mg/day (0.091 mg/kg per day). The medication was dosed in the morning, at noon, at 4 P.M., and at bedtime. Guanfacine has a half-life of nearly 17 hours and is normally dosed once a day in adult hypertension patients, so the reason for the multiple dosing is not clear. The subjects showed a significant decline in parent ratings of inattention and hyperactivity, although teacher ratings were not obtained. Sedative and hypotensive side effects were minimal.

Chappell et al. (1995) reported on the use of guanfacine in 10 children with comorbid ADHD and Tourette's syndrome. They ranged in age from 8 to 13 years; however, their weights were not reported. Guanfacine total daily doses ranged from 1.5 to 3.0 mg/day; most children were dosed two or three times daily. The length of treatment ranged from 4 to 20 weeks. The authors obtained Conners Continuous Performance Test (CPT) scores and parent ratings before and after treatment, but no teacher ratings data were available. Guanfacine produced a significant reduction in the number of errors on the CPT, but no overall improvement was found on the parent ratings. When the individual data are examined, 4 of the 10 subjects show marked declines in parent ratings of hyperactive behavior, 3 show no change, 3 show worsening of symptoms. In view of the lack of a statistically significant effect, this study cannot be viewed as supporting the use of guanfacine.

Thirteen children with severe ADHD and various comorbid conditions (predominantly ODD, Tourette's syndrome, and learning disorders) underwent an open trial of guanfacine (Horrigan & Barnhill, 1995). The subjects were aged 7–17 years and had failed an average of two other medications before entering the study. The dose of guanfacine ranged from 0.5 to 3 mg/day (mean, 1.27). Parent and teacher ratings of ADHD symptoms were obtained at baseline and at 4–8 weeks of guanfacine treatment. There were no statistically significant effects of guanfacine on either blood pressure or pulse. Both parent and teacher rating scales showed significant declines in ratings of inattention and impulsivity. Further double-blind placebo-controlled studies of guanfacine are needed.

NEUROLEPTICS

Neuroleptics are never used as a treatment for ADHD per se despite evidence that they can decrease symptoms of inattention or hyperactivity (Gittelman-Klein, Klein, Katz, Saraf, & Pollack, 1976; Werry & Aman,

1975). There are certain complex cases, however, where these medications can be useful—such as in the treatment of severe aggression (Chapter 6) or in treatment of children with developmental disabilities who show prominent hyperactivity and aggressiveness (Chapter 10). A discussion of the use of neuroleptics in children must be preceded by an overview of the issue of tardive dyskinesia (TD), their most serious long-term side effect. It is important to distinguish TD from withdrawal dyskinesia (WD). Both consist of abnormal motor movements—lip smacking, rolling of the tongue, tic-like movements of the head, neck, trunk, and extremities. WD occurs when neuroleptic medications are discontinued. They last at least 1 week and resolve within 16 weeks. If the abnormal motor movements persist beyond 16 weeks or if they emerge while the patient is on a steady-state dose of neuroleptic, then TD is diagnosed. TD may be permanent in many patients; in others it will gradually resolve if the patient is left off neuroleptic for months or years. In young adult schizophrenics chronically treated with neuroleptic, 19% will show signs of TD by year 4; by year 6 the prevalence of TD increases to 26% (Kane, 1995; Kane, Woerner, & Lieberman, 1988). How prevalent is WD or TD in children chronically treated with neuroleptic?

Gualtieri, Quade, Hicks, Mayo, and Schroeder (1984) reported on 41 mentally retarded children (mean IQ = 45) who were chronically treated with neuroleptic for behavioral disturbance. Fifteen (36.6%) developed either WD or TD. Only three of these children meet criteria for TD; in two of these cases, the abnormal movements resolved after a year off neuroleptic. A higher dose of neuroleptic was associated with a increased risk of TD, but dose was confounded with diagnosis, age, and treatment duration. In a second study, 38 mentally retarded individuals were withdrawn from neuroleptic (Gualtieri, Schroeder, Hicks, & Quade, 1986). They had begun neuroleptic treatment at a mean age of 10.9 years, and had received neuroleptic treatment for a mean of 8.33 years (*SD* = 6.6). The mean dose of neuroleptic, in chlorpromazine equivalents, was 225 mg/day. The mean cumulative dose of neuroleptic the subjects had received over their lifetimes was 1,046 grams (*SD* = 2,122). Twelve of the children (31%) had no abnormal movements at all upon withdrawal, 13 (34%) had WD, and 13 had TD. Four of these cases of TD resolved within 12 months. Gualtieri and colleagues calculated that a cumulative 374 of chlorpromazine represented a threshold at which the risk of TD or WD increased markedly. This would translate to 1,000 mg/day of chlorpromazine or 20 mg/day of haloperidol for a year.

M. A. Richardson, Haugland, and Craig (1991) examined a larger sample of 61 children (aged 10–18 years) treated with neuroleptic. The children were treated in a residential facility, and most did not have a psychotic diagnosis; rather, neuroleptics were prescribed chronically for assaultive behavior. Forty-one of these children remained on neuroleptic for longer than 3 months and thus were at risk for TD. Five (12%) of these children developed treatment-emergent TD; that is, they developed TD while on the neuroleptic. There was no difference between those patients with and those without TD in terms of dose or length of exposure to neuroleptic.

In the largest prospective study to date, Campbell et al. (1997) followed 118 autistic children treated with haloperidol. The subjects were kindergarten age upon entry into the study and were followed for up to 5 years, receiving haloperidol drug-free holidays through the study. The mean dose of haloperidol was 1.18–1.98 mg/day (0.06–0.086 mg/kg per day). The children were exposed to these doses for a mean of 1.54 years. Upon withdrawal of haloperidol, 40 (33.9%) of the sample showed dyskinetic movements. Mostly the children showed WD; only four had abnormal movements persistent enough to meet criteria for TD. The haloperidol dose was not higher in the group with WD or TD. Females were more likely to have TD and to have multiple dyskinetic episodes.

Thus the majority of children treated with neuroleptics do not develop dyskinetic movements upon withdrawal of the drug. About a third do develop such problems, but only about 10% meet criteria for TD. The remainder may develop WD, which resolves within 16 weeks; even many cases of TD will resolve within a year. The literature is inconsistent as to whether dosage and length of exposure are related to the risk of TD. Parents must be informed of the risk of TD or WD, but clinicians can point out that most children will not have these difficulties. Increasingly, atypical neuroleptics such as risperidone or olanzapine have fewer acute extrapyramidal symptoms (EPS) than the traditional neuroleptics do, although a number of case reports of TD in patients treated with risperidone have emerged (Anand & Dewan, 1996; Edleman, 1996; Feeney & Klykylo, 1996; Gwinn & Caviness, 1997; Khan, 1997). Thus, while it is assumed that atypical neuroleptics will cause less TD than traditional agents, this has not been proven by long-term studies. Studies of risperidone in children and its effects on hyperactivity and aggression will be reviewed in subsequent chapters. Risperidone has been well tolerated in children in studies performed to date. No EPS was found in 18 children and adolescents with autistic disorder or other pervasive developmental disorders treated with risperidone at doses ranging from 1 to 4 mg/day (McDougle et al., 1997). Findling, Maxwell, and Wiznitzer (1997) treated 6 young (aged 5–9 years) autistic children with risperidone (mean dose, 1.1 mg) and reported only 1 case of EPS, which resolved on reduction of dosage. In contrast, Armenteros, Whitaker,

Welikson, Stedge, and Gorman (1997) found that 2 out of 10 adolescent schizophrenics treated with risperidone had acute dystonic reactions, while three developed EPS requiring treatment with benztropine. In all of these studies significant weight gain was noted as well as somnolence, the latter generally resolving after several weeks of treatment. A chart review of 13 psychotic children treated with risperidone revealed two cases of liver enzyme abnormalities (Kumra, Herion, Jacobsen, Briguglia, & Grothe, 1997). Both showed evidence of fatty infiltration on abdominal ultrasound, and their liver enzymes returned to normal after risperidone was discontinued. Liver functions should be monitored in children and adolescents treated with risperidone, particularly if the child experiences a marked increase in weight. The role of neuroleptics in the treatment of ADHD children with severe aggression or pervasive development disorders is dealt with in Chapters 6 and 10.

SUMMARY

The modern clinician has a wide ranger of psychopharmacological agents at his/her disposal to treat the child or teenager with complicated ADHD. Pharmacology is, however, only one arm of treatment of ADHD and its comorbid conditions. The next chapter will give an overview of behavioral treatments commonly applied in these cases.

5

Behavioral Interventions

Behavioral treatment techniques have been used to address a variety of problem behaviors associated with childhood disorders. The purpose of this chapter is to provide an overview of principles and techniques of behavioral treatment; this information will be a useful starting point for those readers interested in designing and implementing the specific behavioral intervention programs described in Part V of this book. In addition, although it is not within the scope of this volume to describe in detail studies that evaluated behavioral treatments with childhood disorders, this chapter will cite research addressing the efficacy of the interventions described. Those readers who are already well versed in behavioral interventions may choose to move directly to these later chapters (14–16).

Inducing behavior change by manipulating environmental consequences is such a natural and frequent phenomenon that "real-life" examples are plentiful, both in historic and modern contexts. The contemporary field of behavioral psychology, however, credits experimental research in operant and classical learning procedures with providing the basis for the specific application of such techniques to treat psychopathological conditions. Early laboratory studies generated knowledge about conditions under which behaviors are increased and decreased, shaped and extinguished, and maintained and generalized; from these empirical roots sprang both the specific intervention methods and the ideological approach that characterize the field of behavior therapy.

A number of texts exist providing comprehensive discussions of behavioral principles and techniques (e.g., Baldwin & Baldwin, 1998; Kazdin, 1994; Malott, Whaley, & Malott, 1997; Martin & Pear, 1996). We do not attempt to provide an exhaustive description of this topic; rather, the following should be considered a "primer" to familiarize the reader with the distinguishing characteristics of the behavioral approach, identify and describe major relevant behavioral principles, and describe and evaluate specific interventions that have been most commonly used to treat the childhood disorders addressed in this volume.

Behavioral interventions have been criticized as being mechanistic, uncaring, and incompatible with child-rearing goals, such as encouraging independence, individualism, and self-fulfillment. Many of these critics are well meaning, and we do not lightly dismiss their concerns. Rather, we believe that such criticisms reflect misunderstandings of the goals and strategies of behavioral approaches, at least those advocated in this volume. As such, an explicit discussion of these concerns within the context of our treatment philosophy is warranted.

We believe that children feel safer in environments that have well-established rules and limits. Without predictable consequences for behavior, the world can appear to be a random and potentially risky place. It is the responsibility of adults to establish these guidelines, and the behavioral approach provides an ideal framework for doing so in a thoughtful and consistent (rather than a haphazard or indiscriminant) way. Children who are hampered by deviant behavior that places them in conflict with reasonable and established social expectations have less access to opportunities for self-fulfillment. When behavioral techniques can be applied to address such behavioral difficulties, it gives children *more*, not *less*, freedom of choice.

Behavioral interventions need not involve a mechanistic or unemotional approach. Many critics of behavior therapy mistakenly believe that they entail the provision of tangible rewards or consequences divorced from social and emotional cues. Effective behavioral treatment, however, typically involves a strong social support component; children are praised and encouraged for their successes, and negative consequences can be accompanied by an acknowledgment and sharing of the child's frustration and disappointment. We advocate the use of behavioral treatments within the framework of loving and supportive relationships. Indeed, the behavioral focus on attending to children's positive behavior can lead to enhanced adult–child relationships, as can be witnessed in the course of the comprehensive behavioral treatment programs we describe below.

Behavior therapy places the ultimate responsibility for children's welfare directly on parents and teachers. While diagnosis and pharmacological treatment can produce an unintended message of abdication of responsibility on the part of adult caretakers, the behavioral approach relies on caretakers to design and implement programs. As emphasized throughout the volume, this perspective in no way suggests that parents and teachers are to blame for ADHD; it does, however, reflect our philosophical belief that effective intervention depends on the coordinated efforts and investments of adults in children's day-to-day functioning.

CHARACTERISTICS OF BEHAVIOR THERAPY

Kazdin (1994) has identified five major features that characterize behavioral treatment approaches: the primacy of behavior, the importance of learning, the use of directive and active treatments, the importance of assessment and evaluation, and the use of persons in everyday life as treatment agents. A consideration of these features helps to illuminate the unique aspects of the behavioral approach to the treatment of childhood disorders.

Primacy of Behavior

Behavioral approaches consider overt behavior to be of primary importance in conceptualizing psychopathological conditions. As noted previously, this approach diverges somewhat from that of the medical model, which views symptoms as signs of pathology rather than problem behaviors that serve as treatment targets. Thus, the behavioral approach considers the specific manifestation of a symptom (e.g., inattention) on a domain of functioning (e.g., ability to follow instructions on an academic task) to be a problem behavior requiring direct intervention. While the behavioral approach has often been conceptualized as ignoring the role of "nonobservable" symptoms, including those in the affective realm (e.g., sadness) and the cognitive realm (e.g., self-defeating beliefs), behavioral approaches have considered feelings and thoughts to constitute relevant areas of treatment consideration, although there are differing views about the extent to which such symptoms should be considered as intervention targets. While most, if not all, behavior therapists agree that the consideration of thoughts and feelings is a critical component of assessment, some consider such symptoms to be amenable to direct intervention (e.g., with cognitive techniques to directly modify dysphoric thoughts and feelings) whereas others believe that such symptoms will respond to interventions that more directly target the overt problem behaviors associated with them (e.g., increasing activity level to reduce dysphoric thoughts and feelings).

Importance of Learning

The behavioral approach assumes that problem behaviors can be modified by new learning experiences; the goal of intervention is to design programs that will provide such learning experiences. Thus, a child with ADHD with a longstanding history of failing to complete task assignments may learn to do so with the appropriate environmental modifications, such as breaking work assignments into smaller segments and rewarding task completion. It is important to note that the behavioral approach does not negate the role of nonenvironmental factors in the etiology of psychopathological conditions; many of the disorders discussed in this volume have been clearly associated with biological origins. The behavioral approach does focus, however, on the use of environmental manipulations to provide new learning experiences that attempt to modify problem behaviors, regardless of whether those behaviors arise from biological or environmental (or mixed or unknown) factors.

Directive and Active Treatments

The application of behavioral techniques typically involves directive and active approaches. While the development of the treatment plan typically involves a collaborative effort among therapists and clients, the treatment goals are usually addressed by detailed and specific instruction in the prescribed procedures. In contrast to other psychological treatments, behavioral techniques do not place a primary focus on the therapeutic relationship or developing insight. It is important to note, however, that both of these may be important factors in behavioral therapy to the extent that they may effect treatment motivation (and, accordingly, compliance with recommendations); however, it is the actual enactment of the behavioral strategies that is viewed as the effective component of treatment (rather than the relationship quality or insight per se).

Importance of Assessment and Evaluation

A defining feature of behavioral treatment approaches involves a strong emphasis on evaluation of problem behaviors, both initially (as a "baseline"), and throughout treatment (to evaluate progress). The careful assessment of problem behaviors and treatment responsiveness is a major contribution of behavior therapy; as described in Chapters 2 and 3, this approach is applicable to the medical as well as the nonpharmacological components of treatment. Although this hallmark characteristic of the behavioral approach provides a high standard, since assessment results may reveal that treatment is not efficacious, using relevant "data" to drive decisions about the necessity of treatment plan changes seems preferable to less objective criteria, such as clinician judgment. The careful measurement of problem behavior prior to and throughout treatment is considered a critical component of the treatment approach promoted in this volume.

Use of Persons in Everyday Life

In contrast to many psychological therapies, behavioral treatment is often conducted in settings other than the therapist's office, such as at home and in school. Since the behavioral approach advocates environmental manipulations to change problem behavior, it is not surprising that those persons who frequently interact with the client, including parents, teachers, and peers, are often utilized to assist in treatment implementation. In some instances, the therapist will design a treatment program and use another person to monitor a specific behavior and/or provide the agreed-upon consequences. An example would be a therapist-designed system to increase completion of classwork, in which a teacher would be asked to monitor the percentage of classwork completed each day and perhaps provide a reward, such as 10 minutes of free time, when a specified goal is met. In other instances, more extensive training in behavioral principles and techniques is provided, and other persons gradually take on the role of both designing and implementing treatment procedures; this approach characterizes parent-training programs.

MAJOR RELEVANT PRINCIPLES OF BEHAVIOR THERAPY: INTRODUCTORY REMARKS

The following sections briefly describe some of the major principles of behavior therapy; these principles underlie the more specific procedures described in Part V (Chapters 14–16). This chapter is not intended to provide a comprehensive discussion of the many considerations involved in designing behavior therapy programs but serves as a brief introduction to the more extensive and detailed discussion of treatment strategies that follows. Although systems for classifying various techniques associated with learning principles vary somewhat, three broad classes often identified are operant, respondent or classical, and modeling procedures. Each of these broad classes is associated with its own experimental history and principles, although, as will become evident, there is some conceptual overlap among them as well. The following section describes techniques based on operant procedures within an "ABC" framework that analyzes the antecedents and consequences of behaviors. The primary components of behavior change programs are identified, including stimulus control techniques, positive reinforcement, avoidance and escape conditioning, and punishments. Also included is a discussion of factors that promote the generalization and maintenance of changes in behavior. Later, a major section describes principles based on respondent, or classical, learning; though less widely incorporated in interventions for externalizing behavior problems, these techniques and their applicability are worthy of mention. In the next section, the use of modeling approaches is described. Then, other techniques associated with behavior therapy, including cognitive and self-control treatments, are discussed. The final section considers the evaluation of behavior therapy.

OPERANT TECHNIQUES AND THE ABC's OF BEHAVIOR

The operant learning paradigm considers how both their antecedents and their consequences affect behaviors; procedures based on operant techniques are probably the most widely utilized in behavioral treatment approaches. In the ABC framework, two classes of events are considered relevant in understanding people's behavior (the "B" component of the equation): Antecedents ("A") or events that precede behaviors, and consequences ("C") or events that follow behaviors, can both influence the likelihood that a behavior will be emitted. First, antecedent events and their use in designing interventions are described below. Then, the consequent events associated with operant techniques are introduced, based on their use in increasing positive behaviors or decreasing negative behaviors.

Antecedents

The later subsections describing operant and classical learning procedures describe the learning of responses based on events, such as reinforcers or punishers, that follow the emission of a behavior; however, behaviors are also influenced by events that precede them. Antecedent events that can be used in behavior change programs include shaping and fading discussed next, and stimulus control techniques, considered subsequently.

Shaping and Fading

Shaping refers to methods to initially elicit a particular behavior, and fading refers to methods for gradually withdrawing reinforcement once a behavior is occurring. Methods for shaping behaviors are most relevant in instances in which the desired behavior is either initially absent or inadequately performed. For example, language may be absent or of very low quality in some developmentally delayed children; it would therefore be ineffective to merely provide a reward for correct word pronunciation since this behavior is unlikely to arise in the absence of specific procedures to initially elicit the desired response. Similarly, although a long-term goal of a behavior change program to improve academic skills might be to expect the child to complete work with 80% accuracy, it would be unrealistic to provide a reward only upon the occurrence of this level of performance if baseline data indicate that the child is initially completing work with an average accuracy rate of 40%. The term "successive approximations" refers to the process of shaping a desired response; initially, responses that only roughly resemble (or are components of) the desired response are reinforced, with progressively more stringent standards set for receiving reinforcement as the actual behavior comes more and more closely to resemble the desired behavior.

Fading is the process of progressively removing antecedent or consequent events once a behavior comes to be consistently demonstrated. As with many of the other techniques described here, fading occurs naturally in many real-life examples of learning. Thus, although a parent teaching a child to ice-skate initially provides much physical guidance and verbal instruction (i.e, shaping), as the child begins to master skating skills, the level of this assistance is gradually decreased. The fading of reinforcers plays a critical role in efforts to maintain and generalize treatment effects, discussed below.

Stimulus Control

Generally, the task of increasing appropriate behaviors and decreasing inappropriate behaviors is affected by issues, such as in what settings and under what conditions the behaviors should be performed or withheld. Stimulus discrimination training refers to the process by which individuals learn to discriminate the environmental factors that signal whether or not a particular behavior should be performed. In designing effective behavioral interventions, it is usually important to attend to discrimination learning since it influences the appropriateness of particular behaviors. Thus, the desirability of behaviors such as setting the table, practicing the cello, and playing a board game with siblings are all influenced by situational factors; we do not want the table set on an evening when the family is dining out, the cello practiced during baby's nap time, or games played after bedtime. The presence of particular individuals may also serve as discriminative stimuli; for example, children typically behave differently on the playground depending upon whether or not an adult is present. Thus, the presence of an adult serves as a discriminative stimuli for children to emit and withhold certain behaviors—for example, they may be more likely to take turns and less likely to start fights—whereas the absence of an adult serves as a discriminative stimulus for them to emit and withhold other behaviors. In fact, behavior is typically influenced by fairly fine-grained stimulus discriminations; in the above example, the presence of a particular adult may differentially influence behavior relative to another adult.

A classic example of stimulus control was provided by Marholin and Steinman (1977), who investigated two school settings (i.e., teacher present vs. teacher not present in the classroom). This was a complex study that addressed how students of elementary school age learn to respond to antecedents and consequences in the classroom setting. The above authors used two strategies for implementing a behavior modification program in the classroom—by tying token reinforcement to observations of behavior or academic productivity.

For one intervention strategy, Marholin and Steinman (1977) provided feedback (tokens) and reinforcement (free-time activity) based on the teacher's observations of behavior during seatwork. The procedure was very simple: every 30 seconds, the teacher checked and awarded a token if the child was "on task" but did not award a token if the child was "off task." As expected from the extensive literature on behavior modification in the school settings, this was a very effective way to increase academic productivity in the classroom (measured by the number of math problems worked on a probe test). After a few days of exposure to this intervention, the performance (number of problems worked) of students in the class improved substantially.

For another intervention strategy, the same authors provided feedback (again, tokens) and reinforcement (again, free-time activity) based on academic productivity (amount and accuracy of completed assignments) during the seatwork time. This, too, was an effective intervention: after a few days of exposure, this also produced improved performance on the probe task (number of math problems worked).

The purpose of the aforementioned study was to evaluate what happened *after* effective interventions were established. Both of these interventions were established in a classroom setting with the *teacher present* during seatwork time. The research question asked was about a subtle change in the setting when the teacher was *not* present: would either effective intervention generalize to a setting where the teacher was out of the room?

Marholin and Steinman (1977) tested this hypothesis by establishing "probe" conditions when the teacher left the room. What happened? For the students who initially learned to stay busy and work to receive tokens (the "on/off-task" procedure), performance plummeted in the probe conditions when the teacher left the room—the number of problems worked correctly dropped by about 65%! In contrast, for the students who initially learned to complete problems to receive tokens, performance did not change much when the teacher was not present. The number of problems worked dropped only roughly a quarter as much—about 15% compared to about 65%.

Why did the effect of treatment (an increase in academic productivity) fail to generalize when such a simple change in setting occurred? Marholin and Steinman (1977) offered a theoretical explanation that appeals to common sense, too. The presence of the teacher in the classroom became a "cue" to the students about the contingency between behavior and reinforcement. The students learned that reinforcement was not contingent on "staying busy" when the teacher was not looking—so, when the teacher was not looking, the increased behavior (staying on task by working problems) was not manifested. The same principle would hold if the student learned to stay on task in one classroom (where the teacher provided constant surveillance during seatwork) and then transferred to another classroom (where the teacher expected independent work and did not check on students during seatwork). The improved performance learned in one setting (the teacher always checking on students) would probably not generalize to the other setting (the teacher seldom checking and requiring independence or personal responsibility).

This study claimed to show that by focusing on the child's *work products*, rather than focusing on the child's orientation or social behavior, the student would become more independent and less dependent on teacher surveillance. Thus, the effective use of antecedents in influencing behavior must take into account the potential inadvertent confounding of adult presence with stimulus control. If a program for increasing classwork productivity uses as its target the "number of minutes observed on task," children have no incentive to continue working when the teacher is out of the room. In contrast, if the targeted behavior is the "number of math problems completed," stimulus control over children's motivation to complete academic work may be adequately maintained even when the teacher is absent.

Children who display aggressive outbursts are often provoked by particular stimuli or situations. When these stimuli are identified, interventions can target de-escalation of the potential explosive outburst. For example, upon detection of characteristic emotional signs, a teacher might provide a nonverbal cue to signal a child to use a self-instructional strategy for decreasing anger. Two specific instances of stimulus control are rules and goals; both of these strategies precede the behavior they are expected to influence. Rules establish the explicit relationships among stimuli, behaviors, and consequences; for example, "If homework is not completed by dinnertime, video games cannot be played that evening." Another specific type of stimulus control procedure involves goal setting, in which reinforcers contingent upon achieving specified goals are stated. The use of goal setting can be a particularly effective component of programs that utilize self-control techniques; this topic is discussed further in a later section.

Consequences: Operant Learning Procedures

Developing, Increasing, or Improving Desirable Behavior

Positive Reinforcement. Positive reinforcers are defined by their consequences on behavior; any event following a behavior that causes that behavior to be more likely to occur in the future is a positive reinforcer. Inherent in this definition is the reliance on the consequences rather than the nature of an event to define a positive reinforcer; events that may be reinforcing to one person may actually be aversive to another. Thus, although classes of potential reinforcers typically include attention and praise; physical affection, such as hugging and kissing; tangible rewards, such as money, food, or toys; or privileges, such as extra time to play video games; no particular event can be classified as a positive reinforcer unless it has the intended effect of increasing the behavior it follows. For example, adult praise may not be universally positively reinforcing across all children and settings. Thus, a teacher's singling out of a student's excellent paper may be perceived as embarrassing to the student or detrimental to peer relations; in this instance, if the student turns in less excellent papers in the future, teacher praise does not meet the criteria to be classified as a positive reinforcer.

In general, activity reinforcers are often preferable to tangible reinforcers. The Premack principle, sometimes referred to as "Grandma's rule," provides a method of determining what activities are reinforcing. This principle is based on the fact that activities that children perform with high frequency can be used to reinforce those that they perform infrequently. For example, when left to their own devices, many children would strongly prefer playing video games to vacuuming their rooms. Using the Premack principle, children can be induced to vacuum their rooms if video game playing is made contingent upon it; thus, Grandma's rule would state, "No video game playing until your room is vacuumed." Similarly, activities such as playing outside, riding bicycles, spending the night with a friend, and going to the mall may be highly effective reinforcers for some children. Such activity reinforcers are easy to implement and are "natural" in that their link to the activity they are to reinforce is often logical. Children can easily understand that if their homework is not completed, for example, they have not "earned" the privilege of playing. Therefore, we recommend that activity reinforcers be considered before tangible reinforcers whenever appropriate.

Reinforcers that are initially effective may become less effective over time. This can occur for a variety of reasons, including satiation effects when food or candy seems less appealing to a child as he/she becomes full, or when some initially desirable activity, such as choosing dessert, becomes less novel over time. To avoid the dilemmas associated with ineffective reinforcers, it is often helpful to include childen in generating reinforcers for behavior change programs. It can also be useful to have a variety of reinforcers available so that children can choose among several options. Such lists of reinforcers, or "reinforcement menus," can include both tangible and activity reinforcers and can be modified over time as needed.

In some instances, positive reinforcement can "backfire" when some undesirable behavior is inadvertently reinforced. The embarrassed father who purchases candy in the grocery store to quiet an acting-out child provides a reward for tantrum throwing and will likely see an increased frequency of this behavior. This unintended reinforcement of problem behaviors can occur frequently with challenging children, who emit higher levels of such behaviors, leaving the often exhausted parent with a strong temptation to provide a quick fix that will immediately stop the aversive behavior despite the negative long-term consequences of this approach. This problem becomes more complex and difficult to address when the reciprocal effects—that is, how the behavior of parents is affected by children—of such situations are considered; we will return to this example below when we describe avoidance and escape conditioning.

Intermittent Reinforcement for Developing Persistence. A well-documented phenomenon in research on learning involves the intermittent or partial reinforcement effect. In the initial stages of increasing a desired behavior, it is most effective to provide reinforcement for every instance. However, once the behavior is occurring, the use of occasional reinforcement will result in greater persistence than the use of continuous reinforcement. For example, a behavior change program designed to get a child to make her bed each morning might initially involve a daily reward; however, once the behavior is established, the reward might be given only on some days. The term "reinforcement schedule" refers to the method for determining which responses to reinforce; two of the most commonly used are "fixed ratio" and "variable ratio" schedules. In the example above, a fixed ratio schedule would involve giving a reward after a specified number of responses. The child might receive a reward after every fourth time she made her bed; in 20 days, she would receive five rewards. In a random ratio schedule, a proportion of acts to be rewarded is specified, but rewards are given randomly within those parameters; for example, as with the fixed ratio schedule, rewards might be provided for one out of four acts on average, but across 20 days the child might have an opportunity to receive rewards on days 2, 5, 12, 14, and 19. The specific characteristics of various reinforcement schedules with regard to how they affect rates of responding both prior to and after rewards have been studied in great detail; when relevant, these aspects of reinforcement schedules will be considered in suggestions for specific program design. Using a partial reinforcement schedule to encourage persistence is a concept related to both fading and to the maintenance of treatment gains, discussed below.

Escape and Avoidance Conditioning. Although escape and avoidance learning are typically associated with punishment paradigms (discussed in a later subsection), such situations can serve to increase behaviors since aversion relief, via either escaping or avoiding a noxious stimulus, is a powerful reinforcer. One example of a situation in which escaping from an aversive stimulus can increase behavior can be seen in the example of the embarrassed father dealing with a screaming child in the grocery store. When this father gave candy to his child, he reinforced the behavior since it resulted in a cessation of the tantrum and thus allowed him to escape from the exceedingly aversive situation of dealing publicly with a loudly unhappy child. Dysfunctional parent–child interactional patterns such as the one described by this example are understandably difficult to modify given the powerful effects that arise when an act—mollifying a screaming child by giving in to his demands—results in reinforcement for both the child (via positive reinforcement) and the parent (via escape conditioning). These kinds of dysfunctional interactions are one of the areas targeted for intervention in parent management programs, discussed in more detail below, and in Chapter 14.

Avoidance learning refers to a similar situation; responses that are associated with the avoidance of an aversive situation are strengthened. For example, a child who is able to stay home from school by complaining of a stomachache will be more likely to attempt the same strategy in the future, since complaining was reinforced by avoidance learning.

Decreasing Undesirable Behaviors

Intermittent Reinforcement for Decreasing Behavior. While many techniques for decreasing undesirable behaviors involve punishment procedures, problem behaviors can also be addressed by providing reinforcement for behavior that is incompatible with the undesirable response. For example, a child who is praised and rewarded for keeping his/her room neat will increase this behavior. It may not be necessary to specifically punish the child for having a "messy room" since an incompatible behavior—keeping the room neat—was increased with positive reinforcement. As noted earlier, behavioral persistence is particularly enhanced when reinforcement is intermittent and even unexpected, for example, in the form of a "surprise" inspection every week or two in which the child may receive a special privilege contingent upon his/her room being neat.

Extinction. Extinction occurs when reinforcement of a response is terminated, resulting in a decrease or cessation of the response. For instance, if a reward program for completing weekly book reports is suddenly terminated, a child may react by writing fewer book reports. The principle of extinction has been used in behavior change programs to decrease undesirable behaviors, particularly when such behaviors may have been inadvertently reinforced and thus increased by attention or other positive events. This situation was discussed earlier in the example in which a father bought candy for his screaming child, thus unintentionally reinforcing the tantrum behavior. If the father ignores future tantrums, this "nonreinforcement" should lead to an eventual decrease or cessation of tantrums due to extinction. Thus, if the reinforcer maintaining a problem behavior can be identified, extinction may be an effective method for decreasing the behavior. One drawback of extinction as a means of decreasing a negative behavior is that it may entail a somewhat lengthy process. Because of this characteristic of extinction, it is important to consider the "cost" of a more prolonged time period during which the behavior is occurring in deciding whether extinction procedures are appropriate or whether punishment procedures, which tend to more quickly decrease problem behaviors, may be more desirable. The next subsection describes the benefits and limitations of punishment techniques in greater detail.

Punishment. As with positive reinforcement, punishment is defined by the effects of an act on a behavior; a punisher is any event that decreases the likelihood of the behavior it follows. Thus, while verbal reprimands, the removal of privileges, and spanking are typically classified as punishments, it is technically incorrect to consider any of these to be punishers without considering their specific effects on the behavior of a particular child. As discussed previously in reference to positive reinforcement, the issue of whether a particular consequence can be considered a reinforcer depends upon whether it actually results in the desired effect of increasing a behavior. In this case, to be considered a punisher, an act or stimulus must decrease the problem behavior it consequates (i.e., to which it is responsive; see also the subsection on peer-mediated interventions, below). With this caveat in mind, most events considered to be punishers can be classified into those that involve the presentation of an aversive event, such as verbal reprimands and physical punishment, or the withdrawal of a positive event, such as timeout and response cost.

Verbal reprimands, including statements of disapproval, warning, and saying no, are commonly used in combination with other punishing stimuli, such as a loud voice tone, a stern look, and physical guidance. It is critical that warnings—telling a child that continued misbehavior will result in the loss of an anticipated outing to the museum, for example—not be used idly; if such warnings are consistently given without the stated consequence delivered, they will lose effectiveness over time.

Physical punishment as used most frequently by parents may take the form of spankings or pinches. In supervised settings, punishers such as electric shocks, ammonia vapors, or aversive tastes have been used to treat serious negative behaviors, including eye gouging, head banging, and excessive ruminative vomiting. Although in cases of such extreme and sometimes life-threatening behaviors the judicious use of physical punishment is justified, we do not generally advocate its use for the more typical kinds of child misbehavior targeted in this volume. We believe that nonphysical punishments can be equally or more effective in reducing most types of negative behavior; furthermore, they minimize the potential negative side effects that have been attributed to punishment, including aggressive responses by the child and the modeling of aggressive behavior by the punishing agent.

Timeout involves removing the child from the opportunity to obtain reinforcement, and most often takes the form of isolating the child, in a corner or in his/her room, for a specified time period. The factors that impact the efficacy of timeout have been studied fairly extensively and are discussed in greater detail in later subsections.

Response cost involves imposing a "fine" for negative behavior; fines may take the form of the loss of money, privileges, or tokens (within the context of a token economy program, described below). Response cost procedures are typically used in combination with positive reinforcement strategies; for example, a child's allowance may be based on his/her earning money for particular positive behaviors, such as taking out the trash, setting the table, and weeding the garden, and losing money for particular infractions, such as being late to dinner.

It is not surprising that punishment techniques are so frequently used by those who deal with children who display high rates of negative behavior, since punishment can result in rapidly decreasing problem behaviors. However, a number of concerns have been voiced about their use. In addition to concerns that such procedures invoke aggressive responses and serve to model aggressive behavior described above, punishment may result in negative emotional reactions, such as crying and anger, and efforts to escape or avoid the punishing agent or environment in which the punishment is administered. The decision to include punishment procedures in behavior change programs is understandably controversial, although we believe its judicious use is warranted under certain conditions. These include instances when potential alternatives to punishment are first considered, punishment is used in combination with positive procedures that promote appropriate behavior, the efficacy of the techniques is carefully monitored, and potential negative side effects are all taken into account.

Generalization and Maintenance Effects

A critical component of behavior change programs involves the generalization and maintenance of treatment-related changes. Generalization refers to the situation when an effective intervention applied in one setting produces a similar effect in another setting. Maintenance refers to the situation when the initial effect of an intervention continues over time. We hope that children who learn to perform a behavior in a particular environment, such as using the terms "please" and "thank you" at home, will also perform those behaviors in other situations in which they are desirable, such as with teachers and peers. Similarly, although we have specified methods for shaping behavior via the application of specific contingencies, it is often desirable to have children maintain their improved behavior even when the specific consequences under which they were learned are withdrawn. For example, the behaviors of saying "please" and "thank you" have been shaped initially by providing praise for their use; however, in real life, people are not praised each time they engage in social niceties even though they are generally expected to do so.

The bane of behavioral treatment programs is the lack of generalization; that is, when an effective intervention is established in one context (e.g., in a small-group training session), it fails to operate in a different setting (e.g., in the classroom setting). One explanation for lack of generalization is based on the concept of stimulus control. Although the behavior change techniques discussed in this volume often show demonstrated efficacy in bringing about improved behavior in the short run, they have been criticized for failing to adequately take into consideration how to generalize and maintain these improvements. A particular goal of this volume will be to specify procedures for promoting the generalization and maintenance of treatment gains as they relate to the treatment programs detailed in later sections.

RESPONDENT (OR CLASSICAL) LEARNING PROCEDURES

The behavioral procedures discussed in this chapter thus far fall under the broad classification of "operant learning procedures," that is, procedures based on learning that occurs because of the consequences of behaviors. The experimental learning literature has also explored another type of learning—respondent or classical learning—that is based on learning that occurs because particular stimuli and responses, typically "reflexive" responses, such as salivating, sweating, or heart palpitations, are paired together temporally. Although respondent learning procedures have been less utilized than operant learning procedures in designing behavior change programs for disruptive behavior problems, they are reviewed here both because of their historical significance and because of their particular application to fear reduction procedures.

Ivan Pavlov is credited with identifying and experimentally examining learning procedures based on the pairing together of stimuli and responses. During an experiment designed to examine digestion, he noticed that dogs who had received meat powder upon several occasions began salivating at the mere sight of white-coated experimenters who brought them their food. Similar examples can be found in humans. An initially fearless child "learns" to fear dogs after being bitten because of the association between a dog and pain; in this instance, the sight of dogs was initially neutral or even positive but became a "conditioned stimulus" to invoke a "conditioned response" of fear after being paired with the "unconditioned stimulus"—the pain-inducing dog bite. As discussed with regard to operant procedures, extinction can occur with conditioned responses; in such instances, the conditioned response (fear) may be extinguished if the conditioned stimulus (a dog) is presented on several occasions without being accompanied by the unconditioned stimulus of the bite. For example, if the fearful child visits family friends and comes into contact with the friendly pet dog, the fear response might extinguish after a number of visits. However, as also discussed previously with regard to operant extinction, this process may be somewhat slow to occur. Thus, more directive and efficient methods of reducing fears with classical conditioning techniques are described below.

Early applications of classical conditioning techniques focused on their utility in decreasing fear responses via "counterconditioning." Based on the rationale that fears that are learned (because some initially neutral stimuli—the dog in the above example—had become associated with pain) could also be "unlearned" via similar mechanisms, the technique of counterconditioning evolved. In counterconditioning, a fear response is decreased by pairing the fear-invoking stimulus (the dog) with a positive stimuli—food, for example. After an adequate number of presentations of the positive stimulus in the presence of the dog, a counterconditioned response—in this case, the pleasure and satiation invoked by food—replaces the previous fear response. In fact, under the proper conditions, such counterconditioning techniques have been demonstrated to reduce fears; this procedure forms the basis of one of the most commonly used fear reduction techniques, systematic desensitization, which uses the relaxation response as the counterconditioning response. Another use of counterconditioning involves aversion therapy, which involves pairing the undesired behavior with an aversive event. Aversion therapy must be used with great caution and has typically been applied only to fairly serious problem behaviors, such as smoking, excessive drinking, and inappropriate sexual behavior.

While counterconditioning has been used largely to decrease an undesirable behavior (or to "unlearn" an undesirable response such as fear), classical conditioning procedures can also be applied to increase a desirable behavior (or to "learn" a desirable response). One example of this use is the "bell-and-pad" device for treating nocturnal bed-wetting. Placed in the child's bedding, these devices sound a bell upon detecting the first drops of urine, thus waking the child. With continued use, the child typically begins to waken without the bell sounding, in accord with classical conditioning theory. This occurs because the feeling of a full bladder—previously, a "neutral" stimulus that did not waken the child—is paired with the unconditioned stimulus (the bell) and therefore eventually comes to elicit the response of awakening.

MODELING

The learning of some behaviors seems to be dependent upon observation; such learning is attributed to the effects of modeling. Examples of modeling are abundant. Children mimic their parents in acquiring language, motor skills, and even gestures and mannerisms. Children can also learn inappropriate or undesirable behaviors via modeling, as any parent whose child has "picked up" the profane language or aggressive responses of a disruptive peer can attest. Modeling is used in a number of the specific treatment procedures described in the following section; for example, programs to treat social skills deficits often include the demonstration and role-play of appropriate social behaviors, such as joining play activities or complimenting peers. Modeling is frequently combined with other procedures to enhance behavior change; thus, a desired response, such as setting the table, is demonstrated to a child and a reward given when the child sets the table appropriately.

OTHER TECHNIQUES

Self-Mediated Interventions

Although the techniques discussed thus far have focused primarily on procedures implemented by parents or teachers, children have also served as agents for their own behavior change. We divide these into techniques in which children monitor and reinforce their own behavior and those that seek to specifically alter cognitions; both of these approaches are based on the rationale that teaching children to serve as their own behavior change agents may increase the likelihood that treatment gains are maintained and generalized.

Self-Monitoring and Self-Reinforcement Strategies

Some interventions have employed children to monitor and provoke consequences for their own overt behavior. For example, a self-reinforcement program might involve having a child monitor the number of pages read for a classroom assignment and reward him/herself with a 10-minute break after each 15 pages. An example of a self-punishment strategy would involve having a child surrender a token each time he/she was not working on a class assignment at the time that a randomly set timer sounded. Some self-control strategies involve the individual in setting behavioral goals as well as providing reinforcers or punishers for meeting or failing to meet particular performance standards. As with cognitive and cognitive-behavioral strategies, self-control programs are inherently appealing but have not demonstrated rigorous therapeutic efficacy in treating children's behavior problems (particularly externalizing ones).

Cognitive and Cognitive-Behavioral Strategies

All of the learning procedures discussed thus far have focused on altering observable behaviors, such as increasing homework completion and decreasing peer aggression. Some psychological experiences, however, involve private events, such as thoughts and feelings. Although most behavior therapists would contend that such private events are subject to the same learning effects that govern observable behaviors, treatment programs that specifically focus on altering cognitions and emotions are classified as "cognitive" or "cognitive-behavioral" in nature. Examples of such treatments include problem solving, anger management, and cognitive restructuring. Problem solving and anger management entail teaching particular steps or skills to be undertaken in various situations; behavior change is presumably achieved by the practice of these skills. Cognitive restructuring seeks to alter negative or inappropriate thought processes that are believed to contribute to some negative state (e.g., thinking negative self-statements such as "I am a worthless person" may lead to depression) by inducing individuals to adapt more positive or appropriate cognitions. The last 20 years has seen both the rise and the fall in popularity of cognitive-behavioral treatment programs for children. Although such programs seem naturally desirable in their focus on self-reliance, their application has met with limited success in treating children's behavior problems, particularly the externalizing problems of most relevance to the subject of this volume. Furthermore, when such programs do achieve behavioral improvements, it is not clear whether the effective mechanism is actually "cognitive" or whether more traditional operant mechanisms, such as the changes in reinforcers and punishers that accompany behavior changes, are responsible. Despite the lack of empirical data validating their efficacy, some researchers have suggested that the use of cognitive-behavioral strategies should not be abandoned prematurely since their benefits may be in less tangible (and therefore less easily measured) yet potentially important domains such as self-efficacy and reasoning ability (Whalen & Henker, 1987). The data evaluating specific cognitive-behavioral and other self-control treatment programs will be discussed in greater detail with regard to the techniques described later, along with specific suggestions by Whalen and Henker (1987) for the judicious use of these techniques.

Peer-Mediated Interventions

Given the powerful influence of peer attention on children's behavior, it is not surprising that peers also have been used as behavior change agents. Peers have been involved in behavior change programs to monitor and consequate classmates' appropriate behavior, also serving sometimes as participants in a group contingency program in which they receive consequences dependent upon the behavior of classmates. For example, peers can be used to monitor behavior and distribute tokens in a token economy system, or they can be members of a team that earns a reward contingent upon an individual meeting a specified goal. A particularly attractive feature of peer-mediated interventions is the accessibility of peers to a wide variety of settings, some of which may be less easily observed by adults (e.g., playgrounds or restrooms). Interventions utilizing peers must be initiated judiciously, however, to ensure that peers in charge of monitoring and consequating behavior do so appropriately, and especially to minimize any potential negative impact on peer relations that might result if a target child's behavior leads to negative consequences for the group.

EVALUATION OF BEHAVIOR THERAPY

On what basis do we advocate the use of behavior therapy to treat the variety of dysfunctional childhood disorders presented in this volume? A well-conducted meta-analysis examined 108 studies (of the effects of psychotherapy with children) and found that behavioral treatments were more effective than nonbehavioral treatments across treatment problems, client age, and experience level of the therapist (Weisz, Weiss, Alicke, & Klotz, 1987). These authors found the average effect size of behavioral treatments to be .88 (i.e., the average treated youngster was functioning better than 88% of those not treated) compared to the average effect size of .44 for nonbehavioral treatments. Thus, the use of nonbehavioral interventions would be expected to result in only half the gains obtained with behavioral interventions. Considering the argument often voiced by defenders of more traditional treatment approaches that these techniques are of particular benefit for particular problem domains such as depression and anxiety, it is noteworthy that the relative benefits of behavior therapy were apparent for "overcontrolled" as well as "undercontrolled" problems. We believe that the combined use of behavioral and pharmacological therapies currently offers the most powerful intervention for treating the complex disorders addressed in this volume.

IV

Comorbid Conditions

6

Disruptive Behavior Disorders and Substance Abuse

Oppositional behavior, aggression, and antisocial behavior are the psychiatric symptoms most frequently comorbid with ADHD. They are often the symptoms most troubling to parents and teachers. At one point, there was extensive debate as to whether conduct disorders (CDs) and ADHD truly constituted separate entities. A wide body of evidence, reviewed by Hinshaw (1987), clearly indicates that these are separate conditions, though the overlap of these disorders is far above the level of chance. Table 6.1 shows this overlap in both clinical and epidemiological studies. As can be seen there, about half of ADHD children will meet criteria for either oppositional defiant disorder (ODD) or CD, though one study (Milich, Widiger, & Landau, 1987) found only 15% of ADHD children had CD. Similarly, a large percentage of children with ODD/CD will in turn meet criteria for ADHD, though an important distinction emerges with regard to age. Almost all children under the age of 12 who meet criteria for ODD/CD will meet criteria for ADHD; that is, there are few cases of "pure" ODD/CD among preadolescents. This is particularly true for clinical samples. Indeed, Klein et al. (1997), seeking to find a group of pure CD children for a research study, found that 69% of the CD sample concurrently suffered from ADHD. Both Reeves, Werry, Elkind, and Zametkin (1987) and Szatmari, Boyle, and Offord (1989) found that more than 80% of preadolescents with CD had

ADHD. A British epidemiological study showed that all preadolescent children with CD also had ADHD (McArdle, O'Brien, & Kolvin, 1995). In adolescent populations, "pure" CD is more common; Szatmari et al. (1989) found that only about a third of adolescents with CD met criteria for ADHD.

Some of this effect may be due to "halo" effects. That is, when adults (parents or teachers) are presented with oppositional or aggressive behavior in children, they may rate ADHD behaviors as being elevated as well. Abikoff, Courtney, Pelham, and Koplewicz (1993) presented elementary school teachers with three tapes of child actors portraying normal classroom behavior, ADHD behavior only, or ODD behavior only. The teachers were then asked to fill out rating scales regarding each child's behavior. If the child showed only ADHD symptoms, the teachers accurately recorded these behaviors and did not code the presence of ODD behaviors. On the other hand, the teachers not only rated the ODD children as showing the oppositional behavior, but they also coded the presence of ADHD behaviors that were not on the tape. Since teacher ratings are a critical component of the workup for ADHD, this finding presents a conundrum for the clinician. It suggests that a teacher may rate a pure "ODD" child as having high rates of ADHD behavior. While the diagnosis of ADHD should never be based on teacher ratings *alone*, the fact that so many preadolescent ODD and CD children meet criteria for ADHD in both clinical and epidemiological samples clearly

TABLE 6.1. Overlap of ADHD and Oppositional Defiant Disorder (ODD) and Conduct Disorder (CD)

Study	Age range	Study type	ADHD children with ODD/CD	ODD/CD children with ADHD
McGee et al. (1984a, 1984b)	7	Epidemiological	61%	58%
Szatmari et al. (1989)	4–11	Epidemiological	42%	87%
Szatmari et al. (1989)	12–16	Epidemiological	50%	37%
J. C. Anderson et al. (1987)	11	Epidemiological	47%	35%
Bird et al. (1988)	4–16	Epidemiological	57%	47%
S. K. Shapiro & Garfinkel (1986)	7–12	Epidemiological	60%	55%
Reeves et al. (1987)	5–12	Clinical	53%	85%
Koriath et al. (1985)	4–13	Clinical	29%	65%
Milich et al. (1987)	6–12	Clinical	15%	66%

indicates that ADHD should be high on the differential whenever oppositional, antisocial, or aggressive behavior are presenting complaints in this population. One should never assume that ADHD symptoms in a young ODD/CD child are simply part of the "acting-out" syndrome. As we shall see later, there is growing evidence that ODD and CD symptoms respond to stimulant medication; thus prematurely ruling out ADHD might well deprive the child of an important component of his/her treatment. In adolescents, ODD/CD not associated with ADHD is more common, though there is still enough overlap for the clinician to be alert to the possibility of comorbid ADHD. If the acting-out adolescent has a history of inattention and hyperactivity beginning before age 7, then treatment of the ADHD symptoms will be of benefit.

While ODD and CD are often discussed as though there were a single entity of acting-out behavior, it is useful to discuss some of the distinctions between them. Loeber, Keenan, Lahey, Green, and Thomas (1993) summarized the distinguishing features of these two disorders. Almost all children with CD have earlier met criteria for ODD, but not all children with ODD go on to develop CD. Seventy-five percent of a sample of boys with ODD *did not* go on to develop CD after 3 years, but of the children who developed CD more than 80% already had ODD. Clinicians have noted that physical aggression is often the first CD symptom to emerge, around age 7 (Lahey, Loeber, Quay, Frick, & Grimm, 1992). Thus early aggression may be a marker for those ODD children who will go on to develop CD. As CD symptoms emerge, children tend to retain all of their ODD symptoms. Thus while the CD diagnosis supersedes the ODD diagnosis in DSM-IV, most CD children continue to show the ODD symptoms of arguing, stubbornness, etc. ODD and CD children both have high rates of parental psychopathology (particularly substance abuse and antisocial personality) relative to clinical controls, but this pattern is much more prominent in the families of CD children. Not surprisingly, CD children have more school suspensions and police contacts than do ODD children (Frick et al., 1992). While ODD and CD are distinct, most studies of these conditions in ADHD children have lumped the conditions together. The following review examines differences primarily between ADHD-only and ADHD/CD children.

DEMOGRAPHICS AND CLINICAL PRESENTATION

Generally children with ADHD and ADHD/CD have similar ages of onset of their problems. In more than 80% of cases these children have difficulties before age 5 (Stewart, Cummings, Singer, & DeBlois, 1981;

McGee et al., 1984b). Only two studies have compared socioeconomic status in ADHD and ADHD/CD children, with conflicting results. Stewart et al. (1981) found no difference between these groups in socioeconomic status, whereas Lahey et al. (1988) found that ADHD/CD children were from poorer families and were less likely to be Caucasian than children with ADHD alone. The different results were most likely caused by the different settings of the two studies: Stewart et al. (1981) drew subjects from a university clinic in a rural state; the Lahey et al. (1988) sample came from two clinics in a large urban area that included many inner-city children. Teachers rate ADHD/CD children as having more severe inattention and hyperactivity than ADHD children have (S. K. Shapiro & Garfinkel, 1986; Reeves et al., 1987), although laboratory measures of activity level do not distinguish between the two groups (Werry, Elkind, & Reeves, 1987). Stewart et al. (1981) found that their ADHD and ADHD/CD groups were not different in terms of depressive symptoms, but the latter group scored significantly lower than the ADHD group on clinician ratings of egocentricity and antisocial behavior.

COGNITIVE AND LEARNING DEFICITS

Shapiro and Garfinkel (1986) did not find differences between ADHD and ADHD/CD children in the number of errors on the Conners Continuous Performance Test (CPT). Indeed, the CPT was not able to distinguish ADHD children from those with "pure" CD (Koriath, Gualtieri, Van Bourogdien, Quade, & Werry, 1985; Klee & Garfinkel, 1983). Werry et al. (1987) compared ADHD and ADHD/CD children on a wide variety of cognitive laboratory measures including the CPT, the Matching Familiar Figures Test (a measure of impulsivity), and a selective attention task. Interestingly, despite the greater clinical severity of those children in the ADHD/CD group, they were not different from the ADHD-only group on the above tasks. Halperin et al. (1990) showed that a hyperactive–aggressive group made more impulsive errors on the CPT than did hyperactive-only children. In this study, however, the classification was based only on teacher ratings and not on diagnostic interviews. There were no differences on the Matching Familiar Figures Test. Schachar and Tannock (1995) measured impulsivity in ADHD children using the Stop Signal Task. Here, the child had to press a button in response to stimuli on a screen but withhold his response whenever he was presented with a tone after the stimulus. Both ADHD and ADHD/CD children had much more difficulty stopping their button press than controls but did not differ from each other in that respect. Pure CD children did not show an inhibitory deficit on this task, suggesting that a deficit in inhibitory control is specifically related to ADHD in the *absence* of CD. In any case, most laboratory measures of attention or impulsivity have not shown differences between ADHD and ADHD/CD children or have shown differences so small that they are not clinically relevant.

In contrast to the above laboratory measures, measures of academic achievement have shown some striking differences between ADHD and ADHD/CD children. McGee, Williams, and Silva (1984b), examining a group of 7-year-olds, found that 37% of an ADHD/CD group had reading disabilities compared to 19% of the ADHD group. (The rate of reading disorder was about 7% in the clinical controls.) These differences in the rate of reading disorders were still present 2 years later. Moffitt and Silva (1988) performed a neuropsychological battery on a large sample of 13-year-olds who had been followed prospectively since age 3. Controls were compared to ADHD teens who had no history of delinquency, ADHD teens with a delinquent history, and delinquent teens without ADHD. ADHD boys without delinquency did not differ from controls on any neuropsychological measure, whereas ADHD-delinquents were impaired on a wide range of neuropsychological measures of verbal skill, visual–motor integration, visual–spatial skills, and verbal memory. Impairments were most profound on the verbal tasks, but ADHD delinquents showed diffuse deficits and no one pattern of neuropsychological pattern emerged in this group. Moffitt (1990) further analyzed these data, examining Verbal IQs and reading scores obtained at 2-year intervals over an 11-year period when the subjects were aged 3–13. ADHD children who would later become delinquent had lower Verbal IQs at age 3 and were showing evidence of reading difficulties by age 5. Thus the combination of ADHD and neuropsychological deficit (particularly verbal deficits) may play a role in the development of the comborbid ADHD/CD conditions.

MEDICAL HISTORY

ADHD and ADHD/CD children have not been found to differ from one another on a variety of medical and neurological variables. ADHD/CD children do not show a higher number of "soft signs" on neurological examination (August & Stewart, 1983; Reeves et al., 1987; McGee et al., 1984b). Similarly, ADHD/CD children do not have a greater history of perinatal insults or minor physical anomalies than do ADHD-only children, nor do they differ in handedness (Reeves et al., 1987). Both ADHD and ADHD/CD children are similar to normal children in terms of birthweight, head circumference and mean gestational age; there is not any excess of premature birth in either of the ADHD groups (McGee et al., 1984a; Moffitt, 1990). Sprich-Buckminster, Biederman, Milberger, Faraone, and Lehman (1993) did not find perinatal complications to be related to ADHD per se, but children with ADHD and any CD did have higher rates of pregnancy and delivery complications; their sample was not large enough, however, to subdivide the ADHD–comorbid group by individual disorders. Thus, overall, there is no evidence to suggest that ADHD/CD children are any more "brain damaged" due to perinatal insult than are ADHD or normal children. Neurological examination in the office will not yield differences between ADHD and ADHD/CD children.

FAMILY HISTORY

Some of the most striking differences between ADHD and ADHD/CD children are in their family history. Virtually every study has shown that ADHD/CD children have experienced more family stress and have relatives with higher rates of psychopathology than have children with ADHD alone. ADHD/CD children experience higher rates of parental divorce and separation than do ADHD children or psychiatric controls (August & Stewart, 1983), and measures of family adversity were four times higher in ADHD/CD children than in ADHD children without CD (Reeves et al., 1987). Forty percent of the ADHD/CD sample had been in foster care, whereas none of the ADHD children had been so placed. Moffitt (1990) found that ADHD children who lived in families with high levels of adversity at age 5 were more likely to become delinquent than were ADHD children without family stress.

Biederman, Munir, and Knee (1987) also compared ADHD children with and without ODD/CD. They examined the rate of psychiatric disorders among the relatives of these two groups. ADHD was equally prevalent among the relatives of ADHD and ADHD + ODD/CD children, but antisocial disorders were found more frequently among the relatives of the ADHD + ODD/CD children. Lahey et al. (1988) compared children with CD, ADHD, ADHD/CD, and clinic controls on demographic variables and parental psychiatric diagnosis. The family psychiatric histories of children with ADHD were not different from the family histories of clinic controls: ADHD children did not have an excess of antisocial personality disorder or affective disorder among their parents. In contrast, the mothers of ADHD/CD children had high rates of antisocial personality, criminal behavior, and affective disorder (but not alcohol or substance abuse). Affective disorder was not increased among the fathers of ADHD/CD children, but antisocial personality and substance abuse were. These antisocial diagnoses were also prevalent among the parents of a group of CD children who did not have ADHD.

Faraone, Biederman, Keenan, and Tsuang (1991a) examined the rate of psychiatric diagnoses among the first-degree relatives of ADHD children. The ADHD sample was subdivided into those with ADHD alone, those with ADHD and DSM-III oppositional disorder (OD), and those with ADHD and CD. Similarly elevated rates of ADHD were found among the relatives of all three ADHD groups compared to controls. A higher risk of antisocial (OD or CD) disorders was only found among the relatives of the ADHD/CD group.

Biederman et al. (1992) examined the rate of psychiatric diagnoses among the relatives of a large sample of ADHD and ADHD/CD children. The risk for ADHD was the same in both groups of relatives, but the ADHD/CD children had an elevated number of relatives with CD (26%) compared to the ADHD-only group (13%). Furthermore, relatives with CD also tended to have ADHD; that is, the two disorders cosegregated, indicating that ADHD/CD is a distinct familial subtype. This confirms an earlier study (August & Stewart, 1983) which also found that ADHD/CD children were more likely to have sibs who suffered from both ADHD and CD whereas the sibs of children with ADHD alone had only hyperactivity. Thus, there is strong evidence that ADHD with CD and ADHD without CD represent different genetic subtypes of ADHD.

LONG-TERM OUTCOME/SUBSTANCE ABUSE

ADHD/CD children appear to have very different long-term outcomes relative to children with ADHD alone. At one time it was thought that ADHD itself was related to antisocial behavior in adulthood, but in an extensive review Loney and Milich (1979) showed that adult antisocial behavior was related to aggressive symptoms in childhood rather than to hyperactivity. August, Stewart, and Holmes (1983) followed two samples of hyperactive children, one with pure hyperactivity and the other with high aggressivity. At follow-up, the subjects had a mean age of about 14. The hyperactive–aggressive group showed more antisocial and defiant behaviors. There were no cases of drug or alcohol abuse in the hyperactive-only group, whereas 30% of the hyperactive–aggressive group had engaged in substance abuse.

Both hyperactivity and aggression independently contribute to the prediction of criminal behavior in childhood and adolescence, but there is an interactive effect when the symptoms are combined. Loeber, Brinthaupt, and Green (1988) examined a sample of adolescents with multiple criminal offenses. Only 1.7% of these adolescents without ADHD or CD were multiple offenders; among those with ADHD without CD, 3.4% were so classified. In contrast, 20.7% of the adolescents with CD (but no history of ADHD) were multiple offenders. In the comorbid ADHD/CD group, nearly a third (30.8%) had committed multiple crimes. Farrington, Loeber, and Van Kammen (1989) collected data on hyperactivity and conduct problems in a large nonreferred sample of school children and followed up on the number of juvenile convictions the subjects acquired over time. Again, hyperactivity and conduct problems independently predicted delinquency: about 24% of ADHD children had a juvenile conviction (compared to 12.6% of controls), but 46% of the ADHD/CD children had become delinquent; 35% of subjects with CD in the absence of ADHD were later convicted of juvenile offenses.

Mannuzza, Klein, Konig, and Giampino (1989) followed a sample of 89 hyperactive boys from middle childhood to their young adult years: 39% of the ADHD sample had been arrested at least once, compared to 20% of the control group. When the data were examined further, it was shown that only the ADHD subjects with a comorbid antisocial personality had an excess number of arrests. ADHD subjects without an antisocial personality had not been arrested any more often than had controls, even when the ADHD symptoms had persisted into adulthood.

Satterfield, Swanson, Schell, and Lee (1994) divided a large sample of ADHD boys into aggressive and nonaggressive groups based on their Iowa Conners Teacher Aggression/Defiant ratings. Forty-three percent of the ADHD boys rated as aggressive had a felony conviction by age 18, compared to 26% of the ADHD boys rated as nonaggressive by teachers. The rate of felony conviction in the control group was only 8%. Thus ADHD by itself confers a risk for antisocial behavior; that risk is significantly increased by the comorbidity of childhood aggressive and defiant behavior.

ADHD subjects were shown to have a higher rate of substance abuse than controls at follow-up (Mannuzza et al., 1991), but again there was an interaction with CD. Every ADHD subject who developed substance abuse developed CD *before* starting to use illegal drugs. The whole issue of the relationship of substance abuse to ADHD is complex. First, there is no evidence that treatment with stimulant medication during childhood or adolescence predisposes patients to develop substance abuse. Treated and untreated children with ADHD have similar rates of substance abuse at follow-up during adulthood (G. Weiss & Hechtman, 1986). What is less clear is to what degree ADHD itself predisposes children to substance abuse as opposed to other comorbid disorders. ADHD is associated with a higher risk of cigarette smoking, and cigarette smoking runs in ADHD families but not in control families (Milberger, Biederman, Faraone, Chen, & Jones, 1997a, 1997b). For other illegal substances, however, it appears that CD or mood disorder, rather than the ADHD per se, is the major risk factor. Biederman et al. (1997) followed 140 children with ADHD and 120 controls for a 4-year period and assessed rates of substance abuse disorders. Both ADHD children and controls had similar rates of such disorders (15%). ADHD children who did abuse substances tended to develop dependence on substances earlier than did non-ADHD subjects (1.5 years vs. 3 years). Those ADHD children with comorbid mood or CD were more likely to abuse substances that controls. There was no difference in the type of illegal substance abused: in both the ADHD and control groups marijuana and alcohol were the most frequently used drugs; ADHD subjects were no more likely than controls to abuse cocaine or stimulants.

While ADHD children as a group may not be a risk for substance abuse, those children who continue to meet criteria for ADHD as adults may not be so fortunate. Wilens et al. (1997) compared 120 adults with ADHD to 268 adult controls. Childhood CD or bipolar disorder conferred a risk of substance abuse disorders independent of ADHD, consistent with the above studies. Adults with comorbid mood, CD, and ADHD in childhood were at considerable risk for substance abuse. Moreover, after controlling for the effects of comorbid disorders, ADHD that persists into adulthood confers its own risk of substance abuse disorder. Thus, for the child whose ADHD symptoms sharply attenuate by high school, the clinician can feel confident that the risk of substance abuse is not greater than that experienced by the general population; ADHD persistent into late adolescent confers a greater-than-average risk of substance abuse; the ADHD child with comorbid bipolar disorder or CD is at very high risk for the use and abuse of illegal drugs, including chemical dependence.

There is evidence that the substance abuse engaged in by ADHD adults is more severe than that of non-ADHD abusers. Carroll and Rounsaville (1993) found that cocaine abusers with a history of childhood ADHD were more likely to have both childhood conduct disorder and adult antisocial personality than were non-ADHD cocaine addicts. Cocaine addicts with a history of ADHD had more severe habits, consuming cocaine in greater amounts and frequency.

SUMMARY OF DISTINGUISHING FEATURES

The comorbidity of CD with ADHD significantly increases the seriousness of the disorder. ADHD/CD children, compared to ADHD children alone, come from more severely impaired and high-stress families where there is frequently a history of antisocial personality in both parents. Substance abuse may also be present in the family. ADHD/CD children have lower Verbal IQs and may show a wide range of learning disabilities and neuropsychological impairment. In spite of this, the medical histories of ADHD children are not different from ADHD only children; neurological examination will not distinguish them. Over time, ADHD/CD children are more likely to persist in antisocial behavior and are at much greater risk than ADHD children for the development of personality disorder, criminal behavior, and substance abuse.

PSYCHOPHARMACOTHERAPY FOR COMORBID ADHD/CONDUCT DISORDER

Stimulants

A number of studies have looked at whether children with ADHD and comorbid ODD/CD are qualitatively different from those with ADHD alone in terms of the stimulant responsiveness of the inattention and hyperactivity symptoms. Barkley, McMurray, Edelbrock, and Robbins (1989) subdivided a group of ADHD children into those with high or low aggression scores on the Child Behavior Checklist (CBCL); all the subjects then underwent a double-blind placebo-controlled trial of methylphenidate at two different doses. The two groups of ADHD children showed an equal degree of reduction in parent and teacher Conners ratings of inattention and hyperactivity. Similarly, observation room ratings of off-task, out-of-seat, and other ADHD behaviors declined significantly during drug treatment, and the improvement was similar for ADHD children with both high and low aggressivity. Using a similar methodology, Pliszka (1989) compared ADHD children with and without ODD/CD. Again, the groups were similar in terms of improvement on both the Iowa Conners Teacher Rating Scales (CTRS) and observation room ratings of off-task behavior. Finally, Klorman and colleagues (1989) divided an ADHD sample into aggressive and nonaggressive groups based on the Iowa CTRS. Both groups responded equivalently to methylphenidate during a placebo-controlled trial in terms of parent/teacher ratings and Conners Continuous Performance Test (CPT) scores.

The above studies show only that the inattention/hyperactivity symptoms of ADHD/CD children respond well to methylphenidate. What about the effect of methylphenidate on aggressive and antisocial behavior per se? As Hinshaw (1991) has pointed out, clinical lore had always held that acting-out behaviors were not responsive to stimulant medication, presumably because behaviors such as stealing and fighting were so much maintained by the child's psychosocial milieu. More recently, a number of studies have looked at the effect of stimulants on antisocial behavior and produced some surprising results. Klein et al. (1997) studied methylphenidate in ADHD/CD children and adolescents and found that the stimulant produced highly significant reductions in antisocial symptomatology. Hinshaw, Henker, Whalen, Erhardt, and Dunnington (1989) enrolled ADHD boys in a summer treatment program where their behavior was observed using a standardized system. Observers coded the frequency of aggressive behaviors such as verbal abuse, fighting, hitting, kicking, destroying property, and threats. The group was subdivided into high- and low-aggressive samples based on staff ratings. Methylphenidate significantly reduced all forms of aggressive behavior, and the improvement was particularly marked for the ADHD–aggressive group. That group showed a near 80% decline in aggressive symptomatology.

Gadow, Nolan, Sverd, Sprafkin, and Paolicelli (1990) observed the school behavior of 11 ADHD–aggressive children during a double-blind placebo-controlled trial of stimulant. Although drug effects on aggression were not noted during the class or in the lunchroom, the subjects showed a significant decline in physical aggression on the playground; this change was most marked at the higher dosage (0.6 mg/kg per dose) of methylphenidate. Murphy, Pelham, and Lang (1992) measured aggression in the laboratory in addition to observing children's behavior in a summer program. The ADHD subjects again showed significantly fewer conduct problems and negative verbalizations during program activities on methylphenidate relative to placebo. There was no effect of drug on aggressive behavior during a video game task in which the child believed a peer had sabotaged his score, nor did the aforementioned authors find drug effects on a social information-processing task where the child had to interpret intentions of others. The study suggested that stimulants clearly have effects on "real-world" aggression but not on laboratory measures of aggression.

Thus a clinician may reasonably expect that reductions in *overt* aggressive and acting-out behavior will occur in a child with ADHD/CD who is treated with stimulants. The results of Murphy et al. (1992) suggest that such changes may not be seen in office-based evaluations of aggression, but positive changes do occur in naturalistic settings. What is the effect of stimulants on *covert* antisocial behavior, such as stealing and cheating? Hinshaw, Heller, and McHale (1992) placed both ADHD children and controls in situations where they were likely to engage in these behaviors. The subjects were placed in a room by themselves and given word problems to solve. An experimenter "accidentally" left the answer sheet in the room; in addition several toys were placed in plain view of the child. Children were observed through a one-way mirror and performed the task on both placebo and methylphenidate. Control subjects did not receive medication but performed the task on two different days as well. Surprisingly, 38% of control subjects (who had no history of psychiatric disorder) stole at least once during the two sessions, and 25% of them cheated. Among the ADHD subjects on placebo, 64% stole, while 52% looked at the answer sheet while on placebo.

Interesting effects of stimulant medication were found on antisocial behavior. While on stimulant, ADHD boys were significantly less likely to steal or destroy property in the room, but the amount of cheating rose relative to placebo. Children who were impulsive and attempted clumsy, poorly planned thefts were more likely, in the view of the investigators, to show less stealing on stimulant. The increase in cheating on stimulant was felt to be related to greater task involvement by the ADHD children when taking methylphenidate. The data clearly indicate that methylphenidate is effective in reducing covert antisocial behaviors such as stealing and vandalism. Overall, children with ADHD/CD should be aggressively treated with stimulants before trying other pharmacological approaches.

What about the ADHD adolescent with a history of substance abuse, particularly one who has abused stimulants? Surprisingly, a history of substance abuse is a relative, not an absolute, contraindication to stimulant treatment (Gawin & Kleber, 1986; Wilens, Biederman, Spencer, & Frances, 1994). It is important to remember that stimulant treatment of the ADHD in childhood is not associated with a higher prevalence of substance abuse in adulthood (G. Weiss & Hechtman, 1986). As noted earlier, the development of CD appears to mediate the tendency of the ADHD child to engage in substance abuse (Mannuzza et al., 1991). In the treatment of the substance-abusing ADHD/CD teen, the ADHD symptoms themselves may present a major obstacle to attaining abstinence. Impulsiveness makes resisting the temptations of drugs harder; inattentiveness increases the likelihood of failure at school or on the job. The latter results in dysphoria, which may increase the craving for illegal drugs.

Gawin and Kleber (1986) reported on seven adult cocaine abusers with comorbid ADHD who were treated with stimulants (methylphenidate or pemoline). Six of the seven responded well to stimulants, and all remained abstinent of cocaine at 6-month follow-up. Despite its widespread clinical use, there have been only two cases reported of adolescents abusing prescribed methylphenidate (Goyer, Davis, & Rapoport, 1979; Jaffe, 1991). In one of these cases the patient stole methylphenidate from the school nurse and from home; he intranasally abused the drug up to 200 mg at a time. Clinicians should therefore be aware of the potential for such abuse. Methylphenidate does not decrease the craving for cocaine (Gawin & Kleber, 1985); it should not be used in the cocaine addict who does not have ADHD. Table 6.2 lists the clinical factors that should be weighed in determining whether to use stimulants in the ADHD/CD adolescent with substance abuse difficulties.

Brenda is a 13-year-old whose father has a history of cocaine abuse despite being a successful businessman. He was "in rehab" at the time of his daughter's evaluation. She was failing all her subjects in eighth grade and had constant office referrals for talking in class, being rude to teachers, and skipping class. Review of the past history and old report cards showed a long history of severe inattentiveness, which previous therapists had seen as secondary to depression. The depression, in turn, was viewed as arising from the family chaos due to the father's substance abuse and severe marital discord. Brenda was living with her mother.

During the diagnostic interview, Brenda was often sullen and stated she did not want to be there and that there was "nothing wrong with her." She reported periods of depression about once a week, that lasted for an hour or so. She denied neurovegetative signs but stated she enjoyed staying up to 2 A.M. to talk with friends on the telephone. She was always tired in school the next day. She denied pervasive depression and clearly enjoyed her weekend activities. She reported the use of marijuana on the weekends, and she

TABLE 6.2. Factors Influencing the Use of Stimulants in the ADHD Patient with a History of Substance Abuse

Stimulants more likely to be beneficial	Stimulants less likely to be beneficial
Strong childhood history of ADHD	Questionable history of ADHD
History of positive response of ADHD symptoms to stimulant	Parents with current substance abuse problems
Currently abstinent from drugs/alcohol	Acutely abusing drugs/alcohol
Parents reliable, or patient is living in structured setting	Disorganized family
No or limited involvement with criminal activities	History of criminal activities, particularly drug dealing
Cooperative with multimodality substance abuse treatment program	Not cooperative with other aspects of substance abuse treatment program
Stimulant medication can be monitored to prevent theft	Possibility of theft of stimulant medication
Patient agrees to have responsible adult check to see if medication is being taken	Oppositional with parents/nurse over taking the medication; high probability of "cheeking" pills to abuse later

said that she drank wine coolers but rarely more than two or three bottles of them at any given time. Psychological testing by the school did not show any learning disabilities. A trial of an SSRI by the family physician was not successful.

Before we go on, several aspects of the case are of interest: this child was treated by clinicians for many years as "depressed" even though she never met the criteria for major depressive disorder. The history of ADHD, inattentive type, which was clearly present, had been ignored or assumed to be "normal" behavior for a child in her situation. The true comorbidities in this situation were ODD and substance abuse.

A diagnosis of ADHD was made and, through the "Section 504" process, Brenda was admitted to Special Education as an "other health impaired" student on the basis of the ADHD diagnosis. She was started on methylphenidate, 10 mg in the A.M. and at noon. The entire medication bottle was transferred to the school to avoid diversion of the medication to Brenda or her father for abuse. Her school behavior and academic performance improved markedly. Nonetheless, Brenda continued to insist that she did not need the medication and began to refuse to take it. Curiously, she stated that her friends told her that she "was not as much fun" when she took it. There was no sedating effect of the medication; however, Brenda's lack of impulsivity on the medication was disconcerting to her.

The case illustrates how comorbid substance abuse is not an absolute contradiction to stimulant treatment. It also should emphasize the need for early treatment. While Brenda's ADHD symptoms responded, she now identified so strongly with her acting-out peers that their approval was more important than doing well on her schoolwork.

Antihypertensive Agents

In Chapter 4 the use of clonidine in ADHD and its possible cardiac side effects were reviewed. Clonidine has also been studied as an agent to reduce aggressive and explosive behavior. Kemph, DeVane, Levin, Jarecke, and Miller (1993) performed an open trial of 17 children and adolescents with ODD or CD, although the sample was highly heterogeneous and specific data on diagnoses was not available. All of the compliant patients showed reductions in aggressive behavior as measured by physician ratings, with minimal side effects. While blood pressures and pulses were not reported, the above authors stated in their discussion that there were clinically significant changes in these variables. Doses of clonidine ranged from 0.15 to 0.4 mg. Schvehla, Mandoki, and Sumner (1994) performed an open trial of clonidine in 18 prepubertal boys with ADHD/CD who had failed a trial of stimulants; 61% of the subjects showed marked improvement of their aggressive behavior at follow-up. Doses ranged from 0.15 to 0.4 mg/day. In four of these cases, a stimulant was added to the clonidine and additional improvement noted. While no controlled trials of clonidine in impulsive aggression have been performed, the use of alpha agonist may be justified when other agents have failed (see Figure 6.1, at the end of this chapter).

Beta Blockers

For many years, beta blockers have been suggested for the control of aggressive and impulsive behavior in brain-damaged adults (Yudofsky, Williams, & Gorman, 1981; Yudofsky, Silver, & Schneider, 1987), leading to the possibility that these medications might be effective in aggressive behavior in children. The pharmacology of the beta blockers is complicated, as four are available: propranolol, metoprolol, atenolol, and nadolol. The latter two do not cross the blood–brain barrier. Despite the widespread belief that beta blockers are effective in the treatment of aggression, only a few small controlled trials have been performed in adults and none have been done in children or adolescents (Allan et al., 1996; Alpert et al., 1990; Greendyke, Kanter, Schuster, Verstreate, & Wooten, 1986; Ratey et al., 1992). These studies showed modest effects of beta blockers on aggressive behavior, but they all had small numbers of subjects (most of whom were psychotic) and in all of them the patients were being concurrently treated with neuroleptics or mood stabilizers. It was of interest that nadolol, which does not cross the blood–brain barrier, did have some effectiveness on aggression, suggesting a peripheral rather than a central nervous system mechanism of action.

Two open studies have looked at the effects of propranolol on agitation and aggression in children and adolescents. D. T. Williams, Mehl, Yudofsky, Adams, and Roseman (1982) treated 26 children and adolescents who had "uncontrolled rage outbursts." Eighty percent of the sample had ADHD; all but one met criteria for CD. About half the sample had some degree of mental retardation. The dose range for propranolol ranged from 50 to 1,600 mg/day, with a mean dose of 160 mg/day (information on mg/kg per day was not reported). Subjects took other medications during the trial. The above authors suggested that 75% of the sample showed "clinically significant" improvement, though no standardized methods of assessing drug response were used. The number of rage outbursts were significantly reduced. Side effects were viewed as mild: four patients suffered hypotension which limited further dose increases; one patient had significant bradycardia. Another patient with a prior history of affective disorder became more depressed (in spite of improvement of aggressive outbursts). Imipramine was added to his regimen and he was reported to have improved. Today it would be more prudent to add an antidepressant without cardiac side effects to a beta blocker. Some subjects without a history of asthma developed new onset shortness of breath. (Beta blockers are contraindicated in patients with a history of asthma.) Kuperman and Stewart (1987) treated 16 subjects with propranolol with doses similar to those of D. T. Williams et al. (1982): 10 of these subjects were judged to have responded. There were no objective predictors of propranolol response in terms of age, EEG findings, or CT abnormalities. Nonetheless, the authors' subjective impression was that younger, more "organic" patients with higher levels of mental retardation responded better. Interestingly, decreases in blood pressure and pulse were not related to clinical improvement, so actual reductions in these indices should not be a target of dosing.

One small open trial has examined the effects of nadolol in minors. Connor, Ozbayrak, Benjamin, Ma, and Fletcher (1997) treated 12 individuals with autism, pervasive developmental disorder, and mental retardation who showed high levels of aggressive behavior; they ranged in age from 9 to 24. The dose of nadolol ranged from 30 to 120 mg (0.6–3.7 mg/kg per day). Five of the patients were on mood stabilizers or neuroleptics; the rest took no other medications. Nadolol was begun at 10 mg twice a day and titrated upward in an open manner by the clinician. The Overt Aggression Scale and Iowa Conners Teacher Rating Scales were used to assess aggressive behavior. After 11 weeks of treatment, nadolol significantly reduced the patients' aggression scores on these items. Blood pressure and pulse were also significantly reduced. Side effects were mild; the above authors did not report that patients suffered from syncope or dizziness.

Propranolol should not be used in patients with asthma, diabetes, cardiac disease, or hyperthyroidism. Children with no prior history of asthma can experience new onset dyspnea (D. T. Williams et al., 1982). Depression can also be triggered by beta blockers. Patients must be monitored for bradycardia, and the medication held if pulse is below 50/minute or the blood pressure falls below 80/50. Given the controversy surrounding $alpha_2$ agonists, clinicians should avoid the use of beta blockers until more controlled trials are available. They should be viewed as drugs of last resort in the treatment of aggression.

Antidepressants

A full discussion of the use of antidepressants in ADHD children is presented in Chapters 8 and 9 on anxiety and depressive disorders. Only one study has looked at the effectiveness of tricyclic antidepressants (TCAs) in ADHD/CD children. Biederman, Baldessarini, Wright, et al. (1993) compared children with ADHD alone to those with ADHD/CD in terms of response to desipramine. These two groups had an equal degree of response to the TCA; that is, there was no evidence that the TCA was more efficacious in ADHD/CD children than in those with ADHD alone. Coccoro and Kavoussi (1997) randomized 40 adults (mean age, 38 ± 8.7 years) with personality disorder to receive either placebo or fluoxetine. Doses of fluoxetine ranged between 20 and 40 mg/day. At week 10 of the study, fluoxetine was superior to placebo in reducing explosive, aggressive behavior, even in those subjects without a history of past mood disorder. None of the subjects met criteria for major depressive disorder on entry to the study. In a small open trial, 20 mg of fluoxetine added to methylphenidate was found to improve global functioning of children and adolescents with ADHD and other comorbid psychiatric disorders (Gammon & Brown, 1993). Even those patients without mood disorders improved with addition of the SSRI. While no controlled trials of SSRIs in aggressive CD children have been performed, these studies do suggest that serotonergic agonists can reduce acting-out behavior. As noted in Chapter 4, however, the clinician should be alert to the possibility of activation with SSRIs.

Lithium

Lithium is not effective for ADHD symptoms per se. Greenhill, Rieder, Wender, Buchsbaum, and Zahn (1973) treated nine hyperactive children who had been unresponsive to stimulants; most of the children had severe problems with oppositional and aggressive behavior. Only two of the children showed an improvement on lithium, these subjects showing higher levels of "affective symptoms" at baseline—one was noted to be depressed; the other, "euphoric and labile." All the other subjects either worsened or showed no change. DeLong and Aldershot (1987) compiled their long-term experience with lithium in a wide variety of child and adolescent psychiatric patients; none of their 19 attention-deficit disorder (ADD) patients responded to the drug.

Campbell and colleagues (1984) performed a double-blind trial of lithium, haloperidol, and placebo in 61 inpatient children aged 5–13 with aggressive CD. All of the subjects had failed to respond to the hospital milieu during a 2-week placebo run-in prior to beginning the drug study. None of the subjects showed evidence of affective disorder, nor did any of them have a family history of bipolarity. While the number of children with ADHD in the sample was not specified, the sample had high ratings of hyperactivity on the Children's Psychiatric Rating Scale, suggesting that the sample was highly comorbid with ADHD. Lithium was started at a dose of 250 mg/day; the optimal doses ranged from 500 to 2,000 mg/day. The serum levels of lithium ranged from 0.32 to 1.51 mEq/liter (mean, 0.993 mEq/liter). Lithium and haloperidol were significantly more effective in reducing hyperactivity, aggression, and hostility than placebo, but the two active drugs were not different from each other. Lithium showed fewer side effects than haloperidol. A second independent sample of 50 children with aggressive CD (none had a mood disorder) were studied in a 6-week double-blind parallel group study of lithium and placebo The authors essentially replicated the above results (Campbell et al., 1995). Lithium, either alone or in combination with stimulants, is one of the first drugs to be considered in the treatment of explosive aggression (see Figure 6.1 at the end of this chapter).

Anticonvulsants in the Treatment of Aggression

There is a paucity of data on the effectiveness of anticonvulsants as therapeutic agents in childhood behavior disorder. Phenytoin has been shown to be ineffective in children and adolescents with behavior disorder (Conners, Kramer, Rothschild, Schwartz, & Stone, 1971; Lefkowitz, 1969). Egli and Graf (1975) followed up 76 behaviorally disordered children with spike discharges on their EEGs (but no seizures). Fifty-six of these children were treated with anticonvulsants, some for years, yet none were felt to have benefited. Puente (1976) carried out a small double-blind placebo-controlled crossover study of carbamazepine in a heterogeneous group of children with behavior disorders. This study is widely cited in the literature as supporting the use of carbamazepine in the treatment of impulsivity or aggression, so it bears a closer look. Seventy-two children were enrolled, but only 56 completed the study (a 23% dropout rate), a fact the above authors does not explain Eleven of the 27 remaining subjects had mental retardation; most had abnormal EEGs. Furthermore, the symptoms were highly diverse: 85% of the children were aggressive and hyperactive, but 51–77% of the sample showed "perseveration, anxiety and extreme passivity." Each subject served as his/her own control; the sample was randomized to receive either the active drug or the placebo first, with each of the treatment periods lasting 4 weeks. Fixed doses were used during the carbamazepine period: 300 mg/day in the first 2 weeks; 600 mg/day in the second 2 weeks. Seventeen of the subjects improved on carbamazepine, whereas only five improved on placebo. There was an order effect, with subjects who received carbamazepine first appearing to get a greater benefit. Puente's (1976) paper did not provide a statistical analysis of these data. The author claimed, based on subjective clinical opinion, that carbamazepine improved cognitive functioning, but no convincing data were presented.

Kafantaris et al. (1992) performed an open trial of carbamazepine in 10 preadolescent children with CD. The groups showed significant declines from baseline in ratings of aggressiveness after 3 weeks of treatment. A double-blind study did not confirm these results, however (Cueva et al., 1996). Twenty-two children aged 5–11 were randomized to receive placebo or carbamazepine. These children had all shown at least three aggressive outbursts per week during a 2-week baseline period prior to randomization. None of the children had a mood disorder, and they all remained in the hospital for the full 10 weeks of the study. All the subjects in the carbamazepine group obtained therapeutic levels of the drug and were maintained for a full 4 weeks at the optimal level. Both the placebo and carbamazepine groups showed declines in aggression as the study progressed, but the two were not statistically different from each other. Thus carbamazepine has not been established as effective in treatment of childhood aggression. No study has compared carbamazepine to other agents (i.e., stimulants, lithium) in the treatment of aggression in children.

Divalproex sodium has recently been studied in an open trial of 10 adolescents with aggressive behavior (Donovan et al., 1997). These patients ranged in age from 15 to 18 and had diagnoses of CD and substance abuse. Only one patient had ADHD; none had ever had a manic or hypomanic episode. Each patient was titrated up to 1,000 mg/day of divalproex sodium, and serum levels were checked. Mean doses of medication were not reported, but the mean serum level of divalproex was 75 µg/ml (range: 45–113 µg/ml). The number of aggressive outbursts declined significantly from a baseline of 6.5 per week to 0.1 per week by the fifth week of treatment. Global assessment of functioning and a mood lability score also improved significantly. Six patients had a relapse of their aggressive outbursts when they discontinued their medication.

Case reports have appeared suggesting that anticonvulsants can induce irritable and aggressive behavior (Pleak, Birmaher, Gavrilescu, Abichandani, & Williams, 1988). Gabapentin is structurally related to gamma-aminobutyric acid (GABA), one of the principle inhibitory neurotransmitters of the brain. Its anticonvulsant mechanisms are not understood. Lee et al. (1996) reported that, of 55 children treated with gabapentin, seven developed behavioral problems. The seven children were aged 3–11 years, and all had diagnoses of ADHD before starting gabapentin, though none were on psychotropic medication. The dosages of gabapentin ranged from 18 to 50 mg/kg per day. All seven children showed an increase in temper tantrums and difficulty listening, and three developed aggression and oppositional behavior that had not been present prior to the gabapentin. For these children the symptoms resolved when the gabapentin was discontinued. Two further cases of behavior disturbance with gabapentin have been reported (Tallian, Nahata, Lo, & Tsao, 1996). A 16-year-old boy with mental retardation and tuberous sclerosis had gabapentin (dose: 10 mg/kg per day) added to the valproate he was already taking for seizure control. He had no prior history of aggressive behavior. The seizures stopped, but by day 9 of gabapentin treatment he developed aggressive behavior, including biting, slapping, scratching, and growling. He was admitted to the hospital, and the gabapentin was discontinued. The behaviors resolved, but when the gabapentin was reinstated the aggressive behavior immediately returned. A 6-year-girl with complex partial seizures was successfully treated with gabapentin (dose: 27 mg/kg per day) for epilepsy. She also had ADHD and was being treated with pemoline. After 6 months of gabapentin she became physically aggressive and assaulted other children. Her behavior improved modestly with the gabapentin dose was reduced to 18 mg/kg per day. It is of interest that in eight of these nine cases the child had a history of ADHD. This suggests that gabapentin should be avoided in epileptic children with ADHD. While further studies are needed, gabapentin does not show promise as a psychotropic medication. At present, divalproex sodium is the anticonvulsant most likely to be useful in the treatment of aggression.

Neuroleptics

Are neuroleptics ever justified in the treatment of aggressive behavior? Suppose a child's aggressive behavior has not responded to mood stabilizers or stimulants? What if cardiac side effects preclude the use of alpha agonists? The risk of withdrawal dyskinesia (WD) and tardive dyskinesia (TD) with neuroleptic treatment was discussed in Chapter 4. What is the evidence that neuroleptics reduce aggressive behavior in conduct disordered (as opposed to developmentally delayed) children? Campbell et al. (1984) compared haloperidol to lithium and placebo in their treatment of children with undersocialized aggressive conduct disorder. The children received a mean daily dose of 2.95 mg of haloperidol. The range of doses was 0.04–0.21 mg/kg per day (mean, 0.096 mg/day). Twenty children were randomized to the haloperidol group;

haloperidol was superior to placebo and equivalent to lithium in reducing aggressive behavior. Half the sample had acute dystonic reactions, while five children developed tremor and six drooled excessively. Thus, at doses necessary to control aggression, extrapyramidal symptoms (EPS) were a problem with haloperidol.

Werry and Aman (1975) treated 24 "hyperactive" and "unsocialized aggressive" children in a double-blind crossover study of methylphenidate, placebo, and two doses per day of haloperidol (0.025 and 0.05 mg/kg). Haloperidol was equivalent to methylphenidate in improving teacher and physician ratings of behavior (though aggressive behavior was not separated out from the global clinical improvement measures). The higher dose of haloperidol was associated with poorer performance on a laboratory cognitive task. Gittleman-Klein et al. (1976) randomized 166 hyperactive children to receive placebo, methylphenidate, thioridazine (fixed dose of 300 mg/day), or a combination of the two active medications. These children were not aggressive and did not have diagnoses of conduct disorder. Methylphenidate alone and the stimulant–neuroleptic combination were equally effective relative to placebo and thioridazine alone in reducing problems rated by parents, teachers, and clinicians. Side effects were more common in the combination group, and no advantage was found in the combination relative to the methylphenidate alone. These early studies do not give the clinicians carte blanche to use neuroleptics in ADHD children. They should never be used in children with ADHD alone, but their judicious use may be justified in aggressive ADHD children in whom no other option is available.

What about the atypical neuroleptic agents? In open studies of risperidone in autistic and psychotic children and adolescents performed to date, risperidone was found to significantly reduce aggressive and hyperactive behavior (Findling, Maxwell, & Wiznitzer, 1997; McDougle et al., 1997). Findling et al. (1998) showed that doses of risperidone up to 3 mg/day effectively reduced aggressive and antisocial behaviors in a group of CD children. Atypical neuroleptics may be useful in the treatment of the aggressive ADHD children with a lesser risk of WD/TD. The following case illustrates the process:

> Samantha is an 8-year-old girl with severe ADHD since age 3, as well as developmental delays. Her WISC-III Full-Scale IQ is 82, with a Verbal IQ of 71 and a Performance IQ of 90. She suffers from severe aggressive outbursts. She is in a self-contained classroom at school, and often an aide must stay with her the entire day. She overturns desks, bites other children, and lashes out whenever frustrated. She presented to the psychiatric clinic after many unsuc-

cessful trials of various medications. Over the years, stimulants (both methylphenidate and amphetamine), tricyclic antidepressants, and bupropion had been used without success.

At the time of her presentation, she was being seen by a pediatric neurologist. A trial of carbamazepine was unsuccessful, and a trial of valproate resulted in a rash and the medication was discontinued. On mental status examination there was no evidence of psychotic symptoms.

Despite her small size (less than 50 lbs or 22.68 kg) a trial of lithium at 150 mg/day was started. This was gradually increased to 300 mg twice a day, which resulted in a level of 0.6 mEq/liter. There was no marked change in behavior, and she began to experience dizziness and excessive urination. The lithium was discontinued. Her aggressive behavior escalated, and she nearly tipped over her 8-month-old brother's "bouncy seat" (with him in it). Olanzapine was initiated at a dose of 2.5 mg/day. There was a marked reduction in the aggressive outbursts. She began to participate in classroom activities and interact with peers. She no longer was threatening her sibling. She has remained stable on this dose for the last 6 months.

In our view, the serious risk to others, as well as to the patient herself, justified the use of the novel neuroleptic. The small risk of TD is far outweighed by the improvement in the child's quality of life. The parents were aware of this risk but agreed that the benefits far outweighed the potential costs.

SUMMARY

Figure 6.1 is a flow chart to guide the clinician in the choice of psychopharmacological agents for the treatment of the ADHD/CD child or adolescent. Most ADHD children with severe aggression or antisocial behavior will need a combined treatment program that includes behavior therapy (see Part V). This flow chart assumes the absence of a mood disorder; the presence of that conditioning addressed in Chapter 7. Specific dosing instructions for the drugs, as well as recommendations for laboratory tests, can be found in Chapter 4. Stimulants should always be the drugs of first choice in the treatment of the ADHD/CD child; as we have shown, it is quite probable that stimulant treatment will reduce impulsive aggression and antisocial behavior as well as inattention and hyperactivity. At least two different stimulants (methylphenidate and dextroamphetamine) should be tried (Elia et al., 1991). The physician should then determine if the child is a partial responder, complete re-

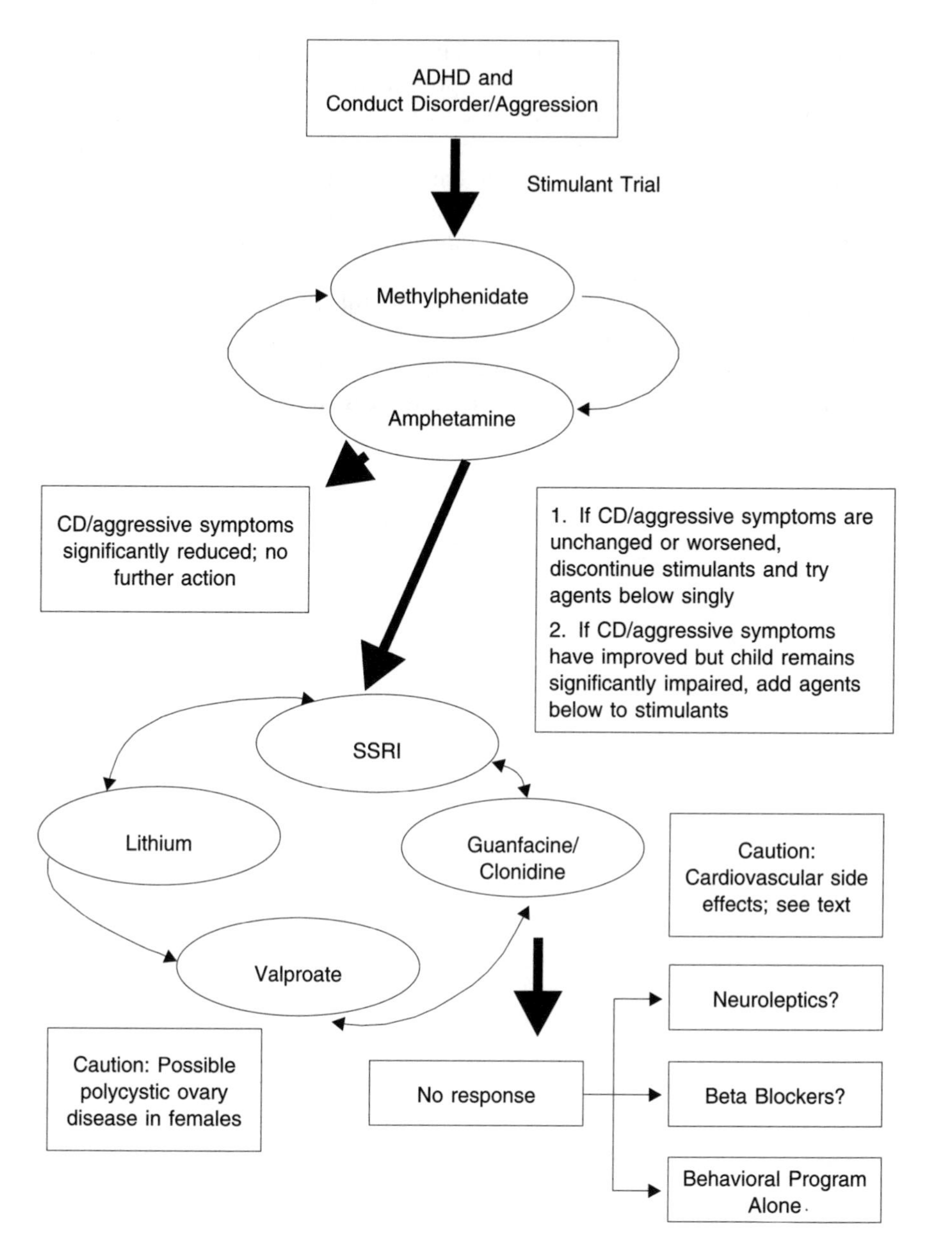

FIGURE 6.1. Decision tree for psychopharmacotherapy of comorbid conduct disorder/aggression.

sponder, or nonresponder. For partial responders, another agent (those in the circle) should be added to the stimulant; but if the child has had a complete nonresponse to stimulants, then the alternative agent should be tried alone. The four agents (lithium, anticonvulsants, SSRIs, and alpha agonists) are arranged in a circle to emphasize that no particular class of medication should automatically be selected first. A given patient may need to be tried on each of them in an empirical fashion to arrive at the regimen most helpful for that child.

If the agents in the circle are not helpful, the physician may then need to move on to other approaches. These include the beta blockers or atypical neuroleptics. Behavioral treatment alone may continue even if pharmacological treatment has been unsuccessful.

7

Neurological Disorders

What is the role of neurological factors in ADHD? Issues related to neuropsychological deficits such as learning disorders are discussed in Chapter 12. This chapter examines the role of central nervous system (CNS) injury in ADHD and aggression. Can neurological factors cause ADHD? Do they produce a syndrome that mimics ADHD but in fact must be treated much differently than ADHD? Several major areas are covered: Do seizures cause impulsive behavior or aggression? What is the role of the neurological workup (i.e., EEG) in the child with inattention or impulsivity? What is the role of head injury in ADHD? Do CNS infections have behavioral sequelae? If a child with ADHD has "soft signs" on neurological examination, how should the clinician respond?

ISSUES IN DIAGNOSTIC CRITERIA

Some behaviors may be so impulsive or inappropriate that parents or teachers become convinced the child suffers from a seizure disorder. They will complain of explosive outbursts that are triggered by minor frustrations or seem to occur for no reason at all. At what point is aggression simply part of the ADHD/CD syndrome, and when does it reach the level of "episodic dyscontrol"? Once such a diagnosis is made, what are implications for treatment, particularly in terms of psychopharmacology? Such behavior is often regarded as "organic" in nature, but in DSM-IV the term "organic" is no longer used. We must be more specific in our terminology, and DSM-IV provides two major diagnoses relevant to this area: *personality change due to a general medical condition (310.1)* and *intermittent explosive disorder (IED) (312.34)*. Since there is often confusion about the use of these diagnoses in childhood, an overview of their criteria is in order.

The diagnosis of personality change due to a general medical condition should be made when there has been a change from a previous (usually healthy) pattern of behavior. In children, the change in behavior must have been present for at least a year. This diagnosis should not be used to describe chronically disturbed behavior, particularly when the behavior has been present since early childhood. Furthermore, there must be strong evidence from the clinical history, physical examination, or laboratory of a medical disorder that has caused the change in behavior. In childhood, head injury, anoxia, or CNS infection are most likely to be the etiological agents involved in this diagnosis. In contrast, degenerative diseases are quite rare in childhood.

The second diagnosis, IED, also causes a fair degree of confusion, and some clinicians mistakenly use this diagnosis for *any* individual who is impulsively aggressive. The criteria for IED clearly spell out that this diagnosis is not to be used if ADHD, CD, or a personality disorder better explains the behavior. A medical condition or the direct physiological effects of a substance are not factors in the outbursts. Such "unexplained" outbursts of aggression in IED are often thought to be neurological in origin, but (as we shall see) the evidence for this view is weak and adhering to it dogmatically can lead to serious clinical error. For instance, a clinician orders an EEG in an aggressive ADHD child and it is found to be "abnormal." The aggression is presumed to be "organic," and perhaps anticonvulsants are prescribed. Is this, however, the best approach? We next review the evidence regarding the role of the EEG and "organic" factors in ADHD and aggression.

Are EEG Findings Important in ADHD?

It is important to note that epileptiform patterns can occur on EEGs in children who have no clinical signs of epilepsy. Cavazzuti, Capella, and Nalin (1980) performed EEGs on more than 3,500 children without epilepsy; 131 (3.54%) showed epileptiform discharges. This included the whole range of spike, polyspike, and spike and wave complexes. Follow-up 8 years later showed that only seven individuals developed seizures; the EEG normalized for most subjects. Eeg-Olofsson (1971) found a prevalence of paroxysmal activity of 15% in children carefully screened for an absence of neurological disorder of any kind. EEG abnormalities should not by themselves be taken as evidence of epilepsy.

Most studies have shown little ability of the EEG to discriminate children with mental disorders from controls. Ritvo, Ornitz, Wolter, and Hanley (1970) examined the prevalence of abnormal EEGs in psychiatrically disordered children with neurotic, behavioral, and psychotic conditions. Importantly, in this study EEGs were read blind to subjects' clinical status. In addition to categorizing psychiatric diagnoses, subjects were further classified as to the presence of "organicity." A subject was classified as having definite organicity if there existed a specific CNS pathology. Probable organicity was defined as the subject having a history of perinatal complications and/or CNS infection or injury. EEGs were abnormal in 21–33% of all three psychiatric diagnostic groups. Organicity was equally prevalent in all three patient groups, and EEGs were twice as likely to abnormal in the "organic" subgroups. No specific psychiatric symptoms were linked to the subgroup with temporal lobe abnormalities. EEGs did not distinguish boys with mental retardation, reading disorder, or psychiatric disorder from controls (Fenton, Fenwick, Dollimore, Rutter, & Yule, 1974). Hsu, Wisner, Richey, and Goldstein (1985) examined EEGs in four groups: inpatient juvenile delinquents, outpatient juvenile delinquents, nonadjudicated adolescent conduct disorders, and adolescents with psychiatric diagnoses other than conduct disorder. There was no excess of any type of EEG abnormality (diffuse, focal, or paroxysmal) among the diagnostic groups. Halperin, Gittelman, Katz, and Struve (1986) found EEG abnormalities in about half of a sample of ADHD boys who did not have seizure disorders. These abnormalities consisted of diffuse or focal slowing, or abnormal spiking activity. There was no relationship of the EEG abnormality to severity of the ADHD or to stimulant response. Cavazzuti et al. (1980) found that 3.54% of their sample of nonepileptic children had epileptiform patterns on the EEG; half of these children did show behavior problems. The EEG normalized with age, however, while the psychiatric problems persisted, suggesting a lack of a direct association between the two. Satterfield and Schell (1984) obtained EEGs on 65 normal and 76 hyperactive children. The hyperactive group was then divided into a delinquent group and nondelinquent group based on whether or not they had an arrest by age 18. The authors attempted to see if the EEG predicted antisocial outcome. Surprisingly, delinquent hyperactive subjects had childhood EEGs that were similar to those of the normal children. In short, the "good outcome" group had *more* abnormal EEGs as children. Thus the EEG is not a simple indicator of "organicity" that foreshadows a poor outcome for a patient. Children who had both ADHD and clearly diagnosed seizure disorders had slightly lower IQs than those of ADHD children without epilepsy, but they were no different in terms of aggressiveness on school achievement, nor did they have any increased prevalence of abnormalities on CT scan (Kinney, Shaywitz, Shaywitz, Sarwar, & Holahan, 1990).

There remains an interest with the supposed relationship between EEG abnormality, epilepsy (particularly that of the temporal lobe), and violence. Can impulsive aggression in an ADHD patient be related to epileptiform activity? Essentially, no study has conclusively shown a positive relationship between abnormal EEGs, epilepsy, and violence; indeed, and considerable negative evidence exists (Stevens & Hermann, 1981; Hermann & Whitman, 1984). Unselected groups of aggressive individuals may have an increased incidence of abnormal EEGs, but it is unclear what this means. Would an abnormal EEG predict response to anticonvulsant medication or other psychopharmacological interventions? An adult psychopharmacology study has shed some light on this issue. Cowdry and Gardner (1988) performed a double-blind placebo-controlled trial of an antianxiety drug, an anticonvulsant (carbamazepine), a neuroleptic, and an antidepressant in patients with borderline personality disorder, which is often associated with episodic dyscontrol. The antianxiety drug appeared to worsen symptoms (according to physician global ratings), whereas the other three drugs were superior to placebo in enhancing global improvement. Neither neurological soft signs nor EEG changes in response to procaine administration predicted specific drug response; that is, those patients who responded positively to carbamazepine were as likely to have normal EEGs as not. Thus an abnormal EEG is not a prerequisite for drug response to anticonvulsant medication when behavior is the target symptom. As noted in Chapter 6, mood stabilizers, whether lithium or divalproex sodium (Depakote), are often useful for treating impulsive aggression, regardless of the child's neurological status.

Overall, the data indicate that the role of seizures in ADHD or comorbid aggression is quite small. Epilepsy does not mimic ADHD, nor is it linked to aggression or rage outbursts. While ADHD children have a higher prevalence of nonspecific EEG abnormalities, these abnormalities do not appear related to any specific clinical variable of importance (drug response, severity, or prognosis). ADHD children with concurrent seizure disorders respond to methylphenidate just as well as neurologically healthy ADHD children do; furthermore, methylphenidate does not lower seizure threshold or effect anticonvulsant blood levels in epileptic ADHD children (Feldman, Crumrine, Handen, Alvin, & Teodori, 1989). There is no reason to obtain an EEG or other neurological workup in an ADHD child unless the history clearly shows evidence of seizures (tonic–clonic movements, loss of consciousness, automatisms).

BEHAVIORAL SEQUELAE OF CENTRAL NERVOUS SYSTEM INFECTION

The mortality rate of childhood meningitis or encephalitis can be quite high (Jadavji, Biggar, Gold, & Prober, 1986; Wald et al., 1986), and there is considerable debate as to the degree of cognitive and behavioral problems in the survivors (B. A. Davies, 1989). We focus here on whether these CNS infections commonly induce ADHD behavior in the recovered children. In the famous encephalitis epidemic of 1917/18 clinicians were presented with children who after recovering from the acute episode showed high levels of impulsivity and hyperactivity (Ebaugh, 1923). The condition became known as "postencephalitic syndrome," and this association of behavior with a brain insult led to hypotheses that hyperactivity had a neurobiological basis (Barkley, 1990). Clearly, the overwhelming number of children with ADHD do not have any history of CNS infection, and it also appears that today few survivors of meningitis or encephalitis show ADHD symptoms, provided they escape major neurological sequelae (deafness, hydrocephalus, or mental retardation). Survivors of bacterial meningitis who do not have such sequelae are no different from siblings or matched controls on teacher or parent ratings of behavior (Feldman & Michaels, 1988; Taylor, Michaels, Mazur, Bauer, & Liden, 1984; Wald et al., 1986). These ratings scales would surely have picked up symptoms of inattention or hyperactivity if ADHD were a common sequela of CNS infection. Only two cases of "hyperkinesia" emerged among 70 children who had recovered from encephalitis, a rate not statistically different from that in control groups (Rantala, Uhari, Saukkonen, & Sorri, 1991).

HEAD INJURY AND ADHD

About 160 per 100,000 children under the age of 15 suffer head injuries each year (Kraus & Norenson, 1994). The clinical outcome of these children is highly dependent on the seriousness of the head injury, which most studies classify according to the Glasgow Coma Scale (GCS; Teasdale & Jennett, 1974), shown in Table 7.1. Kraus and Sorenson (1994) found about 88% of head-injured children had mild head injuries (MHI). These children had initial GCS scores of 9–15, hospital stays of less than 48 hours, and no abnormal CT findings. The remainder had moderate-to-severe injuries involving initial GCS scores above 15, lengthy postinjury hospitalizations, and abnormal CT findings.

What is the relationship between ADHD and head injuries? This is a difficult question to answer, for it has a number of parts. Do children

TABLE 7.1. The Glasgow Coma Scale (GCS)

Domain	Status	Score
Eye opening	Spontaneous	4
	To speech	3
	To pain	2
	None	1
Best verbal response	Oriented	5
	Confused	4
	Inappropriate	3
	Incomprehensible	2
	None	1
Best motor response[a]	Obeying	5
	Localizing	4
	Flexing	3
	Extending	2
	None	1

Note. Severity of the head injury is assessed by the lowest postresuscitation GCS score obtained during the 24–72 hours after injury (see Table 7.2).

[a] The patient is asked to make a movement ("Touch my hand!"). If there is no response, a painful stimulus is applied to more than one site. If the patient moves to avoid the stimulus regardless of where it is applied, it is a localizing response. If the limb to which the stimulus is applied merely flexes or extends, the score is lower.

who sustain head injury develop an increased incidence of ADHD? On the other hand, are children with ADHD perhaps at higher risk for head injury because of their high activity level and impulsivity? Either phenomenon could explain an increased history of head injury in a sample of ADHD children. One must also distinguish between cognitive sequelae of head injury (changes in IQ, language deficits) and behavioral sequelae (ADHD, irritability, aggressiveness).

Mild Head Injury

Head injuries to their children often evoke strong emotions in parents, who fear "brain damage" and may attribute any behavioral change to the injury (Bijur, Haslum, & Golding, 1990). This is particularly true since the scalp is well vascularized and even minor cuts can bleed profusely and require sutures. It also should be noted that the medical definition of MHI (see Table 7.2) is much more severe than the layperson's perception of it. As we shall see, there is no evidence that minor "head bumps" which cause acute pain but no change of consciousness result in long-term problems.

In terms of cognition, it has been shown fairly conclusively that

MHI is not associated with any significant long-term changes in IQ, nor are there permanent deficits in verbal or visual memory (Levin, Ewing-Cobbs, & Fletcher, 1989). The study of behavioral sequelae of MHI is complicated by the fact that 28% of children with MHI have preexisting behavioral problems; 35% had below-average school performance before the injury (Brown, Chadwick, Shaffer, Rutter, & Traub, 1981; Chadwick, Rutter, Shaffer, & Shrout, 1981). In their sample of children with MHI, Brown et al. (1981) did not find any increase in psychiatric disorder 2½ years after injury. Fletcher et al. (1990) found the Vineland Adaptive Behavior Scores of children with MHI to be within the normal range 6 months after injury; they also did not have elevated externalizing symptoms as measured by the Child Behavior Checklist (CBCL). Asarnow et al. (1991) found elevated CBCL scores in a very small sample (n = 10) of children with MHI, but a larger sample *did not* have elevated scores on the Conners Parent Rating Scale at either 3 or 9 months postinjury (Schweizer, Feighner, Mandos, & Rickels, 1994). The performance of children with MHI on standardized laboratory measures of attention was not found to be impaired in two separate studies (Saletu et al., 1992; Murray, Shum, & McFarland, 1992). Max and Dunisch (1997) reviewed the charts of more than a thousand children at a psychiatric outpatient clinic; about 5% had a definite history of MHI. ADHD was not more common among these children relative to clinic attendees without MHI. Twenty-four children with MHI were followed prospectively for 2 years; only three cases of ADHD emerged, which was not statistically different from the one case of ADHD that emerged among a matched group of children with orthopedic injuries (Max et al., 1998).

TABLE 7.2. Definition of Severity of Head Injury

Mild head injury	GCS of 13 or over No loss of consciousness (LOC) or LOC < 20 minutes Nondepressed linear fracture without LOC
Moderate head injury	GCS of 8–12 LOC > 20 minutes Skull fracture with contusions, neurological findings, or hemorrhage CT/MRI abnormal
Severe head injury	GCS of 7 or less Intracranial hematoma Depressed fracture Subarachnoid hemorrhage Cerebral edema

The most comprehensive study of MHI has been performed by Bijur et al. (1990). More than 3,000 children were assessed at age 5 as part of an epidemiological study. Measures of intelligence and mother's ratings of aggression and hyperactivity were obtained. The children were followed up again at age 10, when cognitive and academic assessments were performed in addition to behavioral measures. During the 5-year period, some of the children experienced MHIs or other injuries. Because of national health system in Britain, *all* the children could be followed up, eliminating the bias of only impaired subjects being reported on. Children who experienced MHI were compared to children who had experienced fractures, burns, or lacerations; these groups were then compared to noninjured controls. Children who were aggressive at age 5 were more likely to experience a head injury, consistent with the findings of Brown et al. (1981). Children with MHI were not different from controls on cognitive and academic tests, though teachers did rate them as more active, even after controlling for the mother's rating of hyperactivity at age 5. Formal diagnoses of ADHD were not made, however. Furthermore, it is possible that some of the children had the onset of hyperactivity after age 5 and yet the head injury did not occur until after the behavior became disruptive. Finally, the effect of head injury on teacher hyperactivity ratings was modest: the MHI group was 0.4 of a standard deviation above the mean of the control group. This still would be within the normal range on the Conners Teacher Rating Scale (CTRS). Overall, parents can be assured that MHI will not cause ADHD, and symptoms of ADHD should not be attributed to a past MHI in a child with such a history. This is particularly important in cases involving litigation, where parents may claim a child's ADHD is due to a minor fall or accident; there are clearly no data to justify such a claim.

Severe Head Injury

The picture is quite different for severe head injury (SHI), which is defined in Table 7.2; it involves severe injuries to the skull and brain. In SHI, posttraumatic amnesia (PTA) is usually longer than a week. A number of studies have shown that children with SHI have serious cognitive and behavioral problems postinjury (Chadwick et al., 1981; Brown et al., 1981; Filley, Cranberg, Alexander, & Hart, 1987; Fletcher et al., 1990; Schweizer et al., 1994; Mendels, Johnston, Mattes, & Riesenberg, 1993). Children with SHI show marked deficits in IQ immediately postinjury, and while improvements in cognition clearly occur in the first year, full recovery is not attained in many children (Brown et al., 1981; Schweizer et al., 1994). Visual–motor and visual–spatial functioning appear to more impaired than verbal skills, but there is no one pattern of neuropsychological deficit in children with SHI (Brown et al., 1981). Some 60–75% of children with SHI develop a psychiatric disorder within 2.5 years of the injury (Chadwick et al., 1981; Max, Koele, et al., 1998), and many remain impaired as adults (Mendels et al., 1993). Children with SHI are markedly more deviant on the Vineland Adaptive Behavior Scale than children with MHI (Fletcher et al., 1990). More than just ADHD symptoms characterize children with SHI at follow-up; they also show a "disinhibition" syndrome best described by Brown et al. (1981, p. 74):

> For example, a 9 year old made loud comments to his mother about people next to them on bus: e.g. "I don't like that lady, she smells." At home this same child stripped naked to dance in the living room to music on the record player. A 13 year old habitually got up at 5 am to wander around the house in the nude, making a lot of noise and considerably disturbing the rest of the family. (p. 74)

If a child had been healthy (without ADHD) before the SHI and developed such a severe syndrome of impulsive behavior, the proper diagnosis would be personality change due to a medical condition, rather than ADHD. If the child had ADHD before the SHI, and then developed the severe disinhibited state, the situation is less clear. If the new behaviors are clearly more severe or qualitatively different (i.e., stripping in public), then one would be justified in making *both* the diagnoses of ADHD and personality change.

Max, Arndt, et al. (1998) used the 14 DSM-III-R ADHD criteria items from the K-SADS to look at the "dose–response" curve of head injury in producing symptoms of ADHD in a sample of 50 children with traumatic brain injury. The subjects were all followed prospectively. The lower the child's GCS score at time of injury, the more ADHD symptoms were present at follow-up, even 2 years later. Age at injury, litigation status, and gender were not related to the development of ADHD in this sample. No finding on computed tomography (CT) scan distinguished those head-injured children who would develop high levels of inattention or impulsivity–hyperactivity.

Treatment Issues in Comorbid ADHD/Head Injury

If an ADHD child has experienced a severe head injury or a clinician is faced with a child in a severely disinhibited state, what are the treatment implications? Actually, stimulants are now widely used in the treatment of such children after head injury (Silver & Yudofsky, 1994); the dosages are not different from those used in the standard treatment of ADHD. Thus, the stimulants remain the drugs of first choice. Clonidine and propranolol are used to treat explosive behavior as already described in Chapter 6. It is now clear that there is no one "head injury syndrome," those with severe head injury may also develop psychoses and affective disorders, including manic states, in addition to disinhibition. Psychopharmacology is tailored to the individual's particular symptom pattern, and the guidelines mentioned in Chapter 6 for the treatment of aggression apply to such head-injured patients as well (Silver & Yudofsky, 1994). The following case illustrates the process:

> Gerald is a 17-year-old young man who suffered a severe head injury as a result of a motorcycle accident. Before the injury he had no psychiatric history. Postinjury, he suffered right-side hemiparalysis necessitating a wheelchair. He lost much of his speech and could communicate only through grunts. At the rehabilitation facility, Gerald showed a range of difficult behaviors. He alternated between periods of agitation and excessive sleeping. With his good right hand, he would grab attendants' breast or clothing without warning. He fell asleep during speech therapy. At times, he might simply start yelling streams of four-letter words without any provocation, then wriggle free of his wheelchair. Gerald weighed close to 180 pounds and was 6 feet tall; one nursing staff member injured her back attempting to get Gerald back into his wheelchair.
>
> Gerald had been on phenytoin (Dilantin) and lorazepam (Ativan) since his discharge a year ago from the neurosurgery ward. Since he had no seizure activity, these were discontinued. Gerald's aggressive outbursts became less intense but were no less frequent. He was started on 5 mg of methylphenidate three times a day. His aggressive outbursts fell to less than three a month, and he began to concentrate on speech therapy. His sleep pattern remained erratic, though he fell asleep less during the day. An increase in methylphenidate seemed to cause a return of the aggressive outbursts, and the daily dose was lowered back to the starting level. Sertraline, 50 mg/day, was added once in the morning, and his sleeping resumed a more normal cycle.

If Gerald had not responded to the above combinations, a trial of mood stabilizers would have been initiated next.

ADHD AND PERINATAL COMPLICATIONS

Part of the clinical lore of the "minimal brain dysfunction" era was that brain injury suffered during birth might be an etiological factor in hyperactivity. Controlled studies have never shown a strong relationship between ADHD and perinatal complications, if any. McGee et al. (1984b) compared hyperactive and hyperactive–aggressive children to controls in a large epidemiological study. ADHD children were not different from controls in terms of birthweight, gestational age, or birth complications, and they were not more likely to be small for gestational age. Hadders-Algra, Huisjes, and Touwen (1988) followed 568 children from birth to age 9; they were divided into three groups: normal, those with mild neonatal abnormalities, and those with definite neonatal abnormalities. Ratings of distractibility and "being troublesome" were obtained from parents and teachers; these ratings were similar in all three groups. Neonatal abnormality was associated with more academic problems in school but not with behavior problems. The Ontario Child Health Study (Szatmari, Saigal, Rosenbaum, Campbell, & King, 1990) compared 82 extremely low-birthweight (<1,000 g) children to a group of normal-birthweight children matched for socioeconomic status and family dysfunction. Ratings of ADHD were elevated by parent report in the low-birthweight group, but this was not confirmed by teacher ratings. When parent and teacher ratings were combined, the low-birthweight group had a higher prevalence of ADHD (15.9%) than the normal-birthweight group (6.9%). Rates of conduct disorder and emotional disorder were not different in the low-birthweight group from the controls. Obviously, the majority of low-birthweight children did not have ADHD.

A higher rate of ADHD (40%) was found among 57 low-birthweight (<1,500 g) infants followed up at age 5, although the ADHD subjects also had lower full-scale IQs (Astbury, Orgill, & Bajuk, 1987). A sample of 20 very-low-birthweight infants (500–890 g) had a 50% prevalence of attention deficits and a 40% prevalence of hyperactivity (Stjernquist & Svenningsen, 1995). A sample of infants that was premature (mean gestational age, 29 weeks) was healthier at follow-up at age 7, with only 18% meeting the criteria for ADHD (G. Ross, Lipper, & Auld, 1992). Thus low birthweight, rather than prematurity itself, may the principle risk factor for ADHD. Perinatal factors may be related not to ADHD per se but to other comorbid disorders. Sprich-Buckminster et al. (1993) reviewed the birth histories of 73 ADHD boys and compared them to those of controls and children with other psychiatric disorders. An increased number of perinatal risk factors was found only in the ADHD children who had a comorbid psychiatric disorder. (The specific disorders were not specified.) Also, children with ADHD who did not have a family history of ADHD were more likely to have a history of perinatal complications. No one particular perinatal complication (pregnancy complication, delivery complication, or problems in the nursery) was specifically related to ADHD. For most children with ADHD, perinatal factors are not an etiological factor in their disorder. For children with very low birthweight (500–1,500 g) or very serious perinatal complications such as intracranial hemorrhage, ADHD with comorbid learning disorders (LD) was a more probable outcome (Lou, 1996).

ADHD AND NEUROLOGICAL "SOFT SIGNS"

Soft signs are abnormal findings on neurological examination that do not indicate a specific brain lesion but suggest immaturity of the nervous system. They were the hallmark of "minimal brain dysfunction," and clinical lore has long suggested that soft signs show a unique relationship to ADHD or LD. Soft signs are listed in Table 7.3, along with the prevalence of each sign in an unselected sample (Shaffer, O'Connor, Shafer, & Prupis, 1983). Dysmetria is the inability to touch a finger to one's nose in an efficient manner. Children are asked to rapidly turn their hand from one side to another. "Floppiness" during the motion, or an inability to do an appropriate number of flips during a set time period, is called dysdiadochokinesia. Awkwardness is judged by observing the child walk head to toe and noting balance and smoothness of movement. Even in research studies, soft signs are difficult to assess reliably (Shafer, Shaffer, O'Connor, & Stokman, 1983); in clinical practice, no two neurologists are likely to do a soft signs examination the same way. How are soft signs related to ADHD or other psychiatric disorders in children?

Hyperactive children were found to have a significantly higher number of soft signs relative to normal controls as measured by the physical and neurological examination for soft signs (PANESS; Mikkelson, Brown, Minichiello, Millican, & Rapoport, 1982). Younger children had more soft signs than did older subjects and were more likely to have abnormal EEGs. Once the effects of age were partialed out, there was no relationship of soft signs to the EEG findings. The aforementioned authors pointed out in their discussion that conducting neurological exam-

TABLE 7.3. Neurological "Soft Signs" in a Sample of 7-Year-Olds: Definition and Prevalence

Findings	Males (n = 231)	Females (n = 225)
Movements		
Tremor	0	1
Tic	1	1
Mirror movements	15	5
Other	3	4
Coordination		
Dysmetria	4	1
Dysdiadochokinesia	44	22
Awkwardness	54	25
Astereognosis	12	2

Note. Adapted from Shaffer et al. (1983). Copyright 1983 by The Guilford Press. Reprinted by permission.

inations in hyperactive children is difficult due to behavioral factors such as oppositional behavior and poor concentration. Poor performance on the examination due to these factors may be misconstrued as an abnormal neurological sign. Vitiello, Stoff, Atkins, and Mahoney (1990) also found ADHD and ODD children to have more total soft signs than did normal children; soft signs also correlated with impulsive errors on the Matching Familiar Figures Test.

Shaffer et al. (1983) compared the children in their sample with soft signs to those without; these two groups were not different at age 7 in terms of parent ratings of aggression or hyperactivity, though the group with soft signs did have higher ratings of "dependency and withdrawal." This sample was followed up at age 14; again there was no relationship between soft signs and ADHD or antisocial behavior (Shaffer, O'Connor, et al., 1985). Soft signs were correlated with depressive and anxiety symptoms. Hadders-Algra and Touwen (1992) found that children with definite soft signs were viewed as more distractible than controls by both parents and teachers, though actual diagnoses of ADHD were not made in this study. I. C. Gillberg, C. Gillberg, and Groth (1989) compared ADHD, LD, ADHD/LD, and controls on a neurological soft signs examination. In general, the "pure" ADHD and LD groups were not different from the controls on soft sign abnormalities, whereas the combined ADHD/LD groups was most likely to have increased soft signs. Even here the difference were quite small and of no clinical significance. The number of soft signs is not related to the probability of a positive stimulant response in ADHD children (Halperin et al., 1986). Thus there seems to be no reason to do a soft signs examination as a "screening" tool. ADHD children with soft signs are not different in any clinically meaningful way from those without soft signs.

SUMMARY

It can be seen that traditional neurological factors (mild CNS injury, infections, or abnormalities on neurological examination) have little relationship to ADHD or aggression. While these factors may be present in ADHD more often than in a control population, the vast majority of ADHD children are normal from a neurological perspective. Even when the above neurological factors are present, they do not identify a subgroup of ADHD children that are unique in terms of psychopharmacological treatment. Severe head injury may produce a range of psychiatric symptoms (aggression, depression, or mania), but the clinician can use the treatment algorithms laid out in Chapters 6 and 8 as one would in the noninjured population.

8

Affective Disorders

In many ways, the study of the comorbidity of ADHD and disruptive behavior disorder is made easier by the more "objective" nature of the conduct or oppositional symptoms. Fighting, temper outbursts, and even stealing are behaviors that lend themselves to quantification. The same is not as true for internalizing symptoms such as depression and anxiety, where one is dealing with a more complex set of signs and symptoms. Some are relatively observable, such as weight loss or whether an individual has made a suicide attempt, whereas others, such as guilt or irritability, are highly subjective. These issues cannot help but complicate the assessment of depression in the ADHD child. The following areas are explored in this chapter: How does the presence of depression in ADHD affect the expression of the ADHD symptoms and vice versa? How does this comorbidity influence treatment decisions in terms of psychopharmacology? Should stimulants and antidepressants be combined in the treatment of ADHD children with mood disorders? What is the relationship of bipolar disorder to ADHD? How should mood stabilizers be used in ADHD children with affective disorders?

ADHD AND MAJOR DEPRESSIVE DISORDER

Table 8.1 summarizes the results of studies that have examined the overlap between ADHD and depression; as with oppositional defiant disorder (ODD) and conduct disorder (CD) the overlap is substantial, but there is much more variation in the degree of this overlap between stud-

TABLE 8.1. Overlap of Depressive Disorders and ADHD

Study	Study type	ADHD children with depression	Depressed children with ADHD
J. C. Anderson et al. (1987)	Epidemiological	15%	57%
McGee et al. (1990)	Epidemiological	0%	0%
Bird et al. (1993)	Epidemiological	27%	48%
Costello et al. (1988)	Epidemiological	9%	13%
Gittelman et al.(1985)	Clinical	3%	—
Biederman, Faraone, Keenan, et al. (1991)	Clinical	33%	—
Biederman, Munir, Knee, et al. (1987)	Clinical	32%	—
Biederman et al. (1992)	Clinical	36%	—
Alessi & Magen (1988)	Inpatient	—	MDD, 25%; dysthymia, 22%
Jensen et al. (1993)	Clinical	38%	—
Kovacs et al. (1984)	Clinical	—	23%

ies. As we saw in the studies of CD, more comorbidity is found in clinical samples compared to epidemiological ones. It should be borne in mind that the reliability of both parent and child reports is lower for internalizing symptoms than for externalizing symptoms, both in standard clinical interviews (Piacentini et al., 1993) and research interviews (Jensen et al., 1995; Schwab-Stone et al., 1993). These studies showed that it is not uncommon for both parents and children to report depression during the first interview but for the depressive symptoms to spontaneously remit in the second interview.

The studies in Table 8.1 differ in the degree to which the examiners used parent interviews only, child interviews, or a combination of both to establish the depression diagnosis. As noted in Chapter 2, parent–child agreement on the presence or absence of depressive symptoms is also low (Boyle et al., 1993), for frequently parents are unaware of the child's depression (Angold, 1988). In the literature there are no firmly established procedures enabling us to determine exactly how parent and child data should be combined, no doubt leading to differences among clinicians on this critical point (Piacentini, Cohen, & Cohen, 1992). For example, a child may report that he is depressed, feels guilty, and has trouble sleeping but deny all other problems. The parent may deny that the child is depressed but report concentration difficulties and loss of appetite. Should the total symptoms from the parent and child interview be combined to yield a diagnosis of major depression? This is what is done in many clinical practices, yet each clinician has developed a different method of doing it.

Evaluating depression in ADHD has added dimensions of difficulty. "Irritable mood" in children can be used in the place of depressed mood to make a diagnosis of affective disorder in children, but children with ODD/CD are often irritable as part of their temper outbursts. Even children with ADHD, as part of their impulsiveness, may be emotionally labile. One must be careful not to overdiagnose depression in these children; the critical issue is the pervasiveness of the irritability. Children with ADHD or ODD will have irritable periods that are very short lived and usually associated with a specific frustration. While the outburst may be intense, it ends within minutes and rarely lasts more than a half hour. The irritability rapidly dissipates if the child gets his way or when the punishment is completed. In contrast, children with major depressive disorder (MDD) or dysthymia should be irritable almost *all of the time*. Periods of irritability are not linked solely to disciplinary events or conflicts with others. If the child is irritable only one or two times a day and the periods of irritability last for less than half an hour, one should view this as part of an ODD syndrome. In contrast, if the ADHD child is pervasively irritable and has the requisite number of other symptoms of depression, then the child can be viewed as truly having comorbid ADHD and MDD.

Psychomotor agitation and diminished concentration are easily confused with hyperactivity and inattentiveness in ADHD. Bear in mind that if pervasive depression or irritability are not present, then symptoms of increased motor activity or impaired concentration *do not* count toward an affective diagnosis. Age and timing of onset of symptoms are frequently critical factors in determining whether ADHD is comorbid with depression or not. A child must meet criteria for ADHD by age 7; thus if a child *over* 7 years of age has no history of poor concentration and develops inattentiveness only *after* becoming depressed, the concentration difficulties should be regarded as part of the depressive disorder. This is particularly true if there are no symptoms of impulsivity–hyperactivity.

Serious diagnostic errors arise when clinicians use criteria other than DSM-IV for diagnosing a child as depressed. Often the child's responses on psychological projective testing are used to describe an ADHD child as "emotionally disturbed" or as having an "underlying depression." This is sometimes done by educational diagnosticians in the school setting. A recommendation for antidepressant medication or psychotherapy is made in spite of the fact that both the child and the parent deny any symptoms of depression! This can be a source of great distress to parents, who begin either to believe that they have done something to make their child depressed or that their child's clinician has "missed" the diagnosis. Whatever the values of projective testing, diagnosing depression in children is not one of them. *No child should be given an affective disorder diagnosis unless he meets the appropriate DSM-IV criteria on clinical interview.* Similarly, some clinicians will base the diagnosis of depression on presumed psychodynamic factors. The child may meet overt criteria only for ADHD, but because the child has experienced some stressor such as separation, divorce, or abuse, a diagnosis of depression is added. The child may indeed have emotional conflicts that should be addressed in therapy, but the clinician should never assume they are "causing" the ADHD symptoms, nor should a diagnosis of depression be made based only on the presence of stressors. Overdiagnosing depression when it is not present will lead to serious problems in terms of both medication and psychotherapeutic intervention. Table 8.1 shows, however, that when proper diagnostic procedures are followed, anywhere from 10 to 30% of ADHD children will meet criteria for MDD or dysthymia.

Family Studies of ADHD and Depression

As they have done with ADHD and CD, Biederman and colleagues (Biederman et al., 1992; Biederman, Faraone, Keenan, & Tsuang, 1991; Biederman, Munir, Knee, et al., 1987) have performed family history studies examining the relationship of ADHD and MDD? These studies attempt to answer some basic questions: Are ADHD and MDD completely independent of each other and thus simply overlap in an given individual? Are ADHD and ADHD/MDD distinct subtypes caused by separate genetic factors? Finally, do ADHD and MDD share some common etiological factors? If this is so, what causes an individual to develop ADHD alone, MDD alone, or ADHD with MDD? The theory behind these studies (Pauls, Towbin, Leckman, Zahner, & Cohen, 1986) is as follows: The first-degree relatives of ADHD children with and without MDD are interviewed, and the prevalence of both ADHD and affective disorder in these relatives is determined. The prevalence of these two disorders in the relatives of control subjects is also assessed. If ADHD and depression were etiologically independent, then one would find that depression would be increased *only* in the relatives of the children with comorbid ADHD/MDD. Furthermore, the disorders would not cosegregate; that is, among the relatives of the ADHD/MDD children, some relatives would have ADHD and others would have MDD, but few relatives would have both ADHD and MDD. In contrast, if ADHD and ADHD/MDD were genetically distinct subtypes, cosegregation would occur. The children with ADHD/MDD would have relatives with both disorders, and very few relatives would have ADHD or MDD alone. In the final example, if ADHD and MDD shared familial factors, one would find an increased prevalence of MDD in the relatives of children with ADHD alone. Because ADHD children who are *not* depressed have relatives with MDD, one would conclude that ADHD and MDD share some risk factor. Of course, some additional factor must be involved in terms of how that common risk factor is transformed into either ADHD, MDD, or ADHD/MDD. Biederman et al. (1992) found that if a child has ADHD alone, his relatives have an increased prevalence of both ADHD and MDD, as do the relatives of children with ADHD/MDD.

Cosegregation of ADHD and MDD in single individuals was not found. MDD tended to be found in the mothers and sisters of ADHD probands (Biederman, Faraone, Keenan, & Tsuang, 1991), but there was no evidence of nonrandom mating (i.e., depressed mothers did not appear to be more likely to marry ADHD fathers). Because the ADHD-only children have an increased prevalence of MDD among their relatives, Biederman et al. (1992) concluded that ADHD and MDD share a common familial factor. Biederman, Faraone, Keenan, and Tsuang (1991) *ruled out* intactness of family and socioeconomic status as factors which results in the expression of ADHD alone versus ADHD/MDD. The work of Biederman and his colleagues has implications for the study of MDD and ADHD generally, as it suggests they share some common genetic mechanism. Further work is necessary, however, before this conclusion can be completely accepted. Other studies have not shown a such a strong relationship between ADHD and MDD (Mannuzza & Addalli, 1991; Mannuzza et al., 1991). Young children were not directly interviewed in the above-cited Biederman et al. (1991, 1992) studies, and many of the younger ADHD subjects were not past the age of risk for developing MDD. If the ADHD-only children with depressed relatives all later developed MDD themselves (or in fact had MDD that was not detected by parent interview), we would conclude that the two diagnoses are in fact independent and do not share etiological factors.

Clinical Issues

Surprisingly, no study has directly compared ADHD children with and without MDD on specific clinical measures such teacher ratings scales, symptom severity, or cognitive variables. Indeed, no study to date has even directly compared ADHD children with those who have "pure" MDD. In the Isle of Wight study, Rutter, Tizard, and Whitmore (1970) compared children with "conduct disorders" to those with "emotional disorders" as well as to a group of children with "mixed disorders." Children in the mixed category had symptoms of both conduct and emotional problems. Given the British diagnostic system of the time, a large number of the CD children would have met criteria for ADHD. When the mixed children were compared to the other groups, they appeared much more similar to the "pure" CD group than to the emotional disorder group in terms of symptom severity, family variables, and the degree of reading disorders. Koriath et al. (1985) compared children with combined hyperkinetic and emotional disorders to those with hyperkinesis alone on a variety of measures, but there were surprisingly few differences. The two groups were nearly identical in terms of teacher and parent ratings of conduct, impulsivity, hyperactivity, and inattentiveness. The groups had similar performances on the Continuous Performance Test (CPT), and both the hyperkinetic group and the hyperkinetic–emotional disorder group had equally short (i.e., more impulsive) reaction times on the Matching Familiar Figures Test (MFFT) compared to children with emotional disorders only. This is consistent with Rutter et al. (1970) finding that the mixed group was similar to the pure CD group. ADHD/MDD children have similar rates of comorbid CD and are just as likely to be in Special Education as are ADHD-only children (Biederman, Faraone, Keenan, & Tsuang, 1991).

Depression generally appears many years after the ADHD symptoms (Kovacs, Akiskal, Gatsonis, & Parrone, 1994; Biederman, Faraone, Mick, & Leleon, 1995). How does ADHD affect the expression of depression? Ninety-two percent of children with MDD are euthymic after 1.5 years, whereas the median time for recovery from dysthymia is 3.5 years (Kovacs, Feinberg, Crouse-Novack, Paulauskas, & Finkelstein, 1984). Whether the depressed child has comorbid ADHD or CD does not appear to effect these recovery rates (Kovacs et al., 1994; Kovacs, Paulauskas, Gatsonis, & Richards, 1988). No evidence has emerged that the nature of the depressive symptoms are different in MDD children who have ADHD compared to those who do not. There is a question as to whether the co-occurrence of ADHD in MDD increases the risk for suicide completion over that of MDD-only youth. Suicide completers were found to have an 18% prevalence of ADHD compared to a 5% rate in suicidal inpatients, though the difference did not reach statistical significance (Brent et al., 1988). Further studies did not show any relationship between ADHD and suicide attempts (Brent, Johnson, et al., 1993) or completed suicides (Brent, Perper, et al., 1993). In contrast, the combination of impulsive–aggressive personality disorder and MDD does substantially increase the risk of suicide (Brent, Johnson, et al., 1993, 1994; Kovacs, Goldston, & Gatsonis, 1993). Thus the risk of suicide in the ADHD/MDD child is *not* increased over the risk in a child with MDD alone, but a child with "triple" comorbidity (ADHD/MDD/CD) *is* at such increased risk. CD and substance abuse by themselves are not associated with an increase risk of suicide attempt but do increase when comorbid with affective disorder (Kovacs et al., 1993). It is clear that a great deal remains to learned about the differences between ADHD and ADHD/MDD children, in terms of cognitive style, symptom expression, and etiology.

Psychopharmacotherapy for Comorbid ADHD/Major Depressive Disorder

As shown in Table 8.2, no study has shown that tricyclic antidepressants (TCAs) are effective in children with MDD, yet they have been shown to be effective in ADHD (Pliszka, 1987). TCAs are therefore not indicated in the treatment of childhood or adolescent MDD. Fluoxetine had a significantly higher response rate (56%) than placebo (33%) in a double-blind study in the treatment of MDD (Emslie et al., 1997). Recently paroxetine was found to have a significantly higher response rate (66%) than either imipramine (50%) or placebo (46%) (G. J. Emslie, personal

TABLE 8.2. Summary of Double-Blind Placebo-Controlled Trials of Antidepressants in Children and Adolescents

Study	Drug	Results/comments
Puig-Antich et al. (1987)	Placebo (n = 22) Imipramine (n = 16)	56% of imipramine group responded; 68% of placebo group responded; no significant difference
Preskorn et al. (1987)	Placebo (n = 10) Imipramine (n = 12)	Clinical global impression (CGI): 38% improved in imipramine group; 26% improved in placebo group
Hughes et al. (1990)	n = 27, randomized to placebo or imipramine	Depressed children without conduct disorder showed better response
Kramer & Feiguine (1981)	Placebo (n = 10) Amitriptyline (n = 10)	Drug not different from placebo
B. Geller et al. (1990)	Placebo (n = 19) Nortriptyline (n = 12)	Only one responder in nortriptyline group; 21% of placebo group responded
Kutcher et al. (1994)	Placebo (n = 30) Desipramine (n = 30)	Drug not different from placebo

communication). This study involved 275 adolescents with MDD who were treated with 20–40 mg of paroxetine or up to 200 mg of imipramine. There was a 30% dropout rate in the imipramine group. The study confirmed that TCAs are not effective in pediatric MDD. This finding raises some interesting questions when clinicians are confronting such medication issues with the ADHD/MDD child. Which medications should be tried first, stimulants or antidepressants? Can antidepressants "kill two birds with one stone" and treat both the ADHD and MDD symptoms? Can stimulants and antidepressants be combined, and if so, under what circumstances? First, we will review the use of antidepressants in ADHD.

Tricyclic Antidepressants in the Treatment of ADHD

A number of controlled studies have shown TCAs to be effective in the treatment of ADHD. Rapoport, Quinn, Bradbard, Riddle, and Brooks (1974) randomized boys with hyperactivity to treatment periods consisting of placebo, imipramine, or methylphenidate. The mean dose of imipramine was 80 mg/day. Physician ratings of playroom behavior showed both drugs superior to placebo in improving behavior, though methylphenidate was superior to imipramine. Methylphenidate was also superior to placebo in improving attention to cognitive tasks, whereas imipramine produced only mild improvement in this area. Garfinkel, Wender, Sloman, and O'Neill (1983) treated 12 ADHD boys in a double-blind crossover placebo-controlled trial of desipramine, clomipramine, and methylphenidate. The mean dose of the antidepressants was 85 mg/day (not to exceed 3.5 mg/kg per dose). Methylphenidate was again shown to be superior to placebo in improving symptoms of inattention, with the antidepressants having an effect intermediate between the stimulants and placebo. The antidepressants produced more positive changes in mood than the stimulants did even though none of the subjects met criteria for an affective disorder. Furthermore, the effects of the antidepressants were more noted in the evening hours.

Biederman, Baldessarini, Wright, Knee, and Harmatz (1989) performed an extensive a double-blind placebo-controlled trial of desipramine in children and adolescents with ADHD using a mean dose of 4.6 mg/kg per day. Sixty-eight percent of patients treated with desipramine were rated as significantly improved, whereas only 10% of placebo-treated patients improved. Patients who as a group had been refractory to prior stimulant treatment also showed significant improvement on desipramine. The plasma level of desipramine, however, showed no relationship to the clinical response, though it was related to increased heart rate and electrocardiogram (ECG) changes (Biederman,

Baldessarini, Wright, Knee, Harmatz, & Goldblatt, 1989). As noted in Chapter 4, desipramine has been associated with six cases of sudden death, which has limited its use in the treatment of ADHD.

Combining Tricyclic Antidepressants and Stimulants

Very few data are available on the combination of TCAs and stimulants in children with ADHD and mood disorders. Rapport, Carlson, Kelly, and Pataki (1993) compared placebo, methylphenidate alone, desipramine alone, and a combination of the two drugs in 16 children with comorbid ADHD/MDD or dysthymia. Each child served as his/her own control such that every subject received all four medication conditions in random order. The mean dose of desipramine for the children was 4 mg/kg per day. Methylphenidate doses were in the standard clinical range of 20–40 mg/day, divided between A.M. and noon doses. Methylphenidate was superior to placebo and desipramine alone in producing improvements in cognition. Overall the combination of methylphenidate and desipramine did not induce any clinically significant cognitive deterioration. Side effects such as nausea, dry mouth, and tremor were present in twice as many children on the combination than with either drug alone (Pataki, Carlson, Kelly, Rapport, & Biancaniello, 1993). Heart rate was higher in children on the combination than in those on either drug alone, but the combination did not result in ECG abnormalities above the rate seen in children on desipramine only. Most of these children had mood disorders and ADHD, implying that each drug was separately treating each disorder (stimulants for ADHD; TCAs for mood disorder). There was no strong evidence for the view the TCAs and stimulants work together to ameliorate ADHD symptoms in the *absence* of mood symptoms. Since TCAs are not effective in mood disorder in childhood or adolescence, they could not "kill two birds with one stone" for the ADHD/MDD child. Their only role is in the ADHD child without mood disorder who is unresponsive to two different classes of stimulants.

Novel Antidepressants

A large-scale study of bupropion combined some of the data from the earlier studies (Conners et al., 1996). Children with ADHD were randomized to receive either bupropion ($n = 72$) or placebo ($n = 37$) for a 4-week trial. Three weight classes were established (20–30 kg, 31–40 kg, and > 40 kg); the maximum total daily dose for the three classes was 150, 200, and 250 mg, respectively. The last 2 weeks of the study the children were maintained on 6 mg/kg per day. By the third day of treatment, teachers noted a significant positive behavioral effect of bupropion relative to placebo, an effect that was still present at day 28. Parent ratings also showed significantly greater improvement on bupropion relative to placebo at days 14 and 28. Overall, the effects of bupropion were less robust than those seen with the stimulant. In contrast, Barrickman et al. (1995) found bupropion to be as effective as methylphenidate in a double-blind controlled trial of the two drugs. Unfortunately, no placebo control was used and the study had very few subjects. The dosages used in this study were lower than that used by Conners et al. (1996); starting doses began at 1.5 mg/kg per day and titrated to clinically effective levels; the final mean dose was 3.3 mg/kg per day. Some children took up to 5.7 mg/kg per day. Low starting doses are difficult in smaller children, since bupropion comes in 75- and 100-mg tablets that are not scored. There have been no controlled trials of bupropion in childhood MDD.

No controlled trials of fluoxetine in ADHD have been performed, but Barrickman et al. (1991) performed an open trial of it in 19 adolescents with ADHD unresponsive to stimulants. The dose ranged from 20 to 60 mg/day; the average daily dose was 0.6 mg/kg. About 60% of the sample was at least moderately improved after 6 weeks, though the above authors noted that most subjects improved within the first week. Furthermore, none of the subjects met criteria for mood disorders, suggesting that the improvement in behavior was not secondary to an antidepressant effect of the drug. No serious or unusual side effects of the drug were noted. Gammon and Brown (1993) combined fluoxetine and methylphenidate in children and adolescents with ADHD and comorbid CD or MDD. The patients were taking 17–60 mg of methylphenidate daily and had had at least a partial response to it. Patients were placed on fluoxetine in doses ranging from 2.5 to 20 mg/day, with 60% of the subjects receiving the maximum dose. The titration was very slow, the dose being raised 2.5–5 mg every 3 or 4 days. The aforementioned authors reported significant improvements in attention, conduct, mood, and schoolwork, with no unusual side effects. We should note, however, that fenfluramine, a potent reuptake blocker of serotonin, has been shown to be ineffective in the treatment of ADHD (Donnelly et al., 1989). Until further studies are done, clinicians should not be too optimistic that SSRIs alone can effectively treat symptoms of inattention or hyperactivity.

Which Drug First?

There are no data in the research literature that directly address stimulant or antidepressant treatment in ADHD/MDD. Table 8.3 summarizes

TABLE 8.3. Factors Influencing the Decision to Begin a Child with Comorbid ADHD/MDD on a Stimulant or an Antidepressant

Begin with a stimulant	Begin with an antidepressant
ADHD symptoms more prominent, accounting for 50% or more of the global clinical severity	Depressive symptoms more prominent, accounting for 50% or more of the global clinical severity
Neurovegetative signs minimal	Marked loss of appetite, weight loss, severe insomnia
Suicidal ideation, but no intent or plan	Well-planned suicide attempt and/or strong suicidal intent
No previous drug treatment	Past history of nonresponse or significant side effects to stimulants
History of ADHD precedes depression by more than a year	Onset of depression and ADHD within the past year

factors we have found useful in weighing whether to begin a stimulant or an antidepressant first in an ADHD/MDD child. *One should never begin a combination of stimulants and antidepressants at the same time.* Depression in children and adolescents can be a good deal more labile than that in adults (Lewinsohn, Clarke, Seely, & Rohde, 1994), and depressive mood may remit rapidly in some children to the psychotherapeutic effects of the initial interview. One can never tell for sure when the depressive symptoms are secondary to frustrations of the ADHD symptoms, such that it is possible that the depression will remit in response to successful stimulant treatment of the ADHD. Thus, these two factors may make antidepressant treatment unnecessary in some ADHD/MDD children. If the mood disorder *completely* remits after stimulant treatment alone, one might even question the validity of the MDD diagnosis in that patient. ADHD/MDD children do not become more depressed by taking stimulants (Pataki et al., 1993), and MDD should not be viewed as a contraindication to stimulant treatment.

As noted in Table 8.3, the decision should rest on whether the more prominent clinical symptomatology consists of ADHD or MDD symptoms. In some cases ADHD may be the presenting complaint and the depressive symptoms are discovered as part of the interview process; furthermore, while these cases meet technical DSM-IV criteria for MDD or dysthymia, the clinical picture of depression in terms of neurovegetative signs or suicidal ideation is mild. These are ideal cases for beginning stimulants first. In contrast, if a melancholic or depressed mood is what brought the child to the clinician, a strong case can be made for starting the antidepressant first.

Once the first drug has been titrated to appropriate levels, the clinician should ask some other questions: How good is the response to the first drug? Did the stimulant affect the mood symptoms as well as the ADHD symptoms? Did the antidepressant improve the ADHD symptoms in addition to improving the mood? Figure 8.1 shows the decision tree if one agent alone appears to be unsatisfactory. When a child with ADHD/MDD is started on a stimulant, close monitoring of symptoms is

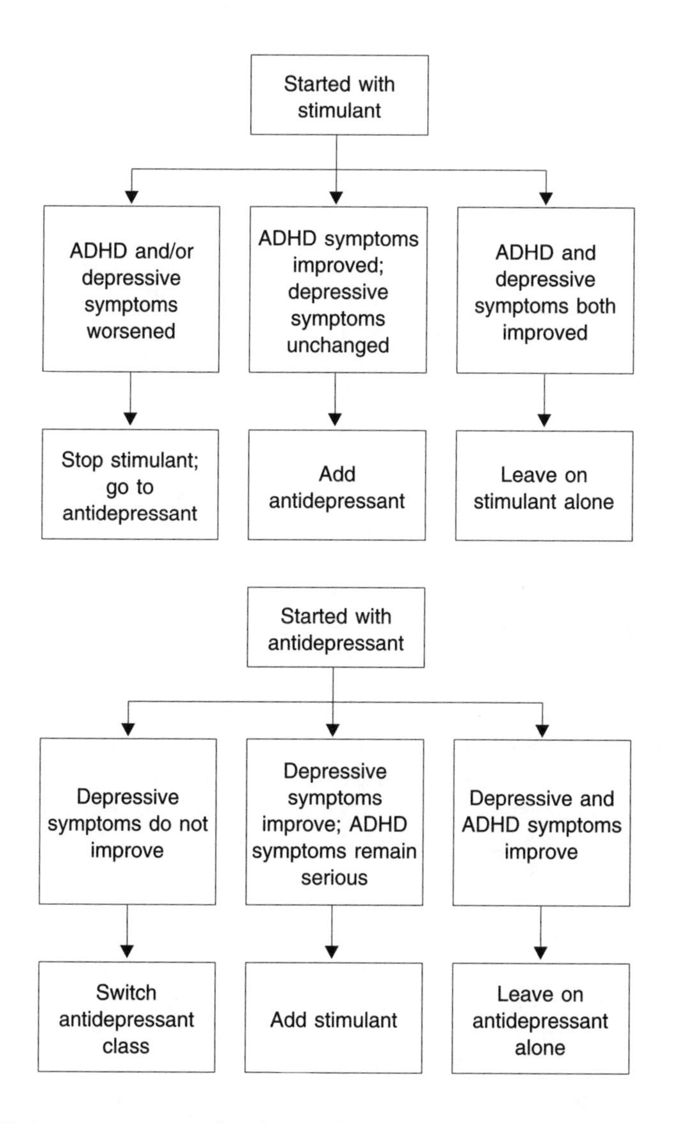

FIGURE 8.1. Decision tree for choice of medication in the child with comorbid ADHD and major depression.

required; if mood symptoms worsen in the first 1–2 weeks of treatment, stimulants should be discontinued and antidepressants started. In other cases, ADHD symptoms may rapidly resolve, but mood symptoms remain serious. Here an antidepressant should be added.

In children with more severe depressive symptoms an antidepressant should be started first. Bupropion is a good choice, as it may effectively treat both ADHD symptoms and mood symptoms. If the mood symptoms do not resolve after 4 weeks at an adequate dose, the clinician should change antidepressant classes, trying at least two different SSRIs. A stimulant can then be added if ADHD symptoms remain problematic after the mood symptoms resolve.

ADHD AND BIPOLAR DISORDER

No studies have examined the prevalence of bipolar disorder in prepubertal children. Lewinsohn, Klein, and Seely (1995) surveyed more than 1,700 high school students and found 16 (0.97%) met DSM-IV criteria for bipolar disorder. Two met criteria for a manic episode only (bipolar I); the remainder met criteria for bipolar II, that is, a history of MDD and hypomanic episodes. There were 97 students (5.7%) who reported having experienced elevated, expanded, or irritable mood but who did not meet full criteria for bipolar disorder. More than half of these adolescents showed significant impairment in social functioning and 14% had made a suicide attempt. B. Geller, Fox, and Clark (1993) followed 79 children (aged 6–12 years) with MDD over a 2- to 5-year period. A third of the sample developed bipolarity during the follow-up period, with a mean age of onset of 11.2 years. About half of these children showed full manic episodes, whereas the other half of the sample met criteria for bipolar II. Family history of affective disorder was predictive of the development of bipolar disorder, but the presence of CD in the depressed child was not. Because CD is so often comorbid with ADHD in prepuberty, this finding suggests that comorbidity of ADHD in MDD does not further increase the already high risk of developing bipolarity in these children.

ADHD children were found to have a higher rate of bipolar disorder than that of a control population (16% vs. 0%) (Biederman et al., 1992), but the prevalence of bipolar disorder is not increased significantly among the first-degree relatives of ADHD children. (Biederman et al., 1992; Biederman, Faraone, Keenan, & Tsuang, 1991; Biederman, Munir, Knee, et al., 1987). Children of bipolar parents show an increased rate of psychiatric disorder relative to the children of control parents, but this rate is not higher than that in the children of non-bipolar psychiatric patients (Carlson & Weintraub, 1993). During childhood, the offspring of bipolar parents do not have a higher rate of bipolar disorder than children of control parents; rather depression, ADHD, and CD are more commonly found (Grigoroiu-Serbanescu et al., 1989). Those offspring of a bipolar parent who experience attentional or behavior disturbances during childhood are more likely to have a mood disorder of any type as young adults, though not necessarily bipolar disorder (G. A. Carlson & Weintraub, 1993).

Biederman and colleagues (Biederman et al., 1996; Wozniak & Biederman, 1996; Wozniak, Biederman, Kiely, et al., 1995; Wozniak, Biederman, Mundy, Mennin, & Faraone, 1995) have ignited a controversy over the prevalence of bipolar disorder in childhood and its relationship to ADHD. A review of their work will set the stage for a discussion of the major issues involved. Wozniak, Biederman, Kiely, et al. (1995) identified 43 children in a psychiatric outpatient clinic who met their criteria (K-SADS) for mania. All but one of these children also met criteria for ADHD. They were compared to 164 nonmanic ADHD children and 84 controls. There was a total of 206 (42 manic and 164 nonmanic) ADHD subjects, which yields a prevalence of mania of 20% among the ADHD sample in this study. There were only two children with euphoric mania, and 77% showed "extreme and persistent mania." That is, they did not cycle or have any prolonged periods of euthymia. Eighty-four percent showed "mixed mania" (in which symptoms of mania and major depression co-occurred). Parents reported the mean age of onset of the manic symptoms to be 4.4 years, whereas the ADHD symptoms had been present since age 2. Compared to nonbipolar ADHD children, the manic children showed a higher rate of reading disorders and lower global functioning scores. They had higher rates of other psychiatric problems, particularly conduct, anxiety, and depressive disorders. This group of researchers studied a second sample of 120 ADHD children and found 29 children (21%) who met criteria for bipolar disorder (14 were diagnosed at the entry to the study; a further 15 were diagnosed at a 4-year follow up) (Biederman et al., 1996). The pattern of more impaired functioning found in the previous study (Wozniak, Biederman, Kiely, et al., 1995) was confirmed. The ADHD/manic children were more likely to be in Special Education or have had a psychiatric hospitalization. Child Behavior Checklist (CBCL) scores of the ADHD/manic children were elevated over the ADHD-only children on nearly all the subscales. Of note, it was the aggression subscale which most differentiated the ADHD/manic group from the ADHD-only group. Relatives of ADHD/manic children had higher rates of bipolar disorder, whereas the prevalence of bipolar disorder among the relatives of ADHD-only children did not exceed that of a control group.

Wozniak, Biederman, Mundy, et al. (1995) next look at the rate of bipolar disorder in the relatives of manic children compared to such rates in controls and non-bipolar children with ADHD. They conducted psychiatric interviews on 46 relatives of 16 manic children (all but one of whom had ADHD) as well as on 305 relatives of 78 ADHD children and 220 relatives of 100 normal controls. Six of the 46 (13%) of the relatives of bipolar children also had bipolar disorder, compared to 7 (2%) of the relatives of the ADHD children and 7 (3%) of the controls. Statistically, the rate of bipolar was higher only among the relatives of the manic children, and the affected relatives tended to have *both* ADHD and bipolar disorder. Faraone, Biederman, Menin, et al. (1997) confirmed this pattern in a second sample of 15 ADHD–bipolar children. That is, children with both ADHD and bipolar children had high rates of bipolarity *and* ADHD in their families, while non-bipolar children with ADHD had elevated rates of ADHD among their relatives, but not bipolar disorder. Furthermore, ADHD and bipolar disorder tended to co-segregate in families (affected relatives having both disorders). As discussed in Chapter 6, this suggests that ADHD–bipolar disorder might be a separate genetic subtype distinct from non-bipolar ADHD.

Before discussing the controversy surrounding the findings, it is important to examine some other studies that have also explored mania in children and adolescents. Using a structured interview, Geller et al. (1995) diagnosed 26 children with bipolar disorder. Nearly 90% of the bipolar children under 12 met criteria for ADHD as well, compared to a third of the adolescent bipolars. Close to 60% of the sample was diagnosed with mixed mania. More than 80% of these subjects showed a pattern of "complex cycling." Research nurses questioned the families closely about the number and length of the bipolar episodes. One parent reported that her child had 104 episodes in a year, each of these episodes lasting from 4 hours to a whole day. Another subject had daily episodes of agitation or depression for a whole year. Only two subjects had episodes that lasted longer than 2 weeks as their only episodes. Psychotic phenomena and suicidality were all common in the sample.

Compared to manic adults, manic adolescents were more likely to be diagnosed with "mixed mania" (63% vs. 52%) and less likely to have psychotic features or other evidence of thought disorder (McElroy, Strakowski, West, Keck, & McConville, 1997). Kovacs and Pollock (1995) studied 26 bipolar adolescents and found that 54% met criteria for ADHD and 69% for CD. CD and non-CD bipolars subjects were similar in terms of the number of hospitalizations, use of psychotropic medication, and severity of the bipolar illness. Bipolar and nonbipolar CD subjects were similar in terms of severity of antisocial behavior. Manic adolescents with ADHD were found to have higher Mania Rating

Scale (MRS) scores than adolescents without ADHD; they were also more likely to be diagnosed with mixed mania (West, McElroy, Strakowski, Keck, & McConville, 1995).

The findings of the Massachusetts General Group have generated intense debate as to how common bipolar disorder is in children and whether it is frequently misdiagnosed as ADHD. Biederman (1998), in summarizing his group's results, stated that bipolar disorder in childhood is chronic, with irritable mood rather than euphoria, and almost always comorbid with ADHD. It is genetically distinct from non-bipolar ADHD. Klein, Pine, and Klein (1998) raise several objections to this viewpoint. First, they argue *chronic* mania violates the DSM-IV criteria for mania, which stipulates that the elevated or irritable mood must be a distinct episode (usually a change from good baseline functioning). Klein et al. (1998) note the high rate of agoraphobia and social phobia in the Wozinak, Biederman, Kiely, et al. (1995) sample; these diagnoses are not usually associated with mania. When the symptoms common to both ADHD and bipolar (hyperactivity, talkativeness, and distractibility) are removed, the rate of bipolar disorder in the Massachusetts General Group's sample falls. Biederman, Faraone, Mick, et al. (1996) found that 2% of the controls developed bipolar disorder at 4-year follow-up, a rate Klein et al. (1998) feel exceeds the rate of bipolar in adult epidemiological studies. Finally, they point out that imipramine has been used to treat ADHD for many years, and no case reports have emerged of ADHD children "switching" to mania, as would be expected if bipolar disorder were common among ADHD. Klein et al. (1998) conclude that many of the bipolar children in the Massachusetts General Group studies are better described as ADHD With comorbid intermittent explosive disorder or severe conduct disorder.

Biederman (1998) replies that DSM-IV does permit a more chronic picture of mania and he points to other studies that do show a higher rate of anxiety disorders among bipolar patients, albeit in adolescents (Lewinsohn, Klein, & Seely, 1995). He argues that bipolar in childhood may be different from bipolar with onset in adulthood. Epidemiological studies of childhood psychiatric disorder with low rates of bipolar disorder may be excluding highly disturbed children who may be in institutional settings or highly dysfunctional families who do not participate in such studies.

How is a clinician to respond to this debate? Clearly, ADHD children likely to be diagnosed as manic fall into a group of severely disturbed ADHD children with high levels of impulsivity, aggression, poor reality testing, and very poor social functioning. They often have multiple neuropsychological deficits (learning disorders). Clinicians tend to use a variety of labels to refer to this group: bipolar disorder not otherwise specified (NOS), agitated depression, psychotic depression, borderline personality disorder, etc. They are 15–20% of the ADHD population. Are they truly bipolar, or do they form a distinct disorder or variant of ADHD altogether? How does a clinician distinguish between a child with "severe" ADHD, a child with bipolar disorder, and a child who has both conditions?

B. Geller and colleagues (Geller, Williams, Zimmerman, Frazier, Beringer, & Warner, 1998) looked at factors that differentiate children with ADHD from those with bipolar disorder. They washed the WASH-U-K-SADS, a version of the K-SADS described in Chapter 2 with items added about hypersexuality and rapid cycling. Their results are shown in Table 8.4, along with clinical pointers on making the distinction between ADHD and mania. In contrast to the Massachusetts General Hospital group, they did find high rates of euphoria, but over 86% did meet criteria for mixed mania. Distractibility and a high energy level did not distinguish the groups. Hypersexual behavior was never seen in the ADHD-only children; its presence in children in the absence of a history of sexual abuse should raise suspicions of mania. Most importantly, disturbances of thought (racing thoughts, delusions, grandiosity) were hallmarks of mania but rarely seen in children with ADHD alone. The following are additional clinical pointers in differentiating ADHD and mania:

1. Do not make a diagnosis of bipolar disorder on the basis of a child's impulsive aggression alone in the absence of any persistent mood symptoms. Lithium will be effective in some children with aggression in the absence of mania (DeLong & Aldershot, 1987; Campbell et al., 1995), so a positive response to lithium in these children cannot be viewed as confirming the bipolar diagnosis. A diagnosis of intermittent explosive disorder justifies treatment with mood stabilizers if aggression is the main complaint.

2. A child with time-limited temper outbursts related only to specific frustrations (not getting his/her way, and the like) should not be viewed as having the persistent irritability needed to make the bipolar diagnosis. Since irritability (temper outbursts) is also found in ODD (see Table 8.4), it must be associated with other first-rank symptoms of mania in order for the diagnosis of bipolar to be made.

3. A family history of bipolar disorder alone should never be used to justify this diagnosis in a child because the child has ADHD. One should never use lithium or any other antimania agent as the treatment of first choice in ADHD simply because the parent has bipolar disorder. The child must meet criteria for bipolar disorder him/herself.

TABLE 8.4. Baseline Percent (*n*) of Mania Items in Bipolar versus ADHD Group

Symptom area	BP (n = 60)	ADHD (n = 60)	χ^2	p
Grandiosity	85.0 (51)	6.7 (4)	74.1	0.001
Elated mood	86.7 (52)	5.0 (3)	80.6	0.001
Daredevil acts	70.0 (42)	13.3 (8)	39.6	0.001
Uninhibited people seeking	68.3 (41)	21.7 (13)	26.4	0.001
Silliness, laughing	65.0 (39)	21.7 (13)	22.9	0.001
Flight of ideas	66.7 (40)	10.0 (6)	40.8	0.001
Racing thoughts	48.3 (29)	0.0 (0)	38.2	0.001
Hypersexuality	45.0 (27)	8.3 (5)	20.6	0.001
Decreased need for sleep	43.3 (26)	5.0 (3)	24.1	0.001
Sharpened thinking	51.7 (31)	23.3 (14)	10.3	0.001
↑ Goal-directed activity	51.7 (31)	21.7 (13)	11.6	0.001
Increased productivity	36.7 (22)	15.0 (9)	7.4	0.007
Irritable mood	96.7 (58)	71.7 (43)	14.1	0.001
Accelerated speech	96.7 (58)	78.3 (47)	9.2	0.002
Hyperenergetic	96.7 (58)	91.7 (55)	F.E.[a]	0.44
Distractibility	91.7 (55)	95.0 (57)	F.E.[a]	0.72

Note. Reprinted with permission of the author from B. Geller, Warner, Williams, and Zimmerman (1998) and B. Geller, Williams, et al. (1998).

[a]F.E. = Fisher's Exact Test.

4. One should not base the diagnosis of bipolar disorder solely on the parent report of the symptoms. The symptoms should be pervasive enough that the clinician can directly observe signs such as flight of ideas, pressured speech, and grandiosity on the child's mental status examination.

Fristad et al. (1992) used the MRS to distinguish ADHD children from those with mania. The MRS was reproduced in full in the Fristad article. It has 11 items, some of which have particular relevance to mania and thus are scored with additional points. ADHD children without mania had a mean MRS score of 7.8; the scores ranged from 0 to 13. In contrast, the manic children had scores ranging from 14 to 39 with a mean of 24. The MRS differentiated the ADHD children from manic children, whereas scores on the Conners Parent and Teacher Rating Scales did not. The MRS is therefore a useful tool in documenting manic symptoms and may be useful in following response to treatment though a high score alone should be used to diagnose mania.

Psychopharmacotherapy for Comorbid ADHD/Bipolar Disorder

Lithium

Controlled trials of lithium have been performed in children and adolescents with both aggressive behavior and bipolar disorder (Campbell et al., 1984, 1995; B. Geller et al., 1998). Despite some clear short-term effects on aggressive behavior, DeLong and Aldershot (1987) found the best long-term outcome with lithium to be in patients with bipolar disorder or non-CD "character disorders" rather than with CD or aggressive patients. In their sample of 59 bipolar children and adolescents, two-thirds were doing well on lithium even after many years of treatment. These patients were diagnosed by the aforementioned authors' clinical judgment rather than by any structured interview. Age of onset of the bipolar disorder was not a predictor of treatment response. Strober et al. (1988) treated 50 hospitalized manic patients with lithium. Two-thirds of the subjects responded after 6 weeks of treatment, but many of the subjects received concomitant neuroleptics or carbamazepine. Those subjects who had childhood onset of ADHD and CD showed a much poorer response rate (40% vs. 60% in those without ADHD/CD). A sample of 37 bipolar adolescents were stabilized on lithium and followed over 18 months (Strober, Morrell, Lampert, & Burroughs, 1990). Thirteen subjects discontinued lithium, and more than 90% of these patients relapsed, compared to a 33% relapse rate in the compliant patients. This latter rate is similar to that in adult bipolar patients.

Early open trials were promising in showing lithium to be effective in children with bipolar disorder (Varanka, Weller, Weller, & Fristad, 1988; Youngerman & Canino, 1995), but the first double-blind study of lithium completed to date has yielded negative results. G. A. Carlson, Rapport, Pataki, and Kelly (1992) treated 11 children with lithium; the children had a wide variety of diagnoses: "affectively unstable" aggression, conduct disorder with manic symptoms, or children with conduct disorder who had a positive family history of bipolar disorder. Those children who improved in an open trial of lithium were randomized to a double-blind crossover of placebo and lithium. No clinically significant differences between placebo and lithium were found for any of the measures of activity, aggression, or mania. Only 3 of the 11 children were felt to be significantly helped by the lithium and ready for discharge from the hospital.

B. Geller et al. (1998) found almost all of their adolescent bipolar patients had co-occurring substance abuse problems—so much so that they elected to specifically treat substance abusing bipolar adolescents in a double-blind placebo-controlled lithium protocol. One of the objectives of the study was to determine if substance-dependent bipolar adolescents would have fewer positive urine samples when treated with lithium. Thirteen bipolar adolescents were randomized to lithium, while 12 were placed on placebo. The mean lithium serum level for the responders was 0.88 + 0.27 mEq/liter, with a mean daily dose of 1,769 mg of lithium. The mean Children's Global Assessment Scale was significantly higher (better functioning) in the lithium group relative to those on placebo, and the active group had significantly fewer positive urine screens.

Combining Lithium and Stimulants

G. A. Carlson, Rapport, Kelly, and Pataki (1992) treated seven prepubertal children with a double-blind placebo crossover study of lithium, methylphenidate, and a combination of the two. While not having classic bipolar disorder, four of the seven children had high levels of manic symptoms and most also met criteria for MDD or dysthymia. All of them had a disruptive behavior diagnosis, and most had a family history of bipolar disorder. Lithium alone was ineffective in reducing inattention and hyperactivity levels, whereas a highly significant effect was seen for the combination of a lithium and a low dose of methylphenidate (5–10 mg) in improving teacher ratings of inattention. Methylphenidate alone was intermediate between the combination and placebo in causing a fall in teachers' ratings of disruptive behavior. While their results were *statistically* significant, the above authors pointed out that the improvement in the individual patients fell far short of *clinical* significance. Children with more clear-cut manic symptoms did not respond any better to lithium than did those without such a presentation. On some cognitive tasks, the combination of lithium and methylphenidate was superior to stimulant alone, whereas on others the lithium appeared to attenuate the positive effect that methylphenidate had when administered by itself. The authors did not report on side effects. The sample was too small to enable definitive conclusions to be drawn, but the data do suggest that lithium and stimulants can be safely combined. This is important in the comorbid ADHD/manic child, as lithium does not treat ADHD symptoms (Greenhill et al., 1973). The findings are also consistent with the clinical impressions of Wozniak and Biederman (1996), who suggested that mood stabilizers do not effectively treat symptoms of inattention and that most of their patients with comorbid ADHD/bipolar disorder required treatment with both a stimulant and a mood stabilizer.

Anticonvulsants in Adolescent Mania

The anticonvulsant valproate has been shown to be superior to placebo and as effective as lithium in the treatment of adult mania (Bowden et al., 1994). Papatheodorou and Kutcher (1993) have reported the results of a pilot study of valproate in six adolescents and young adults with acute manic episodes. Dosages of the drug ranged from 750 to 1,250 mg/day (mean, 1,000 mg/day). All the subjects were receiving neuroleptics at the time of the study. Clinical improvement was highly significant, ranging from 32 to 82% reduction in MRS scores. Side effects were minimal. Eleven adolescent patients with bipolar disorder were treated in an open trial of valproate (West et al., 1994): 6 of the 11 had mixed mania; 64% also had ADHD. Five of the patients were treated concomitantly with lithium, and all were on neuroleptics. Clinical response was assessed through chart review and an interview with a psychiatrist. According to this informal method, 9 of the 11 patients showed moderate-to-marked improvement. While these results are encouraging, further double-blind placebo-controlled trials are needed. Strober (1997) followed 34 adolescents with mixed mania for 3 years: 20 were maintained on lithium, while 14 were treated with valproate. All the patients had an initial good response to the mood stabilizer (lithium or valproate). At follow-up, 50% of those treated with lithium had relapsed, whereas only 34% of those on valproate had relapsed. Thus, consistent with adult data, mixed or dysphoric manic patients may respond better to valproate than to lithium, though this must be confirmed by double-blind trials.

Medication Choices in the ADHD/Bipolar Patient

Figure 8.2 shows the decision tree for a child with comorbid ADHD/mania. The decision to start with a stimulant or mood stabilizer rests on the severity and certainty of the manic symptoms. In the face of full-blown mania, stimulant treatment of ADHD is unlikely to be of benefit and a mood stabilizer should be utilized before attempting treatment of the ADHD. Lithium may be preferred for treatment of females, due to concerns raised about polycystic ovary disease (see Chapter 4). Valproate may be preferred for treatment of mixed manics. If the mania does not respond to the first mood stabilizer tried, the patient should be switched to the alternative. If there is a partial response of the mania, lithium and anticonvulsants may be combined (Strober et al., 1988). When the manic symptoms have stabilized, stimulants can be added to treat the symptoms of inattention and hyperactivity if these are still present. In a child for whom the diagnosis of mania is less clear and the ADHD or ex-

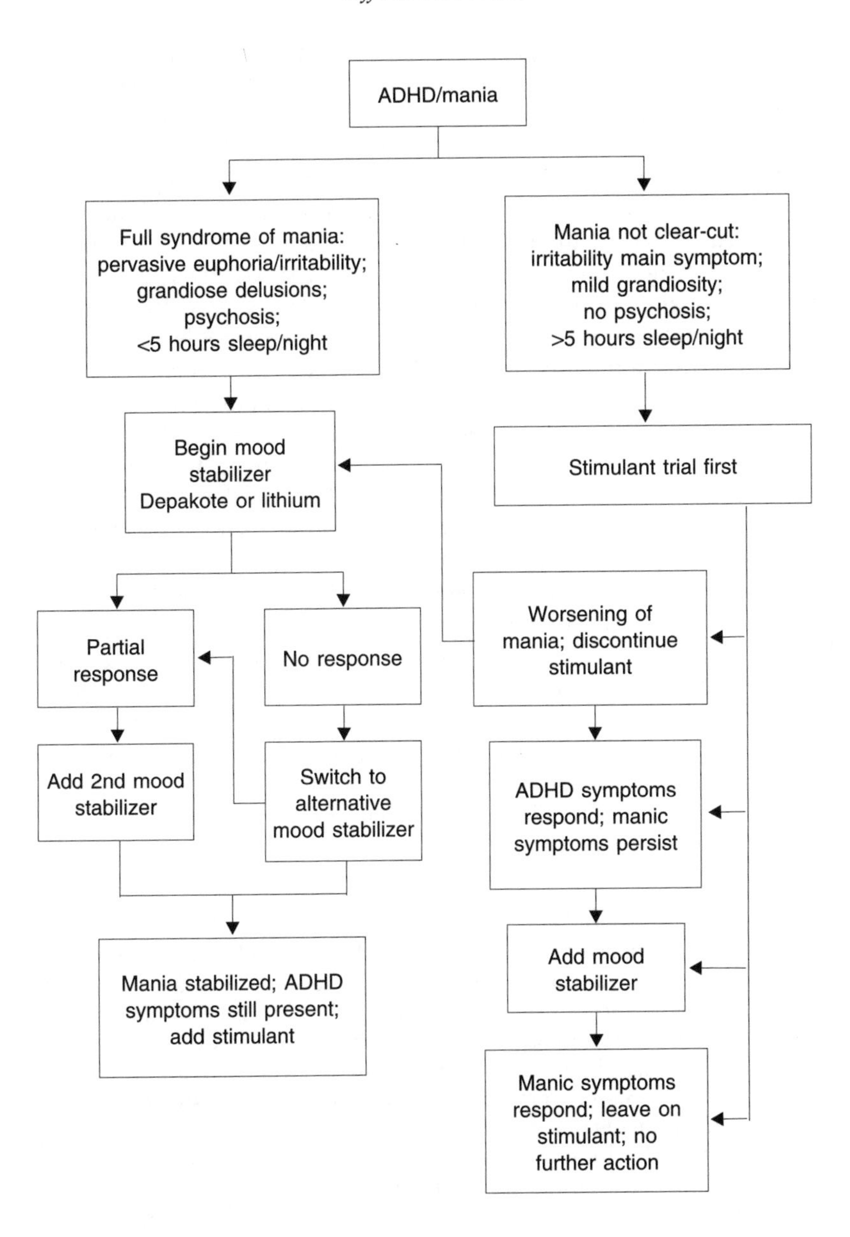

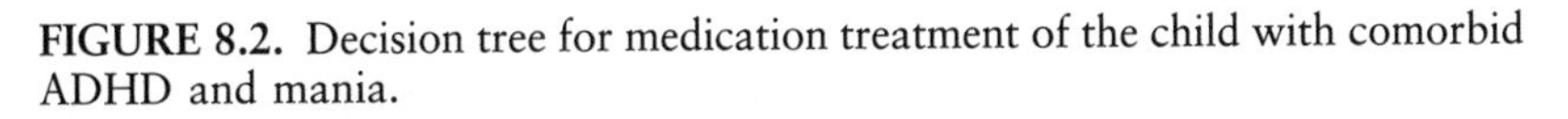
FIGURE 8.2. Decision tree for medication treatment of the child with comorbid ADHD and mania.

plosive rage symptoms are predominant, stimulants should be tried first. Mood stabilizers can then be added to the stimulant if explosive rage or unstable mood persist despite improvement of the ADHD symptoms.

Should an antidepressant also be added in those children that show severe symptoms of ADHD, depression, and mania? This step should be taken only after mood stabilization has been achieved with lithium or valproate; as Wozniak and Biederman (1996) have suggested, certain antidepressant drugs (imipramine, bupropion) treat ADHD symptoms as well as depression. In rare cases, three drug classes (mood stabilizers, stimulants, and an antidepressant) may be used together, but careful attention to possible interactions and side effects is warranted.

Some children will fail to respond to any combination of medication. It is important for the physician to assess at each step whether the particular medication has indeed had its desired effect. If it has not, it should be discontinued. A diagnosis of bipolar disorder should not be used as a reason to continue an ineffective drug regimen indefinitely. Rather, diagnoses of bipolarity in childhood or adolescence should be viewed as provisional. Careful attention should be paid to how the clinical picture evolves. If a pattern more consistent with CD or personality disorder emerges and the mood stabilizer is not effective, then the diagnosis should be reexamined. Children with such complex symptomatology often need more than psychopharmacological treatment alone. Chapters 14–16 provide a wide array of psychosocial interventions to address the multiple impairments that these individuals show. In the case below we discuss a difficult situation that shows the limits of our research knowledge, yet still can be treated successfully:

> Sam is a 13-year-old sixth grader. He presented to the clinician's office after discharge from a psychiatric hospital. He had been admitted there after the police found him in the middle of a busy street, wandering in and out of traffic. Sam told police he was planning to kill himself. In the hospital he was very sullen until the second day of admission, when an attractive female peer was admitted. He brightened, became very talkative, and began to pester the girl to the point that her parents complained to hospital staff.
>
> Sam had a long history of ADHD and always was "somewhat better" on stimulants, according to his parents. A previous valproate trial was unsuccessful. He was severely learning disabled, reading at a fifth-grade level, and his math was at the third-grade level. His Full Scale IQ was 92. He was poorly coordinated and lacked social skills. He used marijuana weekly but had no history of using other illegal substances. He had only a few casual friends.
>
> He was discharged on stimulant medication. At his first follow-up visit, he was sullen, stated he did not want to be there, and de-

nied depression or suicidal ideation. He did say he "hated himself." He went to bed at 2 A.M. and often slept until 1 P.M. the next day. His mother stated that he continued to be irritable all the time. On a nearly daily basis, he overturned furniture, screamed at his mother and sister, and broke objects in the house.

On mental status examination, he was slightly paranoid ("My parents just want to screw up my life") but had no delusions, nor any flight of ideas, pressured speech, or grandiosity.

The stimulant was discontinued, and there was no marked change in his clinical picture. He was started on lithium, and therapeutic levels were obtained after 3 weeks. There was a marked reduction in his aggressive outbursts. He responded to limits better. He continued to be very distracted and disorganized at school, although he no longer was being sent to on-campus suspension. Adderall was added at a dose of 10 mg in the A.M., but he became more irritable. It was discontinued, and he was started on bupropion (150 mg slow release twice a day; he weighed 145 pounds, or 65.8 kg). His attention span improved, though not dramatically. Nonetheless, he progressed in school with Special Education placement. No further psychiatric hospitalizations have been necessary.

For Sam any number of diagnoses would be appropriate: bipolar disorder not otherwise specified, intermittent explosive disorder, or borderline personality disorder. He never did, however, meet full criteria for a manic episode. Patient, orderly trials of different classes of medications led to improvements in his social functioning. Only long-term follow-up will determine whether Sam evolves into a more classic picture of bipolar disorder or personality disorder.

9

Anxiety Disorders

Anxiety disorders are the most common of psychiatric disorders in childhood, and their comorbidity with ADHD is far above chance (Klein, 1994; Tannock, 1994). Unlike the studies of depression and ADHD, a more consistent finding has emerged as to the degree of overlap between these conditions. As shown in Table 9.1, about a quarter of the children with ADHD will meet criteria for a least one anxiety disorder; similarly, approximately a quarter of the children with anxiety disorders will meet concurrent criteria for ADHD. This raises a number of issues not unlike those discussed in Chapter 8 with respect to depression: How does one determine if a child with a primary anxiety disorder has developed hyperactivity or inattentiveness as secondary complications of the anxiety disorder? Do children with ADHD simply develop anxiety due to "demoralization," and can this be distinguished from a bona fide anxiety disorder? For those children who clearly show both ADHD and an anxiety disorder, how do clinical presentation and response to treatment differ from those with ADHD alone?

OVERVIEW OF ANXIETY DISORDERS

Some 5–15% of the childhood population will meet criteria for one of the anxiety disorders, with overanxious disorder (OAD) and separation anxiety being slightly more common than phobias in most studies (R. G. Klein, 1994; Cohen et al., 1993; Tannock, 1994). One recent study, however, showed simple phobia to be much more common than the

TABLE 9.1. Overlap of Anxiety Disorders and ADHD

Study	Study type	ADHD children with anxiety disorder	Anxious children with ADHD
Anderson et al. (1987)	Epidemiological	26%	24%
Bird et al. (1988)	Epidemiological	23%	21%
Pliszka (1989)	Clinical	28%	—
Strauss et al. (1988)	Clinical		
	<12 years	—	35%
	>12 years	—	9%
Last et al. (1987)	Clinical		
	Separation anxiety	—	23%
	Overanxious	—	15%
	Separation anxiety/ overanxious	—	24%
Biederman et al. (1991)	Clinical	30%	—
Faraone et al. (1991b)	Clinical	29%	—
Biederman et al. (1992)	Clinical	29%	—

other anxiety disorders (Silverman & Eisen, 1992). Studies relying on each child's report of anxiety generally produce higher rates of these disorders. As with depressive disorders, parents may frequently be unaware of the child's anxiety symptoms (Pliszka, 1992). In an epidemiological study (Cohen et al., 1993), 15% of the girls and 13% of the boys meet criteria for OAD at age 10, by age 18 only 5% of boys but 13% of the girls still meet criteria for the disorder. In contrast, about 12% of both sexes met criteria for separation anxiety at age 10, but by age 18 the prevalence of this disorder had fallen to less than 3%, regardless of gender. While the above anxiety disorders are common in childhood, panic disorder (in the absence of separation anxiety) is quite rare before adolescence (D. F. Klein, Mannuzza, Chapman, & Fyer, 1992). Children with separation anxiety were found to be younger than children with OAD at the time of presentation and came from families of lower socioeconomic status (Last, Hersen, Kazdin, Finkelstein, & Strauss, 1987). Children with OAD had much higher rates of anxiety disorders among their first-degree relatives than did children with separation anxiety (Last, Hersen, Kazdin, Orvaschel, & Perrin, 1991). This study also uncovered the surprising finding that children with OAD, rather than those with separation anxiety, had a higher prevalence of panic disorder among their relatives. Previous indirect evidence had suggested that children with separation anxiety were more likely than children with other anxiety disorders to develop panic disorder (R. G. Klein, 1994), but at present the question remains unresolved. Children with any type of anxiety disorder (overanxious, separation anxiety, phobia) are equally likely to meet criteria for ADHD (Last et al., 1987). Younger children with OAD are more likely to meet criteria for ADHD than are adolescent OAD subjects (Strauss, Lease, Last, & Francis, 1988).

Despite the fact the test–retest reliability of OAD is comparable to other anxiety disorders of childhood (Silverman & Eisen, 1992), the validity of OAD has been frequently questioned. R. G. Klein (1994) noted that the wording of the criteria was vague; but more importantly, there was an absence of data suggesting that OAD was really separate from other anxiety disorders, given that so many children with OAD also meet criteria for separation anxiety or phobia (Last et al., 1987). Biedel (1991) compared children with social phobia and OAD to normal controls on a number of measures. Children with social phobia experienced higher levels of stress during their daily lives and had more pronounced changes in heart rate during a cognitive task than did normal controls. OAD children were intermediate between these two groups, and the aforementioned author felt that their higher level of trait anxiety did not appear to impair their daily functioning. Based partly on such findings, DSM-IV elected to merge OAD with generalized anxiety disorder (GAD). The criteria for GAD are shown in Table 9.2; note that children need only meet one of the six symptoms of "physical" anxiety under item C of the table. The new GAD criteria may create new problems for clinicians dealing with anxious ADHD children. Restlessness and poor concentration are symptoms of ADHD; they should not count toward a GAD diagnosis unless the child is experiencing clear-cut anxiety and worry.

ISSUES IN CLINICAL DIAGNOSIS

Item A in the DSM-IV criteria for GAD (Table 9.2) is vague. Precisely what type of "anxiety and worry" about "events or activities" should be regarded as significant? The Diagnostic Interview Schedule for Children (DISC) uses a number of questions to operationalize this item (Shaffer et al., 1993; Jensen et al., 1995). For instance, does the child worry about upcoming tests or school projects?—About his/her performance in upcoming sports events?—Whether the family has enough money?—About looking foolish when he/she does things?—About dying or getting sick? Also, does he/she exaggerate minor aches and pains? Note that these anxieties do not include simple fear of punishment for things that the child has done wrong. Many ADHD children have no foresight and *lack*

TABLE 9.2. DSM-IV Criteria for Generalized Anxiety Disorder (GAD)

A. The person is beset by excessive anxiety and worry (apprehensive expectation), occurring more days than not for at least 6 months, about a number of events or activities (such as work or school performance).

B. The person finds it difficult to control the worry.

C. The anxiety and worry are associated with three (or more) of the following six symptoms (with at least some symptoms present for more days than not for the past 6 months):

(1) restlessness
(2) being easily fatigued
(3) difficulty concentrating
(4) irritability
(5) muscle tension
(6) sleep disturbance

Note: Only one of the above items is required in children.

D. The focus of the anxiety and worry is not due to another Axis I disorder.

E. The anxiety, worry, or physical symptoms cause clinically significant distress or impairment in social, occupational, or other important areas of functioning.

F. The anxiety or worry is not directly due to substance/alcohol abuse.

Note. Adapted from the American Psychiatric Association (1994). Copyright 1994 by the American Psychiatric Association. Adapted by permission.

the appropriate amount of anticipatory anxiety for events (such as studying for a test). When the test is over and they are grounded for a poor grade, they may express dysphoria or nervousness. This is critical when the interviewer is taking a history from the parent to distinguish between true performance anxiety and unhappiness about the consequences of misbehavior. Next, the symptoms should have sufficient frequency to impair functioning. A child who is anxious for only a few minutes a time about something should not be diagnosed as having GAD; for that diagnosis, anxiety should be present for at least an hour, three to five times per week.

Older children and adolescents may use the word "nervous" to describe their ADHD symptoms. How is this to be distinguished from true anxiety? There is no research on this matter, but clinical experience suggests that there are distinct qualitative factors which separate the two feelings. When asked to give an example of their "nervousness," ADHD adolescents will describe a symptom more akin to motor restlessness or impatience: "When I'm in algebra class, it's so boring I want to jump up and scream," or "My mom says I bother the whole family the way I shake my leg when I'm sitting at the dinner table." One 16-year-old girl had a chief complaint of "being too nervous," as evidenced by her inability to stop talking in class or impulsively laughing at inappropriate times. Anxiety has a more painful quality; it is an internal experience as opposed to a reaction to immediate environmental stimuli.

Clinicians should avoid the error of assuming that because the child has experienced a life stressor the ADHD symptoms are reflective of "unconscious conflicts," the so-called masked depression. If children with psychodynamic conflicts due to psychosocial stressors commonly developed a "pseudo-ADHD," then the clinician might expect that overall ADHD children with a history of such stressors would show a less robust response to stimulants. In fact, Taylor et al. (1987) did not find this to be the case. Hyperactive and inattentive boys with a wide variety of stressors such as single-parent families, placement in foster care, and parental separation responded just as well to stimulants as did those without such histories. Children should not be diagnosed as anxious unless they meet DSM-IV criteria for one of the several anxiety disorders.

This being said, we confront the following question: Whose history of anxiety is most important, the parent's or the child's? Pliszka (1992) found that half of the ADHD children who met criteria for OAD *by their own report* were not described as anxious by their parents, suggesting that (as with depression) parents may often be unaware of their child's internalizing symptoms. Bird et al. (1992) found that parents and children agree on the presence of anxiety symptoms only about half the time. Tannock (1994) compared two groups of ADHD/anxiety disorder children: one group met criteria by child report, whereas in the other group the children denied anxiety but the parent reported anxiety symptoms in the child. Only the ADHD/anxiety children who themselves endorsed anxiety showed lower levels of self-confidence and impairment in daily activities. This suggests that it is the child interview, rather than that with the parent, which is more important in making the diagnosis of anxiety, but further research is needed to resolve this issue.

How are ADHD children with and without comorbid anxiety different? A small body of research literature has emerged that examines this issue. Pliszka (1989, 1992) found that children with ADHD and OAD were older at the time of presentation than children with ADHD alone. In the initial study, Pliszka (1989) found than ADHD/OAD children were less likely to meet criteria for conduct disorder (CD) and had lower teacher ratings of inattention/hyperactivity than did ADHD-only children. However, when a structured interview was used in a larger follow-up study, these findings were not confirmed (Pliszka, 1992). Biederman, Faraone, Keenan, Steingard, and Tsuang (1991) also did not find differences in the rate of CD in children with ADHD and those with ADHD/anxiety. In contrast, Tannock (1994) found higher rates of CD among ADHD/anxiety children. Neither Tannock nor Biederman and colleagues (in the above studies) found differences between ADHD children with anxiety and those without it in terms of the prevalence of learning disabilities. While ADHD/anxiety and ADHD-only subjects were not found to be different in school performance (Biederman, Faraone, Keenan, Steingard, & Tsuang, 1991), ADHD/anxiety children reported more school problems than did ADHD-only children (Biederman, Faraone, & Chen, 1993). Indeed, children with ADHD/anxiety reported a wider variety of social difficulties than did children with ADHD alone (Biederman, Faraone, & Chen, 1993).

Mothers of children with ADHD/anxiety reported higher levels of problems during pregnancy and developmental delays than did mothers of children with ADHD alone (Tannock, 1994). Children with ADHD/anxiety have generally experienced more stressful life events than have ADHD-only children (Jensen et al., 1993; Tannock, 1994). Biederman, Faraone, Keenan, Steingard, and Tsuang (1991) found much higher rates of divorce and separation among the families of ADHD/anxiety children (59%) compared to ADHD-only children (27%).

Pliszka (1989, 1992) used the observation technique of Barkley (1990) to assess the motor behavior of ADHD children with and without OAD. Children were placed in an observation room with a one-way mirror and required to perform arithmetic while being watched by a research assistant blind to the clinical information. Children were rated in terms of off-task behaviors, fidgeting, vocalizing, getting out of their seats, and playing with objects. In both studies, children with ADHD/OAD were less likely to display these impulsive–hyperactive behaviors than were ADHD-only children. The second study (Pliszka, 1992) compared both ADHD groups to controls. When the total number of ADHD behaviors were summed, the ADHD-only children were significantly more off task and disruptive than were the ADHD/OAD children, who in turn were significantly more disruptive than the normal controls.

The cognitive performance of ADHD children with and without anxiety have been compared using a variety of measures. Pliszka (1989) used the Memory Scanning Test. The child had to memorize four numbers, and then the computer screen presented one of three displays: a number by itself, a 4 × 4 grid of letters in which one number was imbedded, or a 4 × 4 grid of numbers. The child had to scan the display and determine if one of the four numbers he/she memorized was present in the display. The child's reaction time was measured for each response. Normally, more time is required to respond to the number display than to the letter display, since in the latter the target is embedded in similar distractors. The single-number display is the quickest to respond to. In the most difficult condition (number distracters), the ADHD group had shorter reaction times than the ADHD/OAD group and a higher number of errors. This suggested that as the task became more cognitively difficult the ADHD-only children became more impulsive, whereas the ADHD/OAD children slowed their reaction times.

In a follow-up study, Pliszka (1992) compared ADHD children with and without OAD to normal controls on the inhibition version of the Conners Continuous Performance Test (CPT). On this task children were required to press a button every time a shape appeared on the screen; if they saw a blue square they had to withhold their response. Children with ADHD alone had a much higher number of errors of commission than children with ADHD/OAD, who in turn were not different from normal controls. Thus the co-occurrence of OAD in ADHD appeared to attenuate impulsivity; this finding was confirmed in a follow-up study using an alternative measure of impulsivity, the Stop Signal Task (Pliszka, Borcherding, Spratley, Leon, & Irick, 1997)

Tannock, Ickowitz, and Schachar (1995) examined the differences between ADHD children with anxiety and without it on a working memory task. In contrast to the CPT and Stop Signal Task, which involve only simple inhibition and do not require active information processing, working memory tasks require the manipulation of information. ADHD children with and without anxiety performed the Children's Paced Auditory Serial Addition Task. Subjects were presented a series of digits (i.e., 4, 5, 1, 7, etc.) by a tape recorder. They had to add the first two digits in the sequence (4 + 5 = 9). When they heard the third digit, they had to add it to the second (5 + 1 = 6), and when they heard the fourth digit they had to add it to the third (1 + 7 = 8), and so on. The digits were presented in three different blocks of varying speeds. When the digits are presented at longer intervals, working memory is taxed because the information must be retained longer. The children with ADHD/anxiety made more errors when the digits were presented at longer intervals, implying a greater impairment of working memory relative to the ADHD-only children. Reviewing the data on cognitive performance, Tannock (1994) suggested that the effect of anxiety in ADHD is to decrease impulsiveness, on the one hand, but to increase difficulties with working memory and effortful processing, on the other. Thus clinically, children with ADHD/anxiety are more likely to appear less overtly hyperactive and disruptive, but they are also more likely to be "slowed down" or inefficient, compared to ADHD-only children.

Family Studies

Biederman and colleagues (Biederman, Faraone, Keenan, Steingard, & Tsuang, 1991; Biederman et al., 1992) have performed family studies similar to those reviewed in Chapter 8 to explore the pattern of inheritance of ADHD and anxiety. As in the depression studies, the relatives of ADHD-only or ADHD/anxiety probands were examined for the presence of ADHD or anxiety. Compared to controls, the rate of anxiety disorders was elevated only in the relatives of ADHD/anxiety children and not in the relatives of ADHD-only children. This is most consistent with the hypothesis that ADHD and anxiety are separate disorders inherited independently of each other. A subsequent family study has confirmed this pattern of inheritance for the two disorders (Perrin & Last, 1996).

PSYCHOPHARMACOTHERAPY FOR COMORBID ADHD/ANXIETY DISORDERS

Stimulants

Pliszka (1987) suggested, based on a review of the literature, that children with comorbid ADHD and anxiety might show a less robust response to stimulant medications than would ADHD children without internalizing disorders. Seeking to determine predictors of stimulant response, E. Taylor et al. (1987) treated a heterogeneous group of boys with behavior problems with a double-blind placebo-controlled trial of methylphenidate. Boys who at baseline had more symptoms of depression or anxiety were least likely to respond to the drug. Pliszka (1989) examined this issue by treating 43 ADHD children (13 of whom had a comorbid OAD) in a double-blind placebo-controlled trial of methylphenidate. Children received a week long placebo run-in, and then were randomized to a 3-week double-blind crossover study of placebo and two doses of methylphenidate. Teachers who were blind to medication status rated the children each of the study weeks. Once a week the children returned to the laboratory, where they performed arithmetic problems for 15 minutes while being observed through a one-way mirror. The observer was also blind to medication status. More than 80% of the nonanxious ADHD children responded to the stimulant, whereas only 30% of the ADHD/OAD children were felt to clearly benefit from the drug. There were a larger number of responders to placebo in the ADHD/OAD group, while there were virtually no such responders in the nonanxious ADHD group. Nonanxious ADHD children had a highly significant reduction in ratings of off-task and fidgeting behaviors in response to methylphenidate, whereas ADHD/OAD children showed little improvement on this measure. There was no evidence that the ADHD/OAD children suffered any unusual side effects, nor did they appear to get more anxious. Of course, 30% of the ADHD/OAD children did respond well to stimulants and continued treatment with methylphenidate; thus the study *did not* show that stimulants are absolutely contradicted in ADHD/anxiety. Further guidelines for the use of stimulants in ADHD/anxiety will be elucidated below.

In contrast, Tannock, Ickowicz, and Schachar (1991) did find that side effects of stimulants appear greater in the ADHD/anxiety group relative to the ADHD-only group. Furthermore, these ADHD children were followed while they received long term methylphenidate treatment (more than 12 months). ADHD/OAD children not only had less behavioral improvement but what improvement there was tended to decline over time (Tannock, 1994). Recently, Tannock, Schachar, and Logan (1993) compared ADHD/anxious children and ADHD-only children on a working memory task. Children performed the task on placebo and several dosages of methylphenidate ranging from 0.3–0.9 mg/kg per dose. ADHD children without anxiety showed clear improvements in performance on methylphenidate, which linearly related to dose. In contrast, ADHD/anxious children showed only modest improvements on the low dose that were not enhanced by the higher dose.

Finally, Dupaul, Barkley, and McMurray (1994) divided ADHD children into internalizers and noninternalizers based on the child's baseline Child Behavior Checklist score. Like Pliszka (1989), they found that ADHD children with comorbid internalizing symptoms had a less robust response to stimulants than did nonanxious ADHD children. On the other hand, Diamond, Tannock, Rimer, Bockus, and Schachar (1998) compared 22 ADHD/anxious children to 34 nonanxious ADHD children who were treated with methylphenidate for up to 3 years. He found that both groups responded very well to the stimulant; indeed, the anxious children showed greater academic gains. Since there are conflicting data in the literature, there is a need for caution in the use of stimulants in children with ADHD/anxiety disorder but a significant minority of ADHD/anxious children will respond well to stimulant (Pliszka, 1989). Table 9.3 shows some of the factors to be weighed in choosing between stimulants and alternative agents; the reasoning is similar to that which we used in selecting a psychopharmacological treatment for the ADHD/depressed child.

If stimulants are selected as the psychopharmacological treatment, careful monitoring of behavior and school performance in particular is indicated. The child should be watched for signs of increased anxiety or overfocusing and the medication should be discontinued if this occurs. On the other hand, if the stimulant response is robust, the clinician should inquire as to the anxiety symptoms. If they remitted along with the ADHD symptoms, the clinician would be justified in concluding that the anxiety was secondary to the problems arising secondary to the ADHD. If stimulants are not effective, then one of the antidepressant medications may be considered.

TABLE 9.3. Factors Influencing the Decision to Begin a Child with Comorbid ADHD/Anxiety Disorder on Stimulants versus Other Agents

Begin with a stimulant	Begin with an alternative agent
Generalized anxiety in the absence of strong physiological symptoms of overarousal	Overt panic-type symptoms such as heart racing, shortness of breath, excessive sweating
Feelings of distress on separation from caretaker but no overt behaviors (clinging, school refusal)	School refusal or acute agitation on separation from caretaker
No history of stimulant treatment	Prior history of poor stimulant response
Long history of severe ADHD; anxiety symptoms of more recent onset	Anxiety symptoms preceded or closely parallel the ADHD symptoms
Chief complaint ADHD symptoms; anxiety disorder discovered only through interview	Chief complaint, anxiety symptoms

Tricyclic Antidepressants

Several controlled trials of tricyclic antidepressants (TCAs) had been performed in children with separation anxiety, with conflicting results. Gittelman-Klein and Klein (1970) treated 35 school refusers (aged 7–15) as part of a double-blind placebo-controlled trial of imipramine (mean dose, 159 mg/day). (All of the subjects also received a behavioral intervention.) Eighty-one percent of the imipramine group returned to school versus only 47% of the placebo group; the imipramine group also had significantly greater reductions in subjective anxiety. Berney et al. (1981) did not find a therapeutic effect of clomipramine in 9- to 15-year-old school refusers, but the dosages used were not adequate (40–75 mg daily). Recently, however, there have been a number of studies that have not shown TCAs to be particularly effective in separation anxiety or school refusal. Bernstein, Garfinkel, and Borehardt (1990) randomized 24 children aged 7–17 to one of three groups: placebo, imipramine, or alprazolam. By chance, children randomized to the alprazolam groups had higher baseline anxiety scores. All subjects participated in a "school reentry plan" that involved intensive therapy and case management. Children in all three groups responded well, with increases in school attendance and decreases in anxiety. While there was a trend for the medication groups to have a more robust reduction in anxiety, the differences were not statistically significant. Similarly, Klein, Koplewicz, and Kanner (1992) did not find that imipramine was superior to placebo in the treatment of separation anxiety. Seventeen children (mean age, 9.5 years) with separation anxiety who had not responded to behavioral intervention were randomized to placebo or the TCA (mean dose, 153 mg/day); they continued their behavioral treatment throughout the study. There was no effect of drug on any of the behavioral or anxiety measures. There has never been a study of TCAs in any form of childhood anxiety disorders other than separation anxiety. Pliszka (1987) had suggested, based on a review of the literature, that TCAs might be more effective in ADHD children with comorbid anxiety; however, Biederman, Baldessarini, Wright, et al. (1993) found that anxious and nonanxious ADHD children responded equally well to desipramine. Thus, while there is evidence that ADHD/anxious children have a less robust response to stimulants, there is not clear evidence that they respond better to TCAs. Given the concern about TCAs expressed in previous chapters, the clinician should look at other approaches.

Benzodiazepines

The benzodiazepines have hardly been studied in childhood anxiety disorders, and no study has examined their effects in the children with comorbid ADHD and anxiety. Preliminary results from a double-blind placebo-controlled protocol suggest that clonazepam is effective in adolescent panic disorder (Kutcher, Reiter, Gardner, & Klein, 1992), whereas two controlled trials show that it is *ineffective* in childhood GAD and separation anxiety disorder (Graae, Milner, Rizzotto, & Klein, 1994; Simeon et al., 1992). Thus there is no strong evidence documenting the effectiveness of benzodiazepines in childhood and adolescence. Furthermore, work with adults who have impulse control disorders suggest that extreme caution should be used when dispensing these medications to individuals with ADHD. Gardner and Cowdry (1985) found dramatic increases in aggression toward both self and others when female patients with borderline personality disorder were treated with alprazolam. In a later larger study these results were confirmed (Cowdry & Gardner, 1988), although some patients with borderline personality disorder improved on the benzodiazepine. Particularly in adolescence, many ADHD children with CD have borderline personality traits; the agitation and mood lability common in these teens should not be mistaken for anxiety. Indeed, benzodiazepines should be avoided in ADHD/anxious children until further studies elucidate the risks and benefits of these drugs in children.

Specific Serotonin Reuptake Inhibitors

Fluoxetine has been used in the treatment of childhood obsessive–compulsive disorder (OCD) with good results (Riddle et al., 1992; Simeon, Dinicola, Ferguson, & Copping, 1990; Simeon, Thatte, & Wiggins, 1990). Birmaher et al. (1994) treated 30 anxious children and adolescents (mean age, 14 years) with an open trial of fluoxetine. The children, who were all nonresponders to psychotherapy, had a variety of anxiety diagnoses other than OCD; two-thirds had failed trials of TCAs. The mean dose of fluoxetine was 25.7 mg/day: only one patient received 10 mg/day; all the others were on 20–60 mg/day. Side effects were mild and transient; none of the subjects had worsening of anxiety symptoms. Anxiety severity scores showed a highly significant reduction, with 56% of the patients rated as moderately or markedly improved. Similar find-

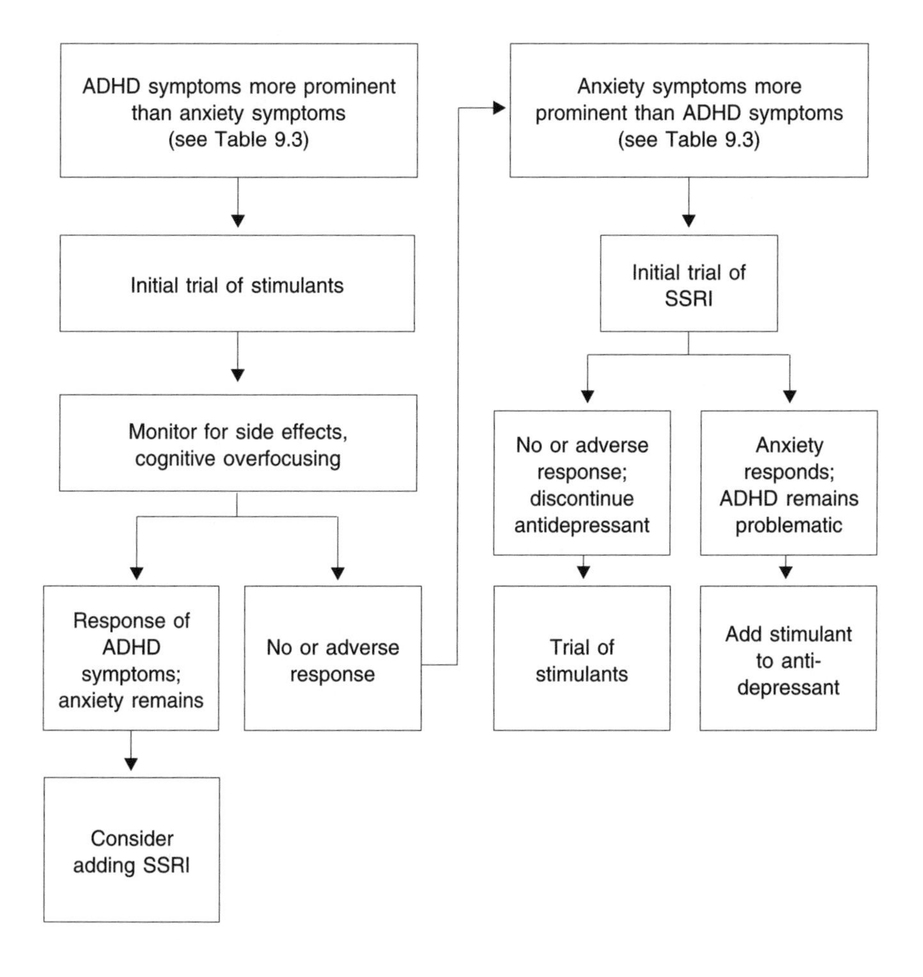

FIGURE 9.1. Decision tree for selection of medication in the child with comorbid ADHD and anxiety.

ings of positive effects of fluoxetine emerged from a second open trial (Fairbanks et al., 1997). In that study, children were treated with a mean dose of 24 mg/day, while adolescents received a mean dose of 40 mg/day. No patient developed disinhibition, akathisia, or suicidality. Given that Gammon and Brown (1993) have shown that fluoxetine can be safely combined with stimulants, these studies suggest that SSRIs are an alternative agent that could be combined with stimulants in the ADHD/anxious child. Figure 9.1 shows a decision tree in dealing with the patient with comorbid ADHD and anxiety.

10

Mental Retardation and Pervasive Developmental Disorders

ADHD AND MENTAL RETARDATION

At one time clinical lore suggested that ADHD did not occur in children with mental retardation (MR); any inappropriate behavior these children showed was presumed to be secondary to their mental impairment. Subsequently, stimulant medications were rarely, if ever, used in this population. In early studies, stimulants were tried in heterogeneous populations of MR children and adults without regard to whether the subjects showed ADHD symptoms or not. These studies, conducted over two decades, consistently showed that stimulants did not improve learning in MR subjects (Aman, 1982). This lead to the common view that stimulants were contraindicated in MR children and that neuroleptics were first-line agents for behavioral control in retarded individuals despite the risk of tardive dyskinesia. In a series of studies, Gualtieri and colleagues (Gualtieri et al., 1984, 1986) showed that about a third of retarded individuals who had been treated with neuroleptics for an average of 8 years developed tardive dyskinesia when the drugs were withdrawn. Small numbers of the patients developed behavioral symptoms that were not present predrug, such as aggression, though these problems were short lived. In these two studies, only about 30% of the patients needed to be placed back on neuroleptics to achieve behavioral control. These results suggest that other psychopharmacological agents need to be considered before turning to neuroleptics in both children and adolescents with MR.

More recent studies have shown that ADHD occurs in MR children at rates higher than in the general population. Eighteen percent of "educable" MR children were found to be at about the cutoff score on the Abbreviated Conners Teacher Rating Scale (Epstein, Cullinan, & Polloway, 1986). Other studies have shown that some 25–40% of MR children are hyperactive (Herbst, 1980; Koller, Richardson, Katz, & McLaren, 1983). Barkley (1990) has suggested that the child's mental age should be used for comparison with the norms on the Conners scale, that is, if a 10-year-old has an IQ of 60, his teacher ratings should be compared to the 6-year norms rather than to the norms for his chronological age. A recent study questions this practice. Pearson and Aman (1994) examined the Conners Teacher Rating Scales (CTRS) in a sample of normal IQ children with psychiatric disorders as well as in a sample of MR children with disruptive behavior. Chronological age, rather than mental age, correlated with teacher ratings of inattention and hyperactivity. Pearson and Aman (1994) further pointed out that using the norms for the child's mental age does not always make clinical sense: an 18-year-old with a mental age of 4 cannot be allowed to act like a 4-year-old. These authors concluded that one should use the chronological age norms even in retarded children such that if, say, a 10-year-old boy with MR has a mental age of 8, the clinician should still compare his teacher ratings with the 10-year-old norms.

Brief Overview of Mental Retardation

MR is subtyped by IQ score: mild, 50–70; moderate, 35–49; severe, 20–34; profound, less than 20. Eighty percent of MR individuals are in the mild range, and only in about 10–25% of those cases can an organic cause be established (Scott, 1994). Down's syndrome and fragile X syndrome are the most common genetic causes, but a heterogeneous number of perinatal, toxic, and traumatic factors may also play a role. Mild MR is found more commonly in groups of lower socioeconomic status, whereas severe MR is equally distributed across income levels, suggesting a role for environmental depravation in the etiology of mild MR (Scott, 1994). Today, MR children remain in the community and are educated in their local public schools; thus the clinician is more likely to be consulted about behavior problems in this group than in past years.

Fragile X syndrome has attracted more interest than other forms of MR, as it has been alleged to be associated with specific psychopathology more than in other forms of MR. Hagerman, Smith, and Mariner

(1983) originally found that 71% of their sample of 24 fragile X males met criteria for ADHD; Fisch (1993) reviewed other uncontrolled studies that showed the prevalence of ADHD among fragile X males averaged about 62%. Fisch (1993) pointed out that these studies did not control for the fact that fragile X children with behavior problems are more likely to come to the clinician's attention. Furthermore, controlled studies have not borne out the relationship of fragile X syndrome and ADHD. Einfeld, Hall, and Levy (1991) compared fragile X patients to age- and IQ-matched nonfragile X MR controls and found no differences in hyperactivity, attention deficits, or aggression. Two other studies using a similar design confirmed that ADHD was not more prevalent among fragile X patients than were other MR subjects (Borghgraef, Fryns, Dielkens, Pyck, & Van den Berge, 1987; Dykens, Leckman, Paul, & Watson, 1988). Thus the increased prevalence of ADHD in fragile X patients relative to the general population is due to the MR and not to the fragile X status per se. As a final note, folic acid, thought at one time to be a specific treatment for fragile X, is ineffective in ameliorating the intellectual or behavioral aspects of the syndrome (Fisch et al., 1988).

The Use of Stimulants for Comorbid ADHD/Mental Retardation

Since 1990, a considerable body of evidence has emerged that stimulants are effective in the treatment of inattention and hyperactivity in MR children. Payton, Burkhart, Hersen, and Hall (1989) performed a preliminary study with three young males with mild MR who also meet criteria for ADHD. The children were placed on alternating weeks of placebo or stimulant, one child receiving dextroamphetamine while the other two received methylphenidate. All three subjects showed marked improvement while on stimulants, with increases in on-task behavior and decreases in hyperactivity. Handen, Breaux, Gosling, Ploof, and Feldman (1990) performed a double-blind placebo-controlled crossover study of methylphenidate in 12 mild MR children with ADHD. Each child received a week of placebo, a week of methylphenidate at low dose (0.3 mg/kg), and a week of methylphenidate at high dose (0.6 mg/kg). The drug–placebo order was randomized for each child. According to teacher ratings, 75% of the groups were stimulant responders, with dramatic reductions in classroom behavior problems similar to those seen in non-MR ADHD children. Each week of the trial, the children attended a Saturday morning session where laboratory testing of behavior and learning was performed. Again, there were significant reductions in restlessness and increases in on-task behavior during the drug weeks. The children made significantly fewer impulsive errors on the Conners Continuous Performance Test (CPT) while on methylphenidate. Similar results were found in a subsequent double-blind crossover study of 14 ADHD children with mild MR (Handen et al., 1992). In this latter study, the authors noted that while overt disruptive behaviors declined when the children were on stimulants, there was no specific improvement in social skills. Nonetheless, the overall response to medication in both studies was quite positive.

Handen, Feldman, Gosling, Breaux, and McAuliffe (1991) examined the rate of side effects in 27 ADHD children with mild MR who completed the double-blind crossover studies of methylphenidate. Overall, methylphenidate was not significantly different from placebo in terms of appetite loss, headaches, or other common side effects of stimulants. Three children developed tics and two developed severe social withdrawal, requiring the medications to be withdrawn. The rate of side effects in MR/ADHD children on stimulants has not been shown to be higher than that in non-MR/ADHD samples (Aman, Kern, McGhee, & Arnold, 1993; Aman, Marks, Turbott, Wilsher, & Merry, 1991).

Methylphenidate has been compared to thioridazine and placebo in a double-blind crossover study (Aman et al., 1991). The dose of methylphenidate was 0.4 mg/kg per day, while the dose of thioridazine was 1.75 mg/day per day in divided doses. Teacher ratings showed a statistically significant effect, with methylphenidate and thioridazine being superior over placebo but not different from each other. However, a psychologist who was blind to drug status performed a global clinical rating of the children each week; on these ratings methylphenidate was clearly superior to the neuroleptic. Interestingly, neither parent ratings nor laboratory measures of attention showed any effects of the drugs. Since the last dose of stimulant was given at noon, the parents may not have observed any effect, as it had worn off by the evening hours. The above authors also found that children with IQs under 45 were less likely to respond to either drug. The study clearly does not show any advantage of thioridazine over methylphenidate in the MR/ADHD patient, despite its traditional use in this population.

Dickerson-Mayes et al. (1994) directly compared the stimulant response rates of MR and normal IQ ADHD children in a double-blind placebo-controlled protocol and found similar numbers of positive responders in both groups. Specifically, 68% of ADHD/MR children were stimulant responders, compared to 88% of children with normal IQ, a difference that was not statistically significant. Thus the evidence conclusively shows that stimulants are effective and safe in ADHD/MR children and should be considered agents of first choice.

ADHD AND PERVASIVE DEVELOPMENT DISORDERS

It is difficult to imagine the stress experienced by caretakers of children with autism and other pervasive developmental disorders (PDDs). These children present with a bewildering array of symptomatic behavior, often impulsiveness, aggression, and hyperactivity are among the most problematic. It may be, however, difficult to apply the ADHD criteria to these children, since the criteria imply a normal level of social relatedness in a child. If an autistic child repeats a television commercial over and over while in class, should this be regarded as "talking excessively" and thus a symptom of ADHD? DSM-IV states that if the symptoms of inattention and hyperactivity occur "exclusively" in the course of a PDD, then ADHD should not be diagnosed. Before pondering how a diagnosis of ADHD should be made in the autistic or PDD child, a brief overview of the PDDs is required.

Brief Overview of the Pervasive Developmental Disorders

The PDDs are now subdivided into five main categories: autistic disorder (formerly infantile autism), Rett's disorder, childhood disintegrative disorder, Asperger's disorder, and PDD–not otherwise specified (PDD–NOS). The criteria for autism serve as a kind of template for all the PDDs. A child with autistic disorder must have impairment in social interaction, language, and also show abnormal stereotyped patterns of behavior. Onset must be before age 3. MR may or may not be present, but autistic individuals of normal intelligence rarely can use their talents in a socially adaptive way.

While males are predominately more affected in autistic disorder, Rett's disorder is found principally in females; it is also distinguished by a characteristic deacceleration of head growth between the ages of 5 and 48 months, despite normal head circumference at birth. Severe of profound MR is almost always present, and gait and trunk movements become poorly coordinated. Language and social interactions are extremely impaired.

In childhood disintegrative disorder, head circumference is normal and, unlike what occurs in autistic disorder, development in language and social interaction is normal for the first 2 years of life. Then, before age 10, the child experiences loss of *previously* acquired skills in at least two of the following areas: language, social skills, bowel or bladder control, and play or motor skills. As in autistic disorder, there must be impairments of social interaction, including communication, and there must be the presence of repetitive, stereotyped behavior. Asperger's disorder is the least impairing of the PDDs. Individuals with this disorder do not have cognitive impairment, and their intelligence is generally within the normal range; general adaptive behavior for activities of daily living is intact. Asperger's disorder is characterized by impairments in social interaction and odd stereotyped behavior similar to that seen in criterion A3 for autistic disorder. The reader is referred to Lord and Rutter (1994) for more details regarding the PDDs and their possible etiologies. ADHD behaviors are not known to be any more prevalent in any particular subtype of PDD.

When is it appropriate to diagnose ADHD in the presence of PDD? How is one to judge inattentiveness in an autistic child or a child with PDD? PDD children, particularly those with autistic disorder, chronically attend to inappropriate (and meaningless) stimuli and rarely focus on normal stimuli. The whole array of symptoms under the inattention section of the ADHD criteria are difficult to apply to PDD children. What is a "careless" mistake for an autistic child? The failure of autistic children to listen to directions may be due to their communication deficits. PDD children do not, as a part of the syndrome, organize their behavior or keep track of their things. We cannot expect autistic children to remember a fact or request for any length of time. Their lack of social relatedness means we cannot judge their failure to comply with our requests as signs of distractibility. If they are drawn from what we want them to do to something in their environment (i.e., spinning objects), this also may not be due to distractibility but to the autistic child's "stereotyped and restricted pattern of interest."

While it would be inappropriate for PDD children to be diagnosed as having ADHD, inattentive type, it is quite possible for such a child to meet criteria for ADHD, impulsive–hyperactive type. As can be seen, *general* increased motor activity is not a symptom of the PDDs. A child might have a *specific* stereotypy (i.e., finger flapping), but if this is the only motor symptom present, then the hyperactivity criterion of ADHD is not met. If, on the other hand, the child is climbing on furniture or impulsively running into the street, then these gross motor activities are not stereotypies and should not be regarded as part of the PDD syndrome. Similarly being "on the go" or "driven like a motor" are purely ADHD symptoms unless they are only present during the performance of a stereotypy. Yelling out, loud laughter, and labile mood are also possible signs of ADHD in a PDD child. Certainly they may be the targets of pharmacological intervention.

Psychopharmacotherapy for Comorbid ADHD/Pervasive Developmental Disorders

Stimulants

Campbell and colleagues (1972, 1976) performed two small studies of the effectiveness of stimulants in the treatment of "childhood schizophrenia." These studies did not find the stimulants to be helpful, and many of the subjects worsened in terms of stereotypies, affectivity and activity level. As a result, these studies are widely cited as showing that stimulants are not effective in the treatment of autism or PDD (Aman, 1982; Lord & Rutter, 1994; Sloman, 1991). These studies are hardly definitive, however. The first (Campbell et al., 1972) involved 16 subjects, only 2 of whom were autistic; 2 subjects had genetic abnormalities (Turner's and Klinefelter's syndromes), and the remaining subjects had "childhood schizophrenia." At that time, there were no set criteria for that diagnosis, and all of the subjects were preschoolers, with a mean age of 4.3 years. Only half the subjects in the sample were "hyperactive"; the remaining subjects were regarded as "hypoactive." The children were treated with dextroamphetamine, the doses ranging from 1.25 to 10 mg/day (mean, 7.5 mg/day). Only 6 children showed slight or marked improvement; the other 63% of the subjects showed deterioration, with increases in their inappropriate behaviors. Campbell et al. (1976) next performed a double-blind trial of levoamphetamine in 11 schizophrenic children who had "autistic features." The subjects were also quite young, with a mean age of 5.3 years. Only 2 of the 11 patients improved. These studies seem to indicate that stimulants are not likely to be effective in autistic or PDD individuals in general; they clearly do not ameliorate the core symptoms of the PDD syndromes such as stereotypies or social/communication deficits. More recent studies have focused on autistic/PDD patients who clearly have elevated levels of impulsivity and hyperactivity; these studies strongly suggest that stimulants do have a role in the treatment of this subgroup.

B. Geller, Guttmacher, and Bleeg (1981) reported two cases of children with comorbid PDD and ADHD who showed improved attention and less hyperactivity when treated with dextroamphetamine. There was no worsening of the PDD symptoms. Strayhorn, Rapp, Donina, and Strain (1988) treated one autistic 6-year-old boy with methylphenidate in a double-blind placebo-controlled protocol. Each day, the child was randomly assigned to receive either placebo or 5 mg of methylphenidate twice a day. By the end of the study, the child had been on placebo 14 days and on the active agent for 17 days. Teacher and parents ratings were compared for the two conditions. Teachers rated the child as significantly improved; even the stereotypies were reduced. Parents also rated the child as concentrating better, less destructive, and more obedient. Although both parents and teachers did note an increase in "unhappiness," the parents felt that the overall improvement was sufficient to continue the child on methylphenidate. Birmaher, Quintana, and Greenhill (1988) treated nine autistic children (age range, 5–16 years) in an open trial of methylphenidate. The dose of methylphenidate ranged from 10 to 50 mg/day, with a mean dose of 25 mg/day. Eight of the nine subjects were stimulant responders, and the entire group showed statistically significant improvements on the CTRS. There was no worsening of the autistic or stereotypical behaviors. There were no changes on the Abnormal Involuntary Movements Scale (AIMS). These studies, while preliminary, clearly show that stimulants may be beneficial to the ADHD/PDD child and should always be considered when high levels of impulsive or hyperactive symptoms are present. One should monitor patients, however, for increasing withdrawals or stereotypies.

Clonidine

Jaselskis, Cook, Fletcher, and Leventhal (1992) performed a double-blind placebo-controlled crossover study of clonidine in eight male autistic children who had high levels of inattention, impulsivity, and hyperactivity. The subjects ranged in age from 5 to 13 years (mean age, 8.1 years) and had a mean IQ of 59. Also, all the subjects had failed previous trials of stimulants, antidepressants, and neuroleptics. The children received 6 weeks of placebo and 6 weeks of clonidine, with a 2-week wash-out period between the two series; the order of drug administration was randomized. The dose of clonidine was 0.15–0.20 mg/day in three divided doses. The most significant effect was a 33% reduction in teacher ratings of irritability for those subjects on active drug relative to those on placebo. Clonidine was significantly better than placebo in reducing ratings of ADHD behaviors on both the parent and teacher Conners scales. Clinician ratings, however, did not distinguish placebo from clonidine. After the study, six of the subjects continued on clonidine, but the medication lost its effectiveness in two-thirds of these children. Hypotension and irritability prevented dose increases. Further studies are needed, but the data suggest that clonidine is helpful in the ADHD/autistic child. Guanfacine may also be a useful agent, as it is less likely to cause the sedation and hypotension that limited clonidine's use in the above study. (See Chapter 4 for a fuller discussion of the alpha agonists in the treatment of ADHD.)

Naltrexone

Naltrexone is a potent opiate antagonist that can be taken orally. It began to be used in the treatment of autistic individuals because of the theoretical role of the endogenous opiates in attachment and self-injurious behavior (SIB) (Herman, Hammock, Arthur-Smith, Kuehl, & Appelgate, 1989). The drug has been found to reduce SIB in small samples of severely disturbed patients (Barrett, Feinstein, & Hole, 1989), but a double-blind placebo-controlled trial in retarded adults was negative (Willemsen-Swinkels, Buitelaar, Nijhof, & van Engeland, 1995). After success with naltrexone in small groups of subjects (Campbell, Adams, Small, Tesch, & Curren, 1988; Campbell et al., 1990), Campbell et al. (1993) performed a double-blind trial of 1.0 mg/kg per day of naltrexone and placebo in 45 autistic children with a mean age of 4.9 years. There was no effect of naltrexone on SIB or aggression, but the drug was superior to placebo in reducing hyperactivity ratings on the clinician's ratings; however, parent and teacher ratings showed no differences in this symptoms area .

Recently, Kolemen, Feldman, Handen, and Janosky (1995) confirmed these findings in a controlled trial of naltrexone. The subjects were 16 children who met DSM-III-R criteria for autistic disorder. They had a mean age of 5.4 and a wide range of IQ scores, from 21 to 115 (mean, 62). The above authors used a double-blind crossover study, with each child receiving both placebo and naltrexone. During the active phase the children were started immediately on 1.0 mg/kg of naltrexone, day given as a single daily dose; this dose was maintained for a 2-week study period. Half the sample received naltrexone first and then naltrexone, whereas the other half was given placebo first. Wash-out periods separated the two phases of the study. Highly significant reductions were found in both parent and teacher ratings of hyperactivity and impulsivity on naltrexone relative to the placebo. The physical activity level as directly measured by an actometer was also sharply decreased. Eight of the 13 children were judged to be responders. Naltrexone might be useful for reducing hyperactive behavior in autistic/PDD patients if stimulants have failed, but it is unlikely to be of benefit for SIB or the abnormalities of social interactions.

Specific Serotonin Reuptake Inhibitors

A number of years ago it was discovered that about 25% of autistic individuals have elevated serotonin in platelets (Cook, 1990). While this fact did not turn out to be of great clinical relevance, it led to an interest in serotonergic drugs for the treatment of autistic persons. Fenfluramine, which depletes serotonin from platelets, was found to have only modest effects on autistic behaviors, and concerns about neurotoxicity in children caused it to fall out of favor with clinicians well before it was removed from the market because of cardiovascular effects. The evidence for their effectiveness is sparse. In a small open trial (n = 15) in MR adults, paroxetine was not successful in reducing either aggression or SIB (Davanzo, Belin, Widawski, & King, 1998). Clomipramine was similarly unimpressive in an open trial with eight autistic children (Sanchez et al., 1996); indeed, six of the children worsened during the trial. In the largest study to date, 30 autistic adults were randomized to placebo or fluvoxamine. Fluvoxamine was superior to placebo in reducing aggression, and repetitive thoughts and behavior, on the one hand, and increasing language use and social relatedness, on the other. Further double-blind placebo-controlled studies are needed in autistic and MR children and adolescents, particularly with regard to aggression and SIB.

Neuroleptics

Campbell and colleagues (1978, 1982; L. T. Anderson et al., 1984, 1989; Anderson, Campbell, et al., 1989) pioneered the use of neuroleptics, particularly haloperidol in autistic children. An initial study (Campbell et al., 1978) of 55 young autistic boys showed that haloperidol was superior to placebo in reducing withdrawal and stereotypies, although it did not affect ratings of hyperactivity. A combination of haloperidol and behavior therapy was best for enhancing speech. A follow-up study (Campbell et al., 1982) showed similar results, but haloperidol was also found to superior to placebo in reducing fidgetiness in these children. L. T. Anderson et al. (1989) treated 45 autistic children in a double-blind crossover trial of haloperidol. The mean age of the children was 4.49 years and the average dose of haloperidol was 0.884 mg; the range of doses was 0.160–0.184 mg/kg per day. Each child received 4 weeks of placebo and then 4 weeks of neuroleptic, with the order randomized. Haloperidol was quite effective, relative to placebo, in reducing autistic behaviors such as withdrawal and stereotypies. The neuroleptic was also effective, however, in reducing ratings of hyperactivity and conduct problems on the Children's Psychiatric Scale. The total score on the Conners Parent Rating Scale was also positively affected by haloperidol, with parents rating their children as less hyperactive and impulsive when on the neuroleptic. Eleven of the 45 subjects had dystonic reactions, which were relieved by diphenhydramine.

Atypical neuroleptics are less likely to cause dystonic reactions, and they are gaining far more use in persons with developmental disabilities

(Findling et al., 1997). Both hyperactivity and aggression were decreased in 18 children and adolescents with autism/PDD after 12 weeks of treatment with risperidone (mean dose, 1.8 + 1.0 mg/day); 12 of the 18 subjects experienced weight gain, but none showed signs of dystonia. Lott, Kerrick, and Cohen (1996) found highly significant reductions in aggression and SIB in 33 adults with PDDs in an institutional setting. Of particular interest, patients on risperidone were much more likely to become employed; moreover, wage earnings increased by 37% for the group after 6 months of risperidone treatment. Thus, the patients' quality of life improved, a fact to be borne in mind by the clinician when he/she is balancing the risk of withdrawal against the risk of tardive dyskinesia. Staff injuries secondary to resident aggressive outbursts also declined markedly. Quite often neuroleptics are the only medications that can successfully treat the child with autism or PDD; they should be used when other approaches have failed.

SUMMARY

When confronted with the hyperactive or impulsive MR, autistic, or PDD child, the clinician should consider treatment with stimulants first, being aware of the higher rate of side effects or possible nonresponse. An alpha agonist or SSRI would be the next choice, but neuroleptic treatment, preferably with atypical agents, should be pursued if the first two classes do not reduce the impulsive or aggressive behavior. If the patient exhibits disorganized, bizarre behaviors or SIB, then the clinician should move more quickly to utilize the neuroleptics.

11

Medical Disorders

What sort of medical illnesses complicate the diagnosis and treatment of ADHD? There are no illnesses that perfectly mimic ADHD, and the general health history of ADHD children is often unremarkable. As a result, physical illness is low in the differential diagnosis of hyperactivity and inattention. There are several areas, however, where issues come up about the role of medical factors in ADHD. In this chapter we deal with the more common and controversial of these issues: (1) What is the relationship of thyroid disease to ADHD? (2) Do allergies and diet play any role in the treatment of ADHD? (3) What is the effect of chronic medical illness (cancer, otitis media, asthma, etc.) on attention and learning in children? Do medications commonly used in children with these medical illnesses impair attention or learning? (4) Can stimulants be used in a seriously ill child?

ADHD AND THE THYROID

In recent years, an association between a rare genetic thyroid disorder and ADHD has been suggested (Hauser et al., 1993). This has led to many questions by both clinicians and the lay public as to the role of thyroid disease in ADHD. Exactly what is the condition found to be associated with ADHD in the above study? How does it relate to standard hyper- or hypothyroidism? How common is it in ADHD children? Does it have any implications for diagnosis or treatment? First, a brief overview of thyroid physiology is in order.

Thyroid Physiology

The hypothalamus secretes thyrotropin-releasing hormone (TRH) in response to a variety of stimuli from the central nervous system (CNS) as well as to environmental factors such as cold and stress. TRH, in turn, induces the anterior pituitary to secrete thyroid-stimulating hormone (TSH; thyrotropin). TSH binds to receptors in the follicular cells of the thyroid, which induces the production of cyclic AMP. Iodine and tyrosine are used to manufacture thyroxine (T_4) and triiodothyronine (T_3), both thyroid hormones. After excretion, most thyroid hormone is bound to plasma proteins. Thyroid hormone binds to receptors on cells in many organs, and T_3 is about four times as potent as T_4 in its biological effect. Oxygen consumption and heat production are increased, as is lipid metabolism, and "under hyperthyroid conditions, the overall effects favor consumption rather than storage of fuel" (Hedge, Colby, & Goodman, 1987, p. 111). Thyroid hormones increase the responsiveness of tissues to the effects of the catecholamines norepinephrine and epinephrine. Thus while the plasma levels of catecholamines are not increased in hyperthyroid states, the number of beta receptors rises. Heart rate and blood pressure are increased. Finally, thyroid hormone receptors are present in the CNS, perhaps accounting for the behavioral symptoms of thyroid disease.

Can Hyperthyroidism Mimic ADHD?

Hyperthyroidism is quite rare in childhood, with Graves' disease being the most likely cause (Clayton, 1982). Other, even rarer etiologies include adenoma of the pituitary and thyroid cancer. Graves' disease has a genetic and immunological basis, and there is almost always a strong family history of hyperthyroidism. Clayton (1982) listed the likelihood of presenting signs and symptom in thryotoxicosis as follows: goiter (98%), tachycardia (82%), nervousness (82%), increased pulse pressure (80%), proptosis (65%), increased appetite (60%), tremor (52%), weight loss (50%), and heat intolerance (30%). Thus, while children with hyperthyroidism may present with hyperactivity, several factors set them apart from ADHD children. *Severe anxiety is usually associated with thryotoxicosis, and the above physical signs should accompany the hyperactivity.* Only if these factors are present would thyroid functions be indicated in the workup of ADHD. Elia, Gulotta, Rose, Marin, and Rapoport (1994) measured thyroid functions in 54 boys with ADHD and compared them to a control group. There were no statistically significant differences between the controls and ADHD subjects in terms of T_3, T_4, or TSH; none of the ADHD boys had values in the abnormal range. R. E. Weiss et al. (1993) evaluated thyroid function in 277 ADHD children and found that 14 (5.4%) had mildly abnormal thyroid functions. This is a higher rate of abnormality than is found in the general population of children, but these authors do not state whether the subjects showed any clinical signs of thyroid disease. Furthermore, most of the abnormalities were quite borderline and there was no distinct pattern of abnormalities: 5 subjects showed elevated TSH but normal free thyroxine index (FT_4I) values, 3 subjects had elevated TSH *and* FT_4I, and 5 subjects had *low* FT_4I values. Without more information about the clinical state of the children, the data do not provide justification for routine screening of ADHD children for thyroid disease.

Generalized Resistance to Thyroid Hormone

Generalized resistance to thyroid hormone (GRTH) needs to be distinguished from hypothyroidism. Congenital hypothyroidism presents in infancy with lethargy, feeding problems, skin mottling, and macroglossia. Without treatment, severe developmental delays ensue. Congenital hyperthyroidism is identified by early screening in the nursery. Later in childhood or adolescence, patients may acquire hypothyroidism, though this is quite rare (<1% of the childhood population). Chronic lymphocytic (Hashimoto's) thyroiditis is the most common cause, though in past years ablation of thyroid through iodine exposure was also a factor. Acquired hypothyroidism in children presents with symptoms similar to those seen in adults: lethargy, cold intolerance, low pulse, decreased appetite, and depression. In addition children show delayed growth and puberty, with an increased upper extremity to lower extremity ratio. T_3 and T_4 are low with increased TSH, unless some factor such as a hypothalamic tumor destroys the capacity to produce TSH, leading to "secondary" hypothyroidism (LaFranchi, 1982). In contrast, GRTH is caused by mutations in the human thyroid receptor ß (hTRß) gene located on chromosome 3 (Hodin, Lazar, & Wintman, 1989; Usala, Bale, & Gesundheit, 1988; Usala, Tennyson, & Bale, 1990). To date, 30 mutations in the amino acid sequence of the hTRß gene have been identified, all of these in either exon 9 or 10 (Mixon et al., 1992; Takeda, Weiss, & Refetoff, 1992). (When DNA is translated into mRNA, the mRNA is cleaved into several pieces that are then spliced together before the mRNA leaves the nucleus. The pieces of mRNA that form the final mRNA are termed *exons,* whereas those fragments that remain behind are referred to as *introns.*) The disease is inherited in an autosomal dominant fashion (Magner, Petrick, Menezes-Ferreira, Stelling, & Weintraub, 1986); as a result of the mutation, thyroid receptors in both the peripheral tissues and the pituitary do not respond to normal levels of T_3 and T_4. Subsequently, T_4 cannot inhibit the production of TSH. Patients do not usually have full-blown hypothyroidism but may have goiter and mild hypothyroid symptoms (DeGroot, 1995). Laboratory findings in GRTH show high T_3 and T_4 with normal or inappropriately normal or elevated TSH (Hauser et al., 1993)

Mixson et al. (1992) examined language abilities in 13 kindreds with GRTH. They found an excess of speech and language delays in these kindreds: those with mutations in exon 9 were particularly likely to have low Verbal IQs and articulation defects. While these authors did not report the percentages of their patients with ADHD, they stated that ADHD was present "in most of the kindreds." Hauser et al. (1993) systematically examined the prevalence of ADHD in 104 subjects from 18 families with GRTH. The subjects with GRTH, despite having much higher T_3, T_4, and TSH levels, did not have disturbed basal metabolic rates. ADHD was more prevalent in the subjects with GRTH than in those without the disorder in both the adult (50% vs. 7%) and the child (70% vs. 20%) samples. ADHD was found to some degree among kindred mutations in exon 9 or 10. These results received widespread publicity, and Ciaranello (1993) argued that routine thyroid evaluations should be part of the workup for ADHD. He suggested that "treatment of the underlying thyroid disorder could reduce or eliminate the need for stimulant medication" (p. 1039). Since then, clinicians have received many questions about this, particularly as the general public does not yet understand the difference between classical hypothyroidism and GRTH. At the present time, however, there is no agreed-upon treatment for GRTH. While some children with GRTH may be administered supraphysiological doses of thyroid hormone, this approach has not been extensively studied (DeGroot, 1995). Ciaranello's (1993) proposal was probably premature, as several follow-up studies have showed.

As we noted earlier, R. E. Weiss et al. (1993) examined thyroid function in 277 ADHD children. While some nonspecific abnormalities were detected, none of the children had laboratory findings suggestive of GRTH. Not one of the children in the Elia et al. (1994) sample were found to have GRTH. Clearly, GRTH is not a common cause of ADHD, and a thyroid workup would only be important in children with a family history of GRTH. An accurate history, however, is often difficult to obtain because of the folklore of a "low thyroid" being responsible for generalized malaise or fatigue. Thus many families may report that an older relative had "thyroid problems" without knowing specifics. The exact relationship of GRTH to ADHD is not clear. Since the thyroid hormone affects the responsiveness of tissues to catecholamines, and since catecholamines are clearly involved in the pathophysiology of ADHD, Hauser et al. (1993) suggested that in individuals with GRTH, catecholamine neurotransmitter function is down-regulated. They also suggested that fetal brain development may be impaired by decreased responsiveness to thyroid hormone. Finally, a recent study did not confirm the linkage of ADHD and GRTH, but it did find low intelligence to be more prevalent in family members affected with GRTH (R. E. Weiss et al., 1994). Further study of the issue is needed, but at present there is no indication for routine thyroid testing in the workup of ADHD.

ADHD AND DIET

Everyone remembers the enthusiasm with which the Feingold diet (Feingold, 1974) was greeted in the mid-1970s. At the time, stimulant treatment had become more common, and there was a great deal of suspicion about it in the public mind and in the lay press. The environmental movement had begun to flower, such that the public was predisposed to think that "chemicals" in food or water could cause illnesses of many types. Feingold was a pediatric allergist who noticed that some food additives were similar in structure to salicylates (such as aspirin). As a result, he hypothesized that hyperactivity was a form of salicylate toxicity in genetically predisposed children. While Feingold himself never performed any studies of his diet, other researchers generated a large body of work that examined both the acute and chronic effects of food additives on behavior (Stare, Whelan, & Sheridan, 1980). In an early study, Conners, Goyette, Southwick, Lees, and Andrilonis (1976) observed the behavior of hyperactive children on additive-free and normal diets in a double-blind fashion. Five of the 15 children were thought to be improved on the diet, but a more rigorous follow-up study failed to confirm the results (Goyette, Conners, & Petti, 1978). Harley and colleagues (Harley, Ray, et al., 1978; Harley, Matthews, & Eichman, 1978) conducted several experiments. In one set of studies, children were on an additive-free diet or a control diet in a crossover study; no effect of the diet was found on neuropsychological tests or teacher ratings of behavior. Only 4 of the 36 subjects were rated as improved overall (Harley, Ray, et al., 1978). In the second experiment, children whose parents regarded them as sensitive to additives were fed a large amount of additive or a placebo in a double-blind challenge design. Even in these "sensitive" children, there was no significant effect of the food additive relative to placebo on either behavior ratings or psychological tests (Harley, Matthews, & Eichman, 1978).

Perhaps the most definitive tests of the Feingold diet was carried out by Gross, Tofanelli, Butzirus, and Snodgrass (1987). Thirty-nine children with ADHD and learning disorders were enrolled in a special summer camp where the researchers were in complete control of the children's diet. Since no outside food was available, no cheating was possible. Children were placed on the Feingold diet for 1 week, then on a regular diet for the second week. Children were videotaped during each week and the tapes reviewed by research assistants who were unaware of which diet each child was on. Ratings of motor restlessness, disorganized behavior, and inappropriate behaviors showed no differences between the diets; there was not even a trend toward a positive effect of the diet. Thus, it may be stated conclusively that the Feingold diet is ineffective in the treatment of ADHD.

Sugar and caffeine are also implicated as commonly causing ADHD, but here again the evidence is lacking. Gross (1984) was the first to test the sugar hypothesis in a controlled fashion. Fifty children whose mothers stated that sugar made their child more agitated were given a glass of lemonade containing either sucrose or saccharin in a double-blind, crossover fashion. After drinking the lemonade, the parent observed the child's behavior for several hours and rated him/her on a scale from –5 (much worse) to +5 (much better). None of the 50 subjects showed any consistent response to the sucrose. Recently, Wolraich et al. (1994) performed an extensive, well-controlled trial of sucrose, saccharine, and aspartame in 25 normal preschoolers and 23 children felt by their parents to be sensitive to sugar. For 3 weeks the whole family ate a diet free of food additives, artificial food coloring, and preservatives. In each of these 3 weeks, a different sweetener was used: sucrose, aspartame, or saccharine (placebo). The researchers performed an extensive battery of behavioral and cognitive tests on the children in each of the 3 weeks. None of the tests showed any clinically meaningful changes as a function of which sweetener the child ingested. Also, contrary to popular opinion, caffeine does not impair attention in either ADHD or normal children (Bernstein et al., 1994).

ADHD AND ALLERGY

The results presented in the previous section do not entirely end the debate, as attention has shifted from the dispute as to whether foods or food additives are a general cause of ADHD to the argument over the hypothesis that there is a relationship between allergy and ADHD. In this theory, popularized by Rapp (1991), at least some ADHD children may have their behavior caused by allergic reactions to food or other substances, and each child is allergic to a different agent. Thus, the theory's proponents argue, a study that looks at only one allergen in a large group of ADHD children will always be negative. One must find out which *particular* substance the child is allergic to and eliminate that from the diet. Moreover, Rapp (1991) ascribes to the view that other allergic symptoms such as uticaria (hives), allergic shiners, asthma, and rhinitis are more common in ADHD children.

In some areas, pediatric allergists advocate skin testing to determine the item (or items) to which the child is allergic. The offending item(s) can be removed from the diet and "desensitization" pursued by injecting diluted amounts of the allergen(s) into the skin. Before examining the data on this matter, it is necessary to review some basic aspects of food allergy. A distinction must be made between *food allergy,* which is immunologically mediated, and *food intolerance,* which is not. For instance, lactose intolerance (which leads to gastrointestinal distress) is caused by a genetic lack of the enzyme that breaks down lactose. In an immunological reaction, the patient forms immunoglobulin E (IgE) antibodies to the allergen. The IgE then binds with high affinity to the mast cells and basophils in the blood and tissues; these cells release a series of potent chemical mediators such as histamine, proteoglycans, and leukotrienes. These agents produce the specific allergic reaction, such as rhinitis, wheezing, or uticaria. Anyone with allergies can attest to the fact that such symptoms make one miserable; a child with any of the above symptoms might be irritable or overactive as an indirect effect of the allergy. Whether allergens can produce ADHD behavior in the absence of any other allergic symptoms is highly questionable, as we shall see.

What are children most likely to be allergic to? Metcalfe, Sampson, and Simon (1995) gives a comprehensive overview of this subject. Among "natural foods" the most common allergies include those to cow's milk (primarily to the whey and casein proteins), chicken egg (albumin), peanuts, soybeans, and wheat. Allergies have been reported to nearly every food, and most allergic children may react to multiple foods. In the area of behavior, parents rarely report that their children are allergic to vegetables or fruits, despite the fact that these substances all contain proteins to which the immune system can react. Parents are far more likely to report that the child is allergic to foods containing "additives," meaning processed foods such as candy bars or "fast foods." This raises an interesting issue as to the psychology of diet and behavior, as parents often wish to restrict those foods that their children most enjoy. We will return to this issue later. Food additives that have been identified as causing allergic reactions include sulfites, monosodium glutamate (MSG), tartrazine, and azo dyes. These are added to foods to either enhance coloring or preservation. One of the most common of the food additives, tartrazine (a yellow dye), did not produce ADHD symptoms in a *even one* subject in a double-blind placebo-controlled trial, even though parents of every subject gave a history of their child reacting negatively to the additive (David, 1987).

If ADHD is truly caused by food allergy, then one should find a higher prevalence of allergy among ADHD children, as well as a greater number of abnormal allergy laboratory findings in ADHD individuals. Three common laboratory measures are used in the assessment of allergy: serum IgE (a nonspecific test), skin testing, and allergen-specific IgE antibody tests. The most common example of the latter is the radioimmunoassay test (RAST), in which allergens (i.e., molds) are exposed to the patient's serum. If the patient has had an immunological reaction to the allergen, his/her serum will contain IgE antibodies that bind to the allergen; these can be detected by using a radioactive probe that binds to the patient's IgE. In skin testing, a small amount of the allergen is injected into the patient's skin and the area is observed for hives or other eruptions. Skin testing has been shown to be a very good means of detecting whether a child is allergic to an airborne substance (pollen, mold), but it is useless for detecting food items to which the child might react (Ferguson, 1995; Fireman, 1995; Jewett, Fein, & Greenberg, 1990). Allergists determine food allergy by first placing the child on a very restrictive diet. If the allergic symptoms disappear, then possible offending foods or additives are introduced through a double-blind placebo-controlled food challenge (Bock et al., 1988). If the allergic symptoms reappear reliably only when the food is given but are absent when the placebo is administered, the patient can positively be said to be allergic to that food. A review of the diet shows that it is quite bland and avoids most of the foods that children love. Do ADHD children, who are noncompliant with adults in so many aspects of their lives, willingly submit to these diets? Do children cheat on these diets? This is an issue that has never been researched but bears looking into.

More to the point, is there a relationship between ADHD and allergy? Roth, Beyreiss, Schlenzka, and Berger (1991) compared 81 allergic children with 71 controls. Parents of children in both groups filled out the Conners Parent Rating Scale, and the children performed a number of tests of attention and impulse control, including a reaction time task and the Matching Familiar Figures Test (MFFT). The allergic children scored significantly higher on the Conners Parent Rating Scale than did the controls: about 15% of the allergic children were scored in the clinical range, as opposed to 4% of the controls. There were no differences on the MFFT, although the allergic children were slower and more variable on the reaction time task, in a manner similar to that of ADHD children. There were a number of weakness in the study, however. Actual diagnoses of ADHD was not made, and a sample of ADHD children were not screened for allergy. If allergy is not more prevalent among ADHD children compared to controls, then allergy cannot be the mechanism that accounts for the ADHD behavior. Furthermore, Roth and colleagues' (1991) allergic group was taken from an allergy clinic and thus subject to sampling bias; McGee, Stanton, and Sears (1993) avoided this difficulty by exploring the hypothesis in a large community and sample.

As part of the Dunedin Health and Development Study, 1,037 children were followed from age 3 to 15. At age 9, all the children were assessed both for allergy and ADHD. ADHD was determined using parent and teacher rating scales as well as the Diagnostic Interview Schedule for Children (DISC). Allergy was defined as the presence of rhinitis, asthma, eczema, or urticaria. ADHD children were not more likely to have allergic disorders, and ADHD was not overrepresented among the children with allergies. More significantly, there was absolutely no relationship between ADHD symptoms and the child's reaction to atopic weals on skin testing, nor was there any relationship between ADHD symptoms and serum IgE levels.

Recently, several groups (Boris & Mandel, 1994; Carter et al., 1993; Egger, Carter, Graham, Gumley, & Soothill, 1985) have suggested that food allergies cause ADHD and have advocated restricted diets to treat behavioral problems. Egger et al. (1985) selected 76 hyperactive children who responded to an open trial of the oligoantigenic diet. Individual foods were then introduced in an open fashion by the parents at home to determine if the child's behavior deteriorated. If the parents said the child's behavior was worse, this was accepted as evidence that the child was allergic. Forty-eight foods were or additives incriminated, mostly consisting of food colorings and preservatives. Twenty-eight of the children were then placed on a double-blind placebo-controlled protocol in which the parents gave the child a placebo or active capsule containing the "allergen." Since most of the children were "allergic" to multiple substances, it is not clear how the investigators chose the particular substance that was used for each child's double-blind trial. Parents and clinicians filled out the Conners Abbreviated Rating Scale, and a psychologist also rated behavior during a testing session. Actometric (activity-level) measures and the MFFT were also performed on the children—both those taking the active capsule and those taking the placebo. While the parents and clinicians rated the child as more disturbed when he/she was exposed to the supposedly allergenic substance compared to the placebo, the objective measures of ADHD such as the actometric test and the MFFT showed no changes in response to the "allergens." Two other studies using a similar design (Boris & Mandel, 1994; Carter et al., 1993) also showed that children were rated as more hyperactive during the active administration of the agent as opposed to the placebo, at least according to parent ratings.

There are, however, many problems with these studies in addition to those already noted. Parents who volunteer their children for allergy treatment of ADHD tend to be strong proponents of it, as are the practitioners; thus the need for tight control of the studies is mandatory. All of the studies used uncontrolled parent reports to determine which children reacted to foods in order to select their samples. Even during the double-blind protocols, the parents administered the foods at home. Since these children were attending allergy clinics, many did have bona fide allergic disorders such as asthma or hives. Such children might become irritable or uncooperative when such symptoms are provoked by the food, and parents rate this as ADHD behavior. It also seems odd that these investigators have found so many children "allergic" to the same additives that many previous double-blind studies clearly showed to be innocuous.

While the preponderance of the evidence does not favor the allergy–ADHD hypothesis, the issue may not yet be completely closed. Further well-controlled studies by investigators not invested in the technique are needed. These studies should place ADHD children with no obvious evidence of allergic disorder on a restricted diet and administer foods or food additives in a double-blind fashion in the laboratory under highly controlled conditions. Ideally, children should be in a hospital or residential setting to prevent any cheating on the diet. This may seem to be a great deal of effort, but the claims of the ADHD–allergy theorists are extreme. They advocate not using a safe, convenient, effective treatment (stimulants), favoring instead a tedious, drawn-out, and expensive allergy assessment. While the issue deserves further study, at present the data do not support the use of diets or allergy procedures in the treatment of ADHD.

ADHD AND ASTHMA

There is ample literature on the psychological effects of asthma on child development (Celano & Geller, 1993). While children with mild asthma generally do not show any unusual psychopathology, high rates of affective disorder have been noted in severe asthmatics; depression has been also been associated with a higher mortality (Miller, 1987). The rate of ADHD or school problems in this population has been less well studied, and the subject is complicated by the fact that asthmatic children take medications that might impair concentration (theophylline, steroids). Furthermore, asthmatic children have higher rates of school absenteeism due to their asthma, which might be expected to negatively impact learning. Celano and Geller (1993) reviewed studies that attempted to tease out variables which influence the children's school performance. They noted that when the effects of socioeconomic status and behavior problems were factored out, the school performance of even severely asthmatic children was not different from that of controls and absenteeism did not have the expected deleterious effect on achievement. As noted earlier, asthma and ADHD do not overlap in excess of that expected by chance (McGee et al., 1993).

There has been a long debate about whether medications used to treat asthma impair learning or affect mood in children. Steroids can induce mild depression and impair memory at higher doses, but there are no reports of ADHD-type symptoms in children treated with these agents (Celano & Geller, 1993). For many years, clinical lore suggested that the bronchodilator theophylline can induce hyperactivity or anxiety. Several controlled trials have not borne this out, however. Rappaport et al. (1989) performed a double-blind crossover study of placebo and theophylline in 17 asthmatic children; no effects of the active drug were found on multiple measures of learning and attention. Schlieper et al. (1991) studied 31 asthmatics using a similar design; no overall differences were found between those children on placebo and those on theophylline in terms of parent ratings of behavior. Children also did not rate their own affect as different on the placebo relative to the theophylline. These authors did note that some individual children showed increased problem behaviors on the medication, but these were the children with preexisting attentional or behavior problems. It seems unlikely that theophylline will induce ADHD behavior in a normal asthmatic child, but it may not be a good choice for treating asthma in a youngster with preexisting ADHD. The issue may be moot, however, as theophylline is used less nowadays in the treatment of asthma in favor of mast cell stabilizers such as cromolyn or steroid inhalers. Systemic side effects are rare with these agents.

ADHD AND OTITIS MEDIA

An association between ADHD and ear infections has emerged that is not generally commented upon. Forty-four children in a research day care center were studied over 3 years; physical examinations accurately documented episodes of otitis media. Behavior measures were taken both during the kindergarten (Feagans, Sanyal, Henderson, Collier, & Appelbaum, 1987) and the third grade (Roberts et al., 1989). At both time points, children with a greater number of episodes of otitis media were rated by observers as showing more off-task behavior and less independence than children with fewer ear infections. In children referred to clinics for learning or behavior problems, the number of ear infections correlated significantly both with a diagnosis of ADHD (as opposed to learning disorders) and with the severity of the ADHD (Adesman,

Altshuler, Lipkin, & Walco, 1990; Hagerman & Falkenstein, 1987). Silva, Kirkland, Simpson, Stewart, and Williams (1982) examined the behavior of 47 children with bilateral otitis media to that of 355 controls in an epidemiological study. The presence or absence of otitis media in these subjects was established by rigorous otological and audiological examination. Children with otitis media were not different from controls in terms of socioeconomic status or parenting ability. They were, however, significantly lower in motor development and IQ (107 for controls vs. 100 in children with otitis). A variety of observers rated the children with bilateral otitis as significantly more hyperactive, aggressive, and off task than controls. The nature of the link between otitis media and ADHD behaviors is not clear. Does early hearing loss secondary to the otitis impair the development of attention? Do otitis media and ADHD share a common genetic vulnerability? It is also not known if aggressive treatment of the ear infections reduces the likelihood of ADHD, though most of the children in the above studies had been appropriately treated for their otitis. The issue clearly deserves further study.

ADHD AND CHRONIC ILLNESS

What is the impact of serious illness on the development of attention and learning? A large body of literature examines the effects of chronic illness on the psychological development of children with diabetes or cystic fibrosis, but ADHD has not been studied in these populations (Mrazek, 1994). In contrast, an extensive body of literature has examined the attentional and learning abilities of children who survive cancers, particularly acute lymphocytic leukemia (ALL). ALL was almost uniformly fatal in the 1950s, whereas today nearly 90% of children are in remission after the first course of chemotherapy. Leukemic cells can invade the CNS and become the focus of a relapse, so that most children with ALL receive a prophylactic course of cranial irradiation or intrathecal (injected directly into the spinal canal) methotrexate. These treatments can cause damage to the white matter as well as cortical atrophy, so concerns have been raised that such children will suffer neuropsychological impairment (Brouwers, Riccardi, Fedio, & Poplack, 1985).

As a result, a large number of pediatric oncology centers perform intellectual, academic, and neuropsychological assessment of ALL survivors; the relevant literature has been extensively reviewed by J. M. Williams and Davis (1986). They point out that methodological issues prevent firm conclusions about what the long-term effects of ALL treatment are on behavior and learning, stating that "the resulting pattern of findings is not clear cut. Some studies have found intellectual deficits and others did not. In addition, those that found deficits are not consistent with each other and do not suggest a common neuropathological mechanism to explain the deficits" (p. 114). It is difficult to cull from these studies specific information about ADHD or other behavior problems in ALL survivors, though it has been suggested that attentional deficits are a problem in this population (Brouwers et al., 1985; Brouwers, Riccardi, Poplack, & Fedio, 1984; Goff, Anderson, & Cooper, 1980). Most studies, however, did not look at the prevalence of ADHD defined by clinical interview, but rather assessed children with intellectual testing or rating scales and inferred the presence of absence of attentional problems. Goff et al. (1980) found high distractibility among 37 long-term survivors compared to newly diagnosed leukemic children (who had not yet had radiation treatment), but no normal control group was included in the study. Distractibility was inferred from poor performance on an auditory tasks which is highly dependent on attention. No behavior rating scales were obtained. Brouwers et al. (1984, 1985) used the "attention-switching task" (part of a neuropsychological test battery) to compare ALL survivors subdivided by computed tomography (CT) scan findings. No normal controls were used. ALL survivors with either atrophy or calcifications on CT scan performed much more poorly on the attention task than did survivors with normal scans. It is not possible, however, to diagnose ADHD based on neuropsychological tests alone. A group of 183 cancer survivors was assessed 2 years or more after treatment; 17% of the subjects had "externalizing" scores on the Child Behavior Checklist in the abnormal range, but another study of 48 survivors found only 10% of the children were in the clinical range on the hyperactivity factor of the Personality Inventory for Children (Sanger, Copeland, & Davidson, 1991). Peers of ALL survivors do not, on average, rate them as any more aggressive or disruptive than normal classmates (Noll, LeRoy, Bukowski, Rogosch, & Kulkarni, 1991).

Thus we cannot conclude definitely that ADHD is a significant neuropsychological sequela of treatment of childhood ALL, but the issue is not closed. At least a subgroup perform poorly on neuropsychological tests of attention, and a clinician serving as the psychiatric consultant to a pediatric oncology unit should be aware of this. It is possible that an increased risk of ADHD may yet be found among these children. Poor school behavior should not always be assumed to be a psychological reaction to the cancer; if the child meets the criteria for ADHD, stimulant treatment is generally advisable. Interestingly, stimulants have uses in pediatric oncology apart from ADHD. Large doses of opioid analgesics are commonly used in pediatric cancer patients to control severe pain. Such dosing often results in somnolence, impairing the child's interaction with family members. Yee and Berde (1994) reported on 11 adolescent cancer patients who received stimulant treatment in combination with opioid analgesics. Patients were treated either with methylphenidate (mean dose, 14.6 mg/day) or dextroamphetamine (mean dose, 6.9 mg/day). These doses were halved for administration twice a day and thus were low considering that this was a sample with a mean age of 15.5 years. Five of the 11 patients showed decreased somnolence and increased social interactions. One patient developed hallucinations. Recently, stimulants were shown to be superior to placebo in improving cognitive function in adult cancer patients receiving narcotics for pain (Bruera, Miller, MacMillan, & Kuehn, 1992). Thus the psychiatric consultant should consider the use of stimulants in the pediatric cancer patient suffering excessive sedation or cognitive impairment from narcotic medication.

12

Learning Disorders

There is probably more confusion over the comorbidity of learning disorders (or disabilities; LDs) and ADHD than any other topic we will address. At meetings for parents and teachers, it is not uncommon for people to ask, "Is ADHD a learning disability?" Some clinicians assume that *all* children with ADHD have some kind of LD. (Not true, as we shall see.) This concept may have originated in the nomenclature of "minimal brain dysfunction," which included both children with learning problems and those with hyperactivity. But what percentage of ADHD children do in fact have LDs? What types of LD do they have? In what way are comorbid ADHD/LD children different from those with no learning problems? Can ADHD itself "cause" a LD? Do LD symptoms mimic ADHD symptoms in a child who in fact does not have ADHD? All of these questions are predicated on the definition of the various LDs, which is not as straightforward an issue as it seems.

OVERVIEW OF LEARNING DISORDERS

In essence, a LD is the failure to develop an academic skill at the "expected" level despite adequate intelligence and education. This basic definition of LD was laid out by U.S. Public Law 94-142 in 1975 and forms the basis of the DSM-IV definitions of LD (see Table 12.1) Not included in DSM-IV, but an important entity as it relates to attentional functioning, is the nonverbal learning disabilities (NVLD) syndrome (Rourke, 1989), which we discuss later in this chapter. The major DSM-IV LD

TABLE 12.1. DSM-IV Learning Disorders

Learning disorders
- Reading disorders
- Mathematics disorders
- Disorder of written expression

Motor skills disorder
- Developmental coordination disorder

Communication disorders
- Expressive language disorder
- Mixed receptive–expressive disorder
- Phonological disorder[a]
- Stuttering

[a] Formerly developmental articulation disorder.

definitions (reading, mathematics, written expression, and communication disorders) have three features in common: (1) the ability as measured by a standard achievement test must be "substantially" below that predicted by IQ; (2) there is "significant" interference with academic achievement of skills of daily living; and (3) if a sensory deficit is present, the achievement levels of the child are deficient to a degree beyond what would be predicted by it. That is, a blind child can be reading disabled if he/she fails to read (e.g., using Braille) at a level typical for other blind children of the same intelligence.

LDs are defined in clinical practice by showing there is a "significant" discrepancy between a measurement of intelligence (i.e., IQ score) and the child's academic ability as measured by a standard achievement test, such as the Wide Range Achievement Test (WRAT). Thus, whether a child is LD or not depends on the type of test chosen (different IQ or achievement tests will yield somewhat different measures of intelligence or achievement) and on the method of determining what constitutes a "significant discrepancy." Most achievement tests give results in terms of standard scores in which 100 represents the mean of the population and each 15 points is a standard deviation above or below that mean. This allows easy comparison to IQ scores, which are scaled in the same manner. The three methods of defining LDs used in both research and clinical practice are shown in Table 2.2. Method 1 is the most commonly used: the child's score on the achievement test must be at least 15 points below the IQ score. In method 2, a more stringent definition requires that the child's standard score be 2 standard deviations below the IQ. Method 3 is less commonly used: the child achievement score must

TABLE 12.2. Effect of Different Definitions of LD on Clinical Outcome

	Child 1	Child 2	Child 3
IQ test	100	120	85
Reading score	70	100	80
RD or not by method:			
1. Reading 1 *SD* below IQ	Yes	Yes	No
2. Reading 2 *SD* below IQ	Yes	No	No
3. Reading 1 *SD* below IQ and reading score below 85	Yes	No	No

Note. Each 10-point difference in IQ or standard score on an achievement test represents a standard deviation.

be a standard deviation below his/her IQ and that achievement score must be below 85, indicating true impairment. As can be seen in Table 12.2, the various methods diagnose children differently. Child 1, with a quite severe discrepancy, is diagnosed LD by all three methods. Methods 2 and 3 tend to underidentify as LD bright children who are only achieving at grade level when their IQs would predict above average performance. On the other hand, method 1 overidentifies bright children who are simply underachievers and have no "neurologically based" LD. For instance, Barkley (1990) found that 21% of normal control children who had no academic problems were diagnosed as LD in reading using method 1; 35% of them were diagnosed as LD in math! All of the methods are problematic for child 3, whose IQ is in the low average range. Technically, the child is achieving appropriately, but clearly the child's academic progress will be poor. Rutter and Yule (1975) would refer to child 1 as having specific reading retardation; child 3, in contrast, would be defined as having general reading backwardness. Different prevalences of these two conditions have been found as a function of psychosocial factors. General reading backwardness was found in 7% of the middle class children in the Isle of Wight study and in 20% of inner London poor children. In contrast, IQ-discrepant specific reading disorder was found in 4% of Isle of Wight children and 10% of London youngsters (Rutter et al., 1974). As Hinshaw (1992a) points out, this suggests a greater role for psychosocial factors in general reading backwardness.

Reading disorder (RD) is the most common and best studied of the LDs; RD accounts for 80% of the children diagnosed as LD (Cardon et al., 1994; B. A. Shaywitz, Fletcher, & Shaywitz, 1995). Traditionally, RD has been thought to disproportionately affect males, but this may have reflected referral biases in earlier studies. Epidemiological studies show that 8.8% of boys and 6.5% of girls meet criteria for RD (S. E. Shaywitz, Shaywitz, Fletcher, & Escobar, 1990). There is now widespread agreement among researchers that the fundamental deficit in RD is in the phonological processes and not in any gross visual–spatial deficit (Pennington, 1991; B. A. Shaywitz et al., 1995). That is, RD children do not have difficulty visualizing letters or words; rather, they have difficulty recognizing that letters and combinations of letters represent different sounds (Vellutino, 1991). Their "word attack skills" (often referred to as decoding) are poor; they are unable to sound out words very easily. They rely too heavily on "sight" reading, memorizing the shape of words, which leads to errors (reading "rat" for "sat"). They are unable to sound out nonsense words. The gross receptive and expressive language skills of RD children are intact, but they show subtle deficits in spoken language (Pennington, 1991). These children are slow to learn their alphabet, have early articulation deficits, and have trouble naming objects as well as difficulty remembering verbal sequences. Debate has centered on whether IQ-discrepant RD children (like child 1 in the example given in Table 7.2) have a qualitatively different deficit in phonological processes from those children with general reading backwardness or whether poor readers all share a similar deficit. The latter appears to be the case; extensive studies of poor readers have not revealed any neuropsychological differences between these two groups in phonologic processes (S. E. Shaywitz, Escobar, & Shaywitz, 1992; Stanovich & Siegel, 1994; B. A. Shaywitz, Fletcher, Holahan, & Shaywitz, 1992).

Much less research has been done on the other LDs listed in Table 12.1. Issues related to mathematics disorder (MD) will be deferred until the discussion of NVLD in a later section. Children with language disorders have more severe deficits of receptive and expressive language that impair communication with others in daily living. Beyond DSM-IV, language disorders are classified by level of language processing and input–output stages (Pennington, 1991) Language processing includes not only phonology but syntax (using grammar and the rules of language) as well as semantics (extracting meaning from language). A discussion of the subtypes of language disorders is beyond the scope of this chapter, and in any case there is at this time no agreed upon method of such subtyping. Filipek (1995) reviewed magnetic resonance imaging (MRI) studies in dyslexia. A variety of abnormalities have been reported in dyslexics, including differences in cerebral hemisphere asymmetry, lack of the normal asymmetry (left > right) of the planum temporale, and corpus callosum abnormalities. The studies reviewed all involved small numbers of subjects and used widely varying methodologies; in none of these studies have findings been consistently replicated. Thus at present there is no clear-cut indication that neuroimaging studies in children with suspected LD will be any more diagnostically conclusive than they are in children with ADHD, though these techniques remain promising research tools.

Table 12.3 shows studies that have examined the prevalence of LDs in children with ADHD. As can be seen, there are marked discrepancies across studies depending on the sample and method of assessing LDs. Three studies (August & Holmes, 1984; Dalby, 1985; Halperin, Gittelman, Klein, & Rudel, 1984) suggest the prevalence of RD in ADHD is not higher than that in the general population. All others studies indicate that the rate of LDs in reading, spelling, and arithmetic is higher in ADHD children than in controls, but the studies are too inconsistent to enable a precise percentage to be given. Cantwell and Baker (1991) have examined the question from a different angle, looking at the development of psychiatric disorder in children with early speech and language impairments. About half of a sample of 600 speech- or lan-

TABLE 12.3. Overlap of ADHD and LD

Study	Method	Reading	Spelling	Arithmetic
McGee et al. (1984a, 1984b)	IQ discrepancy	Hyp[a]	19%	
		Hyp + CD	37%	
August & Holmes (1984)	IQ discrepancy	Hyp	7%	
		Hyp + CD	8%	
Dalby (1985)	IQ discrepancy	ADHD	9%	
S. E. Shaywitz & Shaywitz (1988)	IQ discrepancy	ADHD	11%	
Halperin et al. (1984)	Combined	Hyp	9%	
Barkley (1990)	IQ discrepancy	41%	60%	60%
	Achievement only	21%	26%	29%
	Combined	19%	24%	26%
Dykman & Ackerman (1991)	Combined	ADDH	53%	
		ADHD/CD	34%	
		ADD[b]	37%	
Frick et al. (1991)	IQ discrepancy		16%	21%
	Combined		8%	12%
Semrud-Clikeman et al. (1992)	IQ discrepancy[c]		38%	55%
	IQ discrepancy[d]		23%	30%
	Combined		15%	33%

[a]Hyp = hyperactive.

[b]ADD = attention-deficit disorder.

[c]WRAT score > 10 standard score points below Full Scale IQ.

[d]WRAT score > 20 standard score points below Full Scale IQ.

guage-impaired children (mean age, 5.6 years) were followed up 4–5 years later at a mean age of 9.1 years: 60% of the sample had a psychiatric diagnosis, with ADHD the most common, representing 37% of the sample. In those speech- or language-impaired children who still met criteria for an LD, 79% had a psychiatric diagnoses, ADHD again being the most common (53%). Similarly, while Shaywitz and Shaywitz (1988) found that while only 11% of ADHD children had an LD, fully a third of LD children have ADHD. Thus a minority of children with ADHD may have LDs, but half or more of LD children may meet criteria for ADHD. The question facing clinicians is whether a child with an LD may develop a "secondary" ADHD simply because of the learning problems. On the other hand, perhaps there is no such thing as "secondary" ADHD and the child is best diagnosed as comorbid ADHD/LD. The first belief, if true, would mean that there is a subgroup of children who would not benefit from stimulant treatment or for whom remedial education addressing their LDs would eliminate or reduce the ADHD symptoms. If, however, ADHD/LD children are truly comorbid, then stimulant treatment might be critical to allow the child to benefit from tutoring or special education. What do the studies show?

ADHD AND READING DISORDERS

How do children with both ADHD and RD (ADHD/RD) differ from those with ADHD alone? This question is complicated by the fact that early studies which compared "ADHD" children to "LD" children did not control for the comorbidity discussed above. Thus many of ADHD subjects had LD and vice versa. It is not surprising that so many of these studies seem to find that ADHD and LD children were quite similar. Only in recent years have carefully controlled studies been performed that compare the groups of most interest: (1) children who meet criteria for ADHD but do not have any LD by psychometric testing; (2) LD children who do not have ADHD (i.e., who have Conners ratings in the normal range); and (3) children with comorbid ADHD and LD. When samples of pure ADHD and LD children are compared to each other on neuropsychological measures, there is no overlap of deficits (McGee, Williams, Moffitt, & Anderson, 1989; Pennington, Groisser, & Welsh, 1993). That is, ADHD children are impaired on measures of impulse control but perform as well as controls on phonological tests; conversely, dyslexic children whose Conners ratings are in the normal range do well on attentional tests but perform poorly on language measures—both findings confirming that ADHD and RD are distinct entities.

An early study showed that ADHD children with and without RD did not differ from each other in severity of hyperactivity, aggression, or anxiety (Halperin et al., 1984). The ADHD/RD groups performed worse on the MFFT than did the ADHD-only group, but this finding was not of great clinical significance. Dykman and Ackerman (1991) have performed extensive studies of ADHD children with and without RD: 122 ADHD children were studied; 64 of these met criteria for RD. A child with RD was defined as one having a WRAT reading score of less than 90 and that score also being at least 10 points below the Full Scale WISC-R IQ. On all measures of ADHD, the ADHD and ADHD/RD groups were exactly the same. Teachers and parents *did not* rate ADHD/RD children as any more inattentive or hyperactive than ADHD children without RD. The two groups were similar to each other in performance on the Gordon Diagnostic Test, a version of the Continuous Performance Test (CPT). McGee et al. (1989) compared groups of ADHD, ADHD/RD, RD, and control children on a number of neuropsychological measures. The two RD groups, regardless of the presence or absence of ADHD, showed impaired performance on an auditory verbal learning test. ADHD children without RD were not different from controls on this measure. The comorbidity of ADHD in RD does not appear to worsen the reading impairments of RD children. The Wisconsin Card Sort Test, a putative measure of executive function, did not distinguish any of the groups. Korkman and Pesonen (1994) compared ADHD, ADHD/RD, and RD groups on neuropsychological measures. Again, ADHD children without RD had a normal performance on language tests, showing impairment on measures of inhibition and control, whereas the RD children showed the reverse pattern. Visual inspection of the above authors' data suggests that the ADHD/RD children had more severe deficits in selective auditory attention and visual–motor integration than did the other groups, but this was not tested statistically.

Pennington et al. (1993) also contrasted RD, ADHD, and ADHD/RD children and controls on various neuropsychological measures of phonological ability and executive function. Consistent with the findings of McGee et al. (1989), ADHD children with normal reading performed just as well as controls on the tests of phonological ability but were impaired on executive function measures. RD children without ADHD performed as well as controls on these measures but had marked impairments on the language measures. Interestingly, the ADHD/RD group did not show deficits on the Wisconsin Card Sort Test or the Hanoi Tower but was deficient on phonological tests. Pennington et al. (1993) suggested that the comorbid ADHD/RD group might have a primary RD with secondary attentional problems. It would not be surprising if RD children, not understanding or having serious difficulty with written material, became distracted and uninterested in schoolwork.

Teachers might view this behavior as representing ADHD. This would suggest that there is a danger that RD children might be misdiagnosed as having ADHD, but several factors argue against this being a common problem in clinical practice.

First, only one the aforementioned studies (Pennington et al., 1993) found that the ADHD/RD group did not show attentional impairment. The Wisconsin Card Sort Test, the principal measure of executive function used in that study, has yielded inconsistent results in other studies of executive function in ADHD (Barkley, Grodzinsky, & DuPaul, 1992). Secondly, if a large portion of the children diagnosed as having ADHD/RD did not in fact have ADHD, one would expect these LD-only children to have responded more poorly to stimulants, as it has been well established that stimulants are not effective in children with pure LDs (Gittelman-Klein & Klein, 1976). Dykman and Ackerman (1991) explored exactly this issue, comparing the response of ADHD and ADHD/RD children to low and high doses of methylphenidate in a double-blind placebo-controlled fashion. *There was no difference between the groups: the ADHD/RD children had a response to the stimulant just as robust as that of the non-RD ADHD group.* This clearly argues against the existence of a large population of RD children who are being misdiagnosed as having ADHD. Other studies regarding learning and stimulants will be reviewed below.

RD does not appear to be more or less prevalent in ADHD as a function of hyperactivity (Barkley, DuPaul, & McMurray, 1990; de Quiros, Kinsbourne, Palmer, & Rufo, 1994; Stanford & Hynd, 1994). As noted in Chapter 6, the "triple" comorbidity of ADHD, CD, and RD is highly predictive of future delinquency (Moffitt, 1990). Recent genetic studies have indicated that ADHD and RD are inherited independently of each other. Faraone and colleagues (1993) examined the prevalence of ADHD and LD in the relatives of children with ADHD. (They combined the various subtypes of LD, but RD was probably the most common form of LD represented.) The ADHD probands were subdivided according to whether they were comorbid for LD or not. ADHD children who were not LD did *not* have an elevated prevalence of LD among their relatives. Children with ADHD/LD had elevated rates of both ADHD and LD in their families relative to a control group, but there was no cosegregation; that is, the ADHD and LD appeared in different relatives. This clearly indicated that the LD and ADHD were inherited separately. Pennington (1991, 1995) has reviewed the genetics of RD: 35–40% of first-degree relatives are affected, with heritability estimates of .5 emerging from twin studies. This means that about 50% of the variability in reading ability is related to genetics. Ability in phonological coding is also highly genetic. Recent twin studies comparing the rates of ADHD and RD in monozygotic and dizygotic twins have shown high heritability for both disorders, with the data clearly suggesting two independent genetic etiologies (Gilger, Pennington, & DeFries, 1992; Gillis, Gilger, Pennington, & DeFries, 1992; Goodman & Stevenson, 1989). This most likely means that the ADHD/RD individual has inherited two separate genetic deficits, though it is possible that there is a distinct ADHD-RD genetic subtype in which one genetic factor leads to the expression of both disorders (Gilger et al., 1992). If such a subtype exists, however, it will account for a minority of ADHD/RD cases; most will be individuals who have inherited the two distinct genetic factors. Recent work has suggested that a marker on chromosome 6 is related to RD (Cardon et al., 1994; Pennington, 1995). If confirmed and found to account for a substantial portion of RD cases, it could be a diagnostic tool for RD in the future.

What happens to RD children as they age? Does the comorbidity of ADHD affect the prognosis of the RD? Kurzweil (1992) followed up 40 children who were rigorously diagnosed with dyslexia at age 7 into their teenage years. Eight of these children were "hyperactive" as determined by notes in their medical records. At follow-up (mean age, 14 years), 40% of the dyslexic subjects were reading at the appropriate grade level (10.1). The remaining 60% of unrecovered dyslexics were still severely delayed, reading at the fifth-grade level. IQ and socioeconomic status were highly predictive of a good outcome: 80% of children with high average IQs recovered, but all of the dyslexic children with low average IQs were still severely impaired. The presence or absence of hyperactivity did not affect the outcome in terms of reading ability. Thus, a codiagnosis of ADHD is not a reason to believe that an RD is more likely to be lifelong, but low IQ is.

PSYCHOPHARMACOTHERAPY FOR COMORBID ADHD/LEARNING DISORDERS

Embedded in this issue are two questions: Does stimulant treatment improve the academic achievement of non-LD ADHD children? If stimulants do not help LD children without ADHD (Gittelman-Klein & Klein, 1976), can they still improve the academic achievement of the ADHD/LD child? It was once thought that stimulants only improved behavior and did not affect academic performance (Barkley & Cunningham, 1978). More recent studies suggest that this is not the case. Pelham et al. (1985) studied 29 ADHD children in a 7-week summer program; 25 of the subjects were below grade level in at least one academic subject. While in the program, each child participated in a double-blind placebo-controlled crossover study of methylphenidate. Marked improvements were noted in mathematics (30%) and reading (18%) productivity were found in the children receiving stimulant relative to those receiving placebo. Increasing doses of methylphenidate correlated with greater gains in academic productivity. Tannock, Schachar, Carr, and Logan (1989) also used a double-blind crossover design to compare methylphenidate to placebo in 12 ADHD children, 8 of whom had LD. Methylphenidate was superior to placebo in improving performance on both a mathematics task and a reading task. Similar results with regard to mathematics were reported by Douglas, Barr, O'Neill, and Britton (1985).

E. Richardson et al. (1988) studied 42 ADHD children, all of whom had RD. All the children received 24 weeks of intensive reading tutoring. They were randomized to receive placebo or one of three doses of methylphenidate in a double-blind parallel groups design. Not only did methylphenidate improve the behavior of the children, but those on stimulant showed much more substantial gains in reading. Indeed, by week 28, children who were good stimulant responders had gained a whole grade level in reading, whereas poor responders gained less than half a grade level. Most likely the children's greater attentiveness while on stimulant allowed them to take advantage of the tutoring. Thus aggressive treatment of the ADHD/LD child's attentional symptoms may be critical for successful remediation of the LD.

Both low (0.3 mg/kg) and high (0.6 mg/kg) doses of methylphenidate increased academic productivity in several domains and accuracy in selected domains for 24 boys with ADHD (11 of whom met discrepancy criteria for either a reading or mathematics disability or both), with no differences between dosages found for any academic measure (C. L. Carlson et al., 1992). A later study using 31 boys with ADHD (17 of whom met discrepancy criteria for an LD in reading, mathematics, written language, or a combination thereof) revealed a similar pattern of findings, with methylphenidate improving rates of seatwork completion, and little incremental value of the high dose over the low dose (Pelham et al., 1993).

It is also noteworthy that none of these studies found beneficial effects of behavior modification on academic performance. Possibly the failure to detect positive effects of the behavioral intervention were at least partially attributable to design elements. The latter two studies used reward procedures to consequate academics and response cost procedures to consequate behavior; given that the behavioral intervention did yield positive effects on behavior, it may be that, within the context of the comprehensive treatment program, the effects of the punishment procedure (for academics) were more salient and therefore stronger than those of the reward procedure (for behavior). Still, the null effects are disappointing. The exploration of behavior therapy effects, either alone or in combination with pharmacological intervention, remains an important area for future investigation.

ADHD AND NONVERBAL LEARNING DISABILITIES

The nonverbal learning disabilities (NVLD) syndrome does not appear in DSM-IV, but it has been the focus of much research in childhood LD over the past decade. Rourke (1989) suggests that those with the syndrome comprise about 5–10% of the LD population, with males and females being equally affected. The NVLD syndrome is a constellation of deficits that apparently cluster in some children: impaired mathematics ability, poor visual–spatial skills, and impaired social cognition, leading to poor social skills and increased signs of depression and anxiety. An issue subject to considerable debate is to what degree attention is impaired in these individuals. Is the NVLD syndrome comorbid with ADHD, or does it simply mimic ADHD symptoms, particularly the inattentive ones?

A brief overview of the development of the NVLD model is helpful in exploring these issues. Rourke (1989) points out that in early LD research in the 1970s, LD children were treated as a homogeneous group: reading-disabled children were combined with arithmetic-disabled children in a single group of "LD" subjects and compared with normal controls on neuropsychological measures. Naturally, little progress was made in understanding LD using this design. Rourke and colleagues (Fuerst, Fisk, & Rourke, 1989; Ozols & Rourke, 1985; Rourke & Finlayson, 1995; Rourke & Strang, 1978; Strang & Rourke, 1983, 1985) found that children with reading delays who nonetheless had good arithmetic performance had a different pattern of neuropsychological deficits from those with arithmetic deficits but intact reading. Rourke and Finlayson (1995) first noted that RD children with good mathematical skills had lower Verbal IQs than Performance IQs on the WISC, whereas MD children who were good readers had higher Verbal IQs than Performance IQs. Earlier, Rourke and Strang (1978) found the MD children to have markedly more impaired tactile–perceptual skills on neuropsychological examination than did RD subjects. The MD group also was well below the RD children on the Category Test, a measure of nonverbal abstract reasoning (Strang & Rourke, 1983).

Rourke (1989) described the clinical course of these MD children, whom he began referring to as having NVLD symptoms. He noted that while they may have mild early language delays, auditory perception, vocabulary, and early reading skills develop very rapidly by kindergarten. Their verbal memory skills are excellent. On the other hand, while speech and vocabulary are normal or advanced, speech prosody is delayed and these children often have flat, nonemotional monotone speech. Visual–perceptual and visual–motor skills are delayed. These children have poor motor coordination and often dislike motor activities. Although somewhat hyperactive during early childhood, they often become hypoactive by late childhood. Difficulties in mathematics are severe, and these individuals rarely advance beyond the fifth-grade level in this subject. They have difficulty with the visual–spatial aspects of mathematics, for instance, in understanding that columns of numbers represent ones, tens, hundreds, and so on. Borrowing and carrying operations are difficult for them. They lack any intuitive feel for weights, measures, or distances. Algebra, with its graphs, equations, and use of nonverbal symbols (*x*, *y*, etc.) is nearly impossible for them.

Studies also indicated that NVLD children show a distinct pattern of emotional disturbance. Porter and Rourke (1985) examined the Personality Inventory for Children (PIC) scores of a large group of LD children: 50% of the sample had an essentially normal profile, 15% were "hyperkinetic," 25% were depressed, and 10% showed high levels of somatic concerns. A follow-up study (Fuerst et al., 1989) found that these types of psychiatric problems were not evenly distributed across LD subtypes. The high Performance IQ/low Verbal IQ subjects (RD) were more likely to have a "normal" profile on the PIC, whereas the low Performance IQ/high Verbal IQ subjects (MD) made a large proportion of the depressed/anxious and hyperkinetic clusters. Ozols and Rourke (1985) compared RD and MD children on four measures of social judgment: the MD group was inferior to the RD group on nonverbal measures of social skills.

Rourke (1989) hypothesized that NVLD represented a right cerebral hemisphere dysfunction, given that (1) these visual–spatial functions have long been thought to be subserved by the right hemisphere and (2) there are similarities between NVLD children and adults who have sustained right hemisphere lesions. Pennington (1991) cautions that MD and poor social skills do not always correlate: there is a population of MD children who do not have impairments in social cognition. Rourke (1989) further postulated that damage to white matter (rather than the hemisphere itself) might produce a NVLD syndrome, as the right hemisphere is more dependent on connections to the rest of the brain to carry out its function. Rourke (1989, 1993) cites some evidence to suggest that NVLD is more prevalent among children with hydrocephalus, children who received intracranial radiation, and children with severe head injury. All of these conditions result in damage to white matter. For instance, Fletcher et al. (1992) performed MRI exams of 32 subjects with hydrocephalus and 12 controls and found a correlation of .54 between corpus callosum size and Performance IQ, whereas the correlation between Verbal IQ and callosum size was only .38. Large right ventricle size was associated with low Performance IQ, whereas enlarged left ventricles correlated with low Verbal IQ. Such neuroimaging variables have not been studied in NVLD children without hydrocephalus. Two studies (Branch, Cohen, & Hynd, 1995; Gross-Tsur, Shalev, Manor, & Amir, 1995) have identified children with signs of "right hemisphere dysfunction" and sought to determine if they showed NVLD. One of the studies (Gross-Tsur et al., 1995) unfortunately confounded the issue by using as inclusion criteria both symptoms of NVLD *and* soft neurological signs on the left side of the body. Thus it was inevitable that this sample of NVLD children would show signs of a right hemisphere deficit. Nonetheless, EEGs were normal in all but 4 of the 20 children, and only 2 of the 4 abnormal EEGs were localized to the right hemisphere. All of the CT scans performed were normal. Interestingly, all of these 20 NVLD children had ADHD, and 16 of the 20 were reported to have responded well to stimulant or desipramine treatment. This finding was consistent with that of Voeller (1986), who found that 14 of 15 subjects with neurological examinations suggestive of right hemisphere deficit met DSM-III criteria for attention-deficit disorder (ADD). Her sample also showed the low Performance IQ, poor social skills, and impaired mathematics skills typical of NVLD children.

Branch et al. (1995) differentiated LD subjects into a left hemisphere group and a right hemisphere group: left hemisphere subjects were defined as having a lower Verbal IQ relative to the Performance IQ or having signs of a left hemisphere lesion on neurological exam; right hemisphere subjects were defined as having a lower Performance IQ relative to the Verbal IQ or a neurological exam suggestive of right hemisphere deficit. Dyslexia was more common in the left hemisphere group, but dyscalculia and dysgraphia were not more common in the right hemisphere group. ADHD and depression were equally common in both the right and left hemisphere groups. In this study, NVLD was not more common in "right hemisphere dysfunction" children.

NVLD is clearly established as a syndrome, though its link to specific right hemisphere damage remains to be proven. Similarly, some small studies (Gross-Tsur et al., 1995; Voeller, 1986) suggest considerable (almost 100%) overlap with ADHD, but these were highly selected subgroups (for neurological abnormality) that may not have been representative of children with NVLD. A study that remains to be done is to select a large sample of children with high Verbal IQ but low Performance IQ and poor social skills and determine the prevalence of ADHD, depression, and neurological signs of right hemisphere dysfunction.

Rourke (1989) suggests that these children have differential attentional abilities: they show good attention to verbal stimuli but are inattentive to nonverbal, visual–spatial stimuli. His hypothesis that activity level declines with age suggests that NVLD might be more represented among children with ADHD, inattentive type, though again this remains to be seen. The clinician should suspect NVLD in an ADHD child when there are reports of marked difficulty in mathematics or when a certain pattern of deficits in social skills appears. Some ADHD children are unpopular because their ADHD results in intrusiveness or aggressiveness; yet these same traits might make them popular with acting-out youngsters who want to be "cool." In contrast, NVLD children are withdrawn, awkward, and often perceived as "weird" by peers (Rourke, 1989; Voeller, 1986). Gross-Tur et al. (1995) suggest that stimulant medication is helpful for the ADHD/NVLD child, but no controlled trials of such medication have been performed. Voeller (1986) stated that 5 of her 15 NVLD subjects received psychotherapy but it was unsuccessful in all cases.

Rourke (1989) is quite pessimistic about the long-term outcome of NVLD, suggesting that almost all patients continuing to suffer deficits in mathematics and social skills as adults. He adopts a "rehabilitation" approach similar to that taken with spinal cord injury: the goal is not to cure but to cope with the deficits. For most NVLD children, this means "teaching to strength," using verbal skills to help them compensate for nonverbal weakness. In the area of social skills, this means taking nothing for granted; parents and teachers should explain verbally all the nuances of a social situation. Before the child is set loose in the playground, the situation might be verbally rehearsed:

PARENT: What are you going to do first?

CHILD: Say hello to the children.

PARENT: Then what?

CHILD: Ask them if I can play.

PARENT: What do you do if they say no?

CHILD: Play by myself for a while.

This is a tedious process, and if a child has ADHD that is not treated, it is not likely to succeed. Finally, Rourke (1989) calls for adoption of a realistic attitude by parents and teachers. This is often the most difficult task of all.

13

Tic and Obsessive–Compulsive Disorders

We have chosen to discuss the comorbidity of tic and obsessive–compulsive disorders (OCD) with ADHD in a single chapter due to the growing body of evidence that tic disorders (both Tourette's disorder and chronic tic disorder) and OCD share common genetic factors (Alsobrook & Pauls, 1997). The comorbidity of tics and ADHD is well known to most clinicians, although there is much debate as to what degree they share etiological factors, if at all (Walkup, Scahill, & Riddle, 1995). The comorbidity of OCD and ADHD is far less studied, and this comorbidity is probability less familiar to clinicians. Indeed, the syndromes of ADHD and OCD appear to be polar opposites: children with ADHD are impulsive, uncontrolled, and fearless, whereas those with OCD are overcontrolled, ritualistic, and neurotic. Nonetheless, nearly every study of children with OCD has shown a high degree of comorbidity with disruptive behavior disorders (e.g., see D. A. Geller, Biederman, Griffin, Jones, & Lefkowitz, 1996).

OVERVIEW OF TIC DISORDERS

There are three tic disorders currently listed in DSM-IV: Tourette's disorder, chronic motor or vocal tic disorder, and transient tic disorder. The following pattern must have been present for at least 1 year to permit a definite diagnosis of Tourette's disorder to be made: (1) both motor and vocal tics must be occurring many times a day; (2) the tics may often "wax and wane," but the patient can never be tic free for longer than 3 months; (3) the onset of the tics must have occurred before 18 years of age; and (4) the tics must cause the patient discomfort or social dysfunction. If one sees a patient whose vocal and/or motor tics have been present for less than a year, one should make a diagnosis of transient tic disorder or tic disorder–NOS (not otherwise specified) until the patient has been followed for a long enough time to enable a definitive Tourette's diagnosis to be made. Chronic tic disorder patients have either vocal or motor tics, but not both. The duration and frequency of the tics must meet the same threshold as for Tourette's disorder.

Several studies have looked at the prevalence of tic disorders. Comings, Himes, and Comings (1990) screened 3,034 students in Southern California and found a very high prevalence of Tourette's disorder. Nearly 1% of the boys and 0.13% of the girls were found to have Tourette's. The male/female ratio was also much higher than that found in other studies. The study was highly biased by the fact the one of the investigators actively recruited subjects into the study and briefed school personnel on how to look for tics. These authors stated that they used a very broad definition of tic disorder. Population studies show much lower estimates. More than 140, 000 elementary students were screened, and 41 were found to meet criteria for Tourette's disorder, giving a point prevalence of 2.9/10,000 (Caine et al., 1988). The average age of onset of the tics was 7 years. Thus, only 0.03% of the population suffered from the disorder according to this study. Apter et al. (1993) screened more than 28,000 people being inducted into the Israeli military: the prevalence of Tourette's disorder was found to be 4.3/10,000, with a male/female ratio of 1.6/1.

ADHD AND TIC DISORDERS

Perhaps more than any comorbid disorder we have looked at, perceptions of the degree of overlap between tics and ADHD are strongly influenced by referral bias. First, it is clear that many persons with pure Tourette's disorder do not seek treatment at all. Others have tics that respond to pharmacological interventions provided by family physicians or neurologists; these patients have no need of mental health intervention and are not represented in psychiatric (clinic-based) studies. Secondly, patients with ADHD who develop tics are likely to be referred to psychiatrists or to specialty clinics that deal with Tourette's syndrome. All the studies cited below utilized such populations.

Comings et al. (1990) found that 100% of their tic disorder patients also met criteria for ADHD. They suggested that ADHD and tic disorders have a common genetic etiology, proposing that the Tourette's gene can actually express itself as ADHD alone. Eleven of 41 Tourette's patients (26.8%) identified by Caine et al. (1988) had ADHD. Robertson, Trimble, and Lees (1988) found that 49% of their Tourette's patients had ADHD, with the onset of the ADHD proceeding the onset of tic disorder by 2.5 years. School teachers rated a sample of 75 children with Tourette's as both "hard to control" (42%) and "hyperative" (25%) (Jagger et al., 1982). Of 400 children with Tourette's recruited through the Tourette's Association, 65–75% were reported by parents to have serious behavior problems including hyperactivity and conduct problems (Stefl, 1984). We should note that samples obtained through support groups often find the most problematic children. Parents of such children are obviously the ones most in need of support. Based on these clinic samples, one might conclude that almost all children with Tourette's disorder have a comorbid disruptive behavior disorder.

An examination of the data compiled by Apter et al. (1993) reveals a very different pattern. Only 1 of the 12 Tourette's patients identified met criteria for ADHD. All the studies have recruited samples of tic disorder patients and examined the prevalence of ADHD. No studies have systematically examined the prevalence of tics in the epidemiological sample of ADHD boys. One striking pattern that can be noted is that very few Tourette's cases are identified in population studies that use strict criteria: only 12 Tourette's cases were found in more than 26, 000 Israelis; Burd, Kerbeshian, Wilkenheiser, and Fisher (1986) found only 22 cases in the entire state of North Dakota. The studies of comorbid clinic samples often consist of hundreds of patients. This raises an intriguing question: are the epidemiological samples using too strict a definition of the disorder, or are the clinical samples using too broad a definition of tics? It is quite conceivable that some symptoms of ADHD—fidgeting and making strange noises in particular—are reported as tics by parents and this would inflate the degree of overlap in clinic samples. The following case illustrates this problem:

> Kyle is a 10-year-old boy whose parents contacted the clinic because he has "Tourette's syndrome and ADD." The parent reported that Kyle had "violent tics." He had destroyed everything in his room on several occasions. The parent reported frequent "coprolalia," but this phenomenon occurred only during Kyle's temper outbursts. Kyle has always been extremely hyperactive since age 2; he was first treated with methylphenidate at age 4. This resulted in the first appearance of "tics," which the mother described as "shaking" of the arms and legs. The methylphenidate was discontinued and a variety of other antidepressant medications were tried without control of either the "tics" or the disruptive behavior. Curi-

ously, the tics were never present when Kyle was playing on his baseball team.

On mental status examination Kyle was fidgety, became bored easily, and became oppositional. No motor tics of the face or shoulders were noted. No vocal tics were observed with the exception of constant sniffing. Kyle also suffered from chronic sinus problems. Kyle denied depression or anxiety, and no other remarkable findings were noted during the examination. Kyle's teacher revealed that he never showed any tics at school, either motor or vocal, although he did talk excessively and frequently was sent to time out for temper outbursts.

The clinician felt that Kyle did not have Tourette's disorder but severe ADHD with comorbid ODD. The mother, however, was highly invested in seeing her child as having Tourette's and became quite upset when the diagnosis was questioned. The teacher, she said, "did not know what to look for." She rejected a repeat trial of stimulant and instead went to a neurologist who prescribed haloperidol.

Clinicians should be suspicious when they never observe the tics on examination or the parent's descriptions of the tics more closely resemble ADHD and/or ODD behaviors.

Pauls, Leckman, and Cohen (1993) performed a large study of families to determine if there was any genetic relationship between tic disorders and ADHD. They studied 85 probands with Tourette's disorder, interviewing 338 of their first-degree relatives. They also studied 27 controls, obtaining interviews from 92 of their relatives. If ADHD and tic disorders share a genetic etiology, then there should be a increased prevalence of ADHD among the relatives of Tourette's syndrome patients. As shown in Table 13.1, this is not the case. While one finds an increased rate of both ADHD and learning disabilities (LDs) among the Tourette's probands themselves, the rate of ADHD among the relatives of Tourette's patients did not exceed that of the control group. While 15.9% of the relatives of Tourette's/ADHD probands had ADHD, only 3.2% of the relatives of Tourette's-only patients met criteria for ADHD. This clearly indicates that Tourette's and ADHD are genetically independent, and in no case can ADHD be viewed as an alternative expression of the Tourette's gene. What, then, is the explanation for the high rate of ADHD seen among the Tourette's probands in this study? Unlike the earlier studies cited, overinclusive diagnosis is not likely, as experienced interviewers used strict DSM-III-R criteria. Pauls et al. (1993) suggested that the Tourette's/ADHD sample contained two subgroups of patients. In one, the onset of ADHD proceeded the onset of tics; these individuals first developed ADHD and then independently developed Tourette's. In the second group, ADHD had its onset after the tics, and

TABLE 13.1. Rates of Diagnoses among First-Degree Relatives of Probands and Controls

	Relatives of					
	Tourette's without ADD		Tourette's with ADD		Controls	
Diagnosis	*n*	%	*n*	%	*n*	%
Tourette's syndrome	17	9.1[a]	11	7.3[b,f]	0	0
Chronic tics	28	15.0[a]	27	17.9[a,f]	1	0.9
OCD	21	11.2[b]	28	18.5[a,e]	2	1.8
ADHD	6	3.2[c]	24	15.9[b,d]	5	4.4

Note. All comparisons between relatives and controls were made with the Fisher's exact test. All comparisons between relatives of Tourette's without ADD and relatives of Tourette's with ADD were made with the chi-square statistic. Adapted from Pauls et al. (1993). Copyright 1993 by D. L. Pauls. Adapted by permission.

[a] Relatives vs. controls, $p < .001$.

[b] Relatives vs. controls, $p < .005$.

[c] Relatives vs. controls, NS.

[d] Relatives of Tourette's without ADD probands vs. relatives of Tourette's/ADD probands, $p < .001$.

[e] Relatives of Tourette's without ADD probands vs. relatives of Tourette's/ADD probands, $p < .06$.

[f] Relatives of Tourette's without ADD probands vs. relatives of Tourette's/ADD probands, NS.

the investigators suggested that the ADHD might be secondary to the Tourette's. For instance, the tics might be distracting and efforts to suppress the tics might lead to less energy being available for other forms of impulsive control. Longitudinal studies will be needed to completely sort out this issue. The possible genetic relationship of tics, OCD, and ADHD is displayed in Figure 13.1

Clinicians will see a high degree of comorbidity of ADHD among tic disorder patients who present for treatment. LD and other cognitive impairments are seen among the Tourette's/ADHD children, whereas the rates of LD in non-ADHD children with Tourette's does not exceed that of a control group (Yeates & Bornstein, 1994). In dealing with tic disorders, clinicians will encounter several different situations:

1. The child presents with both Tourette's and ADHD, with neither disorder having been previously treated. What is the first line of psychopharmacological intervention?

2. A patient presents with ADHD only and is treated with stimulants, but then develops tics. Is this a case of Tourette's or merely a transient tic disorder secondary to stimulant treatment? Should the stimulant be discontinued? What other medications should be tried if use of stimulants exacerbates the tics?

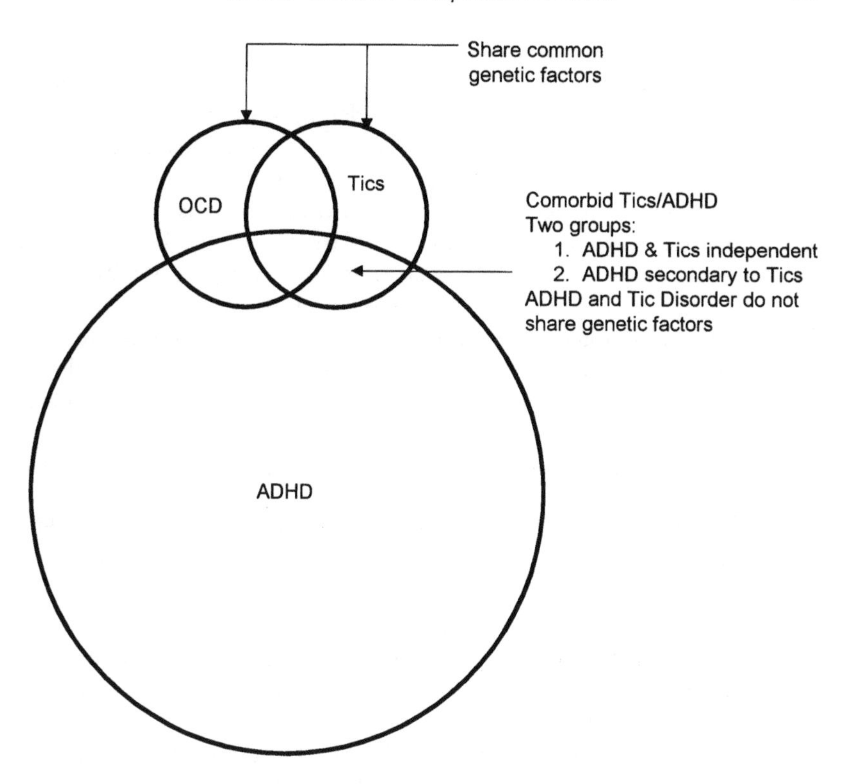

FIGURE 13.1. Representation of the overlap of tic disorder, OCD, and ADHD.

Discussion of these issues first requires an overview of the research concerning the use of stimulant medication in children with tic disorders.

Tics and Stimulants

Clinically, it had long been accepted that stimulants exacerbate tics and thus were contraindicated in children with Tourette's or other tic disorders (Lowe, Cohen, Detlor, Kremenitzer, & Shaywitz, 1982). Recently, two well-controlled trials have examined the efficacy of stimulants in children with comorbid tic disorders and ADHD (Castellanos et al., 1997; Gadow, Sverd, Sprafkin, Nolan, & Ezor, 1995). Gadow et al. (1995) randomized 34 prepubertal boys with combined tics and ADHD to receive placebo or one of three doses of methylphenidate (0.1, 0.3, and 0.5 mg/kg) in a double-blind fashion. The children took the doses twice daily for 2 weeks. The usual behavioral measures to assess stimulant response were gathered, as well as detailed information on tic frequency and severity. Teachers, parents, and physicians made blind ratings of tics, and the children were videotaped with blind observers rating the tics. The stimulant was highly effective in reducing ADHD behaviors, and baseline tic severity did not predict stimulant response; that is, a child might have severe Tourette's disorder, but his behavior was just as likely to improve on methylphenidate as was the behavior of a child with mild tics. Surprisingly, there was no overall statistically significant effect on tic frequency or severity on stimulant relative to placebo. Teachers actually noted a decrease in vocal tics when children were on methylphenidate. The study clearly suggested that stimulants could be used safely in comorbid ADHD/tic disorder but did not address long-term safety issues.

Castellanos et al. (1997) performed a double-blind placebo-controlled trial of methylphenidate and dextroamphetamine in 20 children with a mean age of 9.4 years. All the subjects had comorbid ADHD and Tourette's syndrome, and each subject received all three conditions for 3 weeks. The doses of stimulant used in the study were quite high: doses of methylphenidate could range as high as 1.2 mg/kg per dose, and dextroamphetamine could range up to 0.64 mg/kg per dose. Again, both stimulants were highly efficacious in reducing ADHD behavior. At these higher doses, tics were significantly exacerbated. There was a increase in tics during the second and third week of dextroamphetamine treatment and during the second week of methylphenidate treatment. At the low doses in this study (which were more typical of those used in clinical practice), neither drug significantly increased tics. Fourteen of the 20 subjects continued stimulant treatment for 1–3 years. There was no clear pattern of tic severity worsening over time; rather, tics tended to wax and wane regardless of medication status. These studies tell us that stimulants can be used safely to treat ADHD in children with tic disorders.

Tics Presenting before ADHD Is Treated

What is the best approach for a child who presents with tics but is found to have ADHD as well? As noted above, ADHD occurring after the onset of the tic disorder may in fact represent a situation in which the inattention/impulsivity symptoms are secondary to the tics. Furthermore, if the tics are quite severe and socially disabling, they may require more immediate intervention. In these situations the clinician should treat the patient with either alpha agonists or neuroleptics first and then assess what effect these medications have on the ADHD symptoms. Only one major double-blind placebo-controlled trial of clonidine in Tourette's syndrome has been published (Leckman et al., 1991). The subjects ranged in age from 7 to 48 years; more than half the sample had comorbid ADHD. Nineteen were randomized to the placebo group, whereas 21 received clonidine at a mean dose of 0.25 mg/day Clonidine was superior to placebo in reducing both motor and vocal tics, though the effect was more pronounced on the motor tics. Side effects included sedation (90%) and dry mouth (17%). Steingard, Biederman, Spencer, Wilens, and Gonzalez (1993) performed an open trial of clonidine (mean dose, 0.19 mg/day) in 24 ADHD children with and without tic disorder. ADHD symptoms improved in 96% of the children with comorbid ADHD and tics, whereas only 53% of the children with ADHD alone were judged to have clinically significant improvements in attention and activity level. Tics improved significantly in 75% of the Tourette's patients. The above authors suggested that children with ADHD and tic disorder respond better to alpha agonists than do children with ADHD alone. This was contradicted in another study of children with comorbid ADHD and tic disorder where clonidine was not superior to placebo in reducing inattention or hyperactivity (Gunning, 1992). Thirty-seven children with ADHD/Tourette's participated in a double-blind placebo-controlled crossover study of desipramine, clonidine, and placebo (Singer et al., 1995). Clonidine was dosed at 0.5 mg four times a day. Clonidine was not different from placebo either in reducing tics or improving ADHD behaviors. Chapell et al. (1995) treated 10 patients aged 8–13 with ADHD/tic disorder with guanfacine (mean dose, 1.5 mg/day; range, 1.5–3.0 mg/day) in an open trial. Phonic and motor tics decreased significantly. Thus while the alpha agonists are widely prescribed for tics, the data supporting their use are mixed.

Pimozide, a high-potency neuroleptic, has been compared to placebo and haloperidol in two studies (Sallee, Nesbitt, Jackson, Sine, & Sethuraman, 1997; E. Shapiro et al., 1989). Both studies showed haloperidol to have more extrapyramidal symptoms than pimozide: E. Shapiro et al. (1989) showed that both drugs were equally efficacious relative to placebo in reducing tics; Sallee et al. (1997) found that haloperidol did not differ from placebo in this regard. They also reported more adverse side effects of haloperidol than of pimozide. Thus pimozide appears superior to haloperidol for treatment of tics.

Recently two open trials have suggested that risperidone is an effective treatment for tic disorders. In the first study, Lombroso et al. (1995) treated 38 patients who had failed haloperidol and/or clonidine with doses of risperidone ranging from 0.5 to 9 mg/day: 8 patients discontinued the medication due to side effects (unspecified); 6 patients experienced extrapyramidal side effects, including 2 with dystonic reactions and 4 with akathisia. This lead these authors to speculate that tic patients may be more sensitive to dystonic reactions with risperidone, but other open trials have not shown this. At the end of a 4-week trial, 22 patients (58%) were improved significantly, while 7 patients showed no change; only 1 patient had worsening of tics. Lombroso et al. (1995) treated seven children (5 Tourette's/2 chronic tic disorder) aged 11–16 years with risperidone. The dose of risperidone ranged from 1 to 2.5 mg/day (mean dose, 1.5 mg/day). Compared to baseline, there was statistically significant decrease to tics. In the second study, Nam et al. (1997) randomized 36 children with Tourette's syndrome to either haloperidol or risperidone for a 2-month trial. Risperidone doses ranged from 2 to 9 mg/day (mean, 4.8 mg/day). More than 80% of the patients in the risperidone group was judged to be responders, compared to 60% in the haloperidol group.

The clinician should choose between the use of alpha agonists or neuroleptics for treating a primary tic disorder. Alpha agonists are often preferred as the treatment of first choice since neuroleptics carry the risk of tardive dyskinesia (TD). On the other hand, the lower risk of TD with novel neuroleptics may push the clinician to use these medications first to avoid concerns about the cardiovascular side effects of alpha agonists. The two cases below illustrate different approaches to children with ADHD and tics:

> David is an 11-year-old boy with a history of temper outbursts at home and at school. His parents have also noted that since age 8 David has always blinked frequently and sniffed. He shrugs his shoulders and shakes his hands for no reason. Despite superior intelligence, David is inattentive in class and makes very poor grades. A trial of methylphenidate undertaken when David was in the first grade resulted in a marked worsening of the tic behaviors.
>
> David was given a trial of clonidine 0.05 mg three times a day. He experienced sedation, which gradually improved but never disappeared, over a month's time. It was very difficult to tell if the tics improved. David would go several weeks without tics, but then have "a bad run" of tics that would last for several days. He was given the nickname "Snotter" at school because of his frequent sniffing. The dose of clonidine was increased to 0.1 mg three times a day and his tics *worsened* dramatically. The alpha agonist was discontinued, and the school year ended. There was an immediate decrease in the tics, and no medications were prescribed during the summer. David began the year (sixth grade) without medications, but the tics returned. David also failed all his classes and was threatened with expulsion for fighting. He was treated with risperidone 2 mg/day, but the tics remained persistent.
>
> Pimozide was started at a dose 0.5 mg/day and increased to 2 mg/day. The tics immediately stopped, as did the disruptive behavior. David's grades improved, and he had no further behavioral

problems. He remains on pimozide without extrapyramidal symptoms or other side effects.

This case illustrates how a physician must remain flexible in trying a variety of medications to treat tic disorder. In the above case, there were no clinical indicators to predict that the individual might respond to pimozide rather than other agents.

Tics Emerging after Stimulant Treatment

As noted earlier, the onset of ADHD is on average 2.5 years earlier than the onset of tics (Robertson et al., 1988). The only clue that a child might develop tics later is a family history of Tourette's disorder. While the parents of such a child should be warned of an increased risk of "unmasking" the tics by treating ADHD with stimulants, the genetic evidence cited earlier clearly predicts that tics will develop in time even without stimulant treatment. The previous medication studies clearly show that most children with tic disorder will not experience worsening of their tics with stimulants. The following case describes the management of tics that emerged during treatment with methylphenidate:

> Julie is an 8-year-old girl with a history of inattentiveness and poor school performance since the first grade. At the time of presentation she was in the second grade in a private school. When the teacher gave her one-to-one attention she could complete work without difficulty. During regular class periods she was off task, fidgeted in her chair, and argued with other children. At home her parents noted similarly problems; in addition she would throw major temper tantrums when frustrated. On the psychiatric interview, Julie met criteria for ADHD and ODD by parent report. Neither Julie nor her parents reported significant depressive, anxiety, or OCD symptoms. There was no family history of Tourette's or any other tic disorder.
>
> Julie was started on 5 mg of methylphenidate, A.M. and noon. Her teacher reported immediate and dramatic improvement in her ADHD symptoms. A 5-mg dose was added in the evening; this resulted in dramatic reduction in her temper outbursts. Treatment proceeded without incident for 3 months, when patient's mother contacted the clinic stating that her daughter was blinking frequently. She was told to observe the behavior. Over the next month, the frequency of the blinking increased and Julie began moving her cheek as well. Other children began to make fun of her.
>
> The methylphenidate was discontinued with the intention of allowing the tic to subside before starting another drug. There was, however, an immediate deterioration in her behavior at home and school. While the tic subsided slightly in the first week off stimulant

medication, it did not resolve completely. Because of the deterioration in grades, it was decided to begin imipramine as an alternative. Julie was started on 1 mg/kg per day, divided into two doses, A.M. and noon, and this was gradually increased to 3 mg/kg per day without any response of the ADHD symptoms. Fearful that she might be asked to leave her private school, the parents requested that the methylphenidate be restarted.

The behavioral improvement was equally robust on the second trial of methylphenidate, but the eye-blinking/cheek-twitching tic worsened again. No vocal tics developed. Julie began to complain of pain in her eyes because of the excess blinking. In view of the tremendous improvement in behavior with stimulant treatment and in view of the worsening of the tics, it was elected to begin clonidine in conjunction with the methylphenidate. Clonidine was given at a dose of 0.5 mg three times a day. The tics gradually resolved. No clinically significant changes were noted on ECG after clonidine treatment and no dizziness, fainting, or heart racing was noted.

During the summer the methylphenidate and clonidine were discontinued. When the third grade resumed, only methylphenidate was restarted. Curiously, the tics did not reoccur. Julie had grown, and the dose of methylphenidate was gradually adjusted to 10 mg three times a day. She completed the third grade without difficulties or reemergence of the tics. In fourth grade she again started on methylphenidate. About 4 months into the school year the same tic (eye blinking/cheek twitching) reoccurred. Guanfacine was started but was not effective in reducing the tic. The clonidine was restarted, and the patient remains on methylphenidate (10 mg three times a day) and clonidine (0.05 mg three times a day) and continues to do well.

This case highlight several aspects of ADHD and tic disorders. It may never be known whether this child would have developed tics off stimulants, as the severity of her ADHD would not permit this. Technically, the child does not clearly meet criteria for a tic disorder since the tic may be the direct effect of the methylphenidate. Families often find that the ADHD symptoms are so disabling for the child that are willing to live with the tics. The benefit of the stimulant as well as the severity of the tics justifies the combination of methylphenidate and clonidine despite possible cardiovascular risk of this regimen discussed in Chapter 4. In view of the work of Castellanos et al. (1997), it is clear that some children will tic on one stimulant but not another. Thus the clinician might well consider a trial of Adderall or dextroamphetamine for this child during the next school year; combining risperidone with the stimulant might have been considered if the tic had not responded to clonidine, though this would involve weighing the risk of TD.

ADHD AND OBSESSIVE–COMPULSIVE DISORDER

Lay persons often do not distinguish between *obsessive* and *addictive* symptoms. Parents of ADHD children, particularly those with comorbid ODD or CD, often refer to their being obsessed with some behavior. They describe their child as being obsessed with video games, or their adolescent son as obsessed with his girlfriend. Expressions such as "a compulsive gambler" add to this confusion. Obsessive thoughts and compulsive behaviors are entities from which the patient derives no pleasure. The patient has no reason for the behavior, and often (but not always) recognizes that it is inappropriate. In contrast, addictive behaviors are things that bring the patient pleasure. The patient engages in the behavior for short-term pleasure, ignoring or denying the long-term risks to his/her health, family relationships, or career. Addictive behavior can be found not only with illicit drugs but with sexual acting out and general risk taking. The first step, therefore, in exploring the possibility that an ADHD child has comorbid OCD is to be certain that the parent or patient is not referring to the child's relentless pursuit of pleasurable stimuli as obsessions:

> Jack is a 15-year-old with a history of ADHD since age 5. He is currently in a Special Education high school due to severe disruptive behavior in his regular school. His mother wanted him reevaluated because he has showed signs of "obsessive–destructive behavior." Jack has frequent rage attacks at home in which he destroys furniture. His mother describes his other compulsions as playing the same video game over and over and becoming enraged if she tries to stop him. If his girlfriend calls during one of the games, however, he stops without difficulty. Jack, his mother reports is obsessed with sex. His room is filled with pornographic magazines, and she recently caught him downloading sexual material off the Internet using the family computer. His mother says she read in a pamphlet at her psychiatrist's office that people with OCD often have sexual obsessions.
>
> On examination Jack denies that he had any rituals or repetitive thoughts. He reports that he enjoys video games and can stop any time *he* wants to. Jack is very sexually active but has no guilt or fear about his sexuality. He finds his sexual daydreams pleasurable and fantasizes frequently.

In this case, the mother was informed that her son's behaviors were different from OCD and were more likely part of the externalizing ODD/CD spectrum. She and Jack were referred for family therapy, with the focus on helping the mother to set firmer limits on Jack's behavior.

Five studies have examined the overlap of OCD and ADHD using clinical samples, with widely varying results (D. A. Geller et al., 1996; Hanna, 1995; Riddle et al., 1990; Swedo, Rapoport, Leonard, Lenane, & Cheslow, 1989; Toro, Cervera, Osejo, & Salamero, 1992). These studies are shown in Table 13.2. All the above studies examined the rate of ADHD and other psychiatric disorders in children with OCD, but no study has looked at the rate of OCD in a large sample of ADHD children. Two studies that excluded children with Tourette's disorder found the prevalence of ADHD to be about 10%. Other studies that included Tourette's patients found both higher rates (16%) and lower rates (6%) of ADHD among children with OCD. Thus including children with Tourette's/OCD in a sample does not automatically raise the rate of comorbidity of ADHD among the children with OCD despite the purported comorbidity of Tourette's and ADHD. One study (D. A. Geller et al., 1996) has found very high rates (33%) of ADHD among OCD children, but this sample included psychotic children. Indeed, 30% of this sample was psychotic, but the authors do not describe the nature of the psychotic symptoms; 27% of the sample also met criteria for bipolar disorder. Two children had pervasive developmental disorder (PDD). The authors argued that because they used no exclusionary criteria their sample of OCD children was more representative of what clinicians really experience. On the other hand, the sample was so overweighted with psychotic subjects that it leaves open the possibility that the many obsessions and compulsions the children experienced were secondary to a primary mood or psychotic disorder.

Toro et al. (1992) found that only 72 out of 8,337 patients in a child mental health clinic met criteria for OCD. Only four of these patients met

TABLE 13.2. Prevalence of ADHD in Children with OCD

Study	*n*	Prevalence of ADHD	Comment
Swedo et al. (1989)	70	10%	Tourette's disorder, psychosis excluded
Riddle et al. (1990)	21	10%	Tourette's disorder, psychosis excluded
Hanna (1995)	31	16%	26% had tic disorder, psychosis excluded
Toro et al. (1992)	72	6%	17% had tic disorder, organic mental disorder excluded
D. A. Geller (1996)	30	33%	40% had tic disorder; 27% were manic; 30% were psychotic; 2 subjects had pervasive developmental disorder

criteria for ADHD. This is consistent with our experience that the comorbidity of OCD and ADHD is quite rare outside a tertiary referral center. Rare does not mean never, of course, and the following case describes an interesting combination of OCD and ADHD in an 8-year-old child:

> Michael, an 8-year-old with codiagnoses of ADHD, ODD, and OCD, presented a number of challenges to the staff at a structured behavioral day treatment program. He expressed a variety of obsessive concerns about cleanliness and germs, which manifested themselves in a reluctance to touch other children or items such as sports equipment or games and hand-washing compulsions. Michael also expressed concerns about neatness and orderliness, and was often seen pulling at his hair to "straighten" it and tying and untying his shoes repeatedly in an effort to "get them perfect." His compulsive behaviors frequently interfered with functioning, such as when he refused to pick up a soccer ball because it was "filled with germs," or when his repeated shoe tying prevented him from following a counselor's request for the group to begin a new activity. Michael's IQ and verbal skills were well above average, and he frequently responded to the counselor's requests to desist from his compulsive behaviors with articulately phrased justifications and arguments about his behavior, which often escalated into screaming and physically resisting any attempts at intervention. Not surprisingly, the combination of his oppositional, impulsive, and OCD behaviors led to frequent teasing by his peers and arguments with them, and his social status was extremely poor. At one point, he became angry over "impurities" in the water fountain. When his counselor tried to reassure him, he became so agitated he had to be removed from the group. As he was lead away, he screamed, "What must I do to get a pure, clean, fresh glass of water?" Unfortunately a variety of medications failed to control either his ADHD or OCD symptoms.

Psychopharmacotherapy for Comorbid ADHD/Obsessive–Compulsive Disorder

A number of studies have shown that the SSRIs such as clomipramine and fluvoxamine are effective in the treatment of childhood OCD (Riddle et al., 1992, 1996; Leonard et al., 1989, 1991). Dosing of these agents was discussed in Chapter 4. We do not know how treatment of the OCD affects attention and impulse control in children with ADHD and OCD. SSRIs do not appear to have any effect on tics (Scahill et al., 1997). As we have noted before, stimulants and fluoxetine can be combined safely in doses of fluoxetine up to 20 mg/day (Gammon & Brown, 1993). Thus the clinician may combine these two classes of agents in treating OCD and ADHD, just as one would in the treatment of major depressive disorder (MDD; see Chapter 8).

V

Specific Areas of Impaired Functioning

14

Behavioral Interventions for Problems at Home

BEHAVIORAL PARENT MANAGEMENT TRAINING (PMT)

Overview

Programs for teaching parents to apply basic principles of behavioral techniques to manage their children's behavior problems have been developed by several prominent and highly respected leaders in the field of child psychopathology, including Gerald R. Patterson and his colleagues (Patterson, 1975; Patterson & Forgatch, 1987, 1989), Rex Forehand and his colleagues (Forehand & Long, 1996; Forehand & McMahon, 1981), and Russell A. Barkley (1987). All of these programs utilize the same basic components; after we describe these components and the specific application of behavioral parent management training (PMT) to address the disorders addressed in this volume, research examining the efficacy of PMT will be reviewed.

Parent management techniques typically comprise between 8 and 20 individual or group sessions. Some programs target younger children, while others are designed to specifically address problems in adolescence. In addition to such variations in targeted child age, PMT programs show some variability in their specific theoretical approaches and the component skills taught. Despite these differences, the basic rationale and procedures of the programs show substantial overlap. Each entails teaching parents to apply basic principles of behavior management to their everyday parenting strategies, including specific instruction on topics such as the following: designing and implementing a "token economy" system; the use of praise and other rewards to increase desirable behaviors; the use of ignoring and punishments, such as timeout and token "fines," to decrease undesirable behaviors; and managing specific types of problems, such as homework completion and public misbehavior. In addition to the didactic component, the instructional format typically includes modeling and practice of skills, use of written materials, and homework assignments, with some programs also incorporating videotaped vignettes in their training materials. Like other learned skills, success of PMT is largely dependent upon mastery that comes with practice. Accordingly, parents should be made aware of the critical importance of attending sessions and completing homework assignments.

PMT is a broad-based approach; that is, it presents a particular philosophy and plan of parenting that can be applied to a variety of child problems. We recommend that PMT be routinely recommended as a treatment component for the complex comorbid conditions addressed in this volume. Some families, however, may not be good candidates for this treatment; this issue is discussed in the next section.

Considerations in Implementing PMT

Why Is PMT Hard to Sell?

A critical component of PMT is motivating parents to master and then actually apply the set of behavioral techniques. It is not possible to overestimate the importance of the motivational component of treatment. By the time they enter treatment, parents have often spent months or even years trying to cope with their children's behavior problems and meeting with frustration and limited success. Understandably, they may be skeptical about embracing a new treatment approach, and PMT is a particularly difficult approach to "sell" for several reasons.

First, since parents are targeted as the mechanism of change, it is easy to misconstrue PMT as placing the blame for children's behavior problems squarely on the parents—after all, they, rather than the child, are expected to initiate processes leading to change. Although inaccurate, this perception of the behavioral approach is understandably demoralizing for parents, many of whom have made heroic efforts on behalf of their children. It is important that the treatment rationale specifically address this issue to preempt the misperception that parent management training is predicated on the belief that children's behavior problems are the result of bad parenting.

Second, PMT requires hard work. It should not be surprising that it is more difficult to convince parents to undertake a treatment program that places high demands on their time and energy than it is to convince them to try a less demanding intervention, such as medication, which requires only a once or twice daily administration, or child-centered therapy, which requires merely accompanying the child to a weekly session. This does not mean that parents are reluctant to invest personal effort in treatment for their children; it is natural and expectable, however, that their belief in the efficacy of a proposed treatment is a particularly salient issue when they are being asked to make such a demanding investment.

Third, behavior therapists typically present a realistic picture of the therapeutic process, which requires substantial effort to effect improved but not "cured" behavior; this depiction must compete with therapies for which exaggerated claims are often made. Unfortunately, it is still the case that practitioners treat children with ADHD using individual therapy or play therapy, despite the fact that a recent review (Pelham, Wheeler, & Chronis, 1998) located no studies documenting the efficacy of this treatment. Relatedly, the recent surge of attention to biofeedback treatment of ADHD has likely been fueled by the promise that children's behavior can be "cured"; such claims seem convincing because this treatment can be made to sound particularly scientific and consistent with current theories ascribing ADHD to biological roots. We know of a number of facilities currently offering this treatment; in many instances, the clinicians involved have been trained in biofeedback techniques but are not knowledgeable about ADHD or treatment evaluation (a colleague relates a tale of one such clinician enthusiastically asking to schedule a meeting so that he could show off his portable biofeedback equipment; it apparently never occurred to him that providing data to support the effectiveness of this treatment would be far more impressive!). While we have found most biofeedback practitioners to be genuinely convinced of its utility, well-meaning but naive sincerity is no substitute for clinical results. Nonetheless, when parents are presented with such a seemingly alluring option, it complicates the task of persuading them to undertake a treatment like PMT that is both more demanding and makes less lofty promises about efficacy.

Are All Families Candidates for PMT?

While PMT offers valuable help in managing children's behavior problems, there are some parental and family characteristics that make certain families less suitable candidates for this treatment. We have already noted that PMT places more demands on parents than do many other treatments, so it is not surprising that these variables involve economic, intellectual, psychiatric, or other factors that limit the resources parents have available to devote to this treatment regimen. This issue was apparent in a case in which an attempt was made to implement PMT with the mother of a severely hyperactive and noncompliant 6-year-old girl who had been placed in an inpatient setting because her level of impulsive behavior had led to several life-threatening accidents. This 21-year-old single mother of three children had dropped out of school in junior high, and her dire economic situation required her to exert tremendous effort to keep her family fed and clothed with her minimum-wage job. Despite her admirable efforts—typically bringing her other children on the hour-long bus trip to and from the clinic, she faithfully kept every scheduled appointment—she was simply unable to adequately master and implement the procedures, despite therapist attempts to pare down reading assignments, simplify procedures, and make other modifications. Similarly, parents with their own serious and all-consuming psychiatric problems, such as alcohol or drug abuse, psychosis, or severe depression, are unlikely to be able to summon up the motivation and energy to effectively master PMT. The factors that have been most consistently found in the empirical literature to be associated with poorer treatment outcome are parental depression, marital discord or single-parent status, negative life stressors, and low family socioeconomic status (e.g., Webster-Stratton & Hammond, 1990). In cases in which these problem areas themselves are amenable to treatment, such as parental depression or marital discord, it may be desirable to intervene directly with these problems prior to PMT. Webster-Stratton (1994) suggests that a more broad-based PMT treatment that specifically addresses parental communication and related skills may have some utility in enhancing outcome; as described in more detail below in the subsection on research on the efficacy of PMT, there is some evidence to support this assertion.

Components of PMT

Rationale for PMT

For the reasons identified above, it is crucial to provide a treatment rationale that is convincing and inspires hope so that parents will be motivated to invest the considerable resources required to master and implement the prescribed procedures. In the following paragraphs we outline several points to be included in the rationale for and description of PMT.

1. *ADHD is a disorder with a biological genesis; it is not the result of overindulgent or excessively strict parenting, divorce, sibling rivalry, or any other family environment factor.* As noted earlier, it is particularly important to prevent the misconception that, because this treatment directly addresses the behavior of parents, it embraces the belief that ADHD is caused by bad parenting. Stating at the outset that this is not the case helps to begin the therapeutic process by alleviating the guilt that many parents of problem children feel, both because they have frequently suffered the criticisms of family and friends and because of the pernicious notions of many more traditional psychological treatments (such as psychodynamic and some of the other insight-oriented approaches) that parents bear the responsibility for child maladjustment.

2. *Even though individuals with ADHD have a biological condition, as with other problems with a known biological etiology, it is still the case that environmental manipulations affect how a person functions in the world.* Environments can be designed to promote success or failure. For example, a person confined to a wheelchair was unable to function in most workplaces when faced with the physical obstacles to accessibility that were in place until relatively recently. However, with the advent of devices including hand controls for automobiles, lifts for public transportation, and ramps and wider doors in buildings, the same person is able to demonstrate his/her abilities. Thus, a wheelchair-accessible environment allows a disabled person to succeed, whereas an environment with barriers guarantees failure. It is clearly the case that home and school environments also have a major impact on how well or poorly a child with ADHD functions. PMT helps parents to provide success-maximizing and frustration-minimizing home environments for their children with ADHD.

3. *Because nature gave you a child that presents you with dilemmas that most parents never face, you must be better than the average parent.* This issue rings particularly true with parents who have other children who are less difficult to manage, since they have learned that the parenting strategies that were perfectly adequate with the less demanding siblings are woefully ineffectual with their ADHD child. This point is clearly illustrated with a story related by a mother participating in a parent training group. This mother proudly described her effective handling of a particularly hellish grocery store incident in which her son, Raymond, flung groceries from a shelf, screamed loudly enough to alarm shoppers on several adjacent aisles, and made increasingly grim threats about the consequences that would ensue if she failed to purchase his desired breakfast cereal. Understandably, the mother felt embarrassed about such public misbehavior and had in the past allowed herself to give in to her Raymond's demands because doing so brought the tan-

trum to a blissfully immediate end. Armed with her recently acquired parent management skills, however, she had anticipated such an incident and made prior arrangements with the grocery store manager to leave her groceries and have them put away until she could return later in the day; with this plan in place, she calmly informed Raymond that she was leaving the store and would wait for him in the car. He watched with astonishment as she departed, and, after several minutes, he resigned himself to the fact that she was not backing down this time and dejectedly joined her in the car. This was the last of Raymond's public tantrums. This strategy is not necessarily one that would be recommended in all cases; while it was reasonable in this case since the family lived in a small town and knew the store owners; in other circumstances it might be inadvisable due to concerns about leaving the child alone in the store. Nonetheless, it provides a good example of the necessity for parents with disruptive children to have better-than-average parenting skills to plan and implement strategies for situations that most parents do not experience.

4. *Although learning and implementing parent management techniques will take some work, in the long run these strategies pay off both in improved child behavior and decreased parent stress.* As we acknowledged previously, PMT requires more parental resources than many other treatments. Because of the demands required to master the prescribed parenting techniques, it is important to assure parents that their efforts are worthwhile, particularly in the early stages of treatment, since treatment gains may not be immediately evident. The potential rewards for parents who are able to learn parent management skills were effectively illustrated by a couple who attended meetings of our local ADHD parent support group. While these parents spoke frankly about the demands required to plan and implement strategies (they humorously lamented their lack of "parenting downtime") and shared their frustration about the daily struggles with which they continued to deal, they also conveyed energetic enthusiasm about the many improvements they had witnessed and their optimism about their ability to effectively manage future problems. Their story served as an eloquent and convincing testimony for behavioral PMT, and their enthusiastic yet realistic portrayal helped other parents see that this treatment offered hope for improved child behavior and family relations.

Determinants of Children's Misbehavior

The behavioral PMT model is based on the premise that children's misbehavior can be understood be examining the environmental consequences for this misbehavior. Behavior problems arise because parents unintentionally reinforce negative behaviors (e.g., allowing a tantruming child to stay up later to play one more video game before bedtime), because doing so reinforces the parent—the child immediately ceases the tantrum and happily plays the game. The coercive process of parents and children reciprocally reinforcing dysfunctional behavior has been studied and described extensively by Gerald R. Patterson (e.g., 1975). Over time, this pattern can lead to increasingly disturbed parent–child interactions.

The emphasis on parent–child interactions should not be construed to negate the role of child characteristics in understanding children's behavior problems. As discussed earlier, biological factors are clearly implicated in ADHD, and the contribution of biological factors to individual differences in child characteristics are important factors in understanding parent–child relations. Most parents of children with ADHD express that their children, from very young ages, were more challenging, demanding, and difficult than other children. As infants and toddlers, they may have been fussy and hard to soothe, or slow to establish a regular pattern of eating or sleeping habits, or more irritable and difficult to correct; these characteristics can easily increase family stress and shape the way parents react to children.

Increasing Positive Behavior with Attention and Praise

A major focus of PMT involves helping parents identify those situations in which their children's behavior is positive and ensuring that such positive behavior is acknowledged and encouraged. It is often the case that when parents first enter treatment they perceive their children's behavior to be primarily negative. This perception can undermine efforts to convince them of the utility of mastering techniques that focus on children's positive behavior. An effective method of introducing this point to parents during PMT involves asking them to estimate what percentage of their child's behavior is "positive" and what percentage is "negative"; typically, the negative percentages overwhelm the positive. With this perspective, parents understandably believe that what they most need is a truly effective punishment to decrease the negative behavior category. It is important to help parents see that their goal of improved behavior can also be achieved by increasing the positive behavior category. The phrase, "catch 'em being good" has been coined to emphasize the importance of this perspective; as difficult as it may initially seem, it is possible to identify and increase instances of positive behavior. By beginning PMT with skills that focus on positive rather than negative behavior, parents are shown that their positive attention can be the most powerful tool in their parenting repertoire.

Parents with disruptive children may have adapted the unfortunate habit of, on the one hand, allowing their child's misbehavior to escalate to an intolerable level and then intervening with threats and other punishments, and, on the other hand, ignoring their child when he/she is behaving appropriately, since such times seem infrequent and provide a much-needed respite for the weary parent. Attention can serve as a highly desirable positive reinforcer, and parents can learn to use it to increase the behaviors they like to see in their children. When implementing PMT in families with young children, an exercise called "the child's game" is sometimes utilized to help parents learn to attend to their child's positive behaviors. In the child's game, parents are instructed to sit with their children while they are playing and to simply comment—much as a sportscaster might—on what their child is doing. For example, a parent might say, "Look at those red blocks Erin is stacking together; what a high tower she's building. She's adding some yellow ones now; I wonder what color block she'll try next." The child's game is introduced in session so that therapists can observe the exercise. This is more difficult than it sounds and can be awkward; to assist in the process, a device called a "bug-in-the-ear" (a communication system that enables a therapist in an adjoining observation room to give suggestions and feedback to parents via earphones) is sometimes used. One specific form of positive attention is praise, which entails complimenting some desirable behavior. This skill can be used in the child's game; for example, parents are encouraged to practice praise by noticing and complimenting their child's block-building abilities. Praise is an integral skill that is also utilized in other facets of PMT, discussed below.

With older children, less formal exercises than the child's game are typically employed, but they have the same goal of prompting parents to notice and provide attention to their child simply for being nondisruptive during play, while watching TV, doing chores or homework, or eating dinner. Thus, parents might be asked to monitor their child at home during play and praise him/her (e.g., "I really like it when you play so cooperatively with your sister—you're really helping Dad get dinner ready") for increasingly long periods of nondisruptive behavior.

Decreasing Negative Behaviors with Ignoring, Timeout, and Loss of Privileges

Once skills for increasing positive behaviors are in place, specific techniques are introduced to directly decrease negative behaviors. The techniques most typically included in PMT are ignoring, timeout, and response cost, which can take the form of loss of privileges or tokens.

Ignoring, or the withdrawal of parental attention, is discussed early in PMT due to the role of attention in maintaining behavior problems. Just as children's desire for parental attention makes it possible for parents to promote behavior simply by letting their children know that they are attending to them, undesirable behaviors can be reduced if parents ignore them. The process by which this occurs is *extinction* (discussed in Chapter 5): once attention is withdrawn, the targeted behavior will eventually decrease. When first using ignoring to decrease a negative behavior, parents must be prepared for an initially bumpy ride; one property of extinction is that it takes time to work. In fact, using ignoring may initially result in a temporary *increase* in the problem behavior, a phenomenon known as a "postextinction burst." For example, parents who apply their newly learned ignoring skills to decrease temper tantrums are likely to be met with an initial reaction of increased intensity of anger and defiance; after all, tantruming has been such an effective attention-getting and goody-generating strategy in the past, surely it will continue to work—perhaps if the volume is increased! If the forewarned parent persists, however, eventually the child will learn that tantrums no longer elicit their desired effect and, over time, tantrums will decrease or even cease. Ignoring is useful for a variety of behaviors that are annoying or unpleasant but for which more intrusive or aversive punishments may not be justified, such as whining, begging, or sloppy table manners.

Timeout has much to recommend it as a punishment procedure. It is effective, yet avoids some of the negative outcomes associated with physical punishment (such as modeling of aggression and other concerns reviewed in Chapter 5). Timeout is defined as a temporary loss of the opportunity to earn reinforcement. Typically, it is operationalized as confinement to a specified area—a corner, a stairstep, a timeout chair, or a bedroom—for a specified time interval (perhaps as brief as 5–10 minutes for younger children and longer for older children) during which further misbehavior does not occur and the child does not receive any attention or other positive reinforcement. This latter aspect of the definition is important and argues against making the timeout area one in which reinforcement, such as TV watching or playing with games, is available. Specific procedures regarding the phrasing, timing, and sequencing of steps in implementing timeout are typically provided for this most challenging PMT skill. Timeout is typically reserved for more serious infractions, although parents may apply their own standards in deciding which misbehaviors they wish to consequate with timeout. Timeout may be used as an automatic consequence for some relatively serious behavior problems, such as incidents of aggression to a peer. Alternatively, it can serve as a backup consequence following a warning, such as for repeated noncompliance, as discussed in the following subsection.

Parents typically need a great deal of therapeutic support when first using timeout, since some children may become quite rebellious and combative during the first attempts to implement it. In such instances, parents are instructed to use physical management procedures to prevent the child from leaving the timeout area, ignore crying and yelling, and remain calm and trust that the tantrum will eventually subside if they refuse to cave in. It is critical that such escalated misbehavior not allow a child to successfully avoid or escape from timeout, since this outcome would reinforce such behavior and make it more difficult to implement timeout in the future. To emphasize this point, some therapists will instruct parents to call them at home prior to allowing a child to leave timeout!

Loss of privileges is another effective technique for consequating undesirable behaviors and is utilized particularly frequently with older children and adolescents. It involves not allowing a child to partake of one or more privileges for a specified time period, such as watching TV, playing video games, choosing favorite snack foods at the grocery store, spending the night with friends, or using the family car. To be effective in preventing misbehavior, it is best if the contingent relationship be specified in advance rather than meted out after an infraction has occurred. Thus, parents are encouraged to warn children about the consequences for rule violations ("Joey, if you come home after your curfew tonight, you won't be able to go out with your friends for the next week") and then, importantly, follow through with the stated consequence.

Compliance Training

Compliance training—getting children to do as they are told—is a nearly universal problem area for the parents of disruptive children. Increasing rates of compliance to commands is a major goal of PMT. The previously discussed skills of attention, praise, ignoring, and timeout can all be utilized in compliance training. As with attention and praise, the use of compliance training with younger children often employs a formal exercise, "the parent game." In this exercise, the parent directs the activity by giving explicit commands, such as asking the child to bring a particular toy to the table or put one game away prior to retrieving another. Parents are coached to praise their children for compliance, to ignore whining and complaining that occur while children are complying, and to use a warning ("Janey, if you don't put the game away, you're going to timeout") followed by timeout for repeated noncompliance.

In addition to providing the appropriate consequences for both compliance and noncompliance, the exact nature of commands can influence how likely a child is to comply. There are a number of typical errors that parents make in issuing commands. Three examples of such commands are chain commands, vague commands, and question commands. *Chain commands* (e.g., "Go upstairs to your room, make your bed, get your dirty clothes and put them in the hamper, put on your shoes, and then set the table for dinner") are problematic if they overwhelm children (particularly younger ones) so that they cannot remember all of the components and hence fail to comply because of problems with recall rather than intentional oppositionalism. *Vague commands* are those that do not clearly specify what is being requested of the child. For example, directing a child to "Be a good boy tonight while the babysitter is here" is too imprecise to allow for compliance. A better command is one that clearly specifies what is expected, such as "Go to bed without arguing tonight when the babysitter asks you to." Finally, *question commands* are those that are phrased in the interrogative rather than declarative form; they are problematic because they do not make expectations explicit. Thus, "Would you like to help me wash the car?" is not a true command and should only be posed if a "no" answer is acceptable. Many times, such questions, which are tentative in tone, are actually meant to convey commands; in these cases, it is preferable to phrase them appropriately: "I'd like you to help me wash the car now." After identifying these types of problematic commands, parents receive suggestions and practice in giving more effective commands.

Token Systems

Many PMT programs teach parents to design and implement token economies as a mechanism for providing specified reinforcers for positive behaviors and "costs" for negative behaviors. Token systems involve the following: (1) making a list of behaviors for which tokens will be rewarded; (2) making a list of behaviors for which tokens will be lost (or "costed"); (3) making a list of rewards for which tokens can be exchanged; (4) specifying the number of tokens rewarded for positive behaviors and costed for negative behaviors, and the number of tokens needed to purchase each reward; and (5) devising a logistical system for tracking the token economy, such as whether tokens will be tangible (e.g., chips; tangible tokens are preferable for younger children) or intangible (e.g., stars or checks on a chart) and when and how tokens are awarded, costed, and exchanged for rewards.

Token systems can be quite simple or quite elaborate. They are very flexible, since behaviors to be awarded and costed can be added to or deleted from the list as desired. Similarly, by providing a variety of rewards on the "reinforcer menu," it is unlikely that satiation (i.e., a child becomes less willing to work for tokens) will occur.

Misbehavior in Public Places

Applying successful discipline strategies in public can be particularly challenging because the stimulating and unfamiliar settings often provide temptations that can lead to increased child misbehavior, and parents may find it more difficult to implement procedures due to embarrassment or logistical considerations, such as the lack of an established timeout area. Planning ahead is a critical component in a successful program for managing behavior problems in public. Planning includes establishing simple rules for appropriate behavior and designating both positive consequences for following rules and negative consequences for rule violations. For younger children, these rules might be as simple as "Stay next to me, don't touch, and don't beg." Examples of contingency plans might include rewards such as allowing a child to choose his/her favorite breakfast cereal or snack for a specified time period in which no rule violations occur, and forfeiture of this privilege for rule violations. Timeout can also be used in public. Some parents utilize immediate timeouts by identifying an appropriate timeout area (a relatively quiet corner of the store or the car; obviously, parents must be willing to supervise their children during timeouts that occur in public places), whereas others will implement a "delayed" timeout by informing children that they will serve a timeout at home for public misbehavior. For families that have established token economies, tokens can be awarded for following rules and costed for breaking rules established for public behavior.

Making a Referral for PMT

Numerous parent- and family-oriented treatments exist, and it is not always easy to discern from the names or brief descriptions of such approaches whether they encompass the behavioral PMT techniques described in this chapter. Many of these approaches have not been empirically validated and may not be effective in treating the behavior problems of concern in this book, so it is important that the specific nature of parent or family programs be explored prior to referring families to them. The following specific questions can assist in this evaluation process:

1. *What theoretical orientation does the program endorse?* Behavioral PMT programs are typically described as reflecting behavior modification or behavior therapy orientations. Programs touted as reflecting other orientations may take a very different approach.
2. *Are the procedures based on a particular PMT program?* As described at the beginning of this chapter, several prominent clinicians, in-

cluding Russell A. Barkley, Gerald R. Patterson, and Rex Forehand, have provided comprehensive PMT programs; programs utilizing these specific materials are exemplars of the behavioral approach. We recommend these programs because, unlike some treatments currently offered, they have been demonstrated empirically to be efficacious for treating the problems experienced by children with ADHD.

Research on the Efficacy of PMT

An extensive literature exists supporting the utility of PMT with families with both clinically disordered and nondiagnosed children. A recent review (Pelham et al., 1998) concluded that behavioral PMT is one of two treatments (along with behavioral classroom interventions, reviewed in Chapter 15), that meet task force criteria for well-established empirical treatments for ADHD, with stronger empirical support of its efficacy for younger children than for older ones. The positive effects of PMT have been demonstrated using a variety of measures, including home observations of parent–child interactions, and parent and teacher ratings of children's behavior. Although rates of children's misbehavior and aggression often show significant reduction, with the positive effects of PMT demonstrated to be maintained in follow-up evaluations conducted 1–4 years posttreatment, there are some limitations to this treatment. Despite significant improvement, children whose parents complete PMT are often still perceived by parents and/or teachers to display clinically significant problems; that is, treatment does not lead to "normalization." As noted previously, PMT may be particularly ineffective for families suffering from high levels of stress, depression, marital discord, or economic disadvantage. Nonetheless, the demonstrated efficacy of PMT warrants its inclusion in a treatment package for children with behavior problems, even though most cases will require adjunctive pharmacological and/or additional behavioral treatments.

Webster-Stratton (1994) reported that basic parent management training can be enhanced by the addition of a broader-based treatment package (ADVANCE) including parent training in communication, problem-solving, and self-control skills to improve coping with interpersonal distress. She describes a study in which families with children diagnosed as having oppositional defiant disorder (ODD) or conduct disorder (CD) received either a standard PMT program or a program including the standard and ADVANCE components. The format of both treatments consisted of the presentation of videotaped vignettes and modeled parenting skills, along with therapist-led discussion; results indicated that some, though not all, treatment outcome measures were improved by the combined treatment. Although both treatments attained similar levels of improved child behavior and decreased parental depression and stress, relative to the standard treatment package, families in the ADVANCE treatment program reported that the parenting skills were more useful and easier to implement, and showed greater improvements in parent problem solving and communication, and child problem solving. Interestingly, across treatments, reductions in levels of deviant child behavior were associated with decreases in critical comments by parents to their children. These findings were based on evaluations conducted shortly after the end of treatment; as noted by Webster-Stratton (1994), it is possible that long-term outcomes may be more sensitive to the potential additional benefits of the ADVANCE treatment. For our purposes, it is noteworthy that a relatively cost-effective intervention shows promise in treating not just deviant child behaviors but parental functioning; we suggest that such enhanced treatment packages have great potential in addressing the complex cases described in this volume.

MULTISYSTEMIC THERAPY

While multisystemic therapy (MST) is a more broadly based program than traditional PMT in that it includes educational and individual treatment components as well as elements of PMT, we briefly consider it here because the focus is on family intervention and because the general approach is consistent with the behavioral methods we advocate. Recent work by Scott W. Henggeler and his colleagues has suggested that MST can be useful in treating the more severe problems associated with juvenile delinquency. The rationale for MST is that delinquent behavior is multidetermined and must be considered in light of youth and family variables as well as the many environmental factors, including peer, school, and neighborhood characteristics, that support and encourage it. Treatment is short term but intensive, often involving sessions conducted three or four times per week or even daily, conducted over 3–6 months. MST is characterized by its focus on present concerns, its active orientation, and its individualized and flexible approach to cases. Accordingly, specific interventions may vary widely but might include both intrapersonal interventions and systemic interventions (e.g., mediating with school personnel; integrating the adolescent into more adaptive peer groups such as the Boy Scouts, athletic groups, church choirs, or other youth activities; working with parents to provide specific sanctions for delinquent behavior). The primary goal of MST is to empower parents with both the resources and skills to negotiate the many twists and turns inevitable in raising an adolescent. Specific guidelines for conducting

MST are provided in detail by Borduin and Henggeler (1990) and Henggeler and Borduin (1990).

Research with MST has supported its efficacy with serious juvenile offenders and in a variety of domains, including family functioning and youth recidivism (e.g., Borduin et al., 1995). Compared to families with youth offenders assigned to individual treatment, those who received MST demonstrated decreased parent symptomatology, decreased youth behavior problems, and improved family relations and family interactions. Most impressively, relative to individual therapy, MST resulted in long-term decreases in youths' criminal behaviors. Four years post-treatment, youths receiving MST showed lower rates of rearrest (26.1%) than those receiving individual therapy (71.4%). Furthermore, of those youths who were rearrested, those in the MST group had been arrested less often and for less serious offenses than those in the individual therapy group.

R. W. GREENE'S "PLAN B" APPROACH TO INFLEXIBLE–EXPLOSIVE BEHAVIOR

In *The Explosive Child,* Greene (1998) argues that some children who demonstrate extreme forms of defiant behavior and out-of-control outbursts do so because of specific deficits in flexibility and frustration tolerance. Since most behavioral techniques (according to Greene's jargon, "Plan A") are predicated on rewarding desirable and punishing undesirable behaviors already in a child's repertoire, they may be insufficient when a child's explosive and inflexible behavior stems from a skills deficit. Thus, Greene's approach ("Plan B") is based on the premise that a subset of children showing externalizing behavior problems cannot (as opposed to *will not*) demonstrate more adaptive behavior. According to Greene, particular co-occurring problems—including ADHD–executive function deficits, difficult temperament, language-processing problems, and nonverbal learning disabilities—represent pathways to this form of inflexible/explosive behavior.

The Plan B approach teaches parents to recognize and anticipate situations that elicit "explosions," create environments that decrease the likelihood of such explosions, focus on collaborative problem solving, and progressively help their child develop self-regulation and problem-solving skills. Parents are asked to prioritize their parenting goals and structure their interventions accordingly. For example, good eating habits may be considered low priority, such that parents are advised to tolerate less than optimal diets (at least initially) and focus their parenting energies on more crucial issues. For high priority matters, parents are taught specific skills for negotiating, compromising, and problem solving with their child about acceptable solutions.

The major limitation of Greene's Plan B approach is that it is based primarily on clinical experience and has yet to be empirically validated. It is, however, consistent with social learning theory as advocated in this volume and seems quite promising for those cases in which standard behavioral interventions are ineffective.

15

Behavioral Interventions for Problems at School

GENERAL ISSUES

The Nature of School Problems in Children with ADHD

Most children with ADHD experience a variety of problems in school, often across several domains. Parents may receive complaints that their child is performing inadequately academically, does not follow school rules, and has problems getting along with other children. As with other facets of their functioning, however, there is a great deal of variability among children with ADHD, such that the nature of school problems may vary greatly from child to child. The following subsections briefly outline some of the types of school problems displayed by children with ADHD. These examples provide good areas of inquiry during assessment and treatment planning, which can be assisted by the use of the SKAMP (discussed in Chapter 3).

Academic Problems

Problems can be seen in both quality (numerous errors, failure to follow explicit instructions, sloppiness; in some cases, problems are also related to difficulties in conceptual understanding) and quantity (does not complete classwork, does not complete homework) of academic work. Inconsistent work patterns are very characteristic of children with ADHD, such that it is common to hear teachers complain that "he turns in all of his work one day, and then barely gets started on his assignments the next." This pattern of variable performance can lead to the misperception that the problem is solely one of motivation since it suggests that, because adequate work output is within the child's capability, it should therefore should be achievable at all times. This common misperception provides yet another example of how education about the nature and attributes of ADHD is an important treatment component and should be extended to teachers as well as parents.

Behavioral Problems

Some behavioral problems may be attributable to inattention and impulsivity rather than intentional oppositionalism, such as forgetting to follow established class rules and procedures and speaking out in class rather than waiting to be called upon. In other instances, such as with children with comorbid disruptive behavior disorders, the nature of the behavior problems may be more directly related to oppositional behavior, including active defiance, noncompliance, and argumentativeness.

Problems with Peer Relationships

As in other domains, the nature of peer relationship problems varies across individuals; some children are socially awkward and/or isolated, whereas others may show aggression toward peers. Some peer problems may stem fairly directly from attention deficits and their effects; they are less attentive during sports and games (Pelham et al., 1990), which may lead to poorer performance and peer rejection.

The nature and treatment of school problems of children with ADHD have been addressed by numerous journal articles and book chapters (e.g., Burcham, Carlson, & Milich, 1993; C. L. Carlson & Lahey, 1988; Greene, 1996; Hinshaw & Erhardt, 1993; Pfiffner & O'Leary, 1993; Zentall, 1993). In addition, several general guides for designing and implementing behavioral interventions in the classroom are available (e.g., Buckley & Walker, 1978; Burke, 1992). Two excellent resources were specifically designed to assist classroom teachers in developing behavioral interventions for children with ADHD; one presents a written guide (Pfiffner, 1996) and the other a training program including videotaped as well as written materials (University of Kentucky Departments of Psychiatry and Psychology & Kentucky Department of Education, 1992). These guides offer detailed, step-by-step guidelines for designing behavioral classroom programs to address the kinds of problems described above. Classroom behavioral interventions have been demonstrated to be effective for children with ADHD, meeting task force criteria for a well-established treatment (Pelham et al., 1998).

Working with School Personnel

A critical factor in implementing a successful school intervention is gaining the support and cooperation of school personnel. In our experience, most classroom teachers are quite receptive to working with professionals to address classroom problems; in fact, many are appreciative of having the additional resources since they often feel ill equipped to deal effectively with the problems presented by the child with ADHD. Still, we have occasionally experienced resistance from teachers. Usually, this resistance occurs if the teachers feel that they are being blamed for the child's difficulties, or if they feel that the suggested interventions require them to devote an extraordinary amount of resources to the targeted child, perhaps at the expense of other children in the class. Clinicians should be sensitive to these issues and should strive to maintain a collaborative relationship with school personnel.

Legal Issues

For years, parents and clinicians attempting to address the school problems of children with ADHD worked within a system that did not grant these children the same legal benefits given other groups, such as those with learning or sensory disabilities, to enable them to gain special school accommodations based solely on their ADHD diagnosis. Largely in response to a concerted grassroots effort spearheaded by the national parent support group and professionals working on their behalf, the U.S. Congress remedied this situation in 1991 by issuing a clarification of the existing policy. The U.S. Department of Education's policy memorandum (of September 16, 1991) recognized children as qualifying for Special Education and related services under federal law *solely* on the basis of having "attention-deficit disorder" (ADD, the term officially used to encompass children with both ADD and ADHD) when it impairs educational performance or learning. Furthermore, the memo noted that such protections were granted under both Public Law 94-142, Individuals with Disabilities Education Act (IDEA), Part B ("other health impaired") and Section 504 of the 1973 Rehabilitation Act. The specific guidelines for qualifying for services are somewhat different under IDEA and under Section 504. Specifically, IDEA, under the Part B "other health impaired" category, considers children with ADD to meet qualifying criteria for Special Education and related services "where the ADD is a chronic or acute health problem resulting in limited alertness." Under Section 504, a child with ADD may be considered to be a "handicapped person," defined as any person who has a physical or mental impairment that substantially limits a major life activity (e.g., learning) and is thus entitled to a free appropriate public education. The phrasing of the

Section 504 recommendations are interpreted as being somewhat more inclusive, in that some children with ADHD may qualify for Special Education services under Section 504 even if they do not meet the criteria specified by IDEA.

There are several important implications of this federal legislation for the identification, evaluation, and academic needs of children with ADHD. First, the legislation stipulates that local education agencies (LEAs) must evaluate a child whose parents believe that he/she has ADHD if the school district has reason to believe that the child may need Special Education or related services. In instances in which the school district does not believe the child needs such services, they must notify parents of their due process rights. Second, the legislation notes that appropriate accommodations might only require adjustments in the regular classroom (rather than Special Education) and provides specific examples of such adaptations to include the following: "providing a structured learning environment; repeating and simplifying instructions about in-class and homework assignments; supplementing verbal instructions with visual instructions; using behavioral management techniques; adjusting class schedules; modifying test delivery; using tape recorders, computer-aided instruction, and other audiovisual equipment; selecting modified textbooks or workbooks; and tailoring homework assignments," as well as other provisions, including "reducing class size, use of one-on-one tutorials; classroom aides and note takers; involvement of a 'services coordinator' to oversee implementation of special programs and services, and possible modification of nonacademic times such as lunchroom, recess, and physical education."

While, as noted previously, it has been our experience that teachers and school personnel are nearly universally supportive of our suggestions for classroom interventions for our ADHD clients, there are exceptions. The potential difficulties that can arise with school personnel were apparent in working with the family of a 7-year-old boy with ADHD, Shannon, who was experiencing both learning and behavior problems at school. One component of the treatment involved a medication assessment, the effects of which were to be evaluated in collaboration with Shannon's physician, which was to include daily school behavior ratings during a 2-week assessment period including 5 mg twice daily, 10 mg twice daily, and placebo phases. Upon learning that a placebo phase was to be included, Shannon's teacher refused to participate in the assessment, declaring that she thought the placebo phase was unnecessary and was intended to "test me, not Shannon." Despite attempts to clarify her misunderstanding and explain the importance of the placebo phase to the evaluation, she refused to reconsider her position and it was necessary to bring the matter to the attention of the principal, who requested that she complete the ratings. This incident occurred prior to the 1991 clarification, so fortunately it was possible to gain the necessary cooperation through informal efforts. In those rare instances when such cooperation is not forthcoming, the now existing legislation provides a legal recourse to parents and professionals in meeting the educational needs of children with ADHD.

What Behaviors Should Be Targeted?

It is evident from the above list of problem behaviors often shown by children with ADHD that they may present with multiple difficulties across the domains of academic, behavioral, and peer relationships. In designing a school behavior management program, it is helpful to have some definite rules about which particular problem behaviors are most appropriate as targets for intervention. Although it may seem desirable to begin by targeting behaviors that are most disruptive and annoying to teachers—such as the child leaving his/her seat without permission, making noises, or calling out in class—there are some compelling reasons *not* to do so. An important set of studies (Ayllon, Layman, & Burke, 1972; Ayllon, Layman, & Kandel, 1975; Ayllon & Roberts, 1974) examining the "direct" and "indirect" effects of behavioral classroom interventions revealed an important pattern. Interventions that directly targeted problem behaviors (e.g., "off-task behavior") successfully decreased these behaviors but did not have any effect on academic productivity (even though it was such off-task behavior that presumably led to the lowered work completion). However, when actual work productivity was directly targeted, not only did it increase but behavior problems decreased as an "indirect" effect of the intervention. These results suggest that, when children direct their resources to schoolwork completion and accuracy, they do so at the "expense" of acting out in the classroom; that is, they show decreased levels of problem behavior as a consequence of working at improving their academic work. However, when they direct their resources to simply decreasing their off-task behavior, they do not necessarily show related decreases in problem behavior.

Given that academic learning is a primary goal of school, we recommend that, when appropriate (i.e., for those children with academic problems), academic productivity and quality be directly targeted in classroom interventions. First, this strategy is one that is most defensible from an ethical standpoint. In an influential paper, "Current Behavior Modification in the Classroom: Be Still, Be Quiet, Be Docile," Winett and Winkler (1972) justifiably argue that designing programs that emphasize orderliness over learning is questionable, and that focusing solely on decreasing disruptive behavior may actually detract from academic performance. Thus, programs that target improved academic performance are not subject to many of the concerns raised by Winett and Winkler (1972), since they are more clearly consistent with appropriate educational goals in that only behaviors that are actually incompatible with learning are reduced. Furthermore, as noted, this strategy may be the most efficient one, since in some instances programs that target improved academic performance also result in decreased levels of problem behavior. Finally, targeting academic performance may increase treatment generalization, such as when the teacher is out of the room (Marholin & Steinman, 1977) and maintenance after treatment withdrawal (Broughten & Lahey, 1978; Hay, Hay, & Nelson, 1977).

Despite the above caveat, there are instances in which it may be necessary to design programs that directly address decreasing problem behaviors. Behavior problems that interfere with the educational progress of other students (e.g., disruptive noisiness during academic seatwork) or interfere with a student's functioning in important nonacademic areas, such as peer relations (e.g., hitting other children), represent appropriate areas of educational concern and may require direct intervention. While some such problem behaviors may respond "indirectly" if academic improvement is targeted, direct targeting of these behaviors is justifiable since they are clearly incompatible with the welfare of the child and/or his/her classmates. Having acknowledged this, we would add a final appeal to clinicians to carefully consider the issues raised about whether a particular behavior is actually interfering with a justifiable educational goal or is merely annoying or inconvenient, and to reserve the powerful behavior therapy techniques we describe below only for those behaviors meeting the former, not the latter, criteria.

SPECIFIC INTERVENTIONS

Environmental Variables

The distinctive characteristics of children with ADHD often place them in direct conflict with the environmental demands that most children are able to successfully navigate. Some of the most effective tools for optimizing the classroom performance of children with ADHD are also the least intrusive, including matching teacher and child characteristics, and manipulating aspects of classroom settings and tasks. The importance of these variables was clearly evident in the course of working with Dean, a fourth-grade child with ADHD, and his family. As part of the evaluation, a school visit was conducted in an attempt to understand the reasons for the remarkably poor academic performance that was a major area of concern for the parents of this intellectually gifted child. The first several minutes of the observation revealed a number of important clues about the mismatch between the teacher's style and expectations and the typical ADHD "style" displayed by Dean. This regimented, "by-the-book" teacher showed a worksheet filled with red ×'s as an example of Dean's poor academic work; examination of the "errors" revealed that, although Dean had in all instances correctly known which capital letters matched specific animals, he had indicated this by circling rather than underlining the correct answers. This inattention to detail so typical of the performance of children with ADHD is certainly problematic, but in this instance the importance of conceptual understanding was completely nullified; this inflexibility will penalize the child with ADHD who is striving to understand concepts despite having difficulty with the details. Add to this picture the fact that the teacher's expectations seemed generally developmentally inappropriate (she revealed during an interview that she was not particularly concerned about Dean's poor performance since approximately one-third of the students failed each day to complete sufficient work to earn the designated privilege!), and it is not surprising that Dean disliked school and was performing poorly despite above-average academic skills.

Matching Teacher–Child Characteristics

As illustrated by the case of Dean, some of the school problems characteristic of children with ADHD can become magnified when their style is a particularly poor match for an individual teacher's expectations. The potential role of mismatches between student and teacher characteristics in the poor school outcomes of children with ADHD has been acknowledged by several writers (for a review, see Greene, 1996). Greene (1995, 1996) has used the term, "student–teacher compatibility" to refer to the compatibility between the capacities, motivations, and behavioral style of the student with ADHD and his/her teacher's expectations and demands. From this perspective, it is important to identify those aspects of teachers' expectations that contribute to the "goodness of fit" between students with ADHD and their instructors. Characteristics potentially influencing compatibility between a child with ADHD and a teacher (Greene, 1996) include the following: teacher interpretations of ADHD behaviors, which may vary from being perceived as willful or attention seeking to beyond the child's control; teacher stress related specifically to interacting with the child with ADHD; the degree to which teaching practices are congruent with those identified to be effective for children with "mild handicaps" (Cannon, Idol, & West, 1992), such as willingness to modify materials to meet individual student's needs and also monitoring performance to provide immediate help and corrective feedback when necessary. Unfortunately, the specific teacher characteristics that result in optimal compatibility for children with ADHD have not been empirically investigated. Although such data are lacking, the obvious importance of this issue dictates that it be informally addressed. When possible, this should occur with an eye toward preventing problems, for example, by discussions with school personnel prior to their making decisions as to annual classroom assignments.

Classroom Setting and Task Variables

Early theorizing about how environments affected children with ADHD embraced widely disparate manipulations, ranging from minimal-stimulation classrooms to decrease distractibility, on the one hand, to open classrooms to allow greater flexibility and freedom, on the other. Little evidence supports either of these approaches (D. M. Ross & S. A. Ross, 1982). Using a social ecology framework, Whalen and Henker and their colleagues (Whalen et al., 1978, 1979) have conducted the most comprehensive assessment of the effects of setting and task variables on children with ADHD. Higher rates of inattentive and inappropriate behaviors were found under noisy conditions and when tasks were difficult and paced according to an outside source; in contrast, differences between ADHD children and control children were minimized under low-noise conditions with easy or self-paced tasks.

Guidelines for educational accommodations have been developed to help children with behavior problems (e.g., ADHD and other disruptive behavior disorders) function more successfully in classroom settings. For example, the state of California outlines specific classroom accommodations for instruction and curriculum, including considerations given to where students are seated, increasing the likelihood that a child will follow instructions, and strategies for modifying classroom structure, lesson plans, and task presentation. Table 15.1 outlines these guidelines as they have been adapted for use by a comprehensive school-based day treatment program for children with ADHD and DBDs conducted by James M. Swanson at the University of California at Irvine—Child Development Center (UCI–CDC). This program utilizes many of the behavioral treatment techniques described in this volume, including classroom behavior management, parent training, and social skills training. The UCI–CDC will be discussed further in later subsections in this chapter and Chapter 16 on maintenance and generalization of treatment gains, since it has developed specific procedures for addressing these important areas.

TABLE 15.1. Classroom Accommodations

I. Considerations given to student's seat in the classroom:
  (1) Near the teacher.
  (2) Near positive role models.
  (3) Out of traffic patterns.
  (4) Away from distractors.

II. Strategies for increasing the likelihood that the child will follow teacher directions:
  (1) Make sure you have eye contact with the child.
  (2) Stand near the child and give directions in a soft voice.
  (3) Be specific as to what you want the child to do.
  (4) Make directions short and clear.
  (5) Break complex directions into a series of simple directions.
  (6) Use a declarative rather than an interrogative sentence to give directions.
  (7) Use visual cues or prompts when possible.
  (8) Give the child at least 10 seconds to respond.
  (9) Check for comprehension by:
    (a) Asking the child to repeat directions.
    (b) Giving the child a chance to ask questions.
    (c) Repeating direction when necessary in a calm, clear voice.
  (10) Teach the child to use a classroom organizer (how, where, and when).

III. Strategies for modifying the structure of the classroom to enhance productivity and task completion:
  (1) Place classroom rules in a prominent place.
  (2) Arrange classroom furniture and traffic pattern to maximize learning and minimize distractions.
  (3) Use color coding activities (e.g., math [blue], reading [red]).
  (4) Use a folder on side of desk for completed papers.
  (5) Use a study carrel to control distractions.
  (6) Have a formalized plan of action if the child does not follow directions—10 seconds for compliance, warning of a consequence with repeat of direction, 10 seconds for compliance, consequence.
  (7) Do not get in the habit of repeating directions without a consequence.

IV. Strategies for modifying how a lesson is presented to enhance productivity and task completion:
  (1) Break lesson into small manageable parts (each part builds on what the child has learned).
  (2) Present lesson using a variety of learning modalities (listening, seeing, touching).
  (3) Alternate response methods (use verbal and nonverbal methods to indicate that children are attending and processing the lesson).
  (4) Vary activities (e.g., seatwork, hands-on activity, small-group discussion, cooperative task).
  (5) Shorten assignments (break assignments into smaller parts with more frequent feedback).
  (6) Use questions to probe comprehension of lesson.

(continued)

TABLE 15.1. *(continued)*

V. Strategies for modifying how a task is structured to enhance productivity and task completion:
  (1) Break assignment into small manageable parts (provide feedback and reinforcement for each part of the assignment completed).
  (2) Give frequent feedback (frequency of feedback is related to the child's attention span).
  (3) Use timer to remind the child to stay on task.
  (4) Set individual goals (assist the child in setting a productivity goal and reinforce completion of that goal).

Teacher-Mediated Programs

Not surprisingly, teachers are responsible for implementing and monitoring most school interventions. The following subsections describe teacher-mediated programs using attention, reward and response cost, token economies, and timeout.

Attention

The contingent use of attention is naturally employed by most teachers, who praise appropriate behaviors and ignore or reprimand inappropriate behaviors. As discussed in Chapter 14 with regard to parent management training (PMT), adult attention can exert a powerful influence on children's behavior. The use of praise, ignoring, and reprimands in the classroom have all been examined empirically. It has been consistently demonstrated that praising children for appropriate behavior is effective in decreasing misbehavior in the classroom. With regards to reprimands, some specific guidelines should be followed. There is some evidence that verbal reprimands are most effective in combination with praise; when used alone they may actually increase inappropriate behavior. In addition, the manner in which reprimands are delivered has been shown to influence their efficacy: soft reprimands are effective, especially reprimands delivered with eye contact while standing close to and grasping the child's shoulders.

Reward and Response Cost

Many classroom management programs are based on providing rewards contingent upon specified desirable behaviors and sanctions (such as response cost) contingent upon specified undesirable behaviors. An example of such a system is making some desired activity, such as 30 minutes of free time, contingent upon a child's completing his/her daily seatwork assignment, or not allowing a child to attend recess contingent upon initiating a fight with a classmate. The success of such interventions require that both the behavior (e.g., "completing all three workbook assignments with at least 80% accuracy") and the consequences (e.g., "may leave class at 3:00 to go to the library for 20 minutes") are specified in advance. The use of a token economy program, described below, provides a comprehensive system for defining behaviors and their consequences.

Token Economies

Token economies have been widely utilized in classroom behavior management programs. The steps relevant to designing a token economy program for the classroom are similar to those relevant to designing one for the home. As noted in Chapter 14, these steps include compiling a list of behaviors to be rewarded and costed, specifying the number of tokens rewarded or costed for these behaviors, and designating available rewards and the token "exchange rate." A major benefit of token economy programs is their flexibility, in that they can be adapted to address a broad range of behaviors and, once set up, can be easily modified as necessary. Token economies have been used to target improved academic performance, class participation, social behavior, and deportment. Numerous rewards, both tangible and intangible, can be incorporated in the token system. An example of a classroom token economy program is outlined in Table 15.2.

Timeout

Timeout, in which a child is temporarily denied the opportunity to obtain reinforcement, can be an effective punishment technique for addressing problem behaviors such as aggression. In the classroom setting, timeout usually refers to socially isolating a child by placing him/her in a chair within the classroom in an area away from other students. An alternative timeout technique involves removing a child from the opportunity to earn reinforcement without actually physically moving him/her to an isolated area. For example, "good behavior ribbons," which are worn by children to indicate their eligibility for participation in desirable activities, can be removed as a form of timeout; this procedure has been shown to be effective in reducing disruptive behavior.

School/Home-Mediated Programs

Home-based reinforcement programs to address children's classroom behavior are widely utilized. These programs typically involve having

TABLE 15.2. Example of a Token Economy Program

	Points earned/lost/cost
Earn tokens for:	
Turning in homework	80 or higher accuracy = 5 90 or higher accuracy = 7
Completing seatwork assignment	80 or higher accuracy = 5 90 or higher accuracy = 7
Being ready to work (has materials, turned to correct page)	5 points (each period)
Beginning work when instructed to do so	5 points (each period)
Keeping hands to yourself	5 points (each period)
Lose tokens for:	
Teasing	10 points
Disturbing classmates	5 points
Starting a fight	50 points
Noncompliance to teacher request	20 points
Talking out of turn/making noises	5 points

Reinforcement menu	
A trip to the library	Choose an art activity for the class
Extra dessert at lunch	Choose from the "school supplies" grab bag (colored pencils, decorative folders, and notebooks)
30 minutes free time/recess	Teacher's assistant for the day
Feed the class pet	

teachers rate some specified set of child behaviors and communicate this rating to parents in a letter or report card, with parents then providing rewards at home for a positive teacher report. Such home report cards have a number of attractive features (Atkeson & Forehand, 1979). First, they are less demanding than many of the teacher-mediated programs discussed above, and therefore may provide a desirable and more acceptable alternative to them when limited teacher resources or motivation are an issue. In addition, by providing parents with feedback about their child's behavior, these programs can result in generally enhanced communication and perhaps greater cohesion between parents and teachers. As mentioned, these programs require less teacher time; they also require fewer school resources than techniques such as token programs, and they may benefit from the use of potentially powerful reinforcers that are accessible at home but not at school.

Many of the school behavior problems demonstrated by children with ADHD are appropriate targets for home report cards. The steps that should be taken in designing these programs are as follows: (1) obtain consensus among relevant parties (i.e., teachers, parents, professionals) about the behaviors to be included in the report; (2) designate specific definitions of target behaviors and criteria for receiving a positive and negative report; (3) designate specific rewards to be given at home for positive reports; (4) designate which parties are responsible for which components of the program, i.e., the child must bring the report to school, the teacher must give the rating at the appropriate time (after each class period, at the end of the day, upon occurrence/nonoccurrence of a behavior, etc.), the parent must ensure that the child is rewarded appropriately at home; (5) explain the program to the child; and (6) reassess the program periodically to make needed changes, such as adding or deleting behaviors as needed, raising expectations as the child shows improvement (e.g., requiring increasingly higher levels of accuracy to receive a "yes" on "completed seatwork assignment"), and "troubleshooting" as problems arise. Other considerations in designing home report cards involve setting initial goals at a level at which success is likely to enhance student motivation and, to ensure children's continuing motivation, having parents provide rewards for positive report cards but not punishment for negative ones. This latter consideration is especially important in instances in which there is a history of highly coercive or abusive parent–child interactions; accordingly, home report cards may be inadvisable for such families. An example of a home report card is provided in Figure 15.1.

Peer-Mediated Programs

Considering the strong influence of peer attention on children's behavior, it is not surprising that peers have been used as behavior change agents in classroom behavior management programs. Peers have been used as monitors in token economy programs, as trained dispensers of attention and reinforcement for a classmate's appropriate behavior, and as group members in programs in which group consequences are contingent upon a child's behavior.

Programs using peers to monitor the behavior of classmates can be used for a variety of problem behaviors; in some instances these programs are classwide, whereas in others an individual child may be the specific target of an intervention. For example, children can be coached to ignore inappropriate behavior and attend to and praise classmates for appropriate behaviors such as completing classwork or working without disrupting the class. When a specific child is the target of a program, a peer who the child particularly likes may serve in this role. Social behavior may be a particularly appropriate area in

JILL'S DAILY REPORT CARD

Class (check one)

Language Arts ____

Math ____

Science ____

Art ____

Other ________

Had materials needed for assignment	Yes	No
Started work right away	Yes	No
Completed assignment	Yes	No
Assignment grade of 80% or higher	Yes	No
Kept hands to myself	Yes	No

FIGURE 15.1. Example of a home report card.

which to use a peer intervention program. For example, Grieger, Kauffman, and Grieger (1976) describe a peer-reporting system in which children took turns distributing happy face badges and reporting to the class about friendly acts of peers; this program resulted in increases in cooperative play and decreases in aggressive behavior. The use of peers in programs specifically designed to improve social skills is described further in Chapter 16.

Programs in which group consequences are contingent upon the behavior of a particular child or group of children have been used to increase academic productivity and decrease a variety of problem behaviors. A common form of this is the "good-behavior game" (e.g., Barrish, Saunders, & Wolf, 1969), in which groups of children compete with each other to fulfill a specified criterion of appropriate behavior to receive a reward. Making group consequences contingent upon an individual child meeting some goal may provide a particularly powerful incentive to the targeted child, though it is obvious that such programs must be designed carefully to avoid making the child subject to coercive consequences of social sanctions from peers if the goal is not obtained.

Peer-mediated programs are appealing for many reasons (Strain,

Cooke, & Apolloni, 1976), including practical considerations related to relieving teachers of some of the logistical aspects of maintaining treatment programs, and the potential for greater generalization and maintenance since peers are present and thus able to monitor behavior across more settings (e.g., the restroom, playground, hallway) than teachers are. Accordingly, peer presence may come to serve as discriminative stimuli for good behavior in classrooms. In addition, there may be social benefits that accrue as a consequence of increased peer contact and a motivational pattern elicited when peers are invested in the positive behavioral outcomes of a child. Despite these potential benefits, the use of peers as behavior change agents can sometimes have its pitfalls (O'Leary & Drabman, 1971) if children undermine the system, place untoward pressure on an individual child, or have inadequate skills to perform the required responsibilities.

Self-Mediated Programs

Self-control techniques, including self-monitoring and self-reinforcement techniques in which children assume the responsibility for monitoring and rewarding their own behavior, have also been used in classroom behavior management programs. While cognitive-behavioral interventions might be classified as "self-control" techniques, these programs will not be discussed in detail since research on their use has failed to demonstrate their efficacy for children with ADHD (Pelham et al., 1998).

Although self-control programs have been used as initial interventions, more often they follow a well-established externally administered program as a mechanism for treatment maintenance and generalization. The transfer of control from an external to an internal locus is usually phased in by, for example, rewarding a child for matching teacher reports prior to making rewards contingent entirely upon child reports. Data on self-monitoring and self-reinforcement programs show mixed results. While they sometimes bring about maintenance of gains achieved with externally monitored programs, deterioration of behavior gains can occur. Thus, while the self-control aspect of these programs is intuitively appealing, they may not be effective for all children.

MAINTENANCE AND GENERALIZATION ISSUES

Maintenance and generalization of treatment gains in the school setting can be challenging, especially as children move from classroom to classroom both within and between school years. One method for addressing this area was developed at the UCI–CDC for helping to facilitate placement from the day-treatment program to a regular classroom setting in the child's home district. After children remained in the UCI–CDC placement for up to 1 year, they attended a "transition school" (El Toro Marine School) to allow them to test their new skills in a natural environment—where UCI–CDC staff were placed to provide help if needed—before returning to their "neighborhood school." The El Toro Marine School transition program evolved into the Irvine Paraprofessional Program (IPP), which we now use to provide treatment in the natural school environment to facilitate generalization and transfer from the more restrictive settings of the UCI–CDC school-based day-treatment program. The IPP was chosen as one of the "promising practices" by the ADD Center at the University of Kentucky, which conducted a review for the U.S. Department of Education (Burchan, Carlson, & Milich, 1993). The IPP was adopted by the NIMH Multimodality Treatment Study as the follow-up transition component for a six-site long-term treatment program that included a school-based day-treatment component and a follow-up transition program in the regular school setting (Arnold et al., 1997; Greenhill et al., 1996; Hinshaw et al., 1997).

Transition is initiated 2 months prior to the end of the treatment program. The transition process from the UCI–CDC to an alternative program focuses on matching the child's needs with an appropriate educational and collateral therapeutic program. The staff of the treatment team meets with the school district personnel to describe exactly what strategies need to be in place to maintain the child's progress. A specific classroom and collateral support services are identified based on the specific needs of the child. This may include Special Education services and a referral for follow-up mental health services. A plan is developed with the school to maintain the child's progress through the use of a collaborative home/school program of reinforcement. A daily report card is developed that targets the child's treatment goals. Parents learn in the multiple-family group sessions to support the school program by providing home-based reinforcement for school behavior. The home/school program developed with the alternative school placement is practiced and refined during the last 2 months of the treatment program. The staff also coordinates with physicians and collateral therapists to plan for transition. Children and their families may also participate in an outpatient multiple-family group designed to monitor and maintain gains made while attending the school program. Parents and their children learn to use the skills they have acquired at the CDC to adjust to problems that occur at school, home, and in the community. The group also serves as a support group for families as they struggle with the difficult task of adapting to the new transition placement.

16

Behavioral Interventions for Problems on the Playground

THE NATURE OF PLAYGROUND/SOCIAL PROBLEMS IN CHILDREN WITH ADHD

One of the most widely documented and readily observed areas of dysfunction for children with ADHD involves peer relationships. Just as the symptoms of ADHD often lead to conflict with the demands of home and school settings, they can also disrupt the process of forming and maintaining friendships. Indeed, peer rejection of children with ADHD can surface even after remarkably brief exposure, with research examining groups of previously unfamiliar children showing that children with ADHD evoke negative reactions from other children within the first hour of exposure. Factors linked to the poor peer functioning of children with ADHD include aggression, oppositional and overt antisocial behavior, and social withdrawal (Hinshaw, Zupan, Simmel, Nigg, & Melnick, 1997). Thus, there may be multiple pathways to peer dysfunction in children with ADHD, and consideration of comorbid conditions is likely to be of particular importance in addressing their peer relationship problems.

We recently asked parents of children with ADHD participating in a research project to describe the nature of their child's peer interactions. The following vignette illustrates the pervasive peer problems experienced by these children and their often painful consequences:

One mother of a 10-year-old boy with ADHD describes what she saw when she accompanied him to the playground to observe his peer interactions. His clumsy attempts at engaging other children consisted of his walking up to them, tapping them on the head, and running while they chased him. The entire time she observed him he was either standing by himself or initiating the tap–run strategy to gain the attention of others. Though this intrusive behavior is not an extremely aggressive one, it is clearly an ineffective strategy for initiating or maintaining good peer interactions. Not surprisingly, this mother reports that her son's peer relationships are quite poor.

INTERVENTIONS FOR SOCIAL PROBLEMS: GRESHAM'S MODEL OF DYSFUNCTIONAL PEER RELATIONSHIPS

As described above, the kinds of behaviors exhibited by ADHD children that lead them into troubled peer relationships seem to vary greatly. In some instances, they seem socially awkward and immature, as if they have simply failed to grasp the unwritten and often subtle social rules that most children are able to discern without undue effort. This pattern may lead ADHD children to withdraw socially, or to make repeated, sometimes overly energetic and intrusive overtures that are frequently rebuffed by other children. In still another group of children with ADHD, overt aggression or impulsive responding result in troubled interactions with peers, marked by high levels of conflict and erratic behavior. As in other domains, individual differences are the rule rather than the exception. It is clear, however, from research documenting that peer rejection is correlated with disruptive behavior, achievement deficits, and aggression, that many children with ADHD are at risk for social failure (Landau & Moore, 1991).

Hinshaw (1992b) specifies potential treatment targets for improving the peer relations of children with ADHD, including decreasing negative peer behaviors (particularly aggression), increasing prosocial behaviors, improving social information processing, altering social goals, intervening directly with peer groups to affect social status, and enhancing general social and academic performance. Specific interventions addressing these areas of potential concern will be discussed below within the framework of Gresham's (1988) model of dysfunctional peer relationships.

Gresham (1988) proposed a model for understanding various pathways to peer relationship problems that may illuminate the nature of social deficits in children with ADHD. This model distinguishes between *social skills* deficits, which are related to inadequate knowledge of appropriate social behavior, and *social performance* deficits, which occur when children, despite possessing adequate knowledge, fail to perform the appropriate social action. Gresham further proposes that both social skills and social performance deficits can be linked to specific interfering responses. For example, social withdrawal may be construed as an interfering response that impedes social skills, since it may lead to low levels of social interaction and thus inhibit the learning of social rules. Similarly, for a child confronting a peer who has just cut in front of him in line, aggression may "short-circuit" what he knows to be an appropriate response—asking the peer to observe the rules—and resort instead to pushing the peer aside; in this example, aggression serves as an interfering response leading to a performance deficit.

Gresham's model has been applied to ADHD by Carlson and colleagues (Maedgen & Carlson, 1998; Wheeler & Carlson, 1994) with a specific goal of delineating the nature of social deficits in the combined subtype versus the predominantly inattentive subtype. These authors note that Gresham's distinction between knowledge and performance deficits suggests at least two pathways that can lead to dysfunctional peer relationships for children with ADHD; importantly, they correspond to distinct treatment implications. For children with knowledge deficits, teaching specific social skills would be an important component of treatment, whereas for children with performance deficits, who presumably possess adequate social knowledge, interventions might better focus on self-control strategies that enable them to use that knowledge. In both instances, treatments might also need to address the specific interfering responses contributing to the deficits. This distinction is considered in the specific interventions discussed below.

SOCIAL SKILLS TRAINING PROGRAMS

Specific Components and Programs

A number of specific social skills training packages have been developed. Oden and Asher (1977) identify four classes of social skills: cooperation, communication, participation, and validation. Each of the four social skills have been operationally defined by Pelham and Bender (1982). They used the strategy of providing a definition of the skill and providing examples (appropriate for children) of performing and not performing the "good" and "bad" examples of each skill. Then, they described the reason for using the skill and provided settings for practice with coaching. Examples for each of these social skills are provided in Table 16.1.

TABLE 16.1. Examples of Definitions of and Rationale for Social Skills

What does cooperation mean?
  Sharing; following rules; taking turns; not getting mad; not cheating

What is an example of cooperating?
  Playing well when losing; playing a game when you don't agree with the rules; keeping your temper and not fighting

What is an example of not cooperating?
  Quitting when losing; crying when you don't like the rules; getting mad and hitting

Why is cooperating important?
  People will like playing with you

What does communication mean?
  Talking about interesting things; listening to what others are saying

What is an example of communicating?
  Looking at others when they are talking; asking questions about how to play games

What is an example of not communicating?
  Ignoring someone who is talking; changing the subject; interrupting

Why is communication important?
  If you talk about interesting things when it's your turn and listen when it is not, then others will want to be your friend

What does participation mean?
  Being interested; paying attention; getting involved

What is an example of participating?
  Initiating a game; setting the rules

What is an example of not participating?
  Wanting to play only your game; refusing to play someone else's game

Why is participation important?
  Others will like playing with you

What does validation mean?
  Being helpful; being nice; being friendly

What is an example of validating?
  Saying nice things; cheering; complimenting

What is an example of not validating?
  Complaining about others; making fun of others

Why is validation important?
  If you are nice and helpful, others will feel good when you are around and like being around you

Note. Data from Oden and Asher (1977) and from Pelham, Greiner, and Gnagy (1997).

Hinshaw, Henker, and Whalen (1984) developed a program to help children with ADHD develop anger management and self-control strategies that can be specifically applied to situations in which they are teased. In the teasing module, children learn anger recognition skills, develop personal goals and plans for self-control (e.g., ignoring, looking away, humming, self-talk), and role-play their strategies during sessions in which counselors and other children "tease" the target child using phrases generated by the child as being those that are particularly bothersome. Obviously, this intervention must be undertaken with a great deal of sensitivity to avoid potentially deleterious effects, such as social stigmatization. We have had mixed experience with this intervention. We have experienced instances of some children reacting negatively to the procedure; furthermore, it is not clear to what extent the "in-session" teasing generalizes to real-world settings. On the other hand, the teasing module seems to have been quite helpful with some children. In addition, using the module as a component in an established treatment program (in which children are well acquainted with each other and likely to have fairly well-established bonds) and providing a thoughtful presentation of treatment goals (with an emphasis on the role of in-session teasing as a mechanism for helping group members effectively manage feelings so that they will be more able to handle teasing situations outside the treatment setting) may actually strengthen rather than damage group cohesion. Thus, we recommend that therapeutic judgment be used in deciding whether or not to implement the teasing module. It may also be useful to supplement the training with procedures that support the use of anger control in other settings; this might be accomplished, for example, with a counselor in a treatment program who provides a "cue" to the child to utilize self-control techniques.

An example of a comprehensive social skills training approach is that used in the school treatment program at the University of California at Irvine–Child Development Center (UCI–CDC), described in Chapter 15. The UCI–CDC program uses a high-density reward system adapted from Pelham and colleagues' work (Pelham & Murphy, 1986; Pelham & Bender, 1982; Swanson et al., 1978) and specific skills approaches developed by Oden and Asher (1977) and Michelson, Sugai, Wood, and Kazdin (1983). The specific social skills curriculum from the UCI–CDC program is shown in Table 16.2. The social skills intervention is used to shape behavior and to build peer interaction skills in a group therapy setting in small-group sessions of 8–12 children, with social skills sessions integrated into the school day. The groups are led by specially trained social skills counselors in combination with the child's teacher or behavioral specialist. Teachers and behavioral specialists team with the social skills counselors to ensure consistency in the vocabulary and strategies used to prompt children to use appropriate social skills in the class-

TABLE 16.2. Social Skills Curriculum at the UCI–CDC Program

1. *Good sportsmanship*
   Cooperation: "When two people work together to get something done"
   Nice sayings: "Saying or doing something nice"
   Following directions: "Doing what the teacher told you to do"
   Following rules: "Doing what is allowed"
   Helping: "Doing something for someone else"
   Sharing: "Letting someone else do what you are doing"
   Staying with the game: "Staying on task"
   Participating: "Trying hard"
   Using "Cool Craig" (puppet figure) voice and behavior (body language)

2. *Accepting*
   "When something happens that you don't like and you continue to follow the rules and get along with others"

3. *Asserting*
   "Not being an aggressive 'Mean Max' or a passive 'Wimpy Wally'—being a 'Cool Craig' [puppet figure]"

4. *Ignoring*
   "Not showing that something is bothering you"

5. *Problem solving*
   "Using five steps to get a problem solved and stay out of trouble"

room. To promote the generalization of social skills target behaviors that are changed by the interventions of the daily group therapy session, the training is integrated into the rest of the day-treatment program. The same language (e.g., "accepting," "good sportsmanship," or "Cool Craig"; see Table 16.2) that is learned and used in the group therapy sessions is used throughout the day, and points are awarded for instances of these categories of behaviors.

Four specific steps are characteristic of most social skills training programs: promoting skill acquisition, enhancing skill performance, removing interfering behaviors, and facilitating generalization (Elliot & Gresham, 1993; Gresham, 1988). These steps are discussed in the following subsections.

Skills Acquisition

Social skills are typically taught via instructions, explanations, modeling, coaching, and behavioral rehearsal. The specific skills taught vary across programs but often include prosocial (e.g., sharing) and assertive (e.g., requesting a behavior change) skills. Oden and Asher (1977) describe four general skills: participation, cooperation, communication, and validation.

Michelson et al. (1983) utilize more specific skills, including giving compliments, making a complaint, saying no, requesting a behavior change, having conversations, and coping with conflict. A typical training session involves the following: a didactic presentation of the definition of, rationale for, and steps in performing a particular skill; discussion with children during which examples of both positive and negative use of the skill are elicited; and modeling of the skill via the use of practice scripts illustrating both proper and improper use of the skill and their related consequences. Children are encouraged throughout sessions to actively participate by providing examples from their own experience, practicing the demonstrated skills, and receiving feedback about their performance as well as providing feedback about the performance of others.

Providing children with knowledge about appropriate social behavior is inadequate if they do not perform those behaviors with adequate skill and finesse. It is therefore necessary to assess their actual level of skill performance and provide specific additional training for those whose performance is lacking. This is most often achieved via behavioral rehearsal and role-playing. For example, after receiving instruction and observing an instructor model the specific steps for requesting a behavior change, a child is asked to practice this skill. Feedback about performance deficits, including inadequate mastering of the prescribed steps as well as more subtle deficits, such as inappropriate voice tone or facial expression, is provided, and the child is encouraged to incorporate the feedback in subsequent role-plays. Videotaping of child role-plays may be used to enhance the process of feedback/performance improvement.

Enhancing Skill Performance

A critical component of training programs is to encourage and enhance the use of targeted social skills. This goal is addressed by prompting and reinforcing the appropriate use of skills via techniques including many of the procedures addressed in previous chapters (e.g., positive reinforcement, peer-mediated interventions, and school/home-based reinforcement programs). Token or other reinforcement can be used for the successful demonstration of skills during school, treatment program, or home settings. For example, teachers might incorporate specific social goals into token reinforcement programs; these might include targets such as inviting another child to share a game, having no episodes of physical aggression during lunch, or reducing the number of episodes of teasing other children. School/home programs can also be used to enhance skill performance by including such socially relevant behaviors in report cards so that they can be monitored and reinforced at home.

Similarly, if parents are knowledgeable about the content of social skills sessions (see the description of a parent-mediated generalization procedure, below), they might set specific goals for having a friend for an overnight visit (e.g., "During snack time, I want you to show good cooperation by taking turns doing tasks when we're making cookies, sharing cookies and popcorn when they're done, and volunteering to put the dirty dishes in the sink"). Children can then earn a special privilege (e.g., watching an extra 30 minutes of videos before going to bed) for meeting the specified goal. Although such programs obviously demand additional planning and monitoring by parents, they provide invaluable practice for children during skill acquisition.

Peer-mediated techniques may involve classmates in prompting and reinforcing appropriate skill performance. Such programs allow "treatment" to be conducted in settings—such as on the playground, in hallways, and during lunchtime—which are typically not accessible to adult observation, thus promoting generalization (discussed further in a later subsection). In addition, as described in Chapter 15, peer-mediated interventions may by their nature have the benefit of improving social status. For such programs to work it is critical that the chosen peer monitor be mature and responsible in implementing the procedures, and a high-status peer may be the most effective agent. If peer monitors are included in social skills training groups, they may provide ongoing feedback to target children and/or participate, under the supervision of the social skills counselor, in giving feedback about skills performance after some specified activity, such as recess.

Addressing Interfering Responses

As already noted, many of the potential targets for addressing the peer relationship problems of children with ADHD involve interfering responses. Indeed, the specific behaviors that actually contribute to their poor peer status involve interfering responses such as aggression, overt antisocial acts, and withdrawal. These behaviors should thus be directly targeted for optimizing gains in social skills since, even if children possess adequate social knowledge and abilities, such interfering responses may prevent them from demonstrating them. For externalizing behaviors involving behavioral excesses (e.g., aggression, or antisocial acts such as lying and stealing), punishment procedures are typically implemented. As discussed in previous chapters, such procedures may include the use of response cost, timeout, and removal of other privileges. For social anxiety or withdrawal, it is critical to assess the cause of the behavioral response and design an intervention accordingly. For children whose social withdrawal stems from insecurity arising from negative social experiences (perhaps due to poor social skills), an effective skills intervention program may be adequate to induce them to be more confident about initiating social interactions. For children whose withdrawal is based on more intense or generalized anxiety, additional procedures, such as exposure, relaxation, or other methods directly targeting anxiety, may be necessary. These procedures are discussed in more detail in Chapter 9 concerning ADHD children with comorbid anxiety disorders.

Generalization

A critical aspect of social skills training involves building in mechanisms to promote the generalization of treatment gains. Children who learn to perform flawless role-plays during the course of skills training sessions will not benefit from their new skills if they do not produce them outside of the treatment environment. Some aspects of training sessions themselves are typically aimed at promoting generalization, such as ensuring that didactic information and role-plays address diverse realms of social situations. Indeed, some of the specific skills targeted in many programs, such as problem-solving techniques, are presumed to specifically address generalization by teaching children a process by which to approach problem situations as they arise. It is typically necessary, however, to supplement these techniques with specific manipulations aimed at promoting and reinforcing their use of appropriate social skills in their natural environments.

As discussed in Chapter 15, specific procedures for promoting generalization can involve having counselors who have worked with the child in a therapeutic setting provide a "transition" to a new or "real-world" setting. We have found some success in having social skills training group counselors accompany children on the playground to prompt and reinforce their use of social skills. If this intervention is used, it is obviously important that it be implemented in a way that does not socially stigmatize a child, since this could sabotage rather than promote social success. In our experience, however, when used with younger children the presence of the counselor (especially to the extent that the counselor is perceived by children as a desirable associate) may actually enhance the child's social status. In some situations, such as with older children, a peer may be able to serve this function.

Another mechanism for enhancing treatment generalization is to give parents training aimed at promoting their children's social skills in their daily interactions outside of the treatment setting. At the UCI–CDC program, in addition to the generalization procedures described earlier (social skills are monitored and reinforced during the morning and afternoon recesses, the after-school program, and when the children are being transported to and from school), a parent training session is devoted to "social skills in the real world." The focus of the session is on how to incorporate the social skills taught during the school program into everyday experiences. Parents have an opportunity to observe the CDC staff model strategies for encouraging children to use their social skills, and then parents practice under the supervision of the CDC staff. An enhanced version of this parent-mediated generalization procedure was recently evaluated in a study (Pfiffner & McBurnett, 1997) that compared the efficacy of an 8-week program of social skills training (SST) program for children with ADHD in which children received group social skills training only (SST-only), group social skills training plus the parent-mediated generalization component (SST–PG), or were assigned to a wait-list control group. The SST program followed the format described above, using didactic instruction, modeling, role-playing, and token reinforcement of skill demonstration; the sessions included specific modules addressing good sportsmanship, accepting negative consequences appropriately, assertiveness, ignoring provocation, problem solving, and recognizing and managing feelings. In the SST–PG group, parents met in a group and received general information about social skills and specific didactic instructions and written materials about each module, observed segments of the children's group sessions, and were coached to use token reinforcement at home and meet with their child's teachers to design a home/school report card targeting the use of social skills at school. Children in both SST groups showed improvements in skill knowledge and parent ratings of social skills and disruptive behavior immediately following treatment and at 4-month follow-up. Teacher ratings showed a more inconsistent pattern; only the SST–PG group showed improvements in teacher-rated social skills that were maintained at 4-month follow-up, which was conducted, importantly, with new teachers unacquainted with the SST program. Only the SST-only group, however, showed decreases in teacher-rated disruptive behavior (not maintained at follow-up). These results provide encouraging evidence for the efficacy of SST for children with ADHD but only modest evidence for the benefits of adding a parent-mediated generalization component (SST–PG). As Pfiffner and McBurnett (1997) acknowledge, however, the relatively limited outcome differences between groups may have been partly attributable to the fact that parents in the SST-only group reported such high rates of improvement that it would have been difficult to discern additive effects of the SST–PG component; furthermore, since parents in the SST-only group did receive the written materials (which included tips for parents to reinforce skills at home), they may have actually engaged in some home-implemented generalization strategies.

Self-monitoring procedures have also been implemented as a means of enhancing the use of targeted social skills outside the treatment setting. Specific forms provided to participants can be used for them to record instances of skill use and its consequences, with reinforcers given to children for returning forms to sessions and providing a parent or teacher signature "authenticating" the incidents (Guevremont, 1990).

Epilogue: Future Directions in Research and Treatment

What lies ahead for researchers studying and clinicians treating ADHD children with comorbid disorders? It is quite likely that advances in the understanding of the neurobiology of ADHD will provide us with new ways to intervene with these difficult patients. Several areas will be impacted. When the causes of ADHD (and it is likely there will prove to be several) are understood, it will be possible to accurately subtype ADHD at a genetic or neurological level. We shall be able to tell if a certain comorbidity occurs more frequently with a particular genetic subtype of ADHD. When the genetics of the comorbid disorder are understood (e.g., bipolar disorder), we can then search for this marker in children who meet criteria for both ADHD and bipolar disorder. How many patients have a bipolar gene in addition to an ADHD gene? How many have only the bipolar gene? In the latter case, the ADHD symptoms might be viewed as prodromal symptoms of the bipolar disorder. In the former case, we might view the two conditions as independent, with two disease genes acting in concert in that individual. The process of diagnosis would be much more rational.

Research in ADHD and other psychiatric disorders is advancing both in the area of neuroimaging and genetics. The first positron-emission tomography (PET) studies in adults with ADHD showed decreased global glucose metabolism relative to controls (Zametkin et al., 1990). The results were less straightforward in adolescents (Ernst et al., 1994; Zametkin et al., 1993), and concerns about radiation in young children, particularly control children, has limited the use of PET studies in ADHD research. Attention has turned to the use of magnetic resonance imaging (MRI) studies. At present only structural imaging studies are available, but functional MRI work is underway. Without using any invasive techniques or radiation, oxygen utilization (and hence brain activity) can be assessed in patients and controls while they perform cognitive tasks. Genetic research has focused on genes involved in the control of the brain catecholamine systems, particularly the dopamine system. To conclude, we will (1) present an overview of the major theories of ADHD, (2) summarize important new findings in the both neuroimaging and genetics, and (3) discuss the relevance of such findings to the comorbidities we have discussed.

THEORIES OF ADHD

Theories about ADHD have been constructed along both neuropsychological lines (Barkley, 1997) and neurochemical lines (Castellanos, 1997; Pliszka, McCracken, & Maas, 1996; Solanto, 1984). Most recently, Barkley (1997) has developed a model of ADHD that postulates *behavioral inhibition* as the core deficit in the disorder, as shown in Figure E.1. Four other more complex executive functions are theorized to be dysfunctional in ADHD. These systems normally function together to establish *motor control,* that is, the final output of complex goal-directed behavior guided by internal cognitions rather than by stimuli or reinforcers in the immediate environment. Behavioral inhibition has three functions: inhibiting a prepotent response (i.e., not responding immediately to a stimulus, or delaying gratification), interrupting an ongoing response (e.g., a child stops himself from grabbing a piece of candy when he remembers it is almost dinnertime) and interference control (e.g., a child does not react to an airplane flying overhead as he concentrates on the next spelling word on a test). Barkley (1997) theorizes that behavioral inhibition not only has a direct effect on motor control, but by blocking the immediate motor response it allows the four major executive functions to come "on-line" and participate in the construction of complex motor behaviors. These four executive functions are summarized in the following subsections.

Nonverbal Working Memory

If long-term memory is analogous to the hard drive of a computer, where data are stored, nonverbal working memory is analogous to the

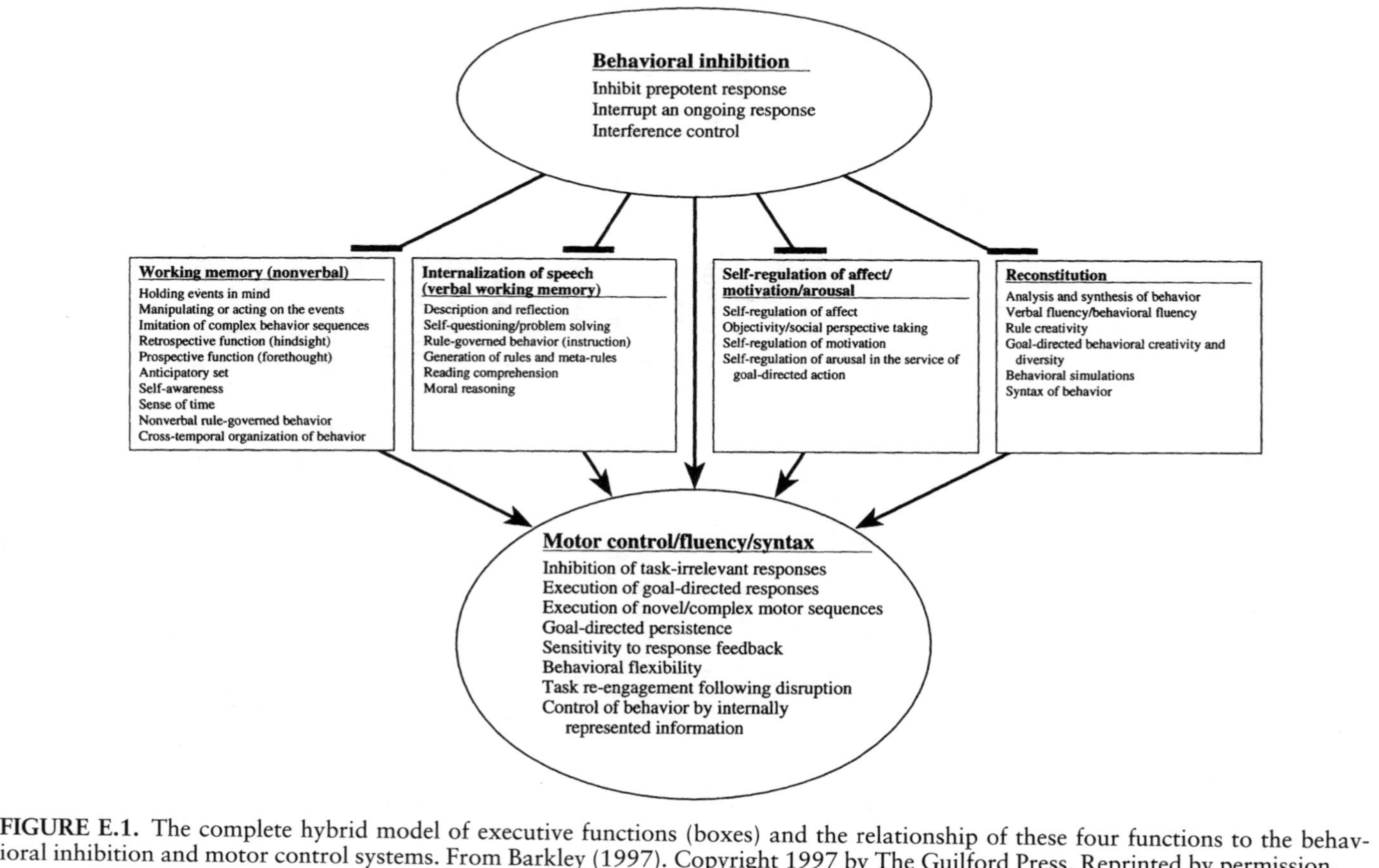

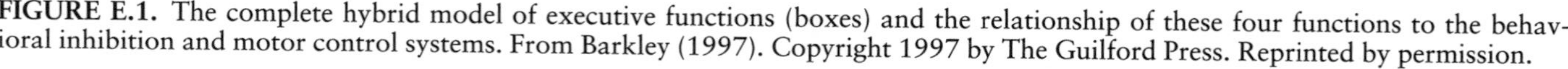
FIGURE E.1. The complete hybrid model of executive functions (boxes) and the relationship of these four functions to the behavioral inhibition and motor control systems. From Barkley (1997). Copyright 1997 by The Guilford Press. Reprinted by permission.

computer's random-access memory (RAM). It is the place where data needed for an operation are stored temporarily and manipulated by the software program. Events are held in the mind, information about the current state is compared to what has happened in the past (hindsight), and attempts are made to estimate how things should be done in light of that experience (forethought). Critical to this is the sense of time. This nonverbal working memory is like a movie of events running in the mind; it is visual–spatial in nature and may be more localized to the right dorsolateral frontal cortex.

Verbal Working Memory

Verbal working memory represents the internalization of speech. As children mature, speech becomes much more than a means to communicate with others. Preschoolers begin to talk to themselves, both in fantasy play and when guiding themselves to perform tasks. Eventually this speech becomes private and rules are internalized. Take the example of the child not taking the piece of candy. The act of stopping his hand from grabbing the candy represents behavioral inhibition, but behavioral inhibition was activated because the child possessed an internal rule ("No candy before dinner"), which he could access. Without such an internal rule, there would be no reason to inhibit behavior. Going back to nonverbal working memory for a moment, the child may also recall the last time he broke the rule—a memory of his mother scolding him or taking away his privileges is conjured up.

Self-Regulation of Affect/Motivation/Arousal

When the child sees the candy, he may become quite excited—perhaps it is his favorite candy and he is hungry. His stomach growls; his mouth waters. The affective aspect of the situation could easily overwhelm inhibitory control. Hence Barkley (1997) postulates a third executive function that suppresses the immediate emotional reaction to a situation and regulates arousal in the service of a goal-directed action. When facing a spelling test, the child must not get overly excited at the start, rush through the test, and then get bored and fail to check his work. Rather, he must maintain a steady level of arousal throughout the task for optimal performance.

Reconstitution

The final executive function represents the individual's ability to create novel goal-directed behaviors. This is accomplished by breaking down a complex behavior into "units" that can then be reassembled to produce a new response to a situation. A batter facing a variety of pitchers is a good example. The basic functions—how to hold the bat, looking for the ball, swinging—are the same at each time at bat. Yet he never bats the same way twice. These behavioral units of batting are adjusted and changed each time to account for the variations of each "at bat"—ball speed, location of the ball, who the umpire is, etc.

Barkley's (1997) model has the advantage of identifying a core deficit in ADHD (poor inhibitory control) while showing how many diverse problems may subsequently arise in the four executive functions. At present this model cannot be fully mapped onto neuroanatomical structures, though Barkley (1997) cites evidence suggesting that the more basic behavioral inhibition functions reside in the orbitomedial frontal cortex (as do those functions involved in the regulation of affect). The more complex executive functions most likely reside in the dorsolateral frontal cortex. Neuroimaging and genetics are beginning to shed more light in this area.

It has been known for many years that stimulants act as agonists of dopamine (DA) and norepinephrine (NE) in both the central and peripheral nervous systems. NE and DA are released from nerve terminals, then cross the synapse to stimulate postsynaptic receptors on target neurons. NE and DA also stimulate prereceptors (or autoreceptors on the neurons that released them; this shuts off the release of further neurotransmitter. There exists on the end of each axon a "transporter," a protein complex that causes the reuptake of DA and NE into the neuron. All of the NE neurons and most DA neurons possess these transporters. Stimulants block the reuptake of NE and DA and thus prolong their lifespan in the neuronal synapse (Castellanos, 1997; Pliszka et al., 1996; Solanto, 1984; Swanson, Sergeant, et al., 1998; Zametkin & Rapoport, 1987). All these researchers suggest that DA or NE functioning is disturbed in ADHD, but there is no agreement on which system is most likely to be involved. Direct study of these catecholamine systems is difficult in children. For years researchers were confined to the study of plasma and urinary catecholamines, which originate in the peripheral sympathetic nervous system (see Pliszka et al., 1996, for a review of these data)

New impetus to the DA theory of ADHD has been caused by the discovery that the brain possesses five DA receptor subtypes. The subtypes have different distributions in the brain, with the D_3 and D_4 having a greater distribution in the limbic areas of the brain most likely to be involved in psychiatric disorders. Animal research has given us a look at role of these different receptors: "knockout" mice can be bred that lack one of the five DA receptors or the dopamine transporter that governs reuptake of DA. These mice exhibit ADHD-like behaviors (Swanson & Castellanos, 1998). Loss of the DA transporter (which causes DA excess at the synapse) results in increased motor activity, as does knockout of the D_1 and D_3 receptors. In contrast, knockout of the D_2 and D_4 receptors produces less active mice. This research shows how different mutations of the various DA receptors might all produce ADHD. It also makes these DA receptor genes prime targets for study in clinical populations. Solanto (1984) proposed that excess dopamine activity in the limbic areas would result in increased motor activity and reward seeking. Castellanos (1997) argued that ADHD children might have a DA excess in the subcortical areas (i.e., the caudate nucleus), which would result in motor excess, while a DA deficit in the area of the anterior cingulate gyrus might result in the cognitive problems. With the new genetic models, we do not have to define "excess" or "deficit" in terms of the amount of neurotransmitter available in the synapse. Rather, a mutant receptor might be hypo- or hypersensitive to the appropriate amount of DA release. Variations in the genes (i.e., differences in DNA sequence) are term "polymorphisms."

It has been noted that drugs that are pure dopamine agonists (as opposed to those that affect both NE and DA) are ineffective in the treatment of ADHD (Pliszka et al., 1996). Also, drugs with no direct effect on the DA system such as the tricyclic antidepressants (TCAs) are effective in the treatment of ADHD. This would seem to implicate the NE system in the pathophysiology of ADHD, although only metabolites of DA in cerebrospinal fluid predicted response to stimulant treatment in ADHD boys (Castellanos, Elia, et al., 1996). Arnsten et al. (1996) reviewed animal data and suggested the NE $alpha_{2a}$ receptors in the frontal cortex are involved in working memory. They suggested that an overactivity of the locus ceruleus results in overarousal (hyperactivity, irritability) whereas subsequent down-regulation of frontal lobe of $alpha_{2a}$ receptors leads to poor concentration and working memory deficits. Pliszka, Maas, Javors, Rogeness, and Baker (1994) found evidence of excess release of NE during a stressful cognitive task in ADHD children. Thus the role of NE system abnormalities has not been ruled out in ADHD.

NEUROIMAGING IN ADHD

Structural MRI has yielded several findings, which while not clinically useful at this time, do suggest that regions of the brain may be involved in ADHD. Two recent studies have found that the right frontal anterior lobes are decreased 6–8% in children with ADHD relative to controls

(Castellanos, Giedd, et al., 1996; Filipek et al., 1997). Abnormalities of the caudate nucleus have also been noted. Castellanos, Giedd, et al. (1996) found the right head of the caudate nucleus to be compromised in children with ADHD; ADHD children lacked a right > left asymmetry seen in their controls. Filipek et al. (1997) also found abnormalities in the caudate nucleus, but they found the left head of the caudate nucleus to be compromised and the controls had a left > right asymmetry. Other studies do not show that controls have any asymmetry of the caudate

TABLE E.1. Summary of Structural MRI Studies in ADHD (Swanson & Castellanos, 1998)

		Estimate of effect size and percent reduction by brain region			
Team and diagnosis	Sample size and age	Corpus callosum	Basal ganglia	Frontal lobes	Cerebellar vermis
University of Georgia[a] DSM-III ADHD	*n* = 7–11 11.1 yr	.51 10.9%	.88 19.0%	.69 3.6%	— —
Harvard[b] DSM-III-R ADHD, all HK	*n* = 15 12.4 yr	.80 12.2%	.72 11.4%	.82 12.7%	— —
NIMH[c] DSM-III-R ADHD, all but 2 HK	*n* = 18–57 12.0 yr	.53 11.2%	.40 5.4%	.64 9.6%	.8 11.1%
John Hopkins[d] DSM-III-R ADHD, all HK	*n* = 10–13 11.3 yr	.44 5.7%	.7 11.8%	.64 9.6%	.79 12.3%

Note. Effect size (ES) = (ADHD mean – control mean)/(standard deviation of control group); effect size allows the magnitude of difference between controls and ADHD to be compared across studies.

Percent reduction = (control mean – ADHD mean)/control mean.

[a]Hynd et al. (1990) (anterior width of frontal lobes on single slice; ES = .69); Hynd et al. (1991) (five areas of corpus callosum; ES = .51); Hynd et al. (1993) (left caudate head; ES = .88).

[b]Semrud-Clikeman et al. (1994) (seven areas of corpus callosum; overall ES = .80); Filipek et al. (1996) (volumetric MRI; left caudate ES = .81; right caudate ES = .63; anterior–superior ES = .74;. anterior–superior white matter ES = .81; anterior–inferior ES = .89); HK = hyperkinetic.

[c]Baumgardner et al. (1996) (area of corpus callosum; overall ES = .44); Aylward et al. (1996) (volume of basal ganglia; left caudate ES = .56; right caudate ES = .34; left globus pallidus ES = 1.1; right globus pallidus ES = .80); Mostofsky et al. (1998) (area of cerebellar vermis lobules VIII–X ES = .79).

[d]Giedd et al. (1994) (seven areas of corpus callosum; rostrum ES = .62; rostral body ES = .81; total ES = .15); Castellanos et al. (1994) (volume of basal ganglia; left caudate ES = .29; right caudate ES = .54); Castellanos, Giedd, et al. (1996) (volumetric MRI; total area corpus callosum ES = .06; left caudate ES = .20; right caudate ES = .52; left globus pallidus ES = .25; right globus pallidus ES = .60; anterior frontal ES = .64); Berquin et al. (1998) (volume of cerebellar vermis lobules VIII–X ES = .80).

(Aylward et al., 1996). There have been similarly inconsistent findings with regard to the volume of white matter connecting the cerebral hemispheres. Recently, decreased cerebellar vermis has been found (see Table E.1).

GENETICS

Two studies have found an association between ADHD and a polymorphism of the DA transporter (Cook et al., 1995; Gill, Daly, Heron, Hawi, & Fitzgerald, 1997). It is not known yet if this polymorphism is related to any deficit in dopamine reuptake. Two studies have also found a relationship between ADHD and a polymorphism for the D_4 receptor termed the "7-repeat" (LaHoste et al., 1996; Swanson, Sunohara, et al., 1998). It is so named because a segment of DNA is repeated seven times within the gene. This particular polymorphism is of interest because it as been associated with novelty-seeking behavior in adults and because the receptor is known to produce a blunted intracellular response to dopamine. La Hoste et al. (1996) found that 49% of the ADHD group had the 7-repeat D_4 gene, compared to only 20% of the controls. Having the 7-repeat D_4 gene was associated with a relative risk of 1.5 for ADHD. That is, if the risk of having ADHD in the general population were 8%, those with the 7-repeat D_4 gene would have a 12% risk of ADHD. Thus having the 7-repeat D_4 gene is neither necessary nor sufficient for having ADHD. It is likely that in the future many different genes will be found that affect the risk for having ADHD.

RELEVANCE FOR COMORBIDITY

Within a few years, the techniques described above will be applied widely in genetic research on ADHD patients and their families. It will be critical to control for comorbidity in this research. For instance, we saw in Chapter 6 that family studies appear to indicate that ADHD and ADHD with comorbid disorder (CD) appear to be distinct genetic subtypes. Let us assume that the D_4 polymorphism discussed above is relevant only to ADHD without CD. Investigators must therefore be careful to control for the presence of CD in studies of the genetic marker, comparing its prevalence in three samples: ADHD/CD, ADHD without CD, and controls. Mixing the first two groups would decrease the prevalence of the D_4 polymorphism in the ADHD group and lead to a "false negative." A similar argument applies to neuroimaging studies. The differences found to date in brain structures between ADHD children and controls have been quite small, and the groups has been very heterogeneous for comorbidities such as CD or LD. It is highly likely that each of these disorders may have structural or functional brain abnormalities associated with them. Enlarging samples and stratifying by comorbid disorder will allow us to make much more sense of our findings. Multicenter studies using similar means of diagnoses will give studies the power to detect small but important differences in brain function between controls and ADHD subjects subdivided by all the major comorbidities.

Eventually, the genetic subtyping may become the independent variable. ADHD children with one genetic polymorphism can be compared to those with another in terms of how prevalent a particular comorbidity is in each group. A group of ADHD children who do not appear to carry any of the discovered genetic markers for ADHD can be identified: this would be an ideal group to study in order to identify any environmental causes of ADHD (severe head injury, toxic exposure, perinatal events, etc.). The ultimate goal of such research is improved treatment. If the D_4 findings are confirmed, then research can proceed toward developing a medication that addresses directly the underlying biological deficit. Perhaps a "D_4 agonist" that would be particularly effective for the 49% of ADHD children who carry this gene is not far off.

A CLOSING NOTE

Children with ADHD and severe psychiatric disorder are among the most challenging patients to treat. Often the clinician feels alone with the child and family; insurance companies, mental health systems, schools—all seem unable or unwilling to help. Unlike the oncologist, who faces cancer with an arsenal of chemotherapeutic agents and volumes of research, the mental health professional feels limited in what he/she can do. The clinician should know that our interventions, both pharmacological and psychosocial, are powerful and useful. When used appropriately, they provide enormous relief to our patients and their families. Research on ADHD is as sound as that in any other branch of science, and it is growing every year. When we are sitting with a boy like Justin (discussed in Chapter 1), we must take heart that answers are being sought for him. In the meantime, we must light our therapeutic candles rather than curse the scientific darkness. It is our hope that this book has provided you with more than a few of those candles.

References

Abikoff, H., Courtney, M., Pelham, W. E., Jr., & Koplewicz, H. S. (1993). Teachers' ratings of disruptive behaviors: The influence of halo effects. *Journal of Abnormal Child Psychology, 21,* 519–533.

Adesman, A. R., Altshuler, L. A., Lipkin, P. H., & Walco, G. A. (1990). Otitis media in children with learning disabilities and in children with attention deficit disorder with hyperactivity. *Pediatrics, 85,* 442–446.

Alessi, N. E., & Magen, J. (1988). Comorbidity of other psychiatric disorders in depressed, psychiatrically hospitalized children. *American Journal of Psychiatry, 145,* 1582–1584.

Allan, E. R., Alpert, M., Sison, C. E., Citrome, L., Laury, G., & Berman, I. (1996). Adjunctive nadolol in the treatment of acutely aggressive schizophrenic patients. *Journal of Clinical Psychiatry, 57,* 455–459.

Alpert, M., Allan, E. R., Citrome, L., Laury, G., Sison, C., & Sudilovsky, A. (1990). A double blind, placebo controlled study of adjunctive nadolol in the management of violent patients. *Psychopharmacology Bulletin, 26,* 367–371.

Alsobrook, J. P., & Pauls, D. L. (1997). The genetics of Tourette syndrome. *Neurologic Clinics, 15,* 381–393.

Aman, M. G. (1982). Stimulant drug effects in developmental disorders and hyperactivity: Toward a resolution of disparate findings. *Journal of Autism and Developmental Disorders, 12,* 385–398.

Aman, M. G., Kern, R. A., McGhee, D. E., & Arnold, L. E. (1993). Fenfluramine and methylphenidate in children with mental retardation and attention deficit hyperactivity disorder: Laboratory effects. *Journal of Autism and Developmental Disorders, 23,* 491–506.

Aman, M. G., Marks, R. E., Turbott, S. H., Wilsher, C. P., & Merry, S. N. (1991). Clinical effects of methylphenidate and thioridazine in intellectually subaverage children. *Journal of the American Academy of Child and Adolescent Psychiatry, 30,* 246–256.

American Psychiatric Association. (1980). *Diagnostic and statistical manual of mental disorders* (3rd ed.). Washington, DC: Author.

American Psychiatric Association. (1987). *Diagnostic and statistical manual of mental disorders* (3rd ed., rev.). Washington, DC: Author.

American Psychiatric Association. (1994). *Diagnostic and statistical manual of mental disorders* (4th ed.). Washington, DC: Author.

Anand, V. S., & Dewan, M. J. (1996). Withdrawal–emergent dyskinesia in a patient on risperidone undergoing dosage reduction. *Annals of Clinical Psychiatry, 8*(8), 179–182.

Anderson, J. C., Williams, S., McGee, R., & Silva, P. A. (1987). DSM-III disorders in preadolescent children: Prevalence in a large community sample. *Archives of General Psychiatry, 44*, 69–76.

Anderson, L. T., Campbell, M., Adams, P., Small, A. M., Perry, R., & Shell, J. (1989). The effects of haloperidol on discrimination learning and behavioral symptoms in autistic children. *Journal of Autism and Developmental Disorders, 19*, 227–239.

Anderson, L. T., Campbell, M., Grega, D. M., Perry, P., Small, A. M., & Green, W. H. (1984). Haloperidol in the treatment of infantile autism: Effects on learning and behavioral symptoms. *American Journal of Psychiatry, 141*, 1195–1202.

Angold, A. (1988). Childhood and adolescent depression: II. Research in clinical populations. *British Journal of Psychiatry, 153*, 476–492.

Angold, A., & Costello, E. J. (1993). Depressive comorbidity in children and adolescents: Empirical, theoretical, and methodological issues. *American Journal of Psychiatry, 150*, 1779–1791.

Apter, A., Pauls, D. L., Bleich, A., Zohar, A. H., Kron, S., Ratzoni, G., Dycian, A., Kotler, M., Weizman, A., Gadot, N., & Cohen, D. J. (1993). An epidemiologic study of Gilles de la Tourette's syndrome in Israel. *Archives of General Psychiatry, 50*, 734–738.

Apter, A., Ratzoni, G., King, R. A., Weizman, A., Iancu, I., Binder, M., & Riddle, M. A. (1994). Fluvoxamine open-label treatment of adolescent inpatients with obsessive–compulsive disorder or depression. *Journal of the American Academy of Child and Adolescent Psychiatry, 33*, 342–348.

Armenteros, J. L., Whitaker, A. H., Welikson, M., Stedge, D. J., & Gorman, J. (1997). Risperidone in adolescents with schizophrenia: An open pilot study. *Journal of the American Academy of Child and Adolescent Psychiatry, 36*, 694–700.

Arnold, L. E., Abikoff, H. B., Cantwell, D. P., Elliot, G., Greenhill, L., Hechtman, L., Hinshaw, S. P., Hoza, B., Jensen, P. S., Kraemer, H. C., March, J. S., Newcorn, J. H., Pelham, W. E., Richters, J. E., Schiller, E., Severe, J. B., Swanson, J. M., Vereen, D., & Wells, K. C. (1997). National Institute of Mental Health collaborative multimodal treatment study of children with ADHD (the MTA). *Archives of General Psychiatry, 54*, 865–870.

Arnsten, A. F., Steere, J. C., & Hunt, R. D. (1996). The contribution of $alpha_2$-noradrenergic mechanisms of prefrontal cortical cognitive function: Potential significance for attention-deficit hyperactivity disorder [Review]. *Archives of General Psychiatry, 53*, 448–455.

Asarnow, R. F., Satz, P., & Light, R. (1991). Behavior problems and adaptive functioning in children with mild and severe closed head injury. *Journal of Pediatric Psychology, 16,* 543–555.

Astbury, J., Orgill, A. A., & Bajuk, B. (1987). Relationship between two-year behavior and neurodevelopmental outcome at five years of very low birthweight survivors. *Developmental Medicine and Child Neurology, 29,* 370–379.

Atkeson, B. M., & Forehand, R. (1979). Home-based reinforcement programs designed to modify classroom behavior: A review and methodological evaluation. *Psychological Bulletin, 86,* 1298–1308.

Atkins, M. S., Pelham, W. E., & Licht, M. H. (1985). A comparison of objective classroom measures and teacher ratings of attention deficit disorder. *Journal of Abnormal Child Psychology, 13,* 155–167.

Atkins, M. S., Pelham, W. E., & Licht, M. H. (1988). The development and validation of objective classroom measures for conduct and attention deficit disorders. *Advances in Behavioral Assessment of Children and Families, 4,* 3–31.

August, G. J., & Holmes, C. S. (1984). Behavior and academic achievement in hyperactive subgroups and learning-disabled boys: A six-year follow-up. *American Journal of Diseases of Children, 138,* 1025–1029.

August, G. J., Realmuto, G. M., MacDonald, A. W., Nugent, S. M., & Crosby, R. (1996). Prevalence of ADHD and comorbid disorders among elementary school children screened for disruptive behavior. *Journal of Abnormal Child Psychology, 24,* 571–595.

August, G. J., & Stewart, M. A. (1983). Familial subtypes of childhood hyperactivity. *Journal of Nervous and Mental Disease, 171,* 362–368.

August, G. J., Stewart, M. A., & Holmes, C. S. (1983). A four-year follow-up of hyperactive boys with and without conduct disorder. *British Journal of Psychiatry, 143,* 192–198.

Ayllon, T., Layman, D., & Burke, S. (1972). Disruptive behavior and reinforcement of academic performance. *Psychological Record, 22,* 315–323.

Ayllon, T., Layman, D., & Kandel, H. J. (1975). A behavioral–educational alternative to drug control of hyperactivity. *Journal of Applied Behavior Analysis, 8,* 137–146.

Ayllon, T., & Roberts, M. (1974). Eliminating discipline problems by strengthening academic performance. *Journal of Applied Behavior Analysis, 7,* 71–76.

Aylward, E. H., Reiss, A. L., Reader, M. J., Singer, H. S., Brown, J. E., & Denckla, M. B. (1996). Basal ganglia volumes in children with attention-deficit hyperactivity disorder. *Journal of Child Neurology, 11*(2), 112–115.

Baldwin, J. D., & Baldwin, J. I. (1998). *Behavior principles in everyday life* (3rd ed.). Upper Saddle River, NJ: Prentice-Hall.

Barkley, R. A. (1987). *Defiant children: A clinician's manual for parent training.* New York: Guilford Press.

Barkley, R. A. (1990). *Attention-deficit hyperactivity disorder: A handbook for diagnosis and treatment.* New York: Guilford Press.

Barkley, R. A. (1997). *ADHD and the nature of self-control.* New York: Guilford Press.

Barkley, R. A., & Cunningham, C. E. (1978). Do stimulant drugs improve the academic performance of hyperkinetic children?: A review of outcome studies. *Clinical Pediatrics, 17,* 85–92.

Barkley, R. A., DuPaul, G. J., & McMurray, M. B. (1990). Comprehensive evaluation of attention deficit disorder with and without hyperactivity as defined by research criteria. *Journal of Consulting and Clinical Psychology, 58,* 775–789.

Barkley, R. A., Grodzinsky, G., & DuPaul, G. J. (1992). Frontal lobe functions in attention deficit disorder with and without hyperactivity: A review and research report. *Journal of Abnormal Child Psychology, 20,* 163–188.

Barkley, R. A., McMurray, M. B., Edelbrock, C. S., & Robbins, K. (1989). The response of aggressive and nonaggressive ADHD children to two doses of methylphenidate. *Journal of the American Academy of Child and Adolescent Psychiatry, 28,* 873–881.

Barrett, R. P., Feinstein, C., & Hole, W. T. (1989). Effects of naloxone and naltrexone on self-injury: A double-blind placebo-controlled analysis. *American Journal of Mental Retardation, 96,* 644–651.

Barrickman, L. L., Noyes, R., Kuperman, S., Schumacher, E., & Verda, M. (1991). Treatment of ADHD with fluoxetine: A preliminary trial. *Journal of the American Academy of Child and Adolescent Psychiatry, 30,* 762–767.

Barrickman, L. L., Perry, P. J., Allen, A. J., Kuperman, S., Arndt, S. V., Herrman, K. J., & Schumacher, E. (1995). Bupropion versus methylphenidate in the treatment of attention deficit hyperactivity disorder. *Journal of the American Academy of Child and Adolescent Psychiatry, 34,* 649–657.

Barrish, H. H., Saunders, M., & Wolf, M. M. (1969). Good behavior game: Effects of individual contingencies for group consequences on disruptive behavior in a classroom. *Journal of Applied Behavior Analysis, 2,* 119–124.

Baumgardner, T. L., Singer, H. S., Denckla, M. B., Rubin, M. A., Abrams, M. T., Colli, M. J., & Reiss, A. L. (1996). Corpus callosum morphology in children with Tourette syndrome and attention deficit hyperactivity disorder. *Neurology, 47*(2), 477–482.

Berney, T., Kolvin, I., Bhate, S. R., Garside, R. F., Jean, J., Kay, B., & Scarth, L. (1981). School phobia: A therapeutic trial with clomipramine and short-term outcome. *Journal of the American Academy of Child and Adolescent Psychiatry, 138,* 110–118.

Bernstein, G. A., Carroll, M. E., Crosby, R. D., Perwien, A. R., Go, F. S., & Benowitz, N. L. (1994). Caffeine effects on learning, performance, and anxiety in normal school age children. *Journal of the American Academy of Child and Adolescent Psychiatry, 33,* 407–415.

Bernstein, G. A., Garfinkel, B. D., & Borchardt, C. M. (1990). Comparative studies of pharmacotherapy for school refusal. *Journal of the American Academy of Child and Adolescent Psychiatry, 29,* 773–781.

Biedel, D. C. (1991). Social phobia and overanxious disorder in school age children. *Journal of the American Academy of Child and Adolescent Psychiatry, 30,* 545–552.

Biederman, J. (1998). Resolved: Mania is mistaken for ADHD in prepubertal children, affirmative. *Journal of the American Academy of Child and Adolescent Psychiatry, 37,* 1091–1093.

Biederman, J., Baldessarini, R. J., Goldblatt, A., Lapey, K. A., Doyle, A., & Hesslein, P. S. (1993). A naturalistic study of 24-hour electrocardiographic recordings and echocardiographic findings in children and adolescents treated with desipramine. *Journal of the American Academy of Child and Adolescent Psychiatry, 32,* 805–813.

Biederman, J., Baldessarini, R. J., Wright, V., Keenan, K., & Faraone, S. V. (1993). A double-blind placebo controlled study of desipramine in the treatment of ADD: III. Lack of impact of comorbidity and family history factors on clinical response. *Journal of the American Academy of Child and Adolescent Psychiatry, 32,* 199–204.

Biederman, J., Baldessarini, R. J., Wright, V., Knee, D., & Harmatz, J. S. (1989). A double-blind placebo controlled study of desipramine in the treatment of ADD: I. Efficacy. *Journal of the American Academy of Child and Adolescent Psychiatry, 28,* 777–784.

Biederman, J., Baldessarini, R. J., Wright, V., Knee, D., Harmatz, J. S., & Goldblatt, A. (1989). A double-blind placebo controlled study of desipramine in the treatment ADD: II. Serum drug levels and cardiovascular findings. *Journal of the American Academy of Child and Adolescent Psychiatry, 28,* 903–911.

Biederman, J., Faraone, S. V., & Chen, W. J. (1993). Social Adjustment Inventory for Children and Adolescents: Concurrent validity in ADHD children. *Journal of the American Academy of Child and Adolescent Psychiatry, 32,* 1059–1064.

Biederman, J., Faraone, S. V., Keenan, K., Benjamin, J., Krifcher, B., Moore, C., Sprich-Buckminster, S., Ugaglia, K., Jellinek, M. S., & Steingard, R. (1992). Further evidence for family-genetic risk factors in attention deficit hyperactivity disorder: Patterns of comorbidity in probands and relatives of psychiatrically and pediatrically referred samples. *Archives of General Psychiatry, 49,* 728–738.

Biederman, J., Faraone, S. V., Keenan, K., Steingard, R., & Tsuang, M. T. (1991). Familial association between attention deficit disorder and anxiety disorders. *American Journal of Psychiatry, 148,* 251–256.

Biederman, J., Faraone, S. V., Keenan, K., & Tsuang, M. T. (1991). Evidence of familial association between attention deficit disorder and major affective disorders. *Archives of General Psychiatry, 48,* 633–642.

Biederman, J., Faraone, S., Mick, E., & Leleon, E. (1995). Psychiatric comorbidity among referred juveniles with major depression: Fact or artifact? *Journal of the American Academy of Child and Adolescent Psychiatry, 34,* 579–590.

Biederman, J., Faraone, S. V., Mick, E., Wozniak, J., Chen, L., Ouellette, C., Marrs, A., Moore, P., Garcia, J., Mennin, D., & Lelon, E. (1996). Attention deficit hyperactivity disorder and juvenile mania: An overlooked comorbidity? *Journal of the American Academy of Child and Adolescent Psychiatry, 35,* 997–1008.

Biederman, J., Munir, K., & Knee, D. (1987). Conduct and oppositional disorder in clinically referred children with attention deficit disorder: A controlled family study. *Journal of the American Academy of Child and Adolescent Psychiatry, 26,* 724–727.

Biederman, J., Munir, K., Knee, D., Armentano, M., Autor, S., Waternaux, C., & Tsuang, M. (1987). High rate of affective disorders in probands with attention deficit disorder and in their relatives: A controlled study. *American Journal of Psychiatry, 144,* 330–333.

Biederman, J., Newcorn, J., & Sprich, S. (1991). Comorbidity of attention deficit hyperactivity disorder with conduct, depressive, anxiety, and other disorders. *American Journal of Psychiatry, 148,* 564–577.

Biederman, J., Thisted, R. A., Greenhill, L. L., & Ryan, N. D. (1995). Estimation of the association between desipramine and the risk for sudden death in 5 to 14 year old children. *Journal of Clinical Psychiatry, 56,* 87–93.

Biederman, J., Wilens, T., Mick, E., Faraone, S. V., Weber, W., Curtis, S., Thornell, A., Pfister, K., Jetton, J. G., & Soriano, J. (1997). Is ADHD a risk factor for psychoactive substance use disorders?: Findings from a four-year prospective follow-up study. *Journal of the American Academy of Child and Adolescent Psychiatry, 36,* 21–29.

Bijur, P. E., Haslum, M., & Golding, J. (1990). Cognitive and behavioral sequelae of mild head injury in children. *Pediatrics, 86,* 337–344.

Bird, H. R., Canino, G., & Rubio-Stipec, M. (1988). Estimates of prevalence of childhood maladjustment in a community survey in Puerto Rico. *Archives of General Psychiatry, 45,* 1120–1126.

Bird, H. R., Gould, M. S., & Staghezza, B. (1992). Aggregating data from multiple informants in child psychiatry epidemiological research. *Journal of the American Academy of Child and Adolescent Psychiatry, 31,* 78–85.

Bird, H. R., Gould, M. S., & Staghezza, B. M. (1993). Patterns of diagnostic comorbidity in a community sample of children aged 9 through 16 years. *Journal of the American Academy of Child and Adolescent Psychiatry, 32,* 361–368.

Birmaher, B., Khetarpal, S., Brent, D., Cully, M., Balach, L., Kaufman, J., & Neer, S. M. (1997). The Screen for Child Anxiety Related Emotional Disorders (SCARED): Scale construction and psychometric characteristics. *Journal of the American Academy of Child and Adolescent Psychiatry, 36,* 545–553.

Birmaher, B., Quintana, H., & Greenhill, L. L. (1988). Methylphenidate treatment of hyperactive autistic children. *Journal of the American Academy of Child and Adolescent Psychiatry, 27,* 248–251.

Birmaher, B., Waterman, G. S., Ryan, N., Cully, M., Balach, L., Ingram, J., & Brodsky, M. (1994). Fluoxetine for childhood anxiety disorders. *Journal of the American Academy of Child and Adolescent Psychiatry, 33,* 993–999.

Bock, S. A., Sampson, H. A., Atkins, F. M., Zeiger, R. S., Lehrer, S., Sachs, M., Bush, R. K., & Metcalfe, D. D. (1988). Double-blind, placebo-controlled food challenge (DBPCFC) as an office procedure: A manual. *Journal of Allergy and Clinical Immunology, 82,* 986–997.

Borduin, C. M., & Henggeler, S. W. (1990). A multisystemic approach to the treatment of serious delinquent behavior. In R. J. McMahon & R. D. Peters (Eds.), *Behavior disorders of adolescence: Research, intervention, and policy in clinical and school settings* (pp. 63–80). New York: Plenum.

Borduin, C. M., Mann, B. J., Cone, L. T., Henggeler, S. W., Fucci, B. R., Blaske, D. M., & Williams, R. A. (1995). Multisystemic treatment of serious juvenile offenders: Long-term prevention of criminality and violence. *Journal of Consulting and Clinical Psychology, 63,* 569–578.

Borghgraef, M., Fryns, J. P., Dielkens, A., Pyck, K., & Van den Berge, H. (1987). Fragile X syndrome: A study of the psychological profile in 23 prepubertal patients. *Clinical Genetics, 32,* 179–186.

Boris, M., & Mandel, F. S. (1994). Foods and additives are common causes of the attention deficit hyperactive disorder in children. *Annals of Allergy, 72,* 462–468.

Boulos, C., Kutcher, S., & Gardner, D. (1992). An open naturalistic trial of fluoxetine in adolescents and young adults with treatment resistant major depression. *Journal of Child and Adolescent Psychopharmacology, 2,* 103–111.

Bourgeois, B., Beaumanoir, A., Blajev, B., de la Cruz, N., Despland, P. A., Egli, M., Geudelin, B., Kaspar, U., Ketz, E., & Kronauer, C. (1987). Monotherapy with valproate in primary generalized epilepsies. *Epilepsia, 28*(Suppl. 2), 8–11.

Bowden, C. L., Brugger, A. M., Swann, A. C., Calabrese, J. R., Janicak, P. G., Petty, F., Dilsaver, S. C., Davis, J. M., Rush, A. J., Small, J. G., Garza-Trevino, E. S., Risch, S. C., Goodnick, P. J., & Morris, D. D. (1994). Efficacy of divalproex vs. lithium and placebo in the treatment of mania. *Journal of the American Medical Association, 271,* 918–924.

Boyle, M. H., Offord, D. R., Racine, Y., Sanford, M., Szatmari, P., Fleming, J. E., & Price-Munn, N. (1993). Evaluation of the Diagnostic Interview for Children and Adolescents for use in general population samples. *Journal of Abnormal Child Psychology, 21,* 663–681.

Branch, W. B., Cohen, M. J., & Hynd, G. W. (1995). Academic achievement and attention-deficit/hyperactivity disorder in children with left- or right-hemisphere dysfunction. *Journal of Learning Disabilities, 28*(1), 35–43, 64.

Brent, D. A., Johnson, B., Bartle, S., Bridge, J., Rather, C., Matta, J., Connolly, J., & Constantine, D. (1993). Personality disorder, tendency to impulsive violence, and suicidal behavior in adolescents. *Journal of the American Academy of Child and Adolescent Psychiatry, 32,* 69–75.

Brent, D. A., Johnson, B. A., Perper, J., Connolly, J., Bridge, J., Bartle, S., & Rather, C. (1994). Personality disorder, personality traits, impulsive violence and completed suicide in adolescents. *Journal of the American Academy of Child and Adolescent Psychiatry, 33,* 1080–1086.

Brent, D. A., Perper, J. A., Goldstein, C. E., Kolko, D. J., Allan, M. J., Allman, C. J., & Zelenak, J. P. (1988). Risk factors for adolescent suicide: A comparison of adolescent suicide victims with suicidal inpatients. *Archives of General Psychiatry, 45,* 451–588.

Brent, D. A., Perper, J. A., Mortiz, G., Allman, C., Friend, A., Roth, C., Schweers, J., Balach, L., & Baugher, M. (1993). Psychiatric risk factors for adolescent suicide: A case-control study. *Journal of the American Academy of Child and Adolescent Psychiatry, 32,* 521–529.

Broughton, S. F., & Lahey, B. B. (1978). Direct and collateral effects of positive reinforcement, response cost, and mixed contingencies for academic performance. *Journal of School Psychology, 16,* 126–136.

Brouwers, P., Riccardi, R., Fedio, P., & Poplack, D. G. (1985). Long term neuropsychologic sequelae of childhood leukemia: Correlation with CT brain scan abnormalities. *Journal of Pediatrics, 106,* 723–728.

Brouwers, P., Riccardi, R., Poplack, D. G., & Fedio, P. (1984). Attentional deficits in long-term survivors of childhood acute lymphoblastic leukemia (ALL). *Journal of Clinical Neuropsychology, 6,* 325–330.

Brown, G., Chadwick, O., Shaffer, D., Rutter, M., & Traub, M. (1981). A prospective study of children with head injuries: III. Psychiatric sequelae. *Psychological Medicine, 11,* 63–78.

Bruera, E., Miller, M. J., MacMillan, K., & Kuehn, N. (1992). Neuropsychological effects of methylphenidate in patients receiving a continuous infusion of narcotics for cancer pain. *Pain, 48,* 163–166.

Buckley, N. K., & Walker, H. M. (1978). *Modifying classroom behavior—Revised: A manual of procedure for classroom teachers.* Champaign, IL: Research Press.

Burcham, B., Carlson, L., & Milich, R. (1993). Promising school-based practices for students with attention deficit disorder. *Exceptional Children, 60,* 174–180.

Burd, L., Kerbeshian, J., Wikenheiser, J., & Fisher, W. (1986). Prevalence of Gilles de la Tourette's syndrome in North Dakota adults. *American Journal of Psychiatry, 143,* 787–788.

Burke, J. C. (1992). *Decreasing classroom behavior problems: Practical guidelines for teachers.* San Diego, CA: Singular Publishing.

Caine, E. D., McBride, M. C., Chiverton, P., Bamford, K. A., Rediess, S., & Shiao, J. (1988). Tourette's syndrome in Monroe County school children. *Neurology, 38,* 472–475.

Campbell, M., Adams, P. B., Small, A. M., Kafantaris, V., Silva, R. R., Shell, J., Perry, R., & Overall, J. E. (1995). Lithium in hospitalized aggressive children with conduct disorder: A double blind and placebo controlled study. *Journal of the American Academy of Child and Adolescent Psychiatry, 34,* 445–453.

Campbell, M., Adams, P. [B.], Small, A. M., Tesch, L. M., & Curren, E. L. (1988). Naltrexone in infantile autism. *Psychopharmacology Bulletin, 24,* 135–139.

Campbell, M., Anderson, L. T., Meier, M., Cohen, I. L., Small, A. M., Samit, C., & Sachar, E. J. (1978). A comparison of haloperidol, behavior therapy and their interaction in autistic children. *Journal of the American Academy of Child Psychiatry, 17,* 640–655.

Campbell, M., Anderson, L. T., Small, A. M., Adams, P. [B.], Gonzalez, N. M., & Ernst, M. (1993). Naltrexone in autistic children: Behavioral symptoms and attentional learning. *Journal of the American Academy of Child and Adolescent Psychiatry, 32,* 1283–1291.

Campbell, M., Anderson, L. T., Small, A. M., Locascio, J. J., Lynch, N. S., & Choroco, M. C. (1990). Naltrexone in autistic children: A double blind placebo controlled study. *Psychopharmacology Bulletin, 26,* 130–135.

Campbell, M., Anderson, L. T., Small, A. M., Perry, R., Green, W. H., & Caplan, R. (1982). The effects of haloperidol on learning and behavior in autistic children. *Journal of Autism and Developmental Disorders, 12,* 167–175.

Campbell, M., Armenteros, J. L., Malone, R. P., Adams, P. B., Eisenberg, Z. W., & Overall, J. E. (1997). Neuroleptic-related dyskinesias in autistic children: A prospective, longitudinal study. *Journal of the American Academy of Child and Adolescent Psychiatry, 36,* 835–843.

Campbell, M., Fish, B., David, R., Shapiro, T., Collins, P., & Koh, C. (1972). Response to triiodothyronine and dextoamphetamine: A study of preschool schizophrenic children. *Journal of Autism and Childhood Schizophrenia, 2,* 343–358.

Campbell, M., Small, A. M., Collins, P. T., Friedman, E., David, R., & Genieser, N. (1976). Levodopa and levoamphetamine: A crossover study of young schizophrenic children. *Current Therapeutic Research, 19,* 70–86.

Campbell, M., Small, A. M., Green, W. H., Jennings, S. J., Perry, R., Bennett, W. G., & Anderson, L. (1984). Behavioral efficacy of haloperidol and lithium carbonate: A comparison in hospitalized aggressive children with conduct disorder. *Archives of General Psychiatry, 41,* 650–656.

Cannon, G. S., Idol, L., & West, J. F. (1996). Educating students with mild handicaps in general classrooms: Essential teaching practices for general and special educators. *Journal of Learning Disabilities, 25,* 300–317.

Cantwell, D. P. (1995). Child psychiatry: Introduction and overview. In H. I. Kaplan & B. G. Sadock (Eds.), *Comprehensive textbook of psychiatry/VI* (pp. 2151–2154). Baltimore: Williams & Wilkins.

Cantwell, D. P., & Baker, L. (1991). Association between attention deficit–hyperactivity disorder and learning disorders. *Journal of Learning Disabilities, 24,* 88–95.

Cantwell, D. P., Swanson, J. [M.], & Connor, D. F. (1997). Case study: Adverse response to clonidine. *Journal of the American Academy of Child and Adolescent Psychiatry, 36,* 539–544.

Cardon, L. R., Smith, S. D., Fulker, D. W., Kimberling, W. J., Pennington, B. F., & DeFries, J. C. (1994). Quantitative trait locus for reading disability on chromosome 6. *Science, 266,* 276–279.

Carlson, C. L., & Lahey, B. B. (1988). Conduct and attention deficit disorders. In J. C. Witt, S. N. Elliott, & F. M. Gresham (Eds.), *Handbook of behavior therapy in education* (pp. 653–677). New York: Plenum.

Carlson, C. L., Pelham, W. E., Jr., Milich, R., & Dixon, J. (1992). Single and combined effects of methylphenidate and behavior therapy on the classroom performance of children with attention-deficit hyperactivity disorder. *Journal of Abnormal Child Psychology, 20,* 213–232.

Carlson, G. A., & Weintraub, S. (1993). Childhood behavior problems and bipolar disorder—Relationship or coincidence? *Journal of Affective Disorders, 28,* 143–153.

Carlson, G. A., Rapport, M. D., Kelly, K. L., & Pataki, C. S. (1992). The effects of methylphenidate and lithium on attention and activity level. *Journal of the American Academy of Child and Adolescent Psychiatry, 31,* 262–270.

Carlson, G. A., Rapport, M. D., Pataki, C. S., & Kelly, K. L. (1992). Lithium in hospitalized children at 4 and 8 weeks: Mood, behavior and cognitive effects. *Journal of Child Psychology and Psychiatry, 33,* 411–425.

Caron, C., & Rutter, M. (1991). Comorbidity in child psychopathology: Concepts, issues and research strategies. *Journal of Child Psychology and Psychiatry, 32,* 1063–1080.

Carroll, K. M., & Rounsaville, B. J. (1993). History and significance of childhood attention deficit disorder in treatment-seeking cocaine abusers. *Comprehensive Psychiatry, 34,* 75–82.

Carter, C. M., Urbanowicz, M., Hemsley, R., Mantilla, L., Strobel, S., Graham, P. J., & Taylor, E. (1993). Effects of a few food diets in attention deficit disorder. *Archives of Diseases of Childhood, 69,* 564–568.

Castellanos, F. X. (1997). Toward a pathophysiology of attention-deficit/hyperactivity disorder. *Clinical Pediatrics, 36,* 381–393.

Castellanos, F. X., Elia, J., Kruesi, M. J. P., Marsh, W. L., Gulotta, C. S., Potter, W. Z., Ritchie, G. F., Hamburger, S. D., & Rapoport, J. L. (1996). Cerebrospinal homovanillic acid predicts behavioral response to stimulants in 45 boys with attention-deficit hyperactivity disorder. *Neuropsychopharmacology, 14,* 125–137.

Castellanos, F. X., Giedd, J. N., Eckburg, P., Marsh, W. L., Vaituzis, C., Kaysen, D., Hamburger, S. D., & Rapoport, J. L. (1994). Quantitative morphology of the caudate nucleus in attention deficit hyperactivity disorder. *American Journal of Psychiatry, 151,* 1791–1796.

Castellanos, F. X., Giedd, J. N., Elia, J., Marsh, W. L., Ritchie, G. F., Hamburger, S. D., & Rapoport, J. L. (1997). Controlled stimulant treatment of ADHD and comorbid Tourette's syndrome: Effects of stimulant and dose. *Journal of the American Academy of Child and Adolescent Psychiatry, 36,* 589–596.

Castellanos, F. X., Giedd, J. N., Marsh, W. L., Hamburger, S. D., Vaituzis, A. C., Dickstein, D. P., Sarfatti, S. E., Vauss, Y. C., Snell, J. W., Lange, N., Kaysen, D., Krain, A. L., Ritchie, G. F., Rajapakse, J. C., & Rapoport, J. L. (1996). Quantitative brain magnetic resonance imaging in attention-deficit hyperactivity disorder. *Archives of General Psychiatry, 53,* 607–616.

Cavazzuti, G. B., Cappella, L., & Nalin, A. (1980). Longitudinal study of epileptiform EEG patterns in normal children. *Epilepsia, 21,* 43–55.

Celano, M. P., & Geller, R. J. (1993). Learning, school performance, and children with asthma: How much at risk? *Journal of Learning Disabilities, 26,* 23–32.

Chadwick, O., Rutter, M., Shaffer, D., & Shrout, P. E. (1981). A prospective study of children with head injuries: IV. Specific cognitive deficits. *Journal of Clinical Neuropsychology, 3,* 101–120.

Chappell, P. B., Riddle, M. A., Scahill, L., Lynch, K. A., Schultz, R., Arnsten, A., Leckman, J. F., & Cohen, D. J. (1995). Guanfacine treatment of comorbid attention-deficit hyperactivity disorder and Tourette's syndrome: Preliminary clinical experience. *Journal of the American Academy of Child and Adolescent Psychiatry, 34,* 1140–1146.

Ciaranello, R. D. (1993). Attention deficit–hyperactivity disorder and resistance to thyroid hormone—A new idea? *New England Journal of Medicine, 328,* 1038–1039.

Clayton, G. W. (1982). Thyrotoxicosis in children. In S. A. Kaplan (Ed.), *Clinical pediatric and adolescent endocrinology* (pp. 110–117). Philadelphia: Saunders.

Coccaro, E. F., & Kavoussi, R. J. (1997). Fluoxetine and impulsive aggressive behavior in personality-disordered subjects. *Archives of General Psychiatry, 54,* 1081–1088.

Cohen, P., Cohen, J., Kasen, S., Velez, C. N., Hartmark, C., Johnson, J., Rojas, M., Brook, J., & Streuning, E. L. (1993). An epidemiological study of disorders in late childhood and adolescence. I: Age and gender specific pattern. *Journal of Child Psychology and Psychiatry, 34,* 851–867.

Comings, D. E., Himes, J. A., & Comings, B. G. (1990). An epidemiologic study of Tourette's syndrome in a single school district. *Journal of Clinical Psychiatry, 51,* 463–469.

Conners, C. K. (1998). Rating scales in attention deficit/hyperactivity disorder. *Journal of Clinical Psychiatry, 59*(Suppl.), 24–30.

Conners, C. K., Casat, C. D., Gualtieri, C. T., Weller, E., Reader, M., Reiss, A., Weller, R. A., Khayrallah, M., & Ascher, J. (1996). Bupropion hydrochloride in attention deficit disorder with hyperactivity. *Journal of the American Academy of Child and Adolescent Psychiatry, 35,* 1314–1321.

Conners, C. K., Goyette, C. H., Southwick, D. A., Lees, J. M., & Andrulonis, P. A. (1976). Food additives and hyperkinesis: A controlled double blind experiment. *Pediatrics, 58,* 154–166.

Conners, C. K., Kramer, R., Rothschild, G. H., Schwartz, L., & Stone, A. (1971). Treatment of young delinquent boys with diphenylhydantoin sodium and methylphenidate. *Archives of General Psychiatry, 24,* 156–160.

Connor, D. F., Ozbayrak, K. R., Benjamin, S., Ma, Y., & Fletcher, K. E. (1997). A pilot study of nadolol for overt aggression in developmentally delayed individuals. *Journal of the American Academy of Child and Adolescent Psychiatry, 36,* 826–834.

Cook, E. H. [Jr.] (1990). Autism: Review of neurochemical investigation. *Synapse, 6,* 292–308.

Cook, E. H., Jr., Stein, M. A., Krasowski, M. D., Cox, N. J., Olkon, D. M., Kieffer, J. E., & Leventhal, B. L. (1995). Association of attention-deficit disorder and the dopamine transporter gene. *American Journal of Human Genetics, 56,* 993–998.

Costello, E. J., Costello, A. J., Edelbrock, C., Burns, B. J., Dulcan, M. K., Brent, D., & Janiszewski, S. (1988). Psychiatric disorders in pediatric primary care: Prevalence and risk factors. *Archives of General Psychiatry, 45,* 1107–1116.

Cowdry, R. W., & Gardner, D. L. (1988). Pharmacotherapy of borderline personality disorder. *Archives of General Psychiatry, 45,* 111–119.

Cueva, J. E., Overall, J. E., Small, A. M., Armentos, J. L., Perry, R., & Campbell, M. (1996). Carbamazepine in aggressive children with conduct disorder: A double blind and placebo controlled study. *Journal of the American Academy of Child and Adolescent Psychiatry, 35,* 480–490.

Dalby, J. T. (1985). Taxonomic separation of attention deficit disorders and developmental reading disorders. *Contemporary Educational Psychology, 10,* 228–234.

Davanzo, P. A., Belin, T. R., Widawski, M. H., & King, G. (1998). Paroxetine treatment of aggression and self injury in persons with mental retardation. *American Journal of Mental Retardation, 102,* 427–437.

David, T. J. (1987). Reactions to dietary tartrazine. *Archives of Diseases of Childhood, 62,* 119–122.

Davies, D. S., Wing, L. M. H., Reid, J. L., Neill, E., Hughes, H., & Davies, D. L. (1977). Pharmokinetics and concentration effect relationships of intravenous and oral clonidine. *Clinical Pharmacology and Therapeutics, 21,* 593–601.

Davies, P. A. (1989). Long term effects of meningitis. *Developmental Medicine and Child Neurology, 31,* 398–406.

de Quiros, G. B., Kinsbourne, M., Palmer, R. L., & Rufo, D. T. (1994). Attention deficit disorder in children: Three clinical variants. *Journal of Developmental and Behavioral Pediatrics, 15,* 311–319.

DeGroot, L. J. (1995). Congenital defects in thyroid hormone formation and action. In L. J. DeGroot (Ed.), *Endocrinology* (pp. 871–892). Philadelphia: Saunders.

DeLong, G. R., & Aldershot, A. L. (1987). Long term experience with lithium treatment in childhood: Correlation with clinical diagnosis. *Journal of the American Academy of Child and Adolescent Psychiatry, 26,* 389–394.

Derivan, A., Aguiar, L., Upton, G. V., Martin, P., D'Amico, D., Troy, S., Ferguson, J., & Preskorn, S. (1995, October). *A study of venlafaxine in children and adolescents with conduct disorder.* Paper presented at the 42nd annual meeting of the American Academy of Child and Adolescent Psychiatry, New Orleans, LA.

Diamond, I. R., Tannock, R., Rimer, P., Bockus, R., & Schachar, R. (1998). *Extended methylphenidate treatment with and without comorbid anxiety.* Paper presented at the 45th annual meeting of the American Academy of Child and Adolescent Psychiatry, Anaheim, CA.

Dickerson-Mayes, S., Crites, D. L., Bixler, E. O., Humphrey, F. J., & Mattison, R. E. (1994). Methylphenidate and ADHD: Influence of age, IQ, and neurodevelopmental status. *Developmental Medicine and Child Neurology, 36,* 1099–1107.

Dodsen, W. E. (1987). Carbamazepine efficacy and utilization in children. *Epilepsia, 28*(Suppl. 3), 17–24.

Donnelly, M., Rapoport, J. L., Potter, W. Z., Oliver, J., Keysor, C. S., & Murphy, D. L. (1989). Fenfluramine and dextroamphetamine treatment of childhood hyperactivity. Clinical and biochemical findings. *Archives of General Psychiatry, 46,* 205–212.

Donovan, S. J., Susser, E. S., Nunes, E. V., Stewart, J. W., Quitkin, F. M., & Klein, D. F. (1997). Divalproex treatment of disruptive adolescents: A report of 10 cases. *Journal of Clinical Psychiatry, 58,* 12–15.

Douglas, V. I., Barr, R. G., O'Neill, M. E., & Britton, B. G. (1985). Short term effects of methylphenidate on the cognitive, learning and academic performance of children with attention deficit disorder in the laboratory and in the classroom. *Journal of Child Psychology and Psychiatry, 27,* 191–211.

Dreifuss, F. E., Langer, D. H., Moline, K. A., & Maxwell, J. E. (1989). Valproic acid hepatic fatalities: II. U.S. experience since 1984. *Neurology, 39*(2, Pt. 1), 201–207.

DuPaul, G. J., Barkley, R. A., & McMurray, M. B. (1994). Response of children with ADHD to methylphenidate: Interaction with internalizing symptoms.

Journal of the American Academy of Child and Adolescent Psychiatry, 33, 894–903.

DuPaul, G. J., Power, T. J., Anastopoulos, A. D., & Reid, R. (1998). *ADHD Rating Scales–IV: Checklists, norms, and clinical interpretation*. New York: Guilford Press.

Dykens, E., Leckman, J., Paul, R., & Watson, M. (1988). Cognitive, behavioral, and adaptive functioning in fragile X and non-fragile X retarded men. *Journal of Autism and Developmental Disorders, 18*, 41–52.

Dykman, R. A., & Ackerman, P. T. (1991). Attention deficit disorder and specific reading disability: Separate but often overlapping disorders. *Journal of Learning Disabilities, 24*, 96–103.

Ebaugh, F. G. (1923). Neuropsychiatric sequelae of acute epidemic encephalitis in children. *American Journal of Diseases of Children, 25*, 89–97.

Edelbrock, C., Costello, A., Dulcan, M. K., Conover, N. C., & Kalas, R. (1986). Parent–child agreement on child psychiatric symptoms assessed via structured interview. *Journal of Child Psychology and Psychiatry, 27*, 181–190.

Edleman, R. J. (1996). TD from risperidone? *Journal of the American Academy of Child and Adolescent Psychiatry, 36*, 867.

Eeg-Olofsson, O. (1971). The development of the electroencephalogram in normal children and adolescents from the age of 1 through 21 years. *Acta Paediatrica Scandinavica, 208*(Suppl.), 1–46.

Egger, J., Carter, C. M., Graham, P. J., Gumley, D., & Soothill, J. F. (1985). Controlled trial of oligoantigenic treatment in the hyperkinetic syndrome. *Lancet, ii*, 540–545.

Egli, M., & Graf, I. (1975). The use of anticonvulsant treatment of behaviorally disturbed children with bioelectric epilepsy. *Acta Paedopsychiatrica, 41*, 54–69.

Einfeld, S., Hall, W., & Levy, F. (1991). Hyperactivity and the fragile X syndrome. *Journal of Abnormal Child Psychology, 19*, 253–262.

Elia, J., Borcherding, B. G., Rapoport, J. L., & Keysor, C. S. (1991). Methylphenidate and dextroamphetamine treatments of hyperactivity: Are there true nonresponders? *Psychiatry Research, 36*, 141–155.

Elia, J., Gulotta, C., Rose, S. R., Marin, G., & Rapoport, J. L. (1994). Thyroid function and attention-deficit hyperactivity disorder. *Journal of the American Academy of Child and Adolescent Psychiatry, 33*, 169–172.

Elliot, S. N., & Gresham, F. M. (1993). Social skills interventions for children. *Behavior Modification, 17*, 287–313.

Emslie, G. J., Rush, A. J., Weinberg, W. A., Kowatch, R., Hughes, C., Carmody, T., & Rintelman, J. W. (1997). Double-blind placebo controlled trial of fluoxetine in depressed children and adolescents. *Archives of General Psychiatry, 54*, 1031–1037.

Epstein, M. H., Cullinan, D., & Polloway, E. D. (1986). Patterns of maladjustment among mentally retarded children and youth. *American Journal of Mental Deficiency, 91*, 127–134.

Ernst, M., Liebenauer, L. L., King, C., Fitzgerald, G. A., Cohen, R. M., & Zametkin, A. J. (1994). Reduced brain metabolism in hyperactive girls. *Journal of the American Academy of Child and Adolescent Psychiatry, 33*, 858–868.

Fairbanks, J. M., Pine, D. S., Tancer, N. K., Dummit, E. S., Kentgen, L. M., Martin, Asche, B. K., & Klein, R. G. (1997). Open fluoxetine treatment of mixed anxiety disorders in children and adolescents. *Journal of Child and Adolescent Psychopharmacology, 7,* 17–29.

Faraone, S. V., Biederman, J., Keenan, K., & Tsuang, M. T. (1991a). Separation of DSM-III attention deficit disorder and conduct disorder: Evidence from a family-genetic study of American child psychiatric patients. *Psychological Medicine, 21,* 109–121.

Faraone, S. V., Biederman, J., Keenan, K., & Tsuang, M. T. (1991b). A family-genetic study of girls with DSM-III attention deficit disorder. *American Journal of Psychiatry, 148,* 112–117.

Faraone, S. V., Biederman, J., Lehman, B. K., Keenan, K., Norman, D., Seidman, L. J., Kolodny, R., Kraus, I., Perrin, J., & Chen, W. J. (1993). Evidence for the independent familial transmission of attention deficit hyperactivity disorder and learning disabilities: Results from a family genetic study. *American Journal of Psychiatry, 150,* 891–895.

Faraone, S. V., Biederman, J., Mennin, D., Wozniak, J., & Spencer, T. (1997). Attention deficit hyperactivity disorder with bipolar disorder: A familial subtype. *Journal of the American Academy of Child and Adolescent Psychiatry, 36,* 1378–1387.

Farrington, D. P., Loeber, R., & Van Kammen, W. B. (1989). Long term criminal outcomes of hyperactivity–impulsivity–attention deficit and conduct problems in childhood. In L. N. Robins & M. R. Rutter (Eds.), *Straight and devious pathways to adulthood* (pp. 62–81). New York: Cambridge University Press.

Feagans, L., Sanyal, M., Henderson, F., Collier, A., & Appelbaum, M. (1987). Relationship of middle ear disease in early childhood to later narrative and attention skills. *Journal of Pediatric Psychology, 12,* 581–594.

Feeney, D. J., & Klykylo, W. (1996). Risperidone and tardive dyskinesia. *Journal of the American Academy of Child and Adolescent Psychiatry, 35,* 1421–1422.

Feingold, B. F. (1974). *Why your child is hyperactive.* New York: Random House.

Feldman, H. [M.], Crumrine, P., Handen, B. L., Alvin, R., & Teodori, J. (1989). Methylphenidate in children with seizures and attention-deficit disorder. *American Journal of Diseases of Children, 143,* 1081–1086.

Feldman, H. M., & Michaels, R. H. (1988). Academic achievement in children 10 to 12 years after *Haemophilus influenzae* meningitis. *Pediatrics, 81,* 339–344.

Fenichel, R. (1995). Combining methylphenidate and clonidine: The role of postmarketing surveillance. *Journal of Child and Adolescent Psychopharmacology, 5,* 155–156.

Fenton, G. W., Fenwick, P. B. C., Dollimore, J., Rutter, M., & Yule, W. (1974). An introduction to the Isle of Wright study. *Electroencephalography and Clinical Neurophysiology, 37,* 325.

Ferguson, A. (1995). Scope and diagnostic criteria of food sensitivity. *Clinical and Experimental Allergy, 25,* 111–113.

Filipek, P. A. (1995). Neurobiologic correlates of developmental dyslexia: How do dyslexic brains differ from those of normal readers? *Journal of Child Neurology, 10*(Suppl.), S62–S69.

Filipek, P. A., Semrud-Clikeman, M., Steingard, R. J., Renshaw, P. F., Kennedy, D. N., & Biederman, J. (1997). Volumetric MRI analysis comparing subjects having attention-deficit hyperactivity disorder with normal controls. *Neurology, 48,* 589–601.

Filley, C. M., Cranberg, L. D., Alexander, M. P., & Hart, E. J. (1987). Neurobehavioral outcome after closed head injury in childhood and adolescence. *Archives of Neurology, 44,* 194–198.

Findling, R. L., Maxwell, K., & Wiznitzer, M. (1997). An open clinical trial of risperidone monotherapy in young children wilth autistic disorder. *Psychopharmacology Bulletin, 33,* 155–159.

Findling, R. L., McNamara, N. K., Branicky, L. A., O'Riordan, M. A., Lemon, E., Schlucter, M., & Blumer, J. L. (1998, December 14–18). *Risperidone in children with conduct disorder.* Paper presented at the 37th annual meeting of the American College of Neuropsychopharmacology, Las Croabas, Puerto Rico.

Fireman, P. (1995). Diagnosis of allergic disorders. *Pediatrics in Review, 16,* 178–183.

Fisch, G. S. (1993). What is associated with the fragile X syndrome? *American Journal of Medical Genetics, 48,* 112–121.

Fisch, G. S., Cohen, I. L., Gross, A. C., Jenkins, V., Jenkins, E. C., & Brown, W. T. (1988). Folic acid treatment of fragile X males: A further study. *American Journal of Medical Genetics, 30,* 393–399.

Fisher, P., Blouin, A. G., & Shaffer, D. (1993). *The C-DISC: A computerized version of the NIMH Diagnositic Interview Schedule for Children, Version 2. 3.* Poster session presented at the annual meeting of the Society for Research in Child and Adolescent Psychopathology, Santa Fe, NM.

Fletcher, J. M., Bohan, T. P., Brandt, M. E., Brookshire, B. L., Beaver, S. R., Francis, D. J., Davidson, K. C., Thompson, N. M., & Miner, M. E. (1992). Cerebral white matter and cognition in hydrocephalic children. *Archives of Neurology, 49,* 818–824.

Fletcher, J. M., Ewing-Cobbs, L., Miner, M. E., Levin, H. S., & Eisenberg, H. M. (1990). Behavioral changes after closed head injury in children. *Journal of Consulting and Clinical Psychology, 58,* 93–98.

Forehand, R., & Long, N. (1996). *Parenting the strong-willed child.* Chicago: Contemporary Books.

Forehand, R., & McMahon, R. (1981). *Helping the noncompliant child: A clinician's guide to parent training.* New York: Guilford Press.

Freeman, T. W., Clothier, J. L., Pazzaglia, P., Lesem, M. D., & Swann, A. C. (1992). A double-blind comparison of valproate and lithium in the treatment of acute mania. *American Journal of Psychiatry, 149,* 108–111.

Frick, P. J., Kamphaus, R. W., Lahey, B. B., Loeber, R., Christ, M. A., Hart, E. L., & Tannenbaum, L. E. (1991). Academic underachievement and the disruptive behavior disorders. *Journal of Consulting and Clinical Psychology, 59,* 289–294.

Frick, P. J., Lahey, B. B., Loeber, R., Stouthamer-Loeber, M., Christ, M. A. G., & Hanson, K. (1992). Familial risk factors to oppositional defiant disorder and conduct disorder: Parental psychopathology and maternal parenting. *Journal of Consulting and Clinical Psychology, 60,* 49–55.

Fristad, M. A., Weller, E. B., & Weller, R. A. (1992). The Mania Rating Scale: Can it be used in children? A preliminary report. *Journal of the American Academy of Child and Adolescent Psychiatry, 31,* 252–257.

Fuerst, D., Fisk, J. L., & Rourke, B. P. (1989). Psychosocial functioning of learning disabled children: Replicability of statistically derived subtypes. *Journal of Consulting and Clinical Psychology, 57,* 275–280.

Gadow, K. D., Nolan, E. E., Sverd, J., Sprafkin, J., & Paolicelli, L. (1990). Methylphenidate in aggressive–hyperactive boys: I. Effects on peer aggression in public school settings. *Journal of the American Academy of Child and Adolescent Psychiatry, 29,* 710–718.

Gadow, K. D., Sverd, J., Sprafkin, J., Nolan, E. E., & Ezor, S. N. (1995). Efficacy of methylphenidate for attention-deficit hyperactivity disorder in children with tic disorder. *Archives of General Psychiatry, 52,* 444–455.

Gammon, G. D., & Brown, T. E. (1993). Fluoxetine and methylphenidate in combination for treatment of attention deficit and comorbid depressive disorder. *Journal of Child and Adolescent Psychopharmacology, 3,* 1–10.

Gardner, D., & Cowdry, R. (1985). Alprazolam induced dyscontrol in borderline personality disorder. *American Journal of Psychiatry, 142,* 98–100.

Garfinkel, B. D., Wender, P. H., Sloman, L., & O'Neill, I. (1983). Tricyclic antidepressant and methylphenidate treatment of attention deficit disorder in children. *Journal of the American Academy of Child Psychiatry, 22,* 343–348.

Gaub, M., & Carlson, C. L. (1997a). Behavioral characteristics of DSM-IV ADHD subtypes in a school-based population. *Journal of Abnormal Child Psychology, 25,* 103–111.

Gaub, M., & Carlson, C. L. (1997b). Gender differences in ADHD: A meta-analysis and critical review. *Journal of the American Academy of Child and Adolescent Psychiatry, 36,* 1036–1045.

Gawin, F. H., & Kleber, H. D. (1985). Methylphenidate treatments of cocaine abusers without ADD: A negative report. *American Journal of Drug and Alcohol Abuse, 11,* 193–197.

Gawin, F. [H.], & Kleber, H. D. (1986). Pharmacologic treatments of cocaine abuse. *Psychiatric Clinics of North America, 9,* 573–583.

Geller, B., Cooper, T. B., Graham, D. L., Marsteller, F. A., & Bryant, D. M. (1990). Double blind placebo controlled study of nortriptyline in depressed adolescents using a "fixed plasma level" design. *Psychopharmacology Bulletin, 26,* 60–85.

Geller, B., Cooper, T. B., Sun, K., Zimerman, B., Frazier, J., Williams, M., & Heath, J. (1998). Double-blind and placebo-controlled study of lithium for adolescent bipolar disorders with secondary substance dependency. *Journal of the American Academy of Child and Adolescent Psychiatry, 37,* 171–178.

Geller, B., Fox, L. W., & Clark, K. A. (1993). Rate and predictors of prepubertal bipolarity during follow-up of 6- to 12-year-old depressed children. *Journal of the American Academy of Child and Adolescent Psychiatry, 33,* 461–468.

Geller, B., Guttmacher, L. B., & Bleeg, M. (1981). Coexistence of childhood onset pervasive developmental disorder and attention deficit disorder with hyperactivity. *American Journal of Psychiatry, 138,* 388–389.

Geller, B., Sun, K., Zimerman, B., Luby, J., Frazier, J., & Williams, M. (1995). Complex and rapid-cycling in bipolar children and adolescents: A preliminary study. *Journal of Affective Disorders, 34,* 259–268.

Geller, B., Warner, K., Williams, M., & Zimmerman, B. (1998). Prepubertal and young adolescent bipolarity versus ADHD: Assessment and validity using the WASH-U-KSADS, CBCL and TRF. *Journal of Affective Disorders, 51,* 81–91.

Geller, B., Williams, M., Zimerman, B., Frazier, J., Beringer, L., & Warner, K. (1998). Prepubertal and early adolescent bipolarity differentiate from ADHD by manic symptoms. *Journal of Affective Disorders, 51,* 93–100.

Geller, D. [A.], Biederman, J., Griffin, S., Jones, J., & Lefkowitz, T. R. (1996). Comorbidity of juvenile obsessive–compulsive disorder with disruptive behavior disorders. *Journal of the American Academy of Child and Adolescent Psychiatry, 35,* 1637–1646.

Geller, D. A., Biederman, J., Reed, E. D., Spencer, T., & Wilens, T. E. (1995). Similarities in response to fluoxetine in the treatment of children and adolescents with obsessive–compulsive disorder. *Journal of the American Academy of Child and Adolescent Psychiatry, 34,* 36–44.

Giedd, J. N., Castellanos, F. X., Casey, B. J., Kozuch, P., King, A. C., Hamburger, S. D., & Rapoport, J. L. (1994). Quantitative morphology of the corpus callosum in attention deficit hyperactivity disorder. *American Journal of Psychiatry, 151,* 665–669.

Gilger, J. W., Pennington, B. F., & DeFries, J. C. (1992). A twin study of the etiology of comorbidity: Attention-deficit hyperactivity disorder and dyslexia. *Journal of the American Academy of Child and Adolescent Psychiatry, 31,* 343–348.

Gill, M., Daly, G., Heron, S., Hawi, Z., & Fitzgerald, M. (1997). Confirmation of association between attention deficit hyperactivity disorder and a dopamine transporter polymorphism. *Molecular Psychiatry, 2,* 311–313.

Gillberg, C., Melander, H., von Knorring, A. L., Janols, L. O., Thernlund, G., Hagglof, B., Eidevall-Wallin, L., Gustafsson, P., & Kopp, S. (1997). Long-term stimulant treatment of children with attention-deficit hyperactivity disorder symptoms: A randomized, double-blind, placebo-controlled trial. *Archives of General Psychiatry, 54,* 857–864.

Gillberg, I. C., Gillberg, C., & Groth, J. (1989). Children with preschool minor neurodevelopmental disorders. V: Neurodevelopmental profiles at age 13. *Developmental Medicine and Child Neurology, 31,* 14–24.

Gillis, J. J., Gilger, J. W., Pennington, B. F., & DeFries, J. C. (1992). Attention deficit disorder in reading-disabled twins: Evidence for a genetic etiology. *Journal of Abnormal Child Psychology, 20,* 303–315.

Gittelman, R., Mannuzza, S., Shenker, R., & Bonagura, N. (1985). Hyperactive boys almost grown up: I. Psychiatric status. *Archives of General Psychiatry, 42,* 937–947.

Gittelman-Klein, R., & Klein, D. F. (1970). Controlled imipramine treatment of school phobia. *Archives of General Psychiatry, 25,* 204–207.

Gittelman-Klein, R., & Klein, D. F. (1976). Methylphenidate effects in learning disabilities. *Archives of General Psychiatry, 33,* 655–664.

Gittelman-Klein, R., Klein, D. F., Katz, S., Saraf, K., & Pollack, E. (1976). Comparative effects of methylphenidate and thioridazine in hyperkinetic children. I. Clinical results. *Archives of General Psychiatry, 33,* 1217–1231.

Goff, J. R., Anderson, H. R., & Cooper, P. F. (1980). Distractibility and memory deficits in long term survivors of acute lymphoblastic leukemia. *Journal of Developmental and Behavioral Pediatrics, 1,* 158–163.

Goldman, L. S., Genel, M., Bezman, R. J., & Slanetz, P. J. (1998). Diagnosis and treatment of attention-deficit/hyperactivity disorder in children and adolescents. Council on Scientific Affairs. *Journal of the American Medical Association, 279,* 1100–1107.

Goodman, R., & Stevenson, J. (1989). A twin study of hyperactivity: I. An examination of hyperactivity scores and categories derived from Rutter teacher and parent questionnaires. *Journal of Child Psychology and Psychiatry, 30,* 671–689.

Goyer, P. F., Davis, G. C., & Rapoport, J. L. (1979). Abuse of prescribed stimulant medication by a 13 year old hyperactive boy. *Journal of the American Academy of Child and Adolescent Psychiatry, 18,* 170–175.

Goyette, C. H., Conners, C. K., & Petti, T. A. (1978). Effects of aritificial colors on hyperkinetic children: A double blind challenge study. *Psychopharmacology Bulletin, 14,* 78.

Graae, F., Milner, J., Rizzotto, L., & Klein, R. G. (1994). Clonazepam in childhood anxiety disorders. *Journal of the American Academy of Child and Adolescent Psychiatry, 33,* 372–376.

Gram, L., & Bentsen, K. D. (1985). Valproate: An updated review. *Acta Neurologica Scandinavica, 72,* 129–139.

Greendyke, R. M., Kanter, D. R., Schuster, D. B., Verstreate, S., & Wootton, J. (1986). Propranolol treatment of assaultive patients with organic brain disease. *Journal of Nervous and Mental Diseases, 174,* 290–294.

Greene, R. [W.] (1995). Students with ADHD in school classrooms: Teacher factors related to compatibility, assessment, and intervention. *School Psychology Review, 24,* 81–93.

Greene, R. [W.] (1996). Students with ADHD and their teachers: Implications of a goodness-of-fit perspective. In *Advances in Clinical Child Psychology, 18,* 205–230.

Greene, R. W. (1998). *The explosive child.* New York: Harper Collins.

Greenhill, L. L. (1998). *Stimulant medications.* Paper presented at the National Institute of Mental Health Consensus Conference, Washington, DC.

Greenhill, L. L., Abikoff, H. B., Arnold, L. E., Cantwell, D. P., Conners, C. K., Elliott, G., Hechtman, L., Hinshaw, S. P., Hoza, B., Jensen, P. S., March, J. S., Newcorn, J. H., Pelham, W. E., Severe, J. B., Swanson, J. M., Vitiello, B., & Wells, K. (1996). Medication treatment strategies in the MTA study: Relevance to clinicians and researchers. *Journal of the American Academy of Child and Adolescent Psychiatry, 34,* 1304–1313.

Greenhill, L. L., Rieder, R. O., Wender, P. H., Buchsbaum, M., & Zahn, T. P.

(1973). Lithium carbonate in the treatment of hyperactive children. *Archives of General Psychiatry, 28,* 636–640.

Gresham, F. M. (1988). Social skills: Conceptual and applied aspects of assessment, training, and social validation. In J. C. Witt, S. N. Elliot, & F. M. Gresham (Eds), *Handbook of behavior therapy in education* (pp. 523–546). New York: Plenum.

Grieger, T., Kauffman, J. M., & Grieger, R. M. (1976). Effects of peer reporting on cooperative play and aggression of kindergarten children. *Journal of School Psychology, 14,* 307–313.

Grigoroiu-Serbanescu, M., Chrstodorescu, D., Jipescu, I., Totoescu, A., Marinescu, E., & Ardelean, V. (1989). Psychopathology in children aged 10–17 of bipolar parents: Psychopathology rate and correlates of the severity of the psychopathology. *Journal of Affective Disorders, 16,* 167–179.

Gross, M. D. (1984). Effect of sucrose on hyperkinetic children. *Pediatrics, 74,* 876–878.

Gross, M. D., Tofanelli, R. A., Butzirus, S. M., & Snodgrass, E. W. (1987). The effects of diets rich in and free from additives on the behavior of children with hyperkinetic and learning disorders. *Journal of the American Academy of Child and Adolescent Psychiatry, 26,* 53–55.

Gross-Tsur, V., Shalev, R. S., Manor, O., & Amir, N. (1995). Developmental right-hemisphere syndrome: Clinical spectrum of the nonverbal learning disability. *Journal of Learning Disabilities, 28,* 80–86.

Gualtieri, C. T., Quade, D., Hicks, R. E., Mayo, J. P., & Schroeder, S. R. (1984). Tardive dyskinesia and other clinical consequences of neuroleptic treatment in children and adolescents. *American Journal of Psychiatry, 141,* 20–23.

Gualtieri, C. T., Schroeder, S. R., Hicks, R. E., & Quade, D. (1986). Tardive dyskinesia in young mentally retarded individuals. *Archives of General Psychiatry, 43,* 335–340.

Guevremont, D. (1990). Social skills and peer relationship training. In R. A. Barkley, *Attention-deficit hyperactivity disorder: A handbook for diagnosis and treatment* (pp. 540–572). New York: Guilford Press.

Gunning, B. (1992). *A controlled trial of clonidine in hyperkinetic children.* Report, Department of Child/Adolescent Psychiatry, Academic Hospital, Rotterdam, The Netherlands.

Gwinn, K. A., & Caviness, J. N. (1997). Risperidone-induced tardive dyskinesia and parkinsonism. *Movement Disorders, 12,* 119–121.

Hadders-Algra, M., Huisjes, H. J., & Touwen, B. C. (1988). Perinatal risk factors and minor neurological dysfunction: Significance for behaviour and school achievement at nine years. *Developmental Medicine and Child Neurology, 30,* 482–491.

Hadders-Algra, M., & Touwen, B. C. (1992). Minor neurological dysfunction is more closely related to learning difficulties than to behavioral problems. *Journal of Learning Disabilities, 25,* 649–657.

Hagerman, R. J., & Falkenstein, A. R. (1987). An association between recurrent otitis media in infancy and later hyperactivity. *Clinical Pediatrics, 26,* 253–257.

Hagerman, R. J., Smith, A. C. M., & Mariner, R. (1983). Clinical features of the fragile X syndrome. In R. J. Hagerman & P. M. McBogg (Eds.), *The fragile X syndrome: Biochemistry, diagnosis, treatment* (pp. 17–54). Dillon, CO: Spectra.

Hagino, O. R., Weller, E. B., Weller, R. A., Washing, D., Fristad, M. A., & Kontras, S. B. (1995). Untoward effects of lithium treatment in children aged four through six years. *Journal of the American Academy of Child and Adolescent Psychiatry, 34,* 1584–1590.

Halperin, J. M., Gittelman, R., Katz, S., & Struve, F. A. (1986). Relationship between stimulant effect, electroencephalogram, and clinical neurological findings in hyperactive children. *Journal of the American Academy of Child Psychiatry, 25,* 820–825.

Halperin, J. M., Gittelman, R., Klein, D. F., & Rudel, R. G. (1984). Reading-disabled hyperactive children: A distinct subgroup of attention deficit disorder with hyperactivity? *Journal of Abnormal Child Psychology, 12,* 1–14.

Halperin, J. M., O'Brien, J. D., Newcorn, J. H., Healey, J. M., Pascualvaca, D. M., Wolf, L. E., & Young, J. G. (1990). Validation of hyperactive, aggressive, and mixed hyperactive/aggressive childhood disorders: A research note. *Journal of Child Psychology and Psychiatry, 31,* 455–459.

Handen, B. L., Breaux, A. M., Gosling, A., Ploof, D. L., & Feldman, H. (1990). Efficacy of methylphenidate among mentally retarded children with attention deficit hyperactivity disorder. *Pediatrics, 86,* 922–930.

Handen, B. L., Breaux, A. M., Janosky, J., McAuliffe, S., Feldman, H., & Gosling, A. (1992). Effects and noneffects of methylphenidate in children with mental retardation and ADHD. *Journal of the American Academy of Child and Adolescent Psychiatry, 31,* 455–461.

Handen, B. L., Feldman, H., Gosling, A., Breaux, A. M., & McAuliffe, S. (1991). Adverse side effects of methylphenidate among mentally retarded children with ADHD. *Journal of the American Academy of Child and Adolescent Psychiatry, 30,* 241–245.

Hanna, G. L. (1995). Demographic and clinical features of obsessive–compulsive disorder in children and adolescents. *Journal of the American Academy of Child and Adolescent Psychiatry, 34,* 19–27.

Harley, J. P., Matthews, C. G., & Eichman, P. (1978). Synthetic food colors and hyperactivty in children: A double blind challenge study. *Pediatrics, 62,* 975–983.

Harley, J. P., Ray, R. S., Tomasi, L., Eichman, P. L., Matthews, C. G., Chun, R., Clelland, C. S., & Traisman, E. (1978). Hyperkinesis and food additives: Testing the Feingold hypothesis. *Pediatrics, 61,* 818–828.

Hauser, P., Zametkin, A. J., Martinez, P., Vitiello, B., Matochik, J. A., Mixson, A. J., & Weintraub, B. D. (1993). Attention deficit–hyperactivity disorder in people with generalized resistance to thyroid hormone. *New England Journal of Medicine, 328,* 997–1001.

Hay, W. M., Hay, L., & Nelson, R. O. (1977). Direct and collateral changes in on-task and academic behavior resulting from on-task versus academic contingencies. *Behavior Therapy, 8,* 431–441.

Hedge, G. A., Colby, H. D., & Goodman, R. L. (1987). *Clinical endocrine physiology*. Philadelphia: Saunders.

Heidemann, S. M., & Sarnaik, A. P. (1990). Clonidine poisoning in children. *Critical Care Medicine, 18,* 618–620.

Henggeler, S. W., & Borduin, C. M. (1990). *Family therapy and beyond: A multisystemic approach to treating the behavior problems of children and adolescents*. Pacific Grove, CA: Brooks/Cole.

Herbst, D. S. (1980). Nonspecific X-linked mental retardation: I. review with information from 24 new families. *American Journal of Medical Genetics, 7,* 443–460.

Herman, B. H., Hammock, M. K., Arthur-Smith, A., Kuehl, K., & Appelgate, K. (1989). Effects of acute administration of naltrexone on cardiocavascular function, body temperature, body weight, and serum concentrations of liver enzymes in autistic children. *Developmental Pharmacology and Therapeutics, 12,* 118–127.

Hermann, B. P., & Whitman, S. (1984). Behavioral and personality correlates of epilepsy: A review, methodological critique, and conceptual model. *Psychological Bulletin, 95,* 451–497.

Hinshaw, S. P. (1987). On the distinction between attentional deficits/hyperactivity and conduct problems/aggression in child psychopathology. *Psychological Bulletin, 101,* 443–463.

Hinshaw, S. P. (1991). Stimulant medication and the treatment of aggression in children with attentional deficits. *Journal of Clinical Child Psychology, 20,* 301–312.

Hinshaw, S. P. (1992a). Academic underachievement, attention deficits, aggression: Comorbidity and implications for intervention. *Journal of Consulting and Clinical Psychology, 60,* 893–903.

Hinshaw, S. P. (1992b). Intervention for social competence and social skill. *Child and Adolescent Psychiatric Clinics of North America, 1,* 539–552.

Hinshaw, S. P., & Erhardt, D. (1993). Behavioral treatment. In V. B. VanHasselt & M. Hersen (Eds.), *Handbook of behavior therapy and pharmacotherapy for children: A comparative analysis* (pp. 233–250). Needham Heigts, MA: Allyn & Bacon.

Hinshaw, S. P., Heller, T., & McHale, J. P. (1992). Covert antisocial behavior in boys with attention-deficit hyperactivity disorder: External validation and effects of methylphenidate. *Journal of Consulting and Clinical Psychology, 60,* 274–281.

Hinshaw, S. P., Henker, B., & Whalen, C. K. (1984). Self-control in hyperactive boys in anger-inducing situations: Effects of cognitive-behavioral training and of methylphenidate. *Journal of Abnormal Child Psychology, 12,* 55–77.

Hinshaw, S. P., Henker, B., Whalen, C. K., Erhardt, D., & Dunnington, R. E., Jr. (1989). Aggressive, prosocial, and nonsocial behavior in hyperactive boys: Dose effects of methylphenidate in naturalistic settings. *Journal of Consulting and Clinical Psychology, 57,* 636–643.

Hinshaw, S. P., Zupan, B. Z., Simmel, C., Nigg, J. T., & Melnick, S. (1997). Peer status in boys with and without ADHD: Predictions from overt and covert antisocial behavior, social isolation, and authoritative parenting beliefs. *Child Development, 68,* 880–896.

Hodin, R. A., Lazar, M. A., & Wintman, B. I. (1989). Identification of a thyroid hormone receptor that is pituitary-specific. *Science, 244,* 76–79.

Horrigan, J. P., & Barnhill, L. J. (1995). Guanfacine for the treatment of attention deficit hyperactivity disorder in boys. *Journal of Child and Adolescent Psychopharmacology, 5,* 215–223.

Hsu, L. K. G., Wisner, K., Richey, E. T., & Goldstein, C. (1985). Is juvenile delinquency related to an abnormal EEG?: A study of EEG abnormalities in juvenile delinquents and adolescent psychiatric inpatients. *Journal of the American Academy of Child Psychiatry, 24,* 310–315.

Hughes, C. W., Preskorn, S. H., Weller, E., Weller, R., Hassanein, R., & Tucker, S. (1990). The effect of concomitant disorders in childhood depression on predicting treatment response. *Psychopharmacology Bulletin, 26,* 235–238.

Hunt, R. D. (1987). Treatment effects of oral and transdermal clonidine in relation to methylphenidate: An open pilot study in ADD-H. *Psychopharmacology Bulletin, 23,* 111–114.

Hunt, R. D., Arnsten, A. F. T., & Asbell, M. D. (1995). An open trial of guanfacine in the treatment of attention deficit hyperactivity disorder. *Journal of the American Academy of Child and Adolescent Psychiatry, 34,* 50–54.

Hunt, R. D., Capper, L. M., Fingeret, M. A., & Ebert, M. H. (1989, October 26–30). *Behavioral effects of clonidine and methylphendiate and both in children with ADHD and conduct disorder.* Paper presented at the 35th annual meeting of the American Academy of Child and Adolescent Psychiatry, Seattle, WA.

Hunt, R. D., Minderaa, R. B., & Cohen, D. J. (1985). Clonidine benefits children with attention deficit disorder and hyperactivity: Report of a double-blind placebo-crossover therapeutic trial. *Journal of the American Academy of Child Psychiatry, 24,* 617–629.

Hynd, G. W., Hem, K. L., Novey, E. S., Eliopulos, D., Marshall, R., Gonzalez, J. J., & Voeller, K. K. (1993). Attention deficit-hyperactivity disorder and asymmetry of the caudate nucleus. *Journal of Child Neurology, 8,* 339–347.

Hynd, G. W., Semrud-Clikeman, M., Lorys, A. R., Novey, E. S., & Eliopulos, D. (1990). Brain morphology in developmental dyslexia and attention deficit disorder/hyperactivity. *Archives of Neurology, 47,* 919–926.

Hynd, G. W., Semrud-Clikeman, M., Lorys, A. R., Novey, E. S., Eliopulos, D., & Lyytinen, H. (1991). Corpus callosum morphology in attention deficit-hyperactivity disorder: Morphometric analysis of MRI. *Journal of Learning Disabilities, 24,* 141–146.

Isojarvi, J. I. T., Laatikainen, T. J., Pakarinen, A. J., Juntunen, K. T. S., & Myllyla, V. V. (1993). Polycystic ovaries and hyperandrogenism in women taking valproate for epilepsy. *New England Journal of Medicine, 329,* 1383–1388.

Jadavji, T., Biggar, W. D., Gold, R., & Prober, C. G. (1986). Sequelae of acute bacterial meningitis in children treated for seven days. *Pediatrics, 78,* 21–25.

Jaffe, S. L. (1991). Intranasal abuse of prescribed methylphenidate by an alcohol and drug abusing adolescent with ADHD. *Journal of the American Academy of Child and Adolescent Psychiatry, 30,* 773–775.

Jagger, J., Prusoff, B. A., Cohen, D. J., Kidd, K. K., Carbonari, C. M., & John, K. (1982). The epidemiology of Tourette's syndrome: A pilot study. *Schizophrenia Bulletin, 8,* 267–277.

Jain, U., Birmaher, B., & Garcia, M. (1992). Fluoxetine in children and adolescents mood disorders: A chart review of efficacy and adverse effects. *Journal of Child and Adolescent Psychopharmacology, 2,* 259–265.

Jaselskis, C. A., Cook, E. H., Jr., Fletcher, K. E., & Leventhal, B. L. (1992). Clonidine treatment of hyperactive and impulsive children with autistic disorder. *Journal of Clinical Psychopharmacology, 12,* 322–327.

Jefferson, J. W., Greist, J. H., & Ackerman, D. L. (1987). *Lithium encyclopedia for clinical practice.* Washington, DC: American Psychiatric Press.

Jensen, P. S., Martin, D., & Cantwell, D. P. (1997). Comorbidity in ADHD: Implications for research, practice, and DSM-V. *Journal of the American Academy of Child and Adolescent Psychiatry, 36,* 1065–1079.

Jensen, P. [S.], Roper, M., Fisher, P., Piacentini, J. [C.], Canino, G., Richters, J., Rubio-Stipec, M., Dulcan, M., Goodman, S., Davies, M., Rae, D., Shaffer, D., Bird, H., Lahey, B., & Schwab-Stone, M. (1995). Test–retest reliability of the Diagnostic Interview Schedule for Children (DISC 2. 1). *Archives of General Psychiatry, 52,* 61–71.

Jensen, P. S., Shervette, R. E., Xenakis, S. N., & Richters, J. (1993). Anxiety and depressive disorders in attention deficit disorder with hyperactivity: New findings. *American Journal of Psychiatry, 150,* 1203–1209.

Jewett, D. L., Fein, G., & Greenberg, M. H. (1990). A double blind study of symptom provocation to determine food sensitivity. *New England Journal of Medicine, 323,* 429–433.

Kafantaris, V., Campbell, M., Padron-Gayol, M. V., Small, A. M., Locascio, J. J., & Rosenberg, C. R. (1992). Carbamazepine in hospitalized aggressive conduct disorder children: An open pilot study. *Psychopharmacology Bulletin, 28,* 193–199.

Kane, J. M. (1995). Tardive dyskinesia: Epidemiological and clinical presentation. In F. E. Bloom & D. J. Kupfer (Eds.), *Psychopharmacology: The fourth generation of progress* (pp. 1485–1496). New York: Raven Press.

Kane, J. M., Woerner, M., & Lieberman, J. (1988). Tardive dyskinesia: Prevalence, incidence and risk factors. *Journal of Clinical Psychopharmacology, 8,* 52S–56S.

Kaufman, J., Birmaher, B., Brent, D., Rao, U., Flynn, C., Moreci, P., Williamson, D., & Ryan, N. (1997). Schedule for Affective Disorders and Schizophrenia for School Age Children—Present and Lifetime Version (K-SADS-PL): Initial reliability and validity data. *Journal of the American Academy of Child and Adolescent Psychiatry, 36,* 980–988.

Kazdin, A. E. (1994). *Behavior modification in applied settings* (5th ed.). Pacific Grove, CA: Brooks/Cole.

Kemph, J. P., DeVane, C. L., Levin, G. M., Jarecke, R., & Miller, R. L. (1993). Treatment of aggressive children with clonidine: Results of an open pilot study. *Journal of the American Academy of Child and Adolescent Psychiatry, 32,* 577–581.

Khan, B. U. (1997). Brief report: Risperidone for severely disturbed behavior and tardive dyskinesia in developmentally disabled adults. *Journal of Autism and Developmental Disorders, 27,* 479–489.

King, R. A., Riddle, M. A., Chappell, P. B., Hardin, M. T., Anderson, G. M., Lombroso, P., & Scahill, L. (1991). Emergence of self-destructive phenomena in children and adolescents during fluoxetine treatment. *Journal of the American Academy of Child and Adolescent Psychiatry, 30,* 179–186.

Kinney, R. O., Shaywitz, B. A., Shaywitz, S. E., Sarwar, M., & Holahan, J. M. (1990). Epilepsy in children with attention deficit disorder: Cognitive, behavioral, and neuroanatomic indices. *Pediatric Neurology, 6,* 31–37.

Klee, S. H., & Garfinkel, B. D. (1983). The computerized continuous performance task: A new measure of inattention. *Journal of Abnormal Child Psychology, 11,* 487–495.

Klein, D. F., Mannuzza, S., Chapman, T., & Fyer, A. J. (1992). Child panic revisited. *Journal of the American Academy of Child and Adolescent Psychiatry, 31,* 112–116.

Klein, R. G. (1994). Anxiety disorders. In M. Rutter, E. Taylor, & L. Hersov (Eds.), *Child and adolescent psychiatry: Modern approaches* (pp. 351–374). Oxford: Blackwell.

Klein, R. G., Abikoff, H., Klass, E., Ganeles, D., Seese, L. M., & Pollack, S. (1997). Clinical efficacy of methylphenidate in conduct disorder with and without attention deficit hyperactivity disorder. *Archives of General Psychiatry, 54,* 1073–1080.

Klein, R. G., Koplewicz, H. S., & Kanner, A. (1992). Imipramine treatment of children with separation anxiety disorder. *Journal of the American Academy of Child and Adolescent Psychiatry, 31,* 21–28.

Klein, R. G., Pine, D. S., & Klein, D. F. (1998). Resolved: Mania is mistaken for ADHD in prepubertal children, negative. *Journal of the American Academy of Child and Adolescent Psychiatry, 37,* 1093-1096.

Klorman, R., Brumaghim, J. T., Salzman, L. F., Strauss, J., Borgstedt, A. D., McBride, M. C., & Loeb, S. (1989). Comparative effects of methylphenidate on attention-deficit hyperactivity disorder with and without aggressive/noncompliant features. *Psychopharmacology Bulletin, 25,* 109–113.

Koller, H., Richardson, S. A., Katz, M., & McLaren, J. (1983). Behavior disturbance since childhood among a 5 year birth cohort of all mentally retarded young adults in a city. *American Journal of Mental Deficiency, 87,* 386–395.

Kolmen, B. K., Feldman, H. M., Handen, B. L., & Janosky, J. E. (1995). Naltrexone in young autistic children: A double blind, placebo controlled crossover study. *Journal of the American Academy of Child and Adolescent Psychiatry, 34,* 223–231.

Koriath, U., Gualtieri, C. T., Van Bourogdien, M. E., Quade, D., & Werry, J. S. (1985). Construct validity of clinical diagnosis in pediatric psychiatry: Relationship among measures. *Journal of the American Academy of Child Psychiatry, 24,* 429–436.

Korkman, M., & Pesonen, A. E. (1994). A comparison of neuropsychological test profiles of children with attention deficit–hyperactivity disorder and/or learning disorder. *Journal of Learning Disabilities, 27,* 383–392.

Kovacs, M. (1998). *Children's Depression Inventory: Manual.* North Tonawanda, NY: Multi-Health Systems.

Kovacs, M., Akiskal, H. S., Gatsonis, C., & Parrone, P. L. (1994). Childhood onset dysthymic disorder: Clinical features and prospective naturalistic outcome. *Archives of General Psychiatry, 51,* 365–374.

Kovacs, M., Feinberg, T. L., Crouse-Novack, M., Paulauskas, S. L., & Finkelstein, R. (1984). Depressive disorders in childhood: I. A longitudinal prospective study of characteristics and recovery. *Archives of General Psychiatry, 41,* 229–237.

Kovacs, M., Goldston, D., & Gatsonis, C. (1993). Suicidal behaviors and childhood onset depressive disorders: A longitudinal investigation. *Journal of the American Academy of Child and Adolescent Psychiatry, 32,* 8–20.

Kovacs, M., Paulauskas, S., Gatsonis, C., & Richards, C. (1988). Depressive disorders in childhood: III. A longitudinal study of comorbidity with and risk for conduct disorders. *Journal of Affective Disorders, 15,* 205–217.

Kovacs, M., & Pollock, M. (1995). Bipolar disorder and comorbid conduct disorder in childhood and adolescence. *Journal of the American Academy of Child and Adolescent Psychiatry, 34,* 715–723.

Kramer, A. D., & Feiguine, R. J. (1981). Clinical effects of amitriptyline in adolescent depression. *Journal of the American Academy of Child Psychiatry, 20,* 636–644.

Kraus, J. F., & Sorenson, S. B. (1994). Epidemiology. In J. M. Silver & S. Yudofsky (Eds.), *Neuropsychiatry of traumatic brain injury* (pp. 3–42). Washington, DC: American Psychiatric Press.

Kumra, S., Herion, D., Jacobsen, L. K., Briguglia, C., & Grothe, D. (1997). Case study: Risperidone-induced hepatotoxicity in pediatric patients. *Journal of the American Academy of Child and Adolescent Psychiatry, 36,* 701–705.

Kuperman, S., & Stewart, M. A. (1987). Use of propranolol to decrease aggressive outbursts in younger patients. *Psychosomatics, 28,* 315–319.

Kurzweil, S. R. (1992). Developmental reading disorder: Predictors of outcome in adolescents who received early diagnosis and treatment. *Journal of Developmental and Behavioral Pediatrics, 13,* 399–404.

Kutcher, S., Boulos, C., Ward, B., Marton, P., Simeon, J., Ferguson, H. B., Szalai, J., Katic, M., Roberts, N., Dubois, C., & Reed, K. (1994). Response to desipramine treatment in adolescent depression: A fixed dose, placebo controlled trial. *Journal of the American Academy of Child and Adolescent Psychiatry, 33,* 686–694.

Kutcher, S. P., Reiter, S., Gardner, D. M., & Klein, R. G. (1992). The pharmacotherapy of anxiety disorders in children and adolescents. *Psychiatric Clinics of North America, 15,* 41–67.

LaFranchi, S. (1982). Hypothyroidism, congential and acquired. In S. A. Kaplan (Ed.), *Clinical pediatric and adolescent endocrinology* (pp. 82–109). Philadelphia: Saunders.

Lahey, B. B., Loeber, R., Quay, H. C., Frick, P. J., & Grimm, J. (1992). Oppositional defiant and conduct disorders: Issues to be resolved for DSM-

IV. *Journal of the American Academy of Child and Adolescent Psychiatry, 31,* 539–546.

Lahey, B. B., Piacentini, J. C., McBurnett, K., Stone, P., Hartdagen, S., & Hynd, G. (1988). Psychopathology in the parents of children with conduct disorder and hyperactivity. *Journal of the American Academy of Child and Adolescent Psychiatry, 27,* 163–170.

LaHoste, G. J., Swanson, J. M., Wigal, S. B., Glabe, C., Wigal, T., King, N., & Kennedy, J. L. (1996). Dopamine D_4 receptor gene polymorphism is associated with attention deficit hyperactivity disorder. *Molecular Psychiatry, 1,* 121–124.

Landau, S., & Moore, L. A. (1991). Social skill deficits in children with ADHD. *School Psychology Review, 20,* 235–251.

Last, C. G., Hersen, M., Kazdin, A. E., Finkelstein, R., & Strauss, C. C. (1987). Comparison of DSM-III separation anxiety and overanxious disorders: Demographic characteristics and patterns of comorbidity. *Journal of the American Academy of Child and Adolescent Psychiatry, 26,* 527–531.

Last, C. G., Hersen, M., Kazdin, A. [E.], Orvaschel, H., & Perrin, S. (1991). Anxiety disorders in children and their families. *Archives of General Psychiatry, 48,* 928–934.

Leckman, J. F., Hardin, M. T., Riddle, M. A., Stevenson, J., Ort, S. I., & Cohen, D. J. (1991). Clonidine treatment of Gilles de la Tourette's syndrome. *Archives of General Psychiatry, 48,* 324–328.

Lee, D. O., Steingard, R. J., Cesena, M., Helmers, S. L., Riviello, J. J., & Mikati, M. A. (1996). Behavioral side effects of gabapentin in children. *Epilepsia, 37,* 87–90.

Lefkowitz, M. M. (1969). Effect of diphenylhydantoin on disruptive behavior: Study of male delinquents. *Archives of General Psychiatry, 20,* 643–651.

Leonard, H. L., Swedo, S. E., Lenane, M. C., Rettew, D. C., Cheslow, D. L., Hamburger, S. D., & Rapoport, J. L. (1991). A double-blind desipramine substitution during long-term clomipramine treatment in children and adolescents with obsessive–compulsive disorder. *Archives of General Psychiatry, 48,* 922–927.

Leonard, H. L., Swedo, S. E., Rapoport, J. L., Koby, E. V., Lenane, M. C., Cheslow, D. L., & Hamburger, S. D. (1989). Treatment of obsessive–compulsive disorder with clomipramine and desipramine in children and adolescents: A double-blind crossover comparison. *Archives of General Psychiatry, 46,* 1088–1092.

Levin, H. S., Ewing-Cobbs, L., & Fletcher, J. M. (1989). Neurobehavioral outcome of mild head injury in children. In H. S. Levin, H. M. Eisenberg, & A. L. Benton (Eds.), *Mild head injury* (pp. 189–213). New York: Oxford University Press.

Levy, F., Hay, D. A., McStephen, M., Wood, C., & Waldman, I. (1997). Attention-deficit hyperactivity disorder: A category or a continuum? Genetic analysis of a large-scale twin study. *Journal of the American Academy of Child and Adolescent Psychiatry, 36,* 737–744.

Lewinsohn, P. M., Clarke, G. N., Seely, J. R., & Rohde, P. (1994). Major depression in community adolescents: Age at onset, episode duration, and time to recurrence. *Journal of the American Academy of Child and Adolescent Psychiatry, 33,* 809–818.

Lewinsohn, P. M., Klein, D. N., & Seeley, J. R. (1995). Bipolar disorders in a community sample of older adolescents: Prevalence, phenomenology, comorbidity, and course. *Journal of the American Academy of Child and Adolescent Psychiatry, 34,* 454–463.

Lilienfeld, S. O., Waldman, I. D., & Israel, A. C. (1994). A critical examination of the use of the term and concept of comorbidity in psychopathology research. *Clinical Psychology: Science and Practice, 1,* 71–83.

Loeber, R., Brinthaupt, V. P., & Green, S. M. (1988). Attention deficits, impulsivity, and hyperactivity with or without conduct problems: Relationships to delinquency and unique contextual factors. In R. J. McMahon & R. D. Peters (Eds.), *Behavior disorders of adolescence: Research, intervention, and policy in clinical and school settings.* New York: Plenum.

Loeber, R., Green, S. M., Lahey, B. B., & Stouthamer-Loeber, M. (1989). Optimal informants on childhood disruptive behaviors. *Development and Psychopathology, 1,* 317–337.

Loeber, R., Keenan, K., Lahey, B. B., Green, S. M., & Thomas, T. (1993). Evidence for developmentally based diagnoses of oppositional defiant disorder and conduct disorder. *Journal of Abnormal Child Psychology, 21,* 377–409.

Lombroso, P. J., Scahill, L., King, R. A., Lynch, K. A., Chappell, P. B., Peterson, B. S., McDougle, C. J., & Leckman, J. F. (1995). Risperidone treatment of children and adolescents with chronic tic disorders: A preliminary report. *Journal of the American Academy of Child and Adolescent Psychiatry, 34,* 1147–1152.

Loney, J., & Milich, R. (1979). The role of hyperactive and aggressive symptomatology in predicting adolescent outcome among hyperactive children. *Journal of Pediatric Psychology, 4,* 93–111.

Loney, J., & Milich, M. (1982). Hyperactivity, inattention, and aggression in clinical practice. *Advances in Behavioral and Developmental Pediatrics, 3,* 113–147.

Lord, C., & Rutter, M. (1994). Autism and pervasive developmental disorders. In M. Rutter, E. Taylor, & L. Hersov (Eds.), *Child and adolescent psychiatry: Modern approaches* (pp. 569–593). Oxford, UK: Blackwell.

Lott, R. S., Kerrick, J. M., & Cohen, S. A. (1996). Clinical and economic aspects of risperidone treatment in adults with mental retardation and behavioral disturbance. *Psychopharmacology Bulletin, 32,* 721–729.

Lou, H. C. (1996). Etiology and pathogenesis of attention deficit hyperactivity disorder (ADHD): Significance of prematurity and perinatal hypoxic–haemodynamic encephalopathy. *Acta Paediatrica, 85,* 1266–1271.

Lowe, T. L., Cohen, D. J., Detlor, J., Kremenitzer, M. W., & Shaywitz, B. A. (1982). Stimulant medications precipitate Tourette's syndrome. *Journal of the American Medical Association, 248,* 1729–1731.

Maedgen, J., & Carlson, C. L. (1998). *Social functioning and emotional regulation in the ADHD subtypes.* Manuscript under review.

Magner, J. A., Petrick, P., Menezes-Ferreira, M. M., Stelling, M., & Weintraub, B. D. (1986). Familial generalized resistance to thyroid hormones: Report of three kindreds and correlation of patterns of affected tissues with the binding of [^{125}I] triiodothyronine to fibroblast nuclei. *Journal of Endrocrinology Investigations, 9,* 459–470.

Malott, R. W., Whaley, D. L., & Malott, M. E. (1997). *Elementary principles of behavior* (3rd ed.). Upper Saddle River, NJ: Prentice-Hall.

Mandoki, M. (1995, October 17–22). *Effects of venlafaxine in major depression in children and adolescents.* Paper presented at the 42nd annual meeting of the American Academy of Child and Adolescent Psychiatry, New Orleans, LA.

Mannuzza, S., & Addalli, K. A. (1991). Young adult mental status of hyperactive boys and their brothers: A prospective follow up study. *Journal of the American Academy of Child and Adolescent Psychiatry, 30,* 743–751.

Mannuzza, S., Klein, R. G., Bonagura, N., Malloy, P., Giampino, T. L., & Addalli, K. A. (1991). Hyperactive boys almost grown up: V. Replication of psychiatric status. *Archives of General Psychiatry, 48,* 77–83.

Mannuzza, S., Klein, R. G., Konig, P. H., & Giampino, T. L. (1989). Hyperactive boys almost grown up: IV. Criminality and its relationship to psychiatric status. *Archives of General Psychiatry, 46,* 1073–1079.

March, J. S., Biederman, J., Wolkow, R., Safferman, A., Mardekian, J., Cook, E. H., Cutler, N. R., Dominguez, R., Ferguson, J., Muller, B., Riesenberg, R., Rosenthal, M., Sallee, F. R., & Wagner, K. D. (1998). Sertraline in children and adolescents with obsessive compulsive disorder: A multicenter, randomized, controlled trial. *Journal of the American Medical Association, 280,* 1752–1756.

March, J. S., Parker, J. D. A., Sullivan, K., Stallings, P., & Conners, C. K. (1997). The Multidimensional Anxiety Scale for Children (MASC): Factor structure, reliability, and validity. *Journal of the American Academy of Child and Adolescent Psychiatry, 36,* 554–565.

Marholin, D., & Steinman, W. M. (1977). Stimulus control in the classroom as a function of the behavior reinforced. *Journal of Applied Behavior Analysis, 10,* 465–478.

Martin, G., & Pear, J. (1996). *Behavior modification: What it is and how to do it* (5th ed.). Upper Saddle River, NJ: Prentice-Hall.

Max, J. E., Arndt, S., Castillo, C. S., Bokura, H., Robin, D. A., Lindgren, S. D., Smith, W. L. Jr., Sato, Y., & Mattheis, P. J. (1998). Attention-deficit hyperactivity symptomatology after traumatic brain injury: A prospective study. *Journal of the American Academy of Child and Adolescent Psychiatry, 37,* 841–847.

Max, J. E., & Dunisch, D. L. (1997). Traumatic brain injury in a child psychiatry outpatient clinic: A controlled study. *Journal of the American Academy of Child and Adolescent Psychiatry, 36,* 404–411.

Max, J. E., Koele, S. H., Smith, W. L., Sato, Y., Lindgren, S. D., Robin, D. A., & Arndt, S. (1998). Psychiatric disorder in children and adolescents after severe traumatic brain injury: A controlled study. *Journal of the American Academy of Child and Adolescent Psychiatry, 37,* 832–840.

McArdle, P., O'Brien, G., & Kolvin, I. (1995). Hyperactivity: Prevalence and relationship with conduct disorder. *Journal of Child Psychology and Psychiatry, 36,* 279–303.

McBurnett, K., Swanson, J. M., Pfiffner, L. J., & Tamm, L. (1997). A measure of ADHD-related classroom impairment based on targets for behavioral intervention. *Journal of Attention Disorders, 2,* 69–76.

McDougle, C. J., Holmes, J. P., Bronson, M. R., Anderson, G. M., Volkmar, F. R., Price, L. H., & Cohen, D. J. (1997). Risperidone treatment of children and adolescents with pervasive developmental disorders: A prospective, open-label study. *Journal of the American Academy of Child and Adolescent Psychiatry, 36,* 685–693.

McElroy, S. L., & Keck, P. E., Jr. (1995). Antiepileptic drugs. In A. F. Schatzberg & C. B. Nemeroff (Eds.), *Textbook of psychopharmacology* (pp. 351–375). Washington, DC: American Psychiatric Press.

McElroy, S. L., Keck, P. E., Jr., Pope, H. G., Jr., & Hudson, J. I. (1992). Valproate in the treatment of bipolar disorder: Literature review and clinical guidelines. *Journal of Clinical Psychopharmacology, 12*(Suppl. 1), 42S–52S.

McElroy, S. L., Strakowski, S. M., West, S. A., Keck, P. E., Jr., & McConville, B. J. (1997). Phenomenology of adolescent and adult mania in hospitalized patients with bipolar disorder. *American Journal of Psychiatry, 154,* 44–49.

McGee, R., Feehan, M., Williams, S., Partridge, F., Silva, P. A., & Kelly, J. (1990). DSM-III disorders in a large sample of adolescents. *Journal of the American Academy of Child and Adolescent Psychiatry, 29,* 611–619.

McGee, R., Stanton, W. R., & Sears, M. R. (1993). Allergic disorders and attention deficit disorder in children. *Journal of Abnormal Child Psychology, 21,* 79–88.

McGee, R., Williams, S., Moffitt, T., & Anderson, J. (1989). A comparison of 13-year-old boys with attention deficit and/or reading disorder on neuropsychological measures. *Journal of Abnormal Child Psychology, 17,* 37–53.

McGee, R., Williams, S., & Silva, P. A. (1984a). Behavioral and developmental characteristics of aggressive, hyperactive, and aggressive–hyperactive boys. *Journal of the American Academy of Child and Adolescent Psychiatry, 23,* 270–279.

McGee, R., Williams, S., & Silva, P. A. (1984b). Background characteristics of aggressive, hyperactive, and aggressive–hyperactive boys. *Journal of the American Academy of Child Psychiatry, 23,* 280–284.

Mendels, J., Johnston, R., Mattes, J., & Riesenberg, R. (1993). Efficacy and safety of b.i.d. doses of venlafaxine in a dose–response study. *Psychopharmacology Bulletin, 29,* 169–174.

Menkes, J. H., & Sankar, R. (1995). Paroxysmal disorders. In J. H. Menkes (Ed.), *Textbook of child neurology* (pp. 725–814). Baltimore: Williams & Wilkins.

Metcalfe, D. D., Sampson, H. A., & Simon, R. A. (1995). *Food allergy: Adverse reactions to foods and food additives.* Boston: Blackwell.

Michelson, L., Sugai, D., Wood, & Kazdin, A. E. (1983). *Social skills assessment and training with children: An empirically based handbook.* New York: Plenum.

Mikkelson, E. J., Brown, G. L., Minichiello, M. D., Millican, F. K., & Rapoport, J. L. (1982). Neurologic status in hyperactive, enuretic, encopretic, and normal boys. *Journal of the American Academy of Child Psychiatry, 21,* 75–81.

Milberger, S., Biederman, J., Faraone, S. V., Chen, L., & Jones, J. (1997a). Further evidence of an association between attention-deficit/hyperactivity disorder and cigarette smoking: Findings from a high-risk sample of siblings. *American Journal on Addictions, 6,* 205–217.

Milberger, S., Biederman, J., Faraone, S. V., Chen, L., & Jones, J. (1997b). ADHD is associated with early initiation of cigarette smoking in children and adolescents. *Journal of the American Academy of Child and Adolescent Psychiatry, 36,* 37–44.

Milich, R., Widiger, T. A., & Landau, S. (1987). Differential diagnosis of attention deficit and conduct disorders using conditional probabilities. *Journal of Consulting and Clinical Psychology, 55,* 762–767.

Miller, B. D. (1987). Depression and asthma: A potentially lethal mixture. *Journal of Allergy and Clinical Immunology, 80,* 48.

Mixon, A. J., Parrilla, R., Ransom, S. C., Wiggs, E. A., McClaskey, J. H., Hauser, P., & Weintraub, B. D. (1992). Correlations of language abnormalities with localization of mutations in the beta-thyroid hormone receptor in 13 kindreds with generalized resistance to thyroid hormone: Identification of four new mutations. *Journal of Clinical Endocrinology and Metabolism, 75,* 1039–1045.

Moffitt, T. E. (1990). Juvenile delinquency and attention deficit disorder: Boys' developmental trajectories from age 3 to age 15. *Child Development, 61,* 893–910.

Moffitt, T. E., & Silva, P. A. (1988). Self-reported delinquency, neuropsychological deficit, and history of attention deficit disorder. *Journal of Abnormal Child Psychology, 16,* 553–569.

Mostofsky, S. H., Reiss, A. L., Lockhart, P., & Denckla, M. B. (1998). Evaluation of cerebellar size in attention-deficit hyperactivity disorder. *Journal of Child Neurology, 13,* 434–439.

Mrazek, D. A. (1994). Psychiatric aspects of somatic disease and disorders. In M. Rutter, E. Taylor, & L. Hersov (Eds.), *Child and adolescent psychiatry: Modern approaches* (pp. 697–710). Oxford, UK: Blackwell.

Murphy, D. A., Pelham, W. E., & Lang, A. R. (1992). Aggression in boys with attention deficit–hyperactivity disorder: Methylphenidate effects on naturalistically observed aggression, response to provocation, and social information processing. *Journal of Abnormal Child Psychology, 20,* 451–466.

Murray, R., Shum, D., & McFarland, K. (1992). Attentional deficits in head-injured children: An information processing analysis. *Brain and Cognition, 18,* 99–115.

Nam, M., Joe, S. H., Jung, I. K., Suh, K. Y., Kwak, D. I., & Hong, K. E. M. (1997, October 14–19). *Comparative efficacy of risperidone and haloperidol in the treatment of Tourette's disorders.* Paper presented at the 44th annual meeting of the American Academy of Child and Adolescent Psychiatry, Toronto, Ontario, Canada.

Noll, R. B., LeRoy, S., Bukowski, W. M., Rogosch, F. A., & Kulkarni, R. (1991). Peer relationships and adjustment in children with cancer. *Journal of Pediatric Psychology, 16,* 307–326.

Oden, S., & Asher, S. R. (1977). Coaching children in social skills for friendship making. *Child Development, 48,* 495–506.

O'Leary, S. G., & Drabman, R. (1971). Token reinforcement programs in the classroom. *Psychological Bulletin, 75,* 379–398.

Olvera, R. L., Pliszka, S. R., Luh, J., & Tatum, R. (1996). An open trial of venlafaxine in children and adolescents with ADHD. *Journal of Child and Adolescent Psychopharmacology, 6,* 241–250.

Ozols, E. J., & Rourke, B. P. (1985). Dimensions of social sensitivity in two types of learning disabled children. In B. P. Rourke (Ed.), *Neuropsychology of learning disabilities: Essentials of subtype analysis* (pp. 281–301). New York: Guilford Press.

Papatheodorou, G., & Kutcher, S. P. (1993). Divalproex sodium treatment in late adolescent and young adult acute mania. *Psychopharmacology Bulletin, 29,* 213–219.

Pataki, C. S., Carlson, G. A., Kelly, K. L., Rapport, M. D., & Biancaniello, T. M. (1993). Side effects of methylphenidate and desipramine alone and in combination in children. *Journal of the American Academy of Child and Adolescent Psychiatry, 32,* 1065–1072.

Patterson, G. R. (1975). *Families: Applications of social learning to family life.* Champaign, IL: Research Press.

Patterson, G. [R.], & Forgatch, M. (1987). *Parents and adolescents living together: Part I. The basics.* Eugene, OR: Castalia.

Patterson, G. [R.], & Forgatch, M. (1989). *Parents and adolescents living together: Part II. Family problem solving.* Eugene, OR: Castalia.

Pauls, D. L., Leckman, J. F., & Cohen, D. J. (1993). Familial relationship between Gilles de la Tourette's syndrome, attention deficit disorder, learning disabilities, speech disorders, and stuttering. *Journal of the American Academy of Child and Adolescent Psychiatry, 32,* 1044–1050.

Pauls, D. L., Towbin, K. E., Leckman, J. F., Zahner, G. E., & Cohen, D. J. (1986). Gilles de la Tourette's syndrome and obsessive–compulsive disorder: Evidence supporting a genetic relationship. *Archives of General Psychiatry, 43,* 1180–1182.

Payton, J. B., Burkhart, J. E., Hersen, M., & Helsel, W. J. (1989). Treatment of ADDH in mentally retarded children: A preliminary study. *Journal of the American Academy of Child and Adolescent Psychiatry, 28,* 761–767.

Pearson, D. A., & Aman, M. G. (1994). Ratings of hyperactivity and developmental indices: Should clinicians correct for developmental level? *Journal of Autism and Developmental Disorders, 24,* 395–411.

Pelham, W. E. (1993). Pharmacotherapy for children with attention deficit hyperactivity disorder. *School Psychology Review, 22,* 199–227.

Pelham, W. E., & Bender, M. E. (1982). Peer relationships in hyperactive children: Description and treatment. In K. D. Gadow & I. Bialer (Eds.), *Advances in behavioral disabilities* (Vol. 1, pp. 365–436). Greenwich, CT: JAI Press.

Pelham, W. E., Bender, M. E., Caddell, J., Booth, S., & Moorer, S. H. (1985). Methylphenidate and children with attention deficit disorder: Dose effects on classroom academic and social behavior. *Archives of General Psychiatry, 42,* 948–952.

Pelham, W. E., Carlson, C., Sams, S. E., Vallano, G., Dixon, M. J., & Hoza, B.

(1993). Separate and combined effects of methylphenidate and behavior modification on boys with ADHD in the classroom. *Journal of Consulting and Clinical Psychology, 61,* 506–515.

Pelham, W. E., Grenier, A., & Gnagy, E. (1997). *Children's STP Manual.* Buffalo, NY: CTADD.

Pelham, W. E., & Hoza, B. (1996). Intensive treatment: A summer treatment program for children with ADHD. In E. Hibbs & P. Jensen (Eds.), *Psychosocial treatments for child and adolescent disorders: Empirically based strategies for clinical practice* (pp. 311–340). New York: APA Press.

Pelham, W. E., McBurnett, K., Harper, G. W., Milich, R., Murphy, D. A., Clinton, J., & Thiele, C. (1990). Methylphenidate and baseball playing in ADHD children: Who's on first? *Journal of Consulting and Clinical Psychology, 58,* 130–133.

Pelham, W. E., & Milich, R. (1991). Individual differences in response to ritalin in classwork and social behavior. In L. L. Greenhill & B. B. Osman (Eds.), *Ritalin theory and patient management* (pp. 203–221). New York: Liebert.

Pelham, W. E., & Murphy, H. A. (1986). Attention deficits and conduct disorders. In M. Hersen (Ed.), *Pharmacological and behavioral treatments: An integrative approach* (pp. 108–148). New York: Wiley.

Pelham, W. E., Jr., Wheeler, T., & Chronis, A. (1998). Empirically supported psychosocial treatments for ADHD. *Journal of Clinical Child Psychology, 27,* 190–205.

Pelletier, G., Geoffroy, G., & Robaey, P. (1996). Mania in children [letter]. *Journal of the American Academy of Child and Adolescent Psychiatry, 34,* 1257

Pellock, J. M. (1987). Carbamazepine side effects in children and adults. *Epilepsia, 28*(Suppl. 3), 64–70.

Pennington, B. F. (1991). *Diagnosing learning disorders.* New York: Guilford Press.

Pennington, B. F. (1995). Genetics of learning disabilities. *Journal of Child Neurology, 10*(Suppl.), S69–S77.

Pennington, B. F., Groisser, D., & Welsh, M. C. (1993). Contrasting cognitive deficits in attention deficit hyperactivity disorder versus reading disability. *Developmental Psychology, 29,* 511–523.

Perrin, S., & Last, C. G. (1996). Relationship between ADHD and anxiety in boys: Results from a family study. *Journal of the American Academy of Child and Adolescent Psychiatry, 35,* 988–996.

Pfiffner, L. J. (1996). *All about ADHD: The complete practical guide for classroom teachers.* New York: Scholastic.

Pfiffner, L. J., & McBurnett, K. (1997). Social skills training with parent generalization: Treatment effects for children with ADD. *Journal of Consulting and Clinical Psychology, 65,* 749–757.

Pfiffner, L. J., & O'Leary, S. G. (1993). Psychological treatments: School-based. In J. L. Matson (Ed.), *Hyperactivity in children: A handbook* (pp. 234–255). Boston: Allyn & Bacon.

Piacentini, J. C., Cohen, P., & Cohen, J. (1992). Combining discrepant diagnostic information from multiple sources: Are complex algorithms better than simple ones? *Journal of Abnormal Child Psychology, 20,* 51–64.

Piacentini, J. [C.], Shaffer, D., Fisher, P., Schwab-Stone, M., Davies, M., & Gioia,

P. (1993). The Diagnositic Interview Schedule for Children—Revised Version (DISC-R). III: Concurrent criterion validity. *Journal of the American Academy of Child and Adolescent Psychiatry, 32,* 658–665.

Pleak, R. R., Birmaher, B., Gavrilescu, A., Abichandani, C., & Williams, D. T. (1988). Mania and neuropsychiatric excitation following carbamazepine. *Journal of the American Academy of Child and Adolescent Psychiatry, 27,* 500–503.

Pliszka, S. R. (1987). Tricyclic antidepressants in the treatment of children with attention deficit disorder. *Journal of the American Academy of Child and Adolescent Psychiatry, 26,* 127–132.

Pliszka, S. R. (1989). Effect of anxiety on cognition, behavior, and stimulant response in ADHD. *Journal of the American Academy of Child and Adolescent Psychiatry, 28,* 882–887.

Pliszka, S. R. (1992). Comorbidity of attention deficit hyperactivity disorder and overanxious disorder. *Journal of the American Academy of Child and Adolescent Psychiatry, 31,* 197–203.

Pliszka, S. R. (1998). Comorbidity of attention-deficit/hyperactivity disorder with psychiatric disorder: An overview. *Journal of Clinical Psychiatry, 59*(Suppl. 7), 50–58.

Pliszka, S. R., Borcherding, S. H., Spratley, K., Leon, S., & Irick, S. (1997). Measuring inhibitory control in children. *Journal of Developmental and Behavioral Pediatrics, 18,* 254–259.

Pliszka, S. R., Maas, J. W., Javors, M. A., Rogeness, G. A., & Baker, J. (1994). Urinary catecholamines in attention deficit hyperactivity disorder with and without comorbid anxiety. *Journal of the American Academy of Child and Adolescent Psychiatry, 33,* 1165–1173.

Pliszka, S. R., McCracken, J. T., & Maas, J. W. (1996). Catecholamines in attention deficit hyperactivity disorder: Current perspectives. *Journal of the American Academy of Child and Adolescent Psychiatry, 35,* 264–272.

Pope, H. G., Jr., McElroy, S. L., Keck, P. E., Jr., & Hudson, J. I. (1991). Valproate in the treatment of acute mania. *Archives of General Psychiatry, 48,* 62–68.

Popper, C. W. (1995). Combining methylphenidate and clonidine: Pharmacologic questions and news reports about sudden death. *Journal of Child and Adolescent Psychopharmacology, 5,* 157–166.

Popper, C. W., & Ziminitzky, B. (1995). Sudden death putatively related to desipramine treatment in youth: A fifth case and a review of speculative mechanisms. *Journal of Child and Adolescent Psychopharmacology, 5,* 283–300.

Porter, J. E., & Rourke, B. P. (1985). Socioemotional functioning of learning disabled children: A subtypal analysis of personality patterns. In B. P. Rourke (Ed.), *Neuropsychology of learning disabilities: Essentials of subtype analysis* (pp. 257–279). New York: Guilford Press.

Preskorn, S. H., & Fast, G. A. (1995). Therapeutic drug monitoring for antidepressants: Efficacy, safety, and cost effectiveness. *Journal of Clinical Psychiatry*(Suppl. 6), 52, 23–33.

Preskorn, S. H., Weller, E. B., Hughes, C. W., Weller, R. A., & Bolte, K. (1987). Depression in prepubertal children: Dexamethasone nonsuppression predicts differential response to imipramine vs. placebo. *Psychopharmacology Bulletin, 23,* 128–133.

Prien, R. F., Himmelhoch, J. M., & Kupfer, D. J. (1988). Treatment of mixed mania. *Journal of Affective Disorders, 15,* 9–15.

Puente, R. M. (1976). The use of carbamazepine in the treatment of behavioral disorders in children. In W. Birkmeyer (Ed.), *Epileptic seizures–Behavior–pain* (pp. 243–247). Baltimore: University Park Press.

Puig-Antich, J., Perel, J. M., Lupatkin, W., Chambers, W. J., Tabrizi, M. A., King, J., Goetz, R., Davies, M., & Stiller, R. L. (1987). Imipramine in prepubertal major depressive disorders. *Archives of General Psychiatry, 44,* 81–89.

Rantala, H., Uhari, M., Saukkonen, A. L., & Sorri, M. (1991). Outcome after childhood encephalitis. *Developmental Medicine and Child Neurology, 33,* 858–867.

Rapoport, J. L., Quinn, P. O., Bradbard, G., Riddle, D., & Brooks, E. (1974). Imipramine and methylphenidate: A double blind comparison. *Archives of General Psychiatry, 30,* 789–793.

Rapp, D. (1991). *Is this your child?* New York: Morrow.

Rappaport, L., Coffman, H., Guare, R., Fenton, T., DeGraw, C., & Twarg, F. (1989). Effects of theophylline on behavior and learning in children with asthma. *American Journal of Diseases of Children, 143,* 368–372.

Rapport, M. D., Carlson, G. A., Kelly, K. L., & Pataki, C. (1993). Methylphenidate and desipramine in hospitalized children: I. Separate and combined effects on cognitive function. *Journal of the American Academy of Child and Adolescent Psychiatry, 32,* 333–342.

Rapport, M. D., & Denny, C. (1997). Titrating methylphendiate in children with attention deficit hyperactivity disorder: Is body mass predictive of clinical response? *Journal of the American Academy of Child and Adolescent Psychiatry, 36,* 523–530.

Rapport, M. D., DuPaul, G. J., Stoner, G., & Jones, T. J. (1986). Comparing classroom and clinic measures of attention deficit disorder: Differential, idiosyncratic, and dose–response effects of methylphenidate. *Journal of Consulting and Clinical Psychology, 54,* 334–341.

Rapport, M. D., Stoner, G., DuPaul, G. J., Birmingham, B. K., & Tucker, S. (1985). Methylphenidate in hyperactive children: Differential effects of dose on academic, learning, and social behavior. *Journal of Abnormal Child Psychology, 13,* 227–243.

Ratey, J. J., Sorgi, P., O'Driscoll, G. A., Sands, S., Daehler, M. L., Fletcher, J. R., Kadish, W., Spruiell, G., Polakoff, S., Lindem, K. J., Bemporad, J. R., Richardson, L., & Rosenfeld, B. (1992). Nadolol to treat aggression and psychiatric symptomatology in chronic psychiatric patients inpatients: A double blind, placebo controlled study. *Journal of Clinical Psychiatry, 53,* 41–46.

Reeves, J. C., Werry, J. S., Elkind, G. S., & Zametkin, A. (1987). Attention deficit, conduct, oppositional, and anxiety disorders in children: II. Clinical charateristics. *Journal of the American Academy of Child and Adolescent Psychiatry, 26,* 144–155.

Reich, W., & Earls, F. (1987). Rules for making psychiatric diagnosis in children on the basis of multiple sources of information: Preliminary strategies. *Journal of Abnormal Child Psychology, 15,* 601–616.

Reynolds, C. R., & Richmond, B. O. (1997). What I think and feel: A revised measure of children's manifest anxiety. *Journal of Abnormal Child Psychology, 25,* 15–20.

Richardson, E., Kupietz, S. S., Winsberg, B. G., Maitinsky, S., & Mendell, N. (1988). Effects of methylphenidate dosage in hyperactive reading-disabled children: II. Reading achievement. *Journal of the American Academy of Child and Adolescent Psychiatry, 27,* 78–87.

Richardson, M. A., Haugland, G., & Craig, T. J. (1991). Neuroleptic use, Parkinsonian symptoms, tardive dyskinesia, and associated factors in child and adolescent psychiatric patients. *American Journal of Psychiatry, 148,* 1322–1328.

Riddle, M. [A.], Claghorn, J., Gaffney, G., Greist, J., Holland, D., Landbloom, R., McConville, B., Pigott, T., Pravetz, M., Walkup, J. T., & Yaryura-Tobias, J. (1996, May). *Fluvoxamine for OCD in children and adolescents: A controlled trial.* Paper presented at the annual meeting of the American Psychiatric Association, San Diego, CA.

Riddle, M. A., Geller, B., & Ryan, N. (1993). Another sudden death in a child treated with desipramine. *Journal of the American Academy of Child and Adolescent Psychiatry, 32,* 792–797.

Riddle, M. A., King, R. A., & Hardin, M. T. (1990). Behavioral side effects of fluoxetine in children and adolescents. *Journal of Child and Adolescent Psychopharmacology, 1,* 193–198.

Riddle, M. A., Scahill, L., King, R. A., Hardin, M. T., Anderson, G. M., Ort, S. I., Smith, J. C., Leckman, J. F., & Cohen, D. J. (1992). Double blind crossover trial of fluoxetine and placebo in children and adolescents with obsessive–compulsive disorder. *Journal of the American Academy of Child and Adolescent Psychiatry, 31,* 1062–1069.

Riddle, M. A., Scahill, L., King, R. [A.], Hardin, M. T., Towbin, K. E., Ort, S. I., Leckman, J. F., & Cohen, D. J. (1990). Obsessive–compulsive disorder in children and adolescents: Phenomenology and family history. *Journal of the American Academy of Child and Adolescent Psychiatry, 29,* 766–772.

Ritvo, E. R., Ornitz, E. M., Walter, R. D., & Hanley, J. (1970). Correlation of psychiatric diagnosis and EEG findings: A double blind study of 184 hospitalized children. *American Journal of Psychiatry, 126,* 988–996.

Roberts, J. E., Burchinal, M. R., Collier, A. M., Ramey, C. T., Koch, M. A., & Henderson, F. W. (1989). Otitis media in early childhood and cognitive, academic, and classroom performance of the school-aged child. *Pediatrics, 83,* 477–485.

Robertson, M. M., Trimble, M. R., & Lees, A. J. (1988). The psychopathology of the Gilles de la Tourette syndrome. *British Journal of Psychiatry, 152,* 383–390.

Ross, D. M., & Ross, S. A. (1982). *Hyperactivity: Current issues, research, and therapy* (Vol. 2). New York: Wiley.

Ross, G., Lipper, E., & Auld, P. A. (1992). Hand preference, prematurity and developmental outcome at school age. *Neuropsychologia, 30,* 483–494.

Roth, N., Beyreiss, J., Schlenzka, K., & Beyer, H. (1991). Coincidence of attention deficit disorder and atopic disorders in children: Empirical findings and hypothetical background. *Journal of Abnormal Child Psychology, 19,* 1–13.

Rourke, B. P. (1989). *Nonverbal learning disabilities: The syndrome and the model.* New York: Guilford Press.

Rourke, B. P. (1993). Arithmetic disabilities, specific and otherwise: A neuropsychologial perspective. *Journal of Learning Disabilities, 26,* 214–226.

Rourke, B. P., & Finlayson, M. A. J. (1995). Neuropsychological significance of variations in patterns of academic performance: Verbal and visual–spatial abilities. *Journal of Abnormal Child Psychology, 6,* 121–133.

Rourke, B. P., & Strang, J. D. (1978). Neuropsychological significance of variations in patterns of academic performance: Motor, psychomotor, and tactile–perceptual abilities. *Journal of Pediatric Psychology, 3,* 62–66.

Rutter, M., Tizard, J., & Whitmore, K. (1970). *Education, Health and Behavior.* London: Longman.

Rutter, M., & Yule, W. (1975). The concept of specific reading retardation. *Journal of Child Psychology and Psychiatry, 16,* 181–197.

Rutter, M., Yule, B., Quinton, D., Rowlands, O., Yule, W., & Berger, M. (1974). Attainment and adjustment in two geographical areas: III. Some factors accounting for areas differences. *British Journal of Psychiatry, 125,* 520–533.

Saletu, B., Grunberger, J., Anderer, P., Linzmayer, L., Semlitsch, H. V., & Magni, G. (1992). Pharmacodynamics of venlafaxine evaluated by EEG brain mapping, psychometry and psychophysiology. *British Journal of Clinical Pharmacology, 33,* 589–601.

Sallee, F. R., Nesbitt, L., Jackson, C., Sine, L., & Sethuraman, G. (1997). Relative efficacy of haloperidol and pimozide in children and adolescents with Tourette's disorder. *American Journal of Psychiatry, 154,* 1057–1062.

Sanchez, L. E., Campbell, M., Small, A. M., Cueva, J. E., Armenteros, J. L., & Adams, P. B. (1996). A pilot study of clomipramine in young autistic children. *Journal of the American Academy of Child and Adolescent Psychiatry, 35,* 537–544.

Sanger, M. S., Copeland, D. R., & Davidson, E. R. (1991). Psychosocial adjustment among pediatric cancer patients: A multidimensional assessment. *Journal of Pediatric Psychology, 16,* 463–474.

Satterfield, J. H., & Schell, A. M. (1984). Childhood brain function differences in delinquent and non-delinquent hyperactive boys. *Electroencephalography and Clinical Neurophysiology, 57,* 199–207.

Satterfield, J. [H.], Swanson, J. [M.], Schell, A., & Lee, F. (1994). Prediction of antisocial behavior in attention-deficit hyperactivity disorder boys from aggression/defiance scores. *Journal of the American Academy of Child and Adolescent Psychiatry, 33,* 185–190.

Scahill, L., Riddle, M. A., King, R. A., Rasmusson, A., Makuch, R. W., & Leckman, J. F. (1997). Fluoxetine has no marked effect on tic symptoms in patients with Tourette's syndrome: A double-blind placebo-controlled study. *Journal of Child and Adolescent Psychopharmacology, 7,* 75–85.

Schachar, R., & Tannock, R. (1995). Test of four hypotheses for the comorbidity of attention deficit hyperactivity disorder and conduct disorder. *Journal of the American Academy of Child and Adolescent Psychiatry, 34,* 639–648.

Schlieper, A., Alcock, D., Beaudry, P., & Feldman, W. (1991). Effect of therapeutic plasma concentrates of theophylline on behavior, cognitive processing and affect in children with asthma. *Journal of Pediatrics, 118,* 449–455.

Schneider, S. M., Atkinson, D. R., & El-Mallakh, R. S. (1996). CD and ADHD in bipolar disorder. *Journal of the American Academy of Child and Adolescent Psychiatry, 35,* 1422–1423.

Schvehla, T. J., Mandoki, M. W., & Sumner, G. S. (1994). Clonidine therapy for comorbid attention deficit hyperactivity disorder and conduct disorder: Preliminary findings in a children's inpatient unit. *Southern Medical Journal, 87,* 692–695.

Schwab-Stone, M. [E.], Fisher, P., Piacentini, J. [C.], Shaffer, D., Davies, M., & Briggs, M. (1993). The Diagnostic Interview Schedule for Children—Revised Version (DISC-R): II. Test–retest reliability. *Journal of the American Academy of Child and Adolescent Psychiatry, 32,* 651–657.

Schwab-Stone, M. E., Shaffer, D., Dulcan, M. K., Jensen, P. S., Fisher, P., Bird, H. R., Goodman, S. H., Lahey, B. B., Lichtman, J. H., Canino, G., Rubio-Stipec, M., & Rae, D. S. (1996). Criterion validity of the NIMH Diagnostic Interview Schedule for Children Version 2.3 (DISC-2.3). *Journal of the American Academy of Child and Adolescent Psychiatry, 35,* 878–888.

Schweizer, E., Feighner, J., Mandos, L. A., & Rickels, K. (1994). Comparison of venlafaxine and imipramine in the acute treatment of depression in outpatients. *Journal of Clinical Psychiatry, 55,* 104–108.

Scott, S. (1994). Mental retardation. In M. Rutter, E. Taylor, & L. Hersov (Eds.), *Child and adolescent psychiatry: Modern approaches* (pp. 616–646). Oxford, UK: Blackwell.

Semrud-Clikeman, M., Biederman, J., Sprich-Buckminster, S., Lehman, B. K., Faraone, S. V., & Norman, D. (1992). Comorbidity between ADDH and learning disability: A review and report in a clinically referred sample. *Journal of the American Academy of Child and Adolescent Psychiatry, 31,* 439–448.

Semrud-Clikeman, M., Filipek, P. A., Biederman, J., Steingard, R., Kennedy, D., Renshaw, P., & Bekken, K. (1994). Attention deficit hyperactivity disorder: Magnetic resonance imaging morphometric analysis of the corpus callosum. *Journal of the American Academy of Child and Adolescent Psychiatry, 33,* 875–881.

Shafer, S. Q., Shaffer, D., O'Connor, P. A., & Stokman, C. J. (1983). Hard thoughts of neurological "soft signs." In M. Rutter (Ed.), *Developmental neuropsychiatry* (pp. 133–143). New York: Guilford Press.

Shaffer, D., Fisher, P., Dulcan, M. K., Davies, M., Piacentini, J., Schwab-Stone, M. E., Lahey, B. B., Bourdon, K., Jensen, P. S., Bird, H. R., Canino, G., & Regier, D. A. (1996). The NIMH Diagnostic Interview Schedule for Children Version 2.3 (DISC 2.3): Description, acceptability, prevalence rates, and performance in the MECA study. Methods for the epidemiology of child and adolescent mental disorders. *Journal of the American Academy of Child and Adolescent Psychiatry, 35,* 865–877.

Shaffer, D., O'Connor, P. A., Shafer, S. Q., & Prupis, S. (1983). Neurological "soft signs": Their origins and significance for behavior. In M. Rutter (Ed.), *Developmental neuropsychiatry* (pp. 144–180). New York: Guilford Press.

Shaffer, D., Schonfeld, I., O'Conner, P. A., Stokman, C., Trautman, P., & Shafer, S. [Q.] (1985). Neurological soft signs: Their relationship to psychiatric disorder and intelligence in adolescence. *Archives of General Psychiatry, 42,* 342–351.

Shaffer, D., Schwab-Stone, M., Fisher, P., Cohen, P., Piacentini, J. [C.], Davies, M., Conners, C. K., & Regier, D. (1993). The Diagnostic Interview Schedule for Children—Revised Version (DISC-R): I. Preparation, field testing, interrater reliability, and acceptability. *Journal of the American Academy of Child and Adolescent Psychiatry, 32,* 643–650.

Shapiro, E., Shapiro, A. K., Fulop, G., Hubbard, M., Mandeli, J., Nordlie, J., & Phillips, R. A. (1989). Controlled study of haloperidol, pimozide, and placebo for the treatment of Gilles de la Tourette's syndrome. *Archives of General Psychiatry, 46,* 722–730.

Shapiro, S. K., & Garfinkel, B. D. (1986). The occurrence of behavior disorders in children: The interdependence of attention deficit disorder and conduct disorder. *Journal of the American Academy of Child Psychiatry, 25,* 809–819.

Shaywitz, B. A., Fletcher, J., Holahan, J. M., & Shaywitz, S. E. (1992). Discrepancy compared to low achievement definitions of reading disabilities: Results from the Connecticut Longitudinal Study. *Journal of Learning Disabilities, 25,* 639–648.

Shaywitz, B. A., Fletcher, J. M., & Shaywitz, S. E. (1995). Defining and classifying learning disabilities and attention-deficit/hyperactivity disorder. *Journal of Child Neurology, 10*(Suppl. 1), S50–S57.

Shaywitz, S. E., Escobar, M. D., & Shaywitz, B. A. (1992). Evidence that dyslexia may represent the lower tail of a normal distribution of reading ability. *New England Journal of Medicine, 326,* 145–150.

Shaywitz, S. E., & Shaywitz, B. E. (1988). Attention deficit disorder: Current perspectives. In J. F. Kavanaugh & T. J. Truss (Eds.), *Learning disabilities: Proceedings of the national conference* (pp. 369–523). Parkton, MD: York Press.

Shaywitz, S. E., Shaywitz, B. A., Fletcher, J. M., & Escobar, M. D. (1990). Prevalence of reading disability in boys and girls: Results of the Connecticut Longitudinal Study. *Journal of the American Medical Association, 234,* 998–1002.

Shire-Richwood. (1997). Open safety investigation of single ingredient amphetamine product in eligible patients with attention deficit hyperactivity disorder. IND #47,301.

Silva, P. A., Kirkland, C., Simpson, A., Stewart, I. A., & Williams, S. M. (1982). Some developmental and behavioral problems associated with bilateral otitis media with effusion. *Journal of Learning Disabilities, 15,* 417–421.

Silver, J. M., & Yudofsky, S. C. (1994). Psychopharmacology. In J. M. Silver, S. C. Yudofsky, & R. E. Hales (Eds.), *Neuropsychiatry of traumatic brain injury* (pp. 631–670). Washington, DC: American Psychiatric Press.

Silverman, W. K., & Eisen, A. R. (1992). Age differences in the reliability of parent and child reports of child anxious symptomatology using a structured interview. *Journal of the American Academy of Child and Adolescent Psychiatry, 31,* 117–124.

Simeon, J. G., Dinicola, V. F., Ferguson, H. B., & Copping, W. (1990). Adolescent depression: A placebo-controlled fluoxetine treatment study and follow-up.

Progress in Neuropsychopharmacology and Biological Psychiatry, 14, 791–795.

Simeon, J. G., Ferguson, H. B., Knott, V., Roberts, N., Gautheir, B., Dubois, C., & Wiggins, D. (1992). Clinical, cognitive, and neurophysiological effects of alprazolam in children and adolescents with overanxious and avoidant disorders. *Journal of the American Academy of Child and Adolescent Psychiatry, 31,* 29–33.

Simeon, J. G., Thatte, S., & Wiggins, D. (1990). Treatment of adolescent obsessive–compulsive disorder with a clomipramine–fluoxetine combination. *Psychopharmacology Bulletin, 26,* 285–290.

Singer, H. S., Brown, J., Quaskey, S., Rosenberg, L. A., Mellits, E. D., & Denckla, M. D. (1995). The treatment of attention-deficit hyperactivity disorder in Tourette's syndrome: A double blind placebo controlled study with clonidine and desipramine. *Pediatrics, 95,* 74–81.

Sloman, L. (1991). Use of medication in pervasive developmental disorders. *Psychiatric Clinics of North America, 14,* 165–182.

Solanto, M. V. (1984). Neuropharmacological basis of stimulant drug action in attention deficit disorder with hyperactivity: A review and synthesis. *Psychological Bulletin, 95,* 387–409.

Solanto, M. V. (1991). Dosage effects of Ritalin on cognition. In L. L. Greenhill & B. B. Osman (Eds.), *Ritalin: Theory and patient management* (pp. 233–245). New York: Liebert.

Spencer, T., Biederman, J., Steingard, R., & Wilens, T. E. (1993). Nortriptyline treatment of children with attention deficit hyperactivity disorder and tic disorder or Tourette's syndrome. *Journal of the American Academy of Child and Adolescent Psychiatry, 32,* 205–210.

Sprague, R. L., & Sleator, E. K. (1977). Methylphenidate in hyperkinetic children: Differences in dose effects on learning and social behavior. *Science, 198,* 1274–1276.

Sprich-Buckminster, S., Biederman, J., Milberger, S., Faraone, S. V., & Lehman, B. K. (1993). Are perinatal complications relevant to the manifestation of ADD? Issues of comorbidity and familiality. *Journal of the American Academy of Child and Adolescent Psychiatry, 32,* 1032–1037.

Stanford, L. D., & Hynd, G. W. (1994). Congruence of behavioral symptomatology in children with ADD/H, ADD/WO, and learning disabilities. *Journal of Learning Disabilities, 27,* 243–253.

Stanovich, K. E., & Siegel, L. S. (1994). Phenotypic performance profile of children with reading disabilities: A regression-based test of the phonological-core variable-difference model. *Journal of Educational Psychology, 86,* 24–53.

Stare, F. J., Whelan, E. M., & Sheridan, M. (1980). Diet and hyperactivity: Is there a relationship? *Pediatrics, 66,* 521–525.

Stefl, M. E. (1984). Mental Health associated with Tourette's syndrome. *American Journal of Public Health, 74,* 1310–1313.

Steingard, R., Biederman, J., Spencer, T., Wilens, T., & Gonzalez, A. (1993). Comparison of clonidine response in the treatment of attention deficit hyperactivity disorder with and without comorbid tic disorders. *Journal of the American Academy of Child and Adolescent Psychiatry, 32,* 350–353.

Stevens, J. R., & Hermann, B. P. (1981). Temporal lobe epilepsy, psychopathology, and violence: The state of the evidence. *Neurology, 31,* 1127–1132.

Stewart, M. A., Cummings, C., Singer, S., & DeBlois, C. S. (1981). The overlap between hyperactive and unsocialized aggressive children. *Journal of Child Psychology and Psychiatry, 22,* 35–45.

Stjernquist, K., & Svenningsen, N. W. (1995). Extremely low-birth weight infants less than 901 g: Development and behavior after 4 years of life. *Acta Paediatrica, 84,* 500–506.

Strain, P. S., Cooke, T. P., & Apolloni, T. (1976). The role of peers in modifying classmates' social behavior: A review. *Journal of Special Education, 10,* 351–356.

Strang, J. D., & Rourke, B. P. (1983). Concept-formation/non-verbal reasoning abilities of children who exhibit specific academic problems with arithmetic. *Journal of Clinical Child Psychology, 13,* 33–39.

Strang, J. D., & Rourke, B. P. (1985). Arithmetic disability subtypes: The neuropsychological signifigance of specific arithmetic impairment in childhood. In B. P. Rourke (Ed.), *Neuropsychology of learning disabilities: Essentials of subtype analysis* (pp. 167–183). New York: Guilford Press.

Strauss, C. C., Lease, C. A., Last, C. G., & Francis, G. (1988). Overanxious disorder: An examination of developmental differences. *Journal of Abnormal Child Psychology, 16,* 433–443.

Strayhorn, J. M., Rapp, N., Donina, W., & Strain, P. S. (1988). Randomized trail of methylphenidate for an autistic child. *Journal of the American Academy of Child and Adolescent Psychiatry, 27,* 244–247.

Strober, M. (1997, October 14–19). *Lithium vs. valproate in the prophylaxsis of adolescent bipolar illness.* Paper presented at the 44th annual meeting of the American Academy of Child and Adolescent Psychiatry, Toronto, Ontario, Canada.

Strober, M., Morrell, W., Burroughs, J., Lampert, C., Danforth, H., & Freeman, R. (1988). A family study of bipolar I disorder in adolescence: Early onset of symptoms linked to increased familial loading and lithium resistance. *Journal of Affective Disorders, 15,* 255–268.

Strober, M., Morrell, W., Lampert, C., & Burroughs, J. (1990). Relapse following discontinuation of lithium maintenance therapy in adolescents with bipolar I illness: A naturalistic study. *American Journal of Psychiatry, 147,* 457–461.

Swanson, J. M. (1992). *School-based assessments and intervention for ADD students.* Irvine, CA: K. C. Publishing.

Swanson, J. M., & Castellanos, F. X. (1998a). *Biological basis of ADHD: Neuroanatomy, genetics, and pathophysiology.* Paper presented at the National Institute of Mental Health Consensus Conference, Washington, DC.

Swanson, J. M., & Castellanos, F. X. (1998b). Cognitive neuroscience of attention deficit hyperactivity disorder and hyperkinetic disorder. *Current Opinion in Neurobiology, 8,* 263–271.

Swanson, J. M., Flockhart, D., Udrea, D., Cantwell, D., Connor, D., & Williams, L. (1995). Clonidine in the treatment of ADHD: Questions about safety and efficacy. *Journal of Child and Adolescent Psychopharmacology, 5,* 301–304.

Swanson, J. M., Kinsbourne, M., Roberts, W., & Zucker, K. (1978). Time–response analysis of the effect of stimulant medication on the learning ability of children referred for hyperactivity. *Pediatrics, 61,* 21–29.

Swanson, J. [M.], Lerner, M., & Williams, L. (1995). More frequent diagnosis of attention deficit hyperactivity disorder. *New England Journal of Medicine, 333,* 944

Swanson, J. M., McBurnett, K., Wigal, T., Pfiffner, L. J., Lerner, M. A., Williams, L., Christian, D. L., Tamm, L., Willcutt, E., Crowley, K., Clevenger, W., Khouzam, N., Woo, C., Crinella, F. M., & Fisher, T. D. (1993). Effect of stimulant medication on children with attention deficit disorder: A "review of reviews." *Exceptional Children, 60,* 154–162.

Swanson, J. M., Sandman, C. A., Deutsch, C. K., & Baren, M. (1983). Methylphenidate hydrochloride given with or before breakfast: I. Behavioral, cognitive, and electrophysiologic effects. *Pediatrics, 72,* 49–55.

Swanson, J. M., Sergeant, J. A., Taylor, E., Sonuga-Barke, E. J., Jensen, P. S., & Cantwell, D. P. (1998). Attention-deficit hyperactivity disorder and hyperkinetic disorder. *Lancet, 351,* 429–433.

Swanson, J. M., Sunohara, G. A., Kennedy, J. L., Regino, R., Fineberg, E., Wigal, T., Lerner, M., Williams, L., LaHoste, G. J., & Wigal, S. (1998). Association of the dopamine transporter D_4 (DRD_4) gene with a refined phenotype of attention deficit hyperactivity disorder (ADHD). *Molecular Psychiatry, 3,* 38–41.

Swanson, J. M., Wigal, S., Greenhill, L. L., Browne, R., Waslick, B., Lerner, M., Williams, L., Flynn, D., Agler, D., Crowley, K. [L.], Fineberg, E., Baren, M., & Cantwell, D. P. (1998). Analog classroom assessment of Adderall in children with ADHD. *Journal of the American Academy of Child and Adolescent Psychiatry, 37,* 519–526.

Swanson, J. [M.], Wigal, S., Greenhill, L. [L.], Browne, R., Waslick, B., Lerner, M., Williams, L., Flynn, D., Agler, D., Crowley, K. L., Fineberg, E., Regino, R., Baren, M., & Cantwell, D. (1998). Objective and subjective measures of the pharmacodynamic effects of Adderall in the treatment of children with ADHD in a controlled laboratory classroom setting. *Psychopharmacology Bulletin, 34,* 55–60.

Swedo, S., Rapoport, J., Leonard, H., Lenane, M., & Cheslow, D. (1989). Obsessive–compulsive disorder in children and adolescents. *Archives of General Psychiatry, 46,* 335–341.

Szatmari, P., Boyle, M., & Offord, D. R. (1989). ADDH and conduct disorder: Degree of diagnostic overlap and differences among correlates. *Journal of the American Academy of Child and Adolescent Psychiatry, 28,* 865–872.

Szatmari, P., Saigal, S., Rosenbaum, P., Campbell, D., & King, S. (1990). Psychiatric disorders at five years among children with birthweights less than 1000 g: A regional perspective. *Developmental Medicine and Child Neurology, 32,* 954–962.

Takeda, K., Weiss, R. E., & Refetoff, S. (1992). Rapid localizations of mutations in thyroid hormone receptor-ß gene by denaturing gradient gel electrophoresis in 18 families with thyroid hormone resistance. *Journal of Clinical Endocrinology and Metabolism, 74,* 712–719.

Tallian, K. B., Nahata, M. C., Lo, W., & Tsao, C. Y. (1996). Gabapentin associated with aggressive behavior in pediatric patients with seizures. *Epilepsia, 37,* 501–502.

Tannock, R. (1994). Attention deficit disorders with anxiety disorders. In T. E. Brown (Ed.), *Subtypes of attention deficit disorders in children, adolescents and adults*. New York: American Psychiatric Press.

Tannock, R., Ickowicz, A., & Schachar, R. [J.] (1991, October 16–20). *Effects of comorbid anxiety disorder on stimulant response in children with ADHD.* Paper presented at the 38th annual meeting of the American Academy of Child and Adolescent Psychiatry, San Francisco.

Tannock, R., Ickowicz, A., & Schachar, R. [J.] (1995). Differential effects of methylphenidate on working memory in ADHD children with and without comorbid anxiety. *Journal of the American Academy of Child and Adolescent Psychiatry, 34,* 886–896.

Tannock, R., Schachar, R. J., Carr, R. P., & Logan, G. D. (1989). Dose–response effects of methylphenidate on academic performance and overt behavior in hyperactive children. *Pediatrics, 84,* 648–657.

Tannock, R., Schachar, R. [J.], & Logan, G. (1993, October 26–31). *Differential effects of methylphenidate on working memory in attention-deficit hyperactivity disorder with and without anxiety.* Paperresented at the 40th annual meeting of the American Academy of Child and Adolescent Psychiatry, San Antonio, TX.

Taylor, E., Schachar, R., Thorley, G., Wieselberg, H. M., Everitt, B., & Rutter, M. (1987). Which boys respond to stimulant medication? A controlled trial of methylphenidate in boys with disruptive behavior. *Psychological Medicine, 17,* 121–143.

Taylor, H. G., Michaels, R. H., Mazur, P. M., Bauer, R. E., & Liden, C. B. (1984). Intellectual, neuropsychological and achievement outcomes in children six to eight years after recovery from *Haemophilus influenzae* meningitis. *Pediatrics, 74,* 198–205.

Teasdale, G., & Jennett, B. (1974). Assessment of coma and impaired consciousness: A practical scale. *Lancet, ii,* 81–84.

Thompson, L. L., Riggs, P. D., Mikulich, S. K., & Crowley, T. J. (1996). Contribution of ADHD symptoms to substance problems and delinquency in conduct-disordered adolescents. *Journal of Abnormal Child Psychology, 24,* 325–347.

Tierney, E., Joshi, P. T., Llinas, J. E., Rosenberg, L. A., & Riddle, M. A. (1995). Sertraline for major depression in children and adolescents: Preliminary clinical experience. *Journal of Child and Adolescent Psychopharmacology, 5*(1), 13–17.

Toro, J., Cervera, M., Osejo, E., & Salamero, M. (1992). Obsessive–compulsive disorder in childhood and adolescence: A clinical study. *Journal of Child Psychology and Psychiatry, 33,* 1025–1037.

University of Kentucky Departments of Psychiatry & Psychology & Kentucky Department of Education. (1992). *ADHD diagnosis and management: A training program for teachers.*

Usala, S. J., Bale, A. E., & Gesundheit, N. (1988). Tight linkage between the syndrome of generalized thyroid hormone resistance and the human c-erbAß gene. *Molecular Endocrinology, 2,* 1217–1220.

Usala, S. J., Tennyson, G. E., & Bale, A. E. (1990). A base mutation of the c-erbAb thyroid hormone receptor in a kindred with generalized thyroid hormone resistance: Molecular heterogeneity in two other kindreds. *Journal of Clinical Investigations, 85,* 93–100.

U.S. Department of Education. (1991, September 16). *Clarification of the policy to address the needs of children with ADD within general and/or special education.*

Varanka, T. M., Weller, R. A., Weller, E. B., & Fristad, M. A. (1988). Lithium treatment of manic episodes with psychotic features in prepubertal children. *American Journal of Psychiatry, 145,* 1557–1559.

Varley, C. K., & McClellan, J. (1997). Case study: Two additional sudden deaths with tricyclic antidepressants. *Journal of the American Academy of Child and Adolescent Psychiatry, 36,* 390–394.

Vellutino, F. R. (1991). Introduction to three studies on reading acquisition: Convergent findings on theoretical foundations of code oriented vs. whole language approaches to reading instruction. *Journal of Educational Psychology, 83,* 437–443.

Vitiello, B., Stoff, D., Atkins, M., & Mahoney, A. (1990). Soft neurological signs and impulsivity in children. *Journal of Developmental and Behavioral Pediatrics, 11,* 112–115.

Voeller, K. K. S. (1986). Right hemisphere deficit syndrome in children. *American Journal of Psychiatry, 143,* 1004–1009.

Wald, E. R., Bergman, I., Taylor, H. G., Chiponis, D., Porter, C., & Kubek, K. (1986). Long term outcome of group B streptococcal meningitis. *Pediatrics, 77,* 217–221.

Walkup, J. T. (1998, October 27–November 1). *The pharmacological treatment of the OCD spectrum disorders.* Paper presented at the 45 annual meeting of the American Academy of Child and Adolescent Psychiatry, Anaheim, CA.

Walkup, J. T., Scahill, L. D., & Riddle, M. A. (1995). Disruptive behavior, hyperactivity, and learning disabilities in children with Tourette's syndrome. *Advances in Neurology, 65,* 259–272.

Weber, M. A. (1980). Discontinuation syndrome following cessation of treatment with clonidine and other antihypertensive agents. *Journal of Cardiovascular Pharmacology, 2,* 573–589.

Webster-Stratton, C. (1994). Advancing videotape parent training: A comparison study. *Journal of Consulting and Clinical Psychology, 62,* 583–593.

Webster-Stratton, C., & Hammond, M. (1990). Predictors of treatment outcome in parent training for families with conduct problem children. *Behavior Therapy, 21,* 319–337.

Weiss, G., & Hechtman, L., (1986). *Hyperactive children grown up: Empirical findings and theoretical considerations.* New York: Guilford Press.

Weiss, R. E., Stein, M. A., Duck, S. C., Chyna, B., Phillips, W., O'Brien, T., Gutermuth, L., & Refetoff, S. (1994). Low intelligence but not attention deficit hyperactivity disorder is associated with resistance to thyroid hormone caused by mutation R316H in the thyroid hormone receptor beta gene. *Journal of Clinical Endocrinology and Metabolism, 78,* 1525–1528.

Weiss, R. E., Stein, M. A., Trommer, B., & Refetoff, S. (1993). Attention-deficit hyperactivity disorder and thyroid function. *Journal of Pediatrics, 123,* 539–545.

Weisz, J. R., Weiss, B., Alicke, M. D., & Koltz, M. L. (1987). Effectiveness of psychotherapy with children and adolescents: A meta-analysis for clinicians. *Journal of Consulting and Clinical Psychology, 55,* 542–549.

Welner, Z., Reich, W., Herjanic, B., Jung, K. G., & Amado, H. (1987). Reliability, validity, and parent–child agreement studies of the Diagnostic Interview for Children and Adolescents (DICA). *Journal of the American Academy of Child and Adolescent Psychiatry, 26,* 649–653.

Werry, J. S., & Aman, M. G. (1975). Methylphenidate and haloperidol in children. *Archives of General Psychiatry, 32,* 790–795.

Werry, J. S., Elkind, G. S., & Reeves, J. C. (1987). Attention deficit, conduct, oppositional, and anxiety disorders in children: III. Laboratory differences. *Journal of Abnormal Child Psychology, 15,* 409–428.

West, S. A., Keck, P. E., McElroy, S. L., Strakowski, S. M., Minnery, K. L., McConville, B. J., & Sorter, M. T. (1994). Open trial of valproate in the treatment of adolescent mania. *Journal of Child and Adolescent Psychopharmacology, 4,* 263–267.

West, S. A., McElroy, S. L., Strakowski, S. M., Keck, P. E. Jr., & McConville, B. J. (1995). Attention deficit hyperactivity disorder in adolescent mania. *American Journal of Psychiatry, 152,* 271–273.

Whalen, C. K., Collins, B. E., Henker, B., Alkus, S. R., Adams, D., & Stapp, S. (1978). Behavior observations of hyperactive children and methylphenidate (Ritalin) effects in systematically structured classroom environments: Now you see them, now you don't. *Journal of Pediatric Psychology, 3,* 177–184.

Whalen, C. K., & Henker, B. (1987). Cognitive behavior therapy for hyperactive children: What do we know? In J. Loney (Ed.), *The young hyperactive child: Answers to questions about diagnosis, prognosis, and treatment* (pp. 123–141). London: Haworth Press.

Whalen, C. K., Henker, B., Collins, B. E., Finck, D., & Dotemoto, S. (1979). A social ecology of hyperactive boys: Medication effects in systematically structured classroom environments. *Journal of Applied Behavior Analysis, 12,* 65–81.

Wheeler, J., & Carlson, C. L. (1994). The social functioning of children with ADD with hyperactivity and ADD without hyperactivity: A comparison of their peer relations and social deficits. *Journal of Emotional and Behavioral Disorders, 2,* 1–12.

Wigal, S. B., Gupta, S., Guinta, D., & Swanson, J. M. (1998). Reliability and validity of the SKAMP rating scale in a laboratory school setting. *Psychopharmacology Bulletin, 34,* 47–53.

Wilens, T. E., Biederman, J., Geist, D. E., Steingard, R., & Spencer, T. (1993). Nortriptyline in the treatment of ADHD: A chart review of 58 cases. *Journal of the American Academy of Child and Adolescent Psychiatry, 32,* 343–349.

Wilens, T. E., Biederman, J., Spencer, T. J., & Frances, R. J. (1994). Comorbidity of attention-deficit hyperactivity and psychoactive substance use disorders. *Hospital and Community Psychiatry, 45,* 421–423, 435.

Wilens, T. E., Spencer, T. J., Biederman, J., & Schleifer, D. (1997). Case study: Nefazodone for juvenile mood disorders. *Journal of the American Academy of Child and Adolescent Psychiatry, 36,* 481–485.

Willemsen-Swinkels, S. H. N., Buitelaar, J. K., Nijhof, G. J., & van Engeland, H. (1995). Failure of naltrexone hydrochloride to reduce self-injurious and autistic behavior in mentally retarded adults. *Archives of General Psychiatry, 52,* 766–733.

Williams, D. T., Mehl, R., Yudofsky, S., Adams, D., & Roseman, B. (1982). The effect of propranolol on uncontrolled rage outbursts in children and adolescents with organic brain dysfunction. *Journal of the American Academy of Child Psychiatry, 21,* 129–135.

Williams, J. M., & Davis, K. S. (1986). Central nervous system prophylactic treatment for childhood leukemia: Neuropsychological outcome studies. *Cancer Treatment Review, 13,* 113–127.

Winett, R. A., & Winkler, R. C. (1972). Current behavior modification in the classroom: Be still, be quiet, be docile. *Journal of Applied Behavior Analysis, 5,* 499–504.

Wolraich, M. L., Lindgren, S. D., Stumbo, P. J., Stegink, L. D., Appelbaum, M. I., & Kiritsy, M. C. (1994). Effects of diets high in sucrose or aspartame on the behavior and cognitive performance of children [see comments]. *New England Journal of Medicine, 330,* 301–307.

Wozniak, J., & Biederman, J. (1996). A pharmacological approach to the quagmire of comorbidity in juvenile mania. *Journal of the American Academy of Child and Adolescent Psychiatry, 35,* 826–828.

Wozniak, J., Biederman, J., Kiely, K., Ablon, S., Faraone, S. V., Mundy, E., & Mennin, D. (1995). Mania-like symptoms suggestive of childhood-onset bipolar disorder in clinically referred children. *Journal of the American Academy of Child and Adolescent Psychiatry, 34,* 867–876.

Wozniak, J., Biederman, J., Mundy, E., Mennin, D., & Faraone, S. V. (1995). A pilot family study of childhood-onset mania. *Journal of the American Academy of Child and Adolescent Psychiatry, 34,* 1577–1583.

Yeates, K. O., & Bornstein, R. A. (1994). Attention deficit disorder and neuropsychological functioning in children with Tourette's syndrome. *Neuropsychology, 8,* 65–74.

Yee, J. D., & Berde, C. B. (1994). Dextroamphetamine or methylphenidate as adjuvants to opioid analgesia for adolescents with cancer. *Journal of Pain and Symptom Management, 9,* 122–125.

Youngerman, J., & Canino, L. A. (1995). Lithium carbonate use in children and adolescents: A survey of the literature. *Archives of General Psychiatry, 35,* 216–224.

Yudofsky, S., Silver, J. M., & Schneider, S. E. (1987). Pharmacologic treatment of aggression. *Psychiatric Annals, 17,* 397–407.

Yudofsky, S., Williams, D. T., & Gorman, J. (1981). Propranolol in the treatment of rage and violent behavior in patients with chronic brain syndrome. *American Journal of Psychiatry, 138,* 218–220.

Zametkin, A. J., Liebenauer, L. L., Fitzgerald, G. A., King, A. C., Minkunas, D. V., Hersovitch, P., Yamada, E. M., & Cohen, R. M. (1993). Brain metabolism in teenagers with attention deficit hyperctivity disorder. *Archives of General Psychiatry, 50,* 333–340.

Zametkin, A. J., Nordahl, T. E., Gross, M., King, A. C., Semple, W. E., Rumsey, J., Hamburger, S., & Cohen, R. M. (1990). Cerebral glucose metabolism in adults with hyperactivity of childhood onset. *New England Journal of Medicine, 323,* 1361–1366.

Zametkin, A. J., & Rapoport, J. L. (1987). Neurobiology of attention deficit disorder with hyperactivity: Where have we come in 50 years? *Journal of the American Academy of Child and Adolescent Psychiatry, 26,* 676–686.

Zentall, S. S. (1993). Research on the educational implications of ADHD. *Exceptional Children, 60,* 143–153.

Index